Rainbow
Family Collections

**Recent Titles in the
Children's and Young Adult Literature Reference Series**

Catherine Barr, Series Editor

☀ ☀ ☀ *Rainbow* ☀ ☀ ☀
Family Collections
Selecting and Using Children's Books with Lesbian, Gay, Bisexual, Transgender, and Queer Content

☀

Jamie Campbell Naidoo

Children's and Young Adult Literature Reference
Catherine Barr, Series Editor

 **LIBRARIES UNLIMITED**

AN IMPRINT OF ABC-CLIO, LLC
Santa Barbara, California • Denver, Colorado • Oxford, England

Library of Congress Cataloging-in-Publication Data
Naidoo, Jamie Campbell.
  Rainbow family collections : selecting and using children's books with lesbian, gay, bisexual, transgender, and queer content / Jamie Campbell Naidoo.
      pages cm. — (Children's and young adult literature reference)
  Includes bibliographical references and index.
  ISBN 978-1-59884-960-8 (hardback) — ISBN 978-1-59884-961-5 (ebook)
  1. Sexual minorities—Juvenile literature—Bibliography. 2. Children of sexual minority parents—Books and reading—United States. 3. Children's libraries—Collection development—United States. 4. Libraries—Special collections—Sexual minorities. 5. Children's libraries—Services to minorities—United States. 6. Libraries and sexual minorities—United States. 7. Sexual minorities in literature. I. Title.
  Z1037.N24 2012
  028.1'624—dc23   2012008362

ISBN: 978-1-59884-960-8
EISBN: 978-1-59884-961-5

16 15 14 13   2 3 4 5

This book is also available on the World Wide Web as an eBook.
Visit www.abc-clio.com for details.

Libraries Unlimited
An Imprint of ABC-CLIO, LLC

ABC-CLIO, LLC
130 Cremona Drive, P.O. Box 1911
Santa Barbara, California 93116-1911

This book is printed on acid-free paper ∞
Manufactured in the United States of America

Dedication

For all the LGBTQ children struggling to find their place in the world and all the rainbow families seeking equality and recognition.

To my Granny for always loving me, supporting my dreams, and accepting me for who I am!

米

Acknowledgments

Behind every book there is a dream team of editors, writers, supporters, assistants, and advocates. I wish to thank my colleagues for their support as I worked on this book, and my partner, who never seems to tire of listening to me rant and rave about children's books.

Catherine Barr and Barbara Ittner at Libraries Unlimited have been extremely gracious and patient in encouraging and overseeing the publication process, particularly during a year full of unexpected family emergencies and natural disasters. A special thanks also goes to Christine McNaull for her assistance with designing, proofing, and typesetting the book, and to my graduate assistants Abby Couch, Jamaica Pouncy, and Katy Olson for their many hours helping me check and recheck bibliographies. My deepest gratitude goes out to all the talented authors and illustrators (as well as their publishers) who create the high-quality children's books representing rainbow families and make them available to children around the world.

No work stands on its own; it builds on the intellect of previous generations. I thank all of the scholars who taught me what I know about children's and young adult literature as well as those who continually publish research about LGBTQ children's literature, especially Joan Atkinson, K. T. Horning, Christine Jenkins, Elizabeth L. Chapman, and Michael Cart. I would especially like to thank Maya Christina Gonzalez, Bobby Combs, Nancy Silverrod, Laura Matanah, and Lesléa Newman for sharing their expertise and passion during our interviews. Finally, I would like to thank the American Library Association Office for Diversity for supporting me with a 2008 Diversity Research Grant, which funded a portion of my research.

Contents

Foreword

Twenty-five years ago, I got a phone call from a friend of a friend, asking me for picture book recommendations for her unborn child. Children's librarians, it seems, are never able to leave work — we're used to new parents who are so eager to share books with their children that they approach us when their children are still in utero — and so this wasn't out of the ordinary. What made the call unusual was that the caller identified herself and her partner as lesbians and told me their baby had been conceived by alternative insemination.

"What kind of books will our daughter find?" she asked me. "Are there books out there about families like ours?"

Unfortunately, I had to tell her that there was hardly anything that showed a child with gay or lesbian parents. At the time, there was just one book about a child with a lesbian mom, *When Megan Went Away*, which had been published by a small press called Lollipop Power in 1979. But it dealt with the break-up of a lesbian relationship, and was hardly the sort of book this mom was looking for. Instead, I found myself recommending picture books that showed single-parent families, books that at least depicted a world from which her child would not feel excluded. I also recommended books that challenged traditional gender roles, reflected diversity and independence, and featured strong girls and women, qualities I came to think of as "lesbian family values." We had to get creative in those early years of the first wave of the lesbian baby boom.

A few years later, Lesléa Newman self-published her groundbreaking picture book *Heather Has Two Mommies,* which would later be picked up as the first title in a new children's imprint from Alyson Books, a well-established gay press. Soon they were publishing original picture books, such as *Daddy's Roommate* by Michael Willhoite and *The Duke Who Outlawed Jellybeans* by Johnny Valentine. Other small presses — particularly feminist presses in the United States and Canada — began to publish a handful of picture books for kids in gay and lesbian families, and some presses, such as Two Lives, were created for this express purpose. But with a few exceptions, they remain outside the mainstream of U.S. trade publishing all these years later, gay penguins notwithstanding.

Although the books themselves represent a minuscule proportion of the total number of children's picture books published, they are disproportionately targeted by would-be censors who either demand that they be moved to a special "parenting" section, or be removed from the library altogether. According to the American Library Association, *Daddy's Roommate* and *Heather Has Two Mommies* were among the top ten most frequently challenged books of the decade, in second and ninth place respectively, and for the past five years *And Tango Makes Three* (Justin Richardson and Peter Parnell's appealing tale of two male penguins hatching an abandoned egg) has had the top position on the list.

The challengers most frequently argue that they don't want their young children exposed to a positive portrayal of homosexuality, or to know that it even exists. But what of the children growing up in families with two dads? They are exposed to countless picture books that show happy heterosexual families, and they rarely see their own families in books or elsewhere in popular culture. Because libraries exist to serve the entire community, it is the duty of every children's librarian to purchase books that reflect community diversity. And that includes books that show gay and lesbian families. Even if a librarian doesn't know of any gay or lesbian families in her community, they are most likely there, whether in a nuclear or extended family, whether they self-identify or not.

This speaks to one of the challenges of serving gay and lesbian families in public libraries — one doesn't always know they are there. They don't always announce themselves. Being out is a deeply personal and individual choice. Not everyone feels as comfortable with outing themselves to a stranger as the friend of a friend who called me at home to ask for book recommendations for her daughter. (And even then she called me at home because she didn't feel safe about approaching me in person at the library.)

One of the best ways to serve gay and lesbian families is simply to include LGBTQ (lesbian, gay, bisexual, transgender and queer/questioning) books in the library's collection. This tells them that their families are valued and that they are welcome in the library. When a gay or lesbian parent easily finds books reflecting their own family's experiences and reality, they can begin to feel that the children's librarian is someone they can trust.

Building trust is important when it comes to serving gay and lesbian families, and it is critical when it comes to serving LGBTQ youth. As with building a gay-friendly picture book collection, selecting books for older children and teens about LGBTQ characters or issues can establish a solid foundation for building trust. Fortunately, there is a rich and diverse body of literature to choose from when it comes to LGBTQ books for older readers. And for those who are just beginning to question their own sexuality, or those who are beginning to come out to themselves or others, books can provide crucial information, as well as a safe place for exploration. Recently established awards and best books lists for LGBTQ literature can guide librarians making selection decisions, and standard library practices such as creating displays and bookmarks can help readers find books they may be too afraid to ask for.

Young people today have free access to a wealth of information and can find support at school and in their communities. But along with this comes free access to misinformation, in addition to the erosion of privacy and the reality of cyber-bullying. Libraries can be a sanctuary for all sorts of kids who feel like outsiders, most especially those who may be LGBTQ. And librarians, just by doing what we do best — providing books, information, and services for those who need them — ensure that all children and families can safely explore the world and feel at home.

Kathleen T. Horning

Introduction

William's grandmother smiled. "He needs [a doll] to hug and to cradle and to take to the park so that when he's a father like you, he'll know how to take care of his baby and feed him and love him and bring him the things he wants, like a doll so that he can practice being a father." (Zolotow 1972, p. 32)

When I was a young boy, this line in Charlotte Zolotow's *William's Doll* (1972) really struck a chord with me. I loved to play with dolls; admittedly I enjoyed playing with race cars and dressing up as a cowboy too, but my dolls brought me the most joy. I had tons of them: baby dolls, Barbie dolls, rag dolls, stuffed toys, and action figures and ponies with hair you can comb. Luckily, I had a grandmother who believed, very much like William's grandmother, that dolls would give me practice being a father. As the matriarch of our rural Kentucky family, she sanctioned my ability to buck gender norms and fostered an environment where it was okay for a boy to play with dolls. Unfortunately, as I grew older and entered school I was made uncomfortably aware that boys did not play with dolls and was often ridiculed as a "sissy." During this time books such as Tomie dePaola's *Oliver Button Is a Sissy* (1979) helped me to realize that it was okay to be different from the other boys and for a while that was enough.

As I grew older, I never encountered other children's books in my classrooms or in the school or public library that explained it was okay for a boy to like sewing, have female friends, or find other boys attractive. I also never came across books that told me I might one day meet another boy who was just like me, and I certainly never found books that showed families with two fathers or two mothers. Perhaps if those books had been available then, my upper elementary, middle school, and high school years would not have been as traumatic and difficult as they were. If my experiences had been normalized or I had been given an opportunity to find children's books that mirrored my life and the lives of other queer children, then I would not have felt so alienated and ashamed of being different from my peers and classmates. Also, these books would have given an opportunity for my classmates to realize that I was not strange and that children around the world shared my budding feelings of queerness. We might even have been afforded the chance to see happy, healthy same-sex families making positive contributions to society. Unfortunately, those books did not exist in the early 1980s and, even if they had, they most likely would not have made it to the shelves of classrooms and libraries in my poor, rural community situated in the heart of the Bible Belt.

Often librarians and educators justify their lack of queer children's materials with the rationale that lesbian, gay, bisexual, transgender, or queer/questioning (LGBTQ) families are not present in the communities served by their libraries, or that they don't have any LGBTQ children or children with LGBTQ families in their classrooms. Lesbian children's author Lesléa Newman highlights this problem and questions the ramifications of sheltering our children from learning about families that are present in almost every county of the United States. She asks educators and librarians:

> How can you possibly assume that every child sitting in your classroom or library comes from a home with a mother and father? How can you presume that there are no children in your classroom or library with lesbian or gay parents, siblings, aunts, uncles, grandparents, neighbors, and friends? What messages are you giving to all children when you pretend there is only one type of family and render the rest invisible? (Newman 2009, n.p.)

Laurent (2009) notes, "Until the 1970s, children's literature that illustrated households with homosexual members was missing from classrooms, bookstores, and libraries, and the importance of children having access to books characteristic of themselves and their families was either dismissed, overlooked, or feared" (p. 125). Prior to this time period, there were a few books that addressed gender nonconformity, but for the most part LGBTQ children's literature surfaced in the very late 1970s and the first picture book appeared in 1979 in the form of Jane Severance's *When Megan Went Away*. However, many of these books were published by small feminist presses and were not readily available to children in most classrooms and libraries in the United Sates.

Fast forward twenty-plus years later, and the situation was much the same. While more children's picture books and novels with queer content had been published, their accessibility to children was still abysmal. In 2001, Clyde and Lobban examined LGBTQ children's books in public libraries and conducted their own research of available titles for their professional book *Out of the Closet and Into the Classroom*. The authors concluded, "For young people and their books, is it really the case that they have come 'out of the closet and into the classroom'? At present, it seems that the closet door is no more than about half open" (p. 27). Today, the same can be said about the availability of gay-themed children's books in public and school libraries as well as classrooms. Compared with the overall number of children's books available at any given time in the United States, there are still few high-quality books and other materials for children eleven years old and younger that depict LGBTQ characters

and topics, and their availability is still pretty scarce in many classrooms, libraries, and bookstores.

This volume that you are holding represents several years of searching to identify as many children's picture books, chapter books, informational books, and other types of media depicting lesbian, gay, bisexual, transgender, queer, and gender nonconformity for children ages birth to eleven. I have included materials from awards lists, bibliographies, blogs, LGBTQ Web sites, publisher catalogs, and any other source that identified these materials. Materials published in the United States and around the world are represented in this collection. The book is divided into four parts: Rainbow Families and Libraries, LGBTQ Content in Children's Literature, Materials with LGBTQ Content for Children, and Resources. In the first section, Chapter 1 provides educators and librarians with a foundation for understanding the various members of rainbow families (LGBTQ families) as well as their informational and recreational needs and the ways in which homophobia in society influences these members. Chapter 2 describes how librarians can create welcoming and inclusive environments for rainbow families, how to introduce children's materials with LGBTQ themes into programming, and how to overcome potential barriers to serving rainbow families.

In Part 2, Chapter 3 opens with an overview of LGBTQ children's literature, including historical milestones and specialized publishers of queer children's materials, and concludes with an examination of censorship challenges and intellectual freedom issues surrounding LGBTQ children's materials. Chapter 4 highlights specialized book awards for LGBTQ children's literature that librarians and educators can use to help identify titles to use with children in their classroom and libraries. The following chapter examines the accessibility of queer children's materials and focuses on both information access concerns in cataloging and the physical arrangement of the materials. Specific selection criteria and evaluation guidelines for choosing LGBTQ children's materials round out Chapter 5.

Part 3 forms the heart of the book, featuring extensive annotated lists of children's materials with LGBTQ content as well as providing information about book reviews and keywords for accessibility purposes. Chapter 6 focuses on picture books, Chapter 7 examines chapter books, and Chapter 8 highlights informational materials and other print and nonprint media for children. Both recommended and non-recommended titles are included, to provide a historical look at all the materials available to date.

In Part 4, Chapter 9 provides an extensive listing of print and nonprint resources, bibliographies, and LGBTQ organizations that will be useful to caregivers in rainbow families as well as the librarians and educators serving this population's informational and literacy needs. Finally, the book concludes with multiple indexes to assist the reader in quickly locating pertinent information relating to a specific author, title, keyword, or subject. The Keyword Index lists keywords used in the bibliographic entries in Chapters 6, 7, and 8 while the Subject Index is used for wider access to subjects discussed throughout the entire book. Librarians and educators seeking books published outside the United States should use the Keyword Index, where they will find keywords such as Australian Literature, British Literature, Canadian Literature,

French Literature, German Literature, Mexican Literature, Spanish Literature, and so forth.

It is my hope that some of the suggestions for library services, collection development, physical arrangement, and recommended books provided in *Rainbow Family Collections* will help improve the access of children and their caregivers to these important materials. However, I would be naïve to think that all librarians and educators will use these materials widely and freely in their programming. As I address various censorship concerns and intellectual freedom issues throughout the book, I am well aware that it will not be easy to incorporate children's materials about rainbow families in all classrooms and libraries. Perhaps the following story will provide a source of inspiration. Recently Molly Raphael, the 2011–2012 president of the American Library Association (ALA), related a story that underscores the importance of children in rainbow families encountering their experiences in children's literature. Raphael states:

> Should you doubt the very real impact that free access to [LGBTQ children's] books can have on just one child, I'll share the story of one little girl. The child's school was celebrating Banned Books Week by reading from banned and challenged works, and a librarian began to read from *And Tango Makes Three*, an award-winning picture book by Peter Parnell and Justin Richardson [2005] that tells the story of two male Emperor Penguins who hatch an egg and raise a chick together in the Central Park Zoo in New York City. The book is ranked as the number one most challenged book in the U.S., based on challenges that claim that the book is unsuitable for its target age group because of its religious viewpoint and homosexual themes. After the librarian finished reading *And Tango Makes Three*, the little girl — the child of same-sex parents — stood up and cheered. It was the first time ever that a book that mirrored her family life had been read and celebrated in public. And it was the first time that she felt as if she belonged. Had the book been banned from her library, all of that would have been taken away from her. (Raphael 2011, par. 9–10)

The young girl in the aforementioned account was lucky enough to have an understanding librarian share a book during a library program that resonated with her experiences. As I've mentioned earlier, I did not have this experience as a child, nor do many other children in rainbow families. Books such as *And Tango Makes Three* provide an important opportunity for all children to make connections with rainbow families. More than thirteen years ago, a young second-grade boy was quoted in *Love Makes a Family: Portraits of Lesbian, Gay, Bisexual and Transgender Parents and Their Families,* saying "I think it's different having two moms, and I think it would be really boring if everybody just had a mom and a dad. It's really special how I have a mom and a mama!" (Gillespie 1999, p. 15). Hopefully librarians and other educators can use the suggestions in this book to better understand the importance of serving LGBTQ families and their children, to celebrate the unique diversity these children

and adults bring to our world, and to help other families understand that rainbow families are special. The time for making rainbow family connections in the library is long overdue!

References

Clyde, Laurel, and Marjorie Lobban. "A Door Half Open: Young People's Access to Fiction Related to Homosexuality." *School Libraries Worldwide* 7, no. 2 (2001): 17–30.

Gillespie, Peggy, ed. *Love Makes a Family: Portraits of Lesbian, Gay, Bisexual and Transgender Parents and Their Families.* Photographs by Gigi Kaeser. Amherst, MA: University of Massachusetts Press, 1999.

Laurent, Dianna. "Children's Literature, Lesbian." In *Encyclopedia of Contemporary LGBTQ Literature of the United States: Volume 1*, ed. by Emmanuel S. Nelson, pp. 125–126. Santa Barbara, CA: Greenwood Press, 2009.

Newman, Lesléa. *Heather Has Two Mommies.* Illus. by Diana Souza. 3rd revised, 20th anniversary ed. New York, NY: Alyson Books, 2009.

Raphael, Molly. "Banned Books Week Reminds Us That Censorship Is Alive and Well in the Internet Age." Huffington Post Online (September 22, 2011). Accessed January 3, 2012, at http://www.huffingtonpost.com/molly-raphael/banned-books-week-censorship_b_977058.html.

Children's Literature

dePaola, Tomie. *Oliver Button Is a Sissy.* New York, NY: Harcourt Brace Jovanovich, 1979.

Richardson, Justin, and Peter Parnell. *And Tango Makes Three.* Illus. by Henry Cole. New York, NY: Simon & Schuster, 2005.

Severance, Jane. *When Megan Went Away.* Illus. by Tea Schook. Chapel Hill, NC: Lollipop Power, 1979.

Zolotow, Charlotte. *William's Doll.* Illus. by William Pène du Bois. New York, NY: Harper and Row, 1972.

PART 1

✳

Rainbow Families and Libraries

CHAPTER 1

Understanding Rainbow Families

Many times throughout my life people have been shocked when they find out my father is gay. "I had no idea," they say. "You'd never know just by looking at you." They make me feel like a rare species as their eyes scan me for any abnormalities they missed that could have tipped them off. Ladies and Gentleman [sic], step right up! Look closely at the child of a gay dad. No horns! No tail! In fact, she could pass for anybody's child. What do people think kids of LGBT parents "look" like? (Garner 2004, p. 13)

Rainbow families can take many different forms and compositions: single or married/partnered, rich or poor, religious or nonreligious, conservative or liberal, urban or rural, biracial or multiracial. These families can have one parent/caregiver, two parents/caregivers, or multiple caregivers. Caregivers can be legal guardians, biological parents, foster parents, stepparents, or surrogate parents. Children in these families can be from previous marriages, from adoption, or from artificial insemination. Children in these families can be straight or lesbian, gay, bisexual, transgender, or queer/questioning (LGBTQ); parents/caregivers or other family members can be straight or LGBTQ.

Regardless of their composition, rainbow families are legitimate members of the community and should receive the same library services and educational opportunities as any other type of family. Rainbow families are found in almost every county in the nation and are most likely being underserved by local schools and public libraries. Because some rainbow families are closeted — meaning they do not want others to know there are LGBTQ members in the family — it can be difficult to identify and serve these families. The purpose of this chapter is to help librarians, teachers, and other educators better understand this population in order to provide the best services, programs, and materials to meet their educational, recreational, informational, and literacy needs.

Rainbow Family Members

For the purposes of this book and for discussing library and literacy services to this population, a rainbow family includes children of LGBTQ caregivers, gender-variant children, children who identify as LGBT, and LGBTQ caregivers or other relatives (aunts, uncles, grandmothers, and so forth). With such a broad and diverse range of people and experiences covered under this term, it is helpful to define the various different members represented.

* *Children of LGBTQ Caregivers or with LGBTQ Relatives:* This group includes children who live in households with caregivers who identify as lesbian, gay, bisexual, transgender, or queer/questioning. It also includes children who have LGBTQ relatives such as a gay uncle, lesbian grandmother, and so forth. These LGBTQ individuals can be single or in relationships.
* *Lesbian or Gay Caregivers or Relatives:* Caregivers or relatives who are attracted to someone of the same sex as themselves. Lesbians are attracted to other women and gay men are attracted to other men. These caregivers, parents, or other relatives can be single or in relationships. (The term gay is also used to describe both gays and lesbians.)
* *Bisexual Caregivers or Relatives:* Caregivers or relatives who are not completely heterosexual or homosexual are considered bisexual. These individuals are attracted to both males and females and may spend parts of their lives in homosexual relationships or heterosexual relationships. Very few overt representations of bisexuals are present in children's literature and materials.
* *Lesbian, Gay, or Bisexual Children:* This group includes children who will eventually grow up to be attracted to the same sex or both sexes. Although most adults prefer to think of children as being asexual, young children are often able to recognize their attractions to other people. When LGBTQ adults are interviewed, many describe knowing at a very young age that they were LGBTQ.
* *Transgender Children and/or Caregivers:* Transgender is an umbrella term used to describe individuals who generally feel that they were born into the wrong physical sex and whose true gender identity differs from their birth sex (male, female, or somewhere in between). *Trans* children and caregivers often believe that their true gender identity is crucial to their survival and are often unhappy until they can claim it. Transgender can include individuals who have had an operation to match their sex with their gender identity, but

it can also include individuals who have not had an operation. Trans children can explicitly express that they are the wrong physical sex, although they would not have any type of operation until they are much older.

✳ *Gender-Variant Children*: Children who are gender-variant (also called gender-nonconforming) choose play activities, toys, and sometimes clothing that is different from that associated with their birth gender. Boys who wear dresses and play with dolls, and girls who play with trucks and sport short "boyish" haircuts are considered gender-variant. Sometimes children who are gender-variant grow up to be transgender. However, according to the Transgender Network of Parents, Families and Friends of Lesbians and Gays (PFLAG), "Not all gender-variant children grow up to be trans people, and not all trans people exhibit gender-variant behaviors in childhood. While some children express the desire to act, dress, play and be treated as a person of the other gender at an early age, the desire wanes in many of them later in childhood" (PFLAG 2007, p. 7).

✳ *Queer/Questioning Children and/or Caregivers*: Individuals who are queer/ questioning include children and/or their caregivers who may or may not be gender-variant but who have lesbian, gay, or bisexual inclinations. Queer/ questioning individuals may not actually be lesbian, gay, or bisexual but they have not ruled out the possibility. Sometimes the term "queer" is also used to represent the entire LGBTQ spectrum.

✳ *Intersex*: Although not explicitly described in many materials for children, intersex individuals are those who are born with both male and female genitalia. Doctors and parents usually decide the sex of the baby and operate to remove one set of genitals. Sometimes the "correct" sex is chosen and the child identifies with his or her assigned gender identity. However, there are times when the "wrong" sex is chosen and the child will identify with the opposite gender.

✳ *Two-Spirit People/Two-Spirited People*: In Native American and First Nations tribes, two-spirit people (sometimes called two-spirited people) are those who exhibit characteristics of both male and female genders and sometimes a third gender (male-female or female-male). Two-spirit people have historically held a place of honor in North American indigenous tribes. Two-spirit people often engage in cross-dressing. Maya Christina Gonzalez's *Gender Now Coloring Book: A Learning Adventure for Children and Adults* (2010) is one of the very few children's books to introduce the concept of two-spirit people and intersex.

For additional information about rainbow family composition consult *Families Like Mine: Children of Gay Parents Tell It Like It Is* (Garner 2004); *Welcoming Children from Sexual-Minority Families in Our Schools* (Lamme and Lamme 2003); the association COLAGE (http://www.colage.org/), which is designed for children with an LGBTQ parent; and PFLAG (http://community.pflag.org/), which represents LGBTQ parents, families, and friends (adults and children). All of these resources include additional defining information on individuals included under the rainbow family umbrella.

Rainbow Families in the United States

Even more difficult than defining rainbow families is identifying their presence in the U.S. population. More than thirteen years ago, Casper and Schultz (1999) lamented the lack of information about lesbian- and gay-headed families in educational research as well as in statistical counts of the U.S. population. Beginning with the 2010 U.S. Census, the federal government began an attempt to identify same-sex households and same-sex households with children. Unfortunately, the questionnaires recording this information were designed in such a way that many same-sex families with children could not fully convey their relationship. This is due partly to the government's definition of marriage, adoption laws for same-sex couples, and U.S. society's predominant view of same-sex households. If it is hard to collect information about same-sex families, then the idea of recording the number of families with LGBTQ children or with bisexual or transgender parents seems unfathomable.

Attempts to determine the number of rainbow families in the United States have been made nonetheless. Same-sex couples raising children live in 96 percent of all counties nationwide, with the highest percentages living in the South, the coastal regions of the country, and along the U.S.-Mexico border (Williams Institute, August 2011; Urban Institute 2003). Almost 7 million LGBTQ parents have school-aged children (GLSEN 2008). According to UCLA School of Law's Williams Institute more than 270,000 children in the United States live with same-sex couples (D'Arcy 2011); this figure does not account for children living with a single lesbian or gay parevnt nor does it account for children living with bisexual or transgender parents. The Urban Institute also reports that an estimated 65,500 adopted children (4 percent of all adopted children in the United States) live with a lesbian or gay parent and that an estimated 14,100 foster children (3 percent of all foster children in the United States) live with lesbian or gay foster parents (Gates et al. 2007). For a breakdown of additional demographic data about same-sex couples with children in the United States, consult Krivickas and Lofquist (2011).

Research studies indicate that children as young as 4 years old are aware of their own sexuality and how it compares with that of their classmates (Rowell 2007). Recent analyses of U.S. Census data from the Williams Institute (April 2011) indicate that almost 4 percent of the current adult population identifies as LGBT. Perhaps this percentage could also be applied to children, to suggest that approximately 4 percent of all U.S. children could now or eventually identify as LGBT. Brill and Pepper (2008) report that 1 in 500 children identify as transgender, and Ehrensaft (2011) indicates that more and more children today are coming out and expressing gender-variant behaviors. Unfortunately, exact percentages and numbers are not available for LGBTQ children[1] because of the stigma associated with sexuality and childhood.

While it is difficult to obtain information about the number of rainbow families in the United States, it is quite easy to encounter numerous myths about rainbow

---

1   Note that information is available on the number of LGBTQ youth (adolescents and young adults) as well as adults. However, specific information on children under the age of 13 is not readily available.

families that include sexual perversion, unfit parenting abilities, recruitment to the "gay lifestyle," and so forth. Figure 1.1 highlights some of the more common myths.

Common Myths About Rainbow Families

Myth 1: Children who live in rainbow families with LGBTQ parents or caregivers will grow up to be LGBTQ themselves.
Reality: The sexual orientation of a parent does not influence the sexual orientation of a child.

Myth 2: LGBTQ parents or caregivers have a "gay agenda" to recruit unsuspecting children, starting with their own, to the "gay lifestyle." This is why they want books about rainbow families in classrooms and libraries.
Reality: LGBTQ parents are not trying to gain new recruits. Actually, many LGBTQ parents have experienced considerable discrimination because of their sexual orientation and would prefer their children to be straight to help them avoid the same discrimination. LGBTQ parents want books about rainbow families in libraries and classrooms to allow their own children to see reflections of their families and to help other children learn about rainbow families. Children who hear stories about rainbow families will not become gay converts after hearing a read-aloud.

Myth 3: Rainbow families seek preferential treatment or "special rights" from the government and society.
Reality: Rainbow families seek the same equal rights that are provided to nuclear and heterosexual families. They want healthcare for themselves and their children, they want to maintain their jobs without fear of losing them because of homophobia, they want the right to marry, and they want to live without fear of discrimination for themselves and their children.

Myth 4: Transgender, gender-variant, queer, or gay children are too young to identify their attraction toward others or determine their gender identity.
Reality: Children as young as two exhibit gender variant behaviors, which are a natural part of their individuality. Children as young as six begin to notice that they prefer playing with children of a particular sex or that they find a particular sex more attractive than another. Young children are able to understand and articulate which gender they identify with and which activities they find appealing. Similarly, intersex children begin noticing in preschool which gender they relate to the best.

Myth 5: Most same-sex couples in rainbow families are white men and are economically advantaged.
Reality: Same-sex couples show racial, ethnic, socioeconomic, religious, and cultural diversity. Same-sex parents can be men or women; bisexual, gay, or transgender; and biological, foster, or adoptive caregivers.

Myth 6: LGBTQ parents or caregivers are sexual deviants and pedophiles who adopt children to molest them.

Figure 1.1   Common Myths About Rainbow Families (continued on page 8).

Reality: Many pedophiles are heterosexual men, followed by heterosexual women. LGBTQ parents and caregivers adopt children because they want to have their own family. Pedophilia and homosexuality are not related.

Myth 7: LGBTQ parents and caregivers are not "real parents," lack parenting skills, and are unfit to raise children.
Reality: In the past, during custody battles between divorced parents, some courts have given custody of children to the straight parent, fearing the gay one lives an unsavory lifestyle. LGBTQ parents are as fit to parent as heterosexual parents. If a rainbow family includes two parents, then both of the parents are "real parents," caring for the physical and emotional needs of their children.

Myth 8: There is always a "man" and a "woman" in each same-sex family with one parent having the "masculine" role and one having the "feminine" role.
Reality: As in heterosexual families, the role of parents in same-sex families varies. Sometimes one dad will do the housework and nurturing, and sometimes the other dad will. There are no defined gender roles in same-sex families.

Myth 9: Rainbow families only live in certain neighborhoods and areas of the country.
Reality: Rainbow families live in various regions and in almost every county in the United States.

Myth 10: If a child has a bisexual or transgender parent or caregiver, they will be unable to form their own gender identity.
Reality: The gender identity or sexual orientation of a parent does not influence that of their child.

Myth 11: LGBTQ parents likely have AIDS and will give the disease to their children.
Reality: Parents in rainbow families are no more likely to have AIDS than their heterosexual counterparts.

Myth 12: All gender-variant children will grow up to be lesbian, gay, bisexual, or transgender.
Reality: Some gender-variant children might identify as lesbian, gay, bisexual, or transgender when they get older but they are just as likely to identify as heterosexual.

Myth 13: Lesbian mothers will keep their children from forming positive relationships with males because they dislike men, or gay fathers will keep their children from forming positive relationships with females because they dislike women.
Reality: Most same-sex parents do not hate the opposite gender and all same-sex parents want the best for their children and would promote positive relationships with others, regardless of gender.

Informational, Educational, Recreational, and Literary Needs of Rainbow Families

Children living in gay families, like all children, mostly need stable, loving parents and a community of peers and significant adults who recognize their parents for who they truly are. They and children all over the world need to be free of homophobia. If they ever are, the gay family, rather than being problematic, may become normal and ordinary in literature for young people. (Wolf 1989, p. 57)

As Wolf surmises, rainbow families are no different from other families in their need to help their children feel accepted, valued, and loved. However, society does not always recognize rainbow families. The U.S. federal government refuses to allow gay marriage, LGBTQ individuals and parents are not allowed to adopt children in some states, and educational curricula often fail to portray rainbow families. Hate crimes occur against individuals in rainbow families, and some states prefer to turn a blind eye to these instances. Libraries have a unique opportunity to create welcoming environments that acknowledge these families and celebrate their differences. By providing children's books and other library materials that represent rainbow families and LGBTQ topics, libraries validate their experiences, provide opportunities for children in rainbow families to make important literary connections, and assist all children in understanding themselves and the world around them (Casement 2002; Chick 2008). Garden (2000) iterates:

Gay and lesbian kids [as well as others in LGBTQ families] need to read about people like themselves, just as kids in other minorities do. They need to read about ordinary people who are gay and lesbian, and, also like kids from other minorities, they need to read about artists, athletes, performers, educators, political figures, and other notables who have come from [the LGBTQ] community. (p. xii)

Many rainbow families may not be "out" and children's librarians often find it hard to identify them and to meet their needs. Privacy is important to both parents and children in rainbow families. This privacy can take the form of confidentiality in the patron records for gender-variant or LGBTQ children or discretion when helping children and parents in rainbow families locate materials.

Having access to up-to-date, accurate information about LGBTQ parenting, gender-variant children, LGBTQ children, LGBT adoptions, and LGBT marriage is highly important not only to rainbow families but to all families. Inaccurate or outdated information can stoke anti-gay sentiment. Access to recreational materials — such as audiobooks, children's and family films, children's literature, music, and children's and parenting magazines — that positively and accurately portray LGBTQ-themed topics and rainbow families is important to all children and parents.

Just as important as having access to these materials is the ability to locate them. Subject headings on LGBTQ topics have been updated over time, but many library catalogs do not update their material records. But the most common problem relating to access is the lack of subject headings or keywords that indicate LGBTQ content. Without adequate and accurate terminology in the MARC record of a library item, children and families naturally will have a difficult time accessing relevant materials.

Finally, rainbow families need a welcoming, safe environment where they can explore their educational and recreational needs. This environment should be free of homophobic attitudes and practices. Often librarians do not realize they are practicing inadvertent heterosexism by selecting materials that only feature nuclear families for their library programs and by using Internet filters that suppress information about LGBTQ topics.

Homophobia and Rainbow Families

> What . . . affect[s] our families negatively is homophobia. It is not good for children to live in a closet, to be shamed by peers or teachers, to be shunned by extended family members, or to be treated unjustly in the eyes of the law. Discriminatory public policy such as the ability to fire parents from their jobs because they are gay, deny them custody of their children because they are transgender, or deny moms the right to marry and therefore both be legally recognized parents does hurt families. It is critical that each and every person in our society work to right these wrongs. (Park-Rogers 2004, p. x)

Homophobia is a term that is all too familiar to rainbow families. Children in these families are subject to bullying, teasing, and physical harassment once their peers and other children discover they have LGBTQ parents or caregivers. The same is true for children who are LGBTQ themselves, and for caregivers and other relatives who are LGBTQ. Sometimes homophobic actions come from peers and sometimes they come from teachers, pastors, and other public figures as well as society at large. Homophobia is the societal belief that individuals who are gay, lesbian, bisexual, transgender, or queer/questioning are demented, evil, harmful to society, disgraceful, perverse, and otherwise unfit to live in society. There are varying levels of homophobia ranging from taunts such as "sissy" or "fag" to violent, brutal beatings and murders of children and adults.

As librarians and educators it is important to understand the harm of homophobia and to discern how best to help children and adults in rainbow families feel safe. The subsequent sections detail how homophobia influences young children.

Understanding the Problem

Children formulate their understanding of family structures from the world around them, which includes the attitudes and behaviors of their classmates, families, and educators; print and electronic media; and larger society. Derman-Sparks and Edwards (2010, p. 113) describe children's experiences and understanding of family structures noting that young children:

- ✳ Have their own definitions of family, based upon their own family composition
- ✳ Perceive their family as an extension of themselves and are hurt when their family is not validated in books, library programs, and the curriculum
- ✳ Are curious about the composition of other families and need reassurance that people choose different ways to be a family but that all families love and care for their children

✳ Seek information from and dialogue with teachers, librarians, educators, and caregivers to understand diverse family compositions

✳ Absorb the biases and attitudes that society presents about various family compositions.

Society's depiction of mainstream families in dominant culture generally features a nuclear family with a mom and dad, children, pets, and a house in the suburbs. This type of family is seen in children's books, educational media, film, video games, sitcoms, advertisements, and children's programming, as well as in materials found in classrooms, libraries, religious organizations, play groups, and community agencies. It is quite possible that children can go through their entire educational career without encountering LGBTQ families in educational and reading materials because nuclear families are an ever-present function of the heteronormative school curriculum (Janmohamed and Campbell 2009; Rowell 2007; Casper 2003; Cahill and Theil-heimer 1999). Accordingly, many young children assume that nuclear families are the norm and any other composition, even if it reflects their own, is wrong. Derman-Sparks and Edwards note:

> These messages can have a harmful impact on young children's developing understanding of family and on their openness to accepting all kinds of families. As a result, it is more common to hear preschoolers question the validity of a family in which the child is being raised by a grandparent, an interracial family, or a gay/lesbian-headed family than the validity of a traditional nuclear configuration. (2010, p. 114)

Questioning the validity of LGBTQ families can be innocent at first, but when fueled by the negative attitudes and prejudices of adults, it can lead children to develop homophobic attitudes. Garner (2004) recalls how as young child she internalized the homophobic attitudes that society held against her gay father. She describes how Anita Bryant's "Save Our Children" campaign to demonize homosexuals harmed her psyche.

> As a five-year-old, I overheard conversations about the "Save Our Children" campaign which I interpreted literally. I feared someone was going to find out my dad was gay and come to take me away to "save" me. I had no way of knowing who those people would be, so to be safe, I assumed it could be anyone at any time. . . . I knew that sometimes people who were gay were attacked or killed . . . [and] in my mind, it was only a matter of time before my family was the next target. (Garner 2004, p. 100)

Pogrebin (1983) observes, "Before children have the vaguest idea about who or what is a homosexual, they learn that homosexuality is something frightening, horrid, and nasty. They become homophobic long before they understand what it is they fear" (p. 12). Lester (2007) also mentions that many gay, lesbian, and bisexual children are aware at a very early age of their attractions, and although they may not be able to describe their feelings, they inherently experience the "wrongness" ascribed to those who are different. This "wrongness" is the result of both overt and covert homophobic messages prevalent in society.

Homophobia is common in elementary school and can begin in preschool. At a very young age, homophobia typically takes the form of name calling with the use of words such as "gay," "sissy," "tomboy," or "fag" to describe children whose activities do not match their gender. Patterns of gender-variant behavior are first noticed in children ages two to four, with boys choosing typical female toys/activities and girls choosing typical male toys/activities (Children's National Medical Center 2006; PFLAG 2007). It has also been noted that children (particularly boys) under the age of two express gender variance by cross-dressing (Zucker and Bradley 1995). These children contradict society's gender expectations by choosing clothes, toys, and play activities associated with the opposite gender. Boys playing house or cradling dolls are called "sissies" by their classmates, and girls who prefer to climb, play ball, or roughhouse are called "tomboys." Teachers, parents, and other educators often overlook these comments as harmless and assume that children are just playing. However, these derogatory labels are harmful to the self-esteem and personality development of gender-variant children, many of whom will eventually identify as gay or lesbian. Left unchecked, this harassment against young children in elementary school escalates into violence as they grow older and can take the form of violent games such as "Smear the Queer" or hate crimes (Gordon 1983; National Gay and Lesbian Task Force 2004). "Smear the Queer" is traditionally played by young children. One child is chosen as the "queer" and is chased and then attacked or tackled by other students until he gives up and another "queer" is chosen. The game is played in schools across the United States. Aside from the negative connotation of attacking someone who is queer, the game also holds extremely negative consequences when older children decide to attack another child they have deemed as "queer" because of gender-variant behavior or the existence of an LGBTQ caregiver or relative. "Smear the Queer" among older children often involves violence and beating of the "queer" until the child is left unconscious or the attackers become tired of the game.

Numerous researchers also indicate that name-calling and homophobia are increasingly more intense toward young boys who do not conform to expected gender roles (Baker 2002; Gordon 1983; Herzog 2009; National Gay and Lesbian Task Force 2004). Baker notes that boys who are gender-nonconforming are often "mercilessly teased and made to feel like outcasts . . . subject to the most extreme rejection and ridicule" (p. 49). Intense homophobia toward gender-variant boys relates to society's need to keep everything in balance and predictable. If a boy dresses as a girl and takes on female characteristics, his behavior calls into question clearly defined sex-role expectations that society has created to maintain order and intimates that he will grow up to become a member of a "stigmatized sexual minority" (Herzog 2009). Apparently this is such a heinous act that the American Psychiatric Association (APA 1980) declared "female" behaviors, such as playing with dolls or wearing a dress, abnormal and worthy of treatment if they are performed by a male child. In 1980 the APA designated these activities as evidence of gender identity disorder (GID). Norton (1999) observes that the "problem" is not with gender-variant boys but with the boys' parents and peers. Parents of gender-variant boys may feel "embarrassed in a male-dominated society [because] their boy is acting like a member of the 'weaker sex'" (p. 416). The peers are often feeding off social cues from adults that identify gender-variant behavior as abnormal. Considering it is not the child but the individuals in his surrounding environment that have the "problem," Norton further suggests that perhaps it is the parents and peers who need treatment if a child is identified as having GID and not the child himself.

Teasing and homophobic actions may come from classmates, but they can also come from teachers, parents, and other adult caregivers. In January 2005 and in August 2006 male caregivers killed two toddler boys in the United States when they tried to "toughen up" the boys for acting like sissies (Rondeaux 2005; Stokely 2006). In both instances, the male caregivers recognized the toddler boys' actions as gender-variant (sissy) and decided that the children should act more manly. To help the boys, the men beat, and in one instance tortured, the boys in an effort to make them behave according to society's prescribed role for males.

Homophobia is also directed toward the children of LGBTQ parents. As mentioned previously in this chapter, a common myth held by parents, educators, and other children is that if a child has an LGBTQ parent then he or she will also identify as LGBTQ. Holding this erroneous assumption, children will often tease and bully the children of LGBTQ parents simply because they are afraid of LGBTQ people. The children's book *How Would You Feel If Your Dad Was Gay?* (Heron and Maran 1991) addresses this problem when a young girl unintentionally outs her dads during a class discussion of family. When the other children learn that Jasmine has two dads they ridicule her, and later older kids pick a fight with Jasmine's brother on the playground. The educators in the school ignore the problem. When Jasmine and her brother explain their problem to one of their dads, he says, "Maybe someday nobody will care if a person is gay or straight. But that's not true now, and I know how other people's prejudice can hurt. I understand that you'd want to protect yourself from it. If you don't want the kids at school to know your dad and I are gay, you should be able to keep that to yourself. It's not your job to stop them when they use bad words about gay people, either. You have to deal with this however is best for you" (pp. 11–12).

The dad's statement is just as relevant today as it was more than twenty years ago. Children are still bullied and teased because of their own or their parents' sexual identity. Lamme and Lamme (2003) and Kosciw and Diaz (2008) describe instances of children in the United States and other countries including Australia being bullied, teased, harassed, and ridiculed by their classmates and peers for having LGBTQ family members. According to Kosciw and Diaz, "In 2007, when a nine-year-old girl at Tucker Elementary School in Milton, MA told her fellow third-graders that her mother is a lesbian, she was verbally abused and physically threatened by her classmates" (2008, p. vii). This case is not unique. The researchers further note that almost half (42 percent) of children with LGBTQ parents have experienced verbal harassment (name-calling and slurs such as "dyke" and "fag") because of their family composition.

Kosciw and Diaz also report that one out of five children with LGBTQ parents have been discouraged from talking about their families by teachers and other educators, and the same number also felt excluded from classroom activities relating to family composition due to the lack of representation of rainbow families. Unfortunately, the lack of representation in classroom activities is one of the least significant ways in which children of LGBTQ parents experience homophobia. Garner (2004) also points out that these children "face discrimination against their families that affects them legally, financially, and emotionally. [And,] because non-LGBT families don't have reason to pay attention to homophobia, they rarely understand the adverse effects on children of LGBT parents" (p. 123). Some of these problems include custody battles as a result of divorce, adoption, or death; financial issues when an LGBTQ caregiver loses a job because of his or her sexuality; and other legal problems resulting from laws that do not recognize gay unions and partnerships and define marriage as between a man and woman.

Strategizing a Solution

You ask yourself: What can I do? I'm just a teacher, librarian, preschool educator, or [insert your role here].

There are numerous ways to promote *cultural understanding* of diverse groups in our pluralistic society: designing and integrating an anti-bias curriculum into existing classes or programs, selecting and developing collections of high-quality children's literature that accurately and authentically represent rainbow families, providing opportunities for children to engage in informed discussion of family and cultural diversity, and putting an end to name-calling and homophobic remarks and behaviors, no matter how small they seem. Notice that cultural understanding is emphasized as the end goal, not the teaching of *tolerance*. The word *tolerance* has a negative connotation, suggesting that a person is not happy with a particular situation but will endure it for the sake of harmony. *Tolerance* implies the underlying attitude that if we suffer rainbow families and their behaviors for a certain period of time, eventually they will go away.

As educators, librarians, and teachers who are invested in stopping hate crimes and homophobic violent acts, we want to promote understanding, empathy, and acceptance of differences, not mere tolerance of them. However, Paley (1997) observes "given the number of sad faces, hurt feelings, and lonely outsiders in our schools, the empathy factor may be more talked about than systematically pursued" (p. i). To ensure we move beyond the mere empathy factor, the implementation of an anti-bias education curriculum is one of the best places to start.

Originally developed in 1989 by Louise Derman-Sparks and the ABC Task-force, an anti-bias education curriculum empowers children to have pride in them-selves and their families, to acknowledge and respect differences, and to identify and challenge bias in other children, their teachers, and their families (Derman-Sparks and Edwards 2010). At the same time, anti-bias education encourages librarians, teach-ers, and other educators not only to help children identify and address bias in books, media, and the environment but also to explore their own deeply rooted biases and suppositions about various groups of people. Relating to serving the informational and literacy needs of rainbow families in particular, the establishment of anti-bias programs in early childhood and elementary education curricula in schools and li-

Anti-Bias Program Goals

Goal 1: Children will develop strong social identities, exhibiting pride in themselves, their abilities, and their families.

Goal 2: Children will expand their awareness of other cultures, expressing respect and using accurate language when describing similarities and differences among themselves and other children.

Goal 3: Children will think critically to identify their own misconceptions and stereotypes as well as elements of unfairness exhibited toward other groups in the world at large. Children will understand that prejudice and unfairness hurt others.

Goal 4: Children will develop the skills necessary to counteract prejudice and unfair treatment of others through words and actions.

Figure 1.2   Anti-Bias Program Goals summarized from Derman-Sparks and Edwards (2010).

braries promotes the self-esteem of children exhibiting gender nonconformity and counteracts homophobic reactions to children with same-sex parents, children exhibiting gender nonconformity, or children with LGBTQ family members. Anti-bias programs can be incorporated into storytimes and other types of library programming for children and their caregivers at both school and public libraries. Figure 1.2 highlights the goals of anti-bias programs.

An anti-bias program includes activities and materials that promote cultural understanding. When librarians and educators select and use high-quality children's literature that accurately and authentically represents diverse cultural groups, they are assisting children with their identity development. Well chosen books can celebrate the diversity within rainbow families and normalize experiences of gender-nonconforming children, LGBTQ family members, and children with LGBTQ parents. Garner (2004) notes that children in LGBTQ families are harmed "every time religious leaders, conservative politicians, . . . [and] radio talk-show hosts express their homo-hostile opinion" (p. 13). Positive children's books about rainbow families in classroom lessons and library programs can help to counter these negative influences.

At the same time, these high-quality books can also provide non-LGBTQ children and families with a window into the lives of rainbow families, thereby fostering cultural literacy as it pertains to rainbow families. Lester (2007) suggests that, "Exposing all children to texts with age-appropriate intimacies and interactions between same-sex characters would validate the experiences of gays or bisexuals . . . [and] counter early manifestations of bold and rampant homophobia" found in early childhood environments (p. 66). Using LGBTQ-themed children's books in classrooms and libraries helps to provide mainstream awareness of rainbow families.

Children feel unimportant and invisible when they do not see representations of their lives and families in books. Derman-Sparks and Edwards (2010) note that "invisibility erases identity and experiences; visibility affirms reality. . . . When young children look at the books or posters in a classroom [or library] and find only two-parent [nuclear] families, they may learn that this is the 'right' kind of family and that all other kinds of families are wrong" (p. 13). Children are very astute and can read the reactions and cues of their peers, teachers, parents, relatives, and others in the world around them and deduce how to respond to a particular cultural group. If a child observes his father laughing at a family with two moms, he or she will internalize that two-mom families are not normal. Similarly, if a girl is told by her aunt that she must act and dress more like a lady in order to find a husband and have a happy life, then she will assume that only women who are feminine and married are happy. In both of these instances the adult's comments and actions influence how the child will relate to lesbians, children with two mothers, girls who want to engage in active play, and so forth. The same thing happens when children are exposed only to books that depict specific races, socioeconomic statuses, abilities, and family compositions. Garden (2000) notes, "There are many causes of homophobia. One of them is ignorance . . . Homophobia is made possible when some people believe that gays and lesbians, or people perceived as being gay and lesbian, are subhuman and/or evil, expendable, and worthy only of contempt; honest, accurate books can help counter this" (p. xii).

Throughout this book educators and librarians will find examples of high-quality children's picture books, chapter books, informational books, coloring books, and other media that they can use in their classrooms or libraries to counter homophobia. The journey to inclusive, anti-homophobic, and welcoming educational settings and communities is about to begin!

References

American Psychiatric Association. *Diagnostic and Statistical Manual of Mental Disorders: Third Edition.* Washington, DC: American Psychiatric Association, 1980.

Baker, Jean M. *How Homophobia Hurts Children: Nurturing Diversity at Home, at School, and in the Community.* Binghamton, NY: Harrington Park Press, 2002.

Brill, Stephanie, and Rachel Pepper. *The Transgender Child: A Handbook for Families and Professionals.* San Francisco, CA: Cleis Press, 2008.

Cahill, Betsy, and Rachel Theilheimer. "'Can Tommy and Sam Get Married?' Questions About Gender, Sexuality, and Young Children." *Young Children* 54, no. 1 (1999): 27–31.

Casement, Rose. "Breaking the Silence: The Stories of Gay and Lesbian People in Children's Literature." *New Advocate* 15, no. 3 (2002): 205–213.

Casper, Virginia. "Very Young Children in Lesbian- and Gay-Headed Families: Moving Beyond Acceptance." *Zero to Three* 23, no. 3 (2003): 18–26.

Casper, Virginia, and Steven B. Schultz. *Gay Parents/Straight Schools: Building Communication and Trust.* New York, NY: Teachers College Press, 1999.

Chick, Kay. "Fostering an Appreciation for all Kinds of Families: Picturebooks with Gay and Lesbian Themes." *Bookbird* 46, no. 1 (2008): 15–22.

Children's National Medical Center. *If You Are Concerned About Your Child's Gender Behaviors: A Parent Guide,* 2006. Accessed August 14, 2011, at http://www.childrensnational.org/files/PDF/DepartmentsandPrograms/Neuroscience/Psychiatry/GenderVariantOutreachProgram/GVParentBrochure.pdf.

D'Arcy, Janice. "Gay Parenting As, Well, Parenting." *The Washington Post,* June 15, 2011. Accessed August 14, 2011, at http://www3.law.ucla.edu/williamsinstitute/press/GayParentingAsWellParenting.html.

Derman-Sparks, Louise, and Julie Olsen Edwards. *Anti-Bias Education for Young Children and Ourselves.* Washington, DC: National Association for the Education of Young Children, 2010.

Ehrensaft, Diane. *Gender Born, Gender Made: Raising Healthy Gender-Nonconforming Children.* New York, NY: The Experiment, 2011.

Garden, Nancy. "Foreword." In *Lesbian and Gay Voices: An Annotated Bibliography and Guide to Literature for Children and Young Adults* by Frances Ann Day, pp. ix–xvi. Westport, CT: Greenwood Press, 2000.

Garner, Abigail. *Families Like Mine: Children of Gay Parents Tell It Like It Is.* New York, NY: HarperCollins, 2004.

Gates, Gary, Lee M. V. Badgett, Jennifer Ehrle Macomber, and Kate Chambers. *Adoption and Foster Care by Lesbian and Gay Parents in the United States.* Washington, DC: Urban Institute, 2007. Accessed July 15, 2011, at http://www.urban.org/publications/411437.html.

GLSEN (Gay, Lesbian, and Straight Education Network). *Involved, Invisible, Ignored: The Experiences of Lesbian, Gay, Bisexual and Transgender Parents and Their Children in Our Nation's K–12 Schools,* 2008. Accessed August 14, 2011, at http://www.glsen.org/binary-data/GLSEN_ATTACHMENTS/file/000/001/1104-1.pdf

Gordon, Leonore. "What Do We Say When We Hear 'Faggot'?" *Interracial Books for Children Bulletin* 14, no. 3/4 (1983): 25–27.

Herzog, Ricky. "Sissies, Dolls, and Dancing: Children's Literature and Gender Deviance in the Seventies." *The Lion and the Unicorn* 33, no. 1 (January 2009): 60–76.

Janmohamed, Zeenat, and Ryan Campbell. *Building Bridges: Queer Families in Early Childhood Education.* Toronto, ON: Atkinson Centre for Society and Child Development, 2009.

Kosciw, Joseph, and Elizabeth M. Diaz. *Involved, Invisible, Ignored: The Experiences of Lesbian, Gay, Bisexual, and Transgender Parents and Their Children in Our Nation's K–12 Schools.* New York, NY: Gay, Lesbian, and Straight Education Network, 2008.

Krivickas, Kristy, and Daphne Lofquist. *Demographics of Same-Sex Couple Households with Children.* Presented at the Annual Meeting of the Population Association of America, Washington, DC, March 31–April 2, 2011.

Lamme, Linda Leonard, and Laurel A. Lamme. *Welcoming Children from Sexual-Minority Families into Our Schools.* Bloomington, IN: Phi Delta Kappa Educational Foundation, 2003.

Lester, Neal. "(Un)Happily Ever After: Fairy Tale Morals, Moralities, and Heterosexism in Children's Texts." *Journal of Gay and Lesbian Issues in Education* 4, no. 2 (2007): 55–74.

National Gay and Lesbian Task Force. *Family Policy: Issues Affecting Gay, Lesbian, Bisexual and Transgender Families.* New York, NY: National Gay and Lesbian

Task Force Policy Institute, 2004. Accessed August 14, 2011, at http://www.thetaskforce.org/downloads/reports/reports/FamilyPolicy.pdf.

Norton, Judy. "Transchildren and the Discipline of Children's Literature." *The Lion and the Unicorn* 23, no. 3 (1999): 415–436.

Paley, Vivian Gussin. "Foreword." In *Starting Small: Teaching Tolerance in Preschool and the Early Grades,* ed. by the Teaching Tolerance Project, pp. i–iii. Montgomery, AL: Teaching Tolerance, 1997.

Park-Rogers, Felicia. "Foreword." In *How It Feels to Have a Gay or Lesbian Parent: A Book by Kids for Kids of All Ages* by Judith E. Snow, pp. ix–xi. New York, NY: Harrington Park Press, 2004.

PFLAG. *Our Trans Children*. Washington, DC: PFLAG, 2007. Accessed on August 16, 2011, and available at http://www.pflag.org/fileadmin/user_upload/Publications/OTC_5thedition.pdf.

Pogrebin, Letty Cottin. "The Secret Fear That Keeps Us from Raising Free Children." *Interracial Books for Children Bulletin* 14, no. 3/4 (1983): 10–12.

Rondeaux, Candace. "Mom Testifies Dad Beat Their 3-Year-Old Son." *The St. Petersburg Times*, July 19, 2005. Accessed, August 10, 2011, at http://www.sptimes.com/2005/07/13/Hillsborough/Mom_testifies_dad_bea.shtml.

Rowell, Elizabeth. "Missing! Picture Books Reflecting Gay and Lesbian Families: Make the Curriculum Inclusive for All Children." *Young Children* 62, no. 3 (2007): 24–30.

Stokely, Sandra. "Mother Receives 6 Years in Prison in Son's Death." *The Press Enterprise*, August 14, 2006. Accessed August 10, 2011, at http://www.pe.com/localnews/inland/stories/PE_News_Local_C_rmikey15.299ce35.html.

Urban Institute. "Gay and Lesbian Families in the Census: Couples with Children," 2003. Accessed August 14, 2011, at http://www.urban.org/publications/900626.html.

The Williams Institute (April 2011). "How Many People Are Lesbian, Gay, Bisexual, or Transgender?" Accessed August 14, 2011, at http://www2.law.ucla.edu/williamsinstitute/pdf/How-many-people-are-LGBT-Final.pdf.

The Williams Institute (August 25, 2011). "901,997 Same-Sex Couples Live in U.S.; Couples Represented in 99% of U.S. Counties." Accessed August 26, 2011, at http://services.law.ucla.edu/williamsinstitute/press/PressReleases/PressRelease8.25.doc.

Wolf, Virginia L. "The Gay Family in Literature for Young People." *Children's Literature in Education* 20, no. 1 (1989): 51–58.

Zucker, Kenneth, and Susan Bradley. *Gender Identity Disorder and Pyschosexual Problems in Children and Adolescents*. New York, NY: Guilford Press, 1995.

Children's Literature

Gonzalez, Maya Christina. *Gender Now Coloring Book: A Learning Adventure for Children and Adults*. San Francisco, CA: Reflection Press, 2010.

Heron, Ann, and Meredith Maran. *How Would You Feel If Your Dad Was Gay?* Illustrated by Kris Kovick. Boston, MA: Alyson Wonderland, 1991.

CHAPTER 2

Library Services to Rainbow Families

Never before did it occur to me to look for books about [same-sex] families like ours. I merely assumed that there would be none. . . . Like the members of any minority, we lived in a mental, if not physical, ghetto. We simply did not expect to see ourselves reflected in the world around us. (Wolf 1989, p. 51)

Both public and school librarians can provide a myriad of services, programs, and collections for rainbow families. Baker (2002) asserts that school librarians "can play a significant role in the lives of gay students" by offering safe havens and providing meeting spaces and creating inclusive displays (p. 130). However, it is important for librarians, educators, and parents to understand the difference between reading books and offering inclusive programs about LGBTQ families, and teaching children about sexuality. Adults too often fixate on the sexual aspect of LGBTQ parents, queer children, and children in LGBTQ families and object to young children learning about sexuality and sexual relationships. Gelnaw and Brickley (2010) observe, "Learning about a gay/lesbian-headed family is no more about sexuality than learning about a heterosexual-headed family is. Children's interest in 'family' has to do with who loves them — not the sexual life of the family's adults" (p. 123). With this in mind, librarians can create various types of programs and services for rainbow families that celebrate and focus on children and family.

As mentioned several times in this book, it is important for children in rainbow families to see representations of their lives in the world around them. When children in rainbow families see reflections of themselves in library programming, their existence is validated and they understand that librarians value and respect their family composition. At the same time, library programs and services that are respectful and inclusive of rainbow families counteract homophobic sentiment and normalize the children and adults in rainbow families, providing a window into their lives and experiences for children and caregivers in other types of families. The following sections provide ideas and considerations for librarians planning programs and creating welcoming, safe environments for rainbow families.

Inclusive and Specialized Programming

Casper and Schultz (1999) and Derman-Sparks and Edwards (2010) mention several ways in which teachers (and librarians) can integrate LGBTQ content into their lessons using books that are not specifically gay-themed. They mention changing pronouns while reading a book with androgynous animal parents, starting a book but allowing children to create the ending by inserting their own personal experiences in a written or oral story, and presenting family composition books (texts describing the structure of a family — the number of caregivers, siblings, and so forth) in class and having children actively explain who the various family members represent. They also suggest that young children can make their own books and bring them to class to share, or create their own page for a classroom book on families. Tunks and McGee (2006) provide a helpful model for librarians and other educators who want to share picture books with gender-variant characters. Their model involves a process of selecting, sharing, discussing, and extending high-quality books that break gender stereotypes and promote the acceptance of gender-variant children. Similarly, Rowell (2007) provides information on how to integrate LGBTQ picture books into various subject areas such as math, science, social studies, and art. Rowell annotates several children's fiction and nonfiction picture books and provides information about the literacy skills that can be modeled by using the books.

Children's author and lesbian mother Vicki Harding offers teachers, educators, and librarians a useful guide, *Learn to Include Teacher's Manual: Teaching and Learning About Diverse Families in a Primary School Setting* (2005), that complements her easy-reader series of rainbow family children's books. Developed by practicing educators and university education professors, the 44-page manual is designed for young children in kindergarten through third grade, helping them learn about family diversity and normalizing the experiences of same-sex families with children. Supported by the New South Wales (Australia) Attorney General's Department and the New South Wales Department of Education and Training, the teacher's guide contains numerous hands-on activities, discussion prompts, and reproducible worksheets. It is available free of charge from http://www.hotkey.net.au/~learn_to_include/pdf/revised%20 manual%20Sept%2005.pdf.

Many ideas for inclusive programming exist in the field of early childhood education and can be adapted for use in public and school libraries. Figure 2.1 takes additional suggestions from Casper and Schultz on creating inclusive classrooms and adapts them for librarians serving rainbow families.

Developing Inclusive Library Programs for Rainbow Families

* **Selecting Your Books:** When searching for books to use in a library program that will include rainbow families, determine what LGBTQ children's books you have available and whether they are developmentally appropriate for your target audience. Ask yourself if these LGBTQ books appear to be "self-help" books rather than stories. Think about how you can use non-LGBTQ-specific children's literature in a creative way to be more inclusive of rainbow families. Choose books that you are comfortable reading and discussing with the children.

* **Choosing Your Words Wisely:** When telling stories or singing songs about families or when discussing families with children, use terms such as "parent" or "caregiver" instead of "mother" and "father." Use words and phrases that are comfortable for you. If it does not feel natural to say "lesbian" or "gay," try saying "two mommies" or "two daddies" instead.

* **Knowing How to Respond to Children:** Children are most likely going to ask you questions or make remarks during story time when they know one of the other children comes from a rainbow family. Librarians must be ready to respond. Determine your comfort level talking about rainbow families with children during a library program. How much can you discuss? Are parents in rainbow families comfortable sharing their experiences with the group? Don't put them on the spot and make them respond in public unless you know they are prepared to share their family dynamic with the group. It's also important to understand the nature of children's questions or comments. Are they truly curious about rainbow families or do they want to express their or their families' personal bias against rainbow families?

* **Knowing How to Respond to Caregivers and Other Adults:** Children aren't the only ones who will make a remark about rainbow families if you incorporate LGBTQ-themed children's books, activities, or other content into your library program. Librarians should determine how to respond to the remarks and questions of caregivers and other adults. Determine whether you will answer questions or address comments during the program or afterward? Think about how you will respond to criticism for including rainbow family content in programming for children. How do you respond to parents who do not want LGBTQ content included in general programming? What do you say to gay fathers who ask you not to read stories about mothers during your programs? If your immediate supervisor or library director is not comfortable with the inclusion of rainbow families in children's programming, what do you say? It may be helpful to practice your answers to various scenarios before they arise.

Figure 2.1   Developing Inclusive Library Programs for Rainbow Families. Ideas loosely adapted from Casper and Schultz (1999).

Partnerships with other organizations are a wonderful way to offer programming to rainbow families or on LGBTQ topics. Public and school libraries often do not have the physical or human resources for targeted library programming. By partnering with groups such as PFLAG (Parents, Families and Friends of Lesbians and Gays) and GLSEN (the Gay, Lesbian and Straight Education Network), libraries can increase their outreach to various populations that might not ordinarily visit the library, and can draw on talent and resources unavailable to the library. A perfect illustration of a community partnership that celebrates the diversity of rainbow families can be seen in the following example.

In May 2011 the Communication Studies Department at San Francisco State University partnered with the Office of Children's Services at the San Francisco Public Library to offer a children's and family program that integrated eight LGBTQ children's picture books with the performing arts. The program, "Dragons & Dresses & Ducklings — Oh My!," highlights various alternative families and gender expressions and promotes cultural literacy. According to the program's director, Amy Kilgard, the show "serves to advocate for non-heterosexual children, children who do not conform to gender norms, and children from non-traditional families, who are frequent targets of bullying." She also notes, "Through the use of color, magic, and laughter, we hope to plant the seeds of social justice in the youth of today and tomorrow" (phone interview, August 2011). "Dragons & Dresses & Ducklings — Oh My!" was presented three times during May, once at the public library and twice on the university campus, and was very well received. Commenting on the importance of the library-university partnership, Kilgard stated, "I believe that developing partnerships between universities and public libraries is an important way to embark upon education and outreach about LGBTQ issues especially around children and families" (phone interview, August 2011). See Figure 2.2 for an example of the promotional material used for this program.

Many public libraries across the United States use the summer reading promotional materials and themes provided by the Collaborative Summer Library Program (CSLP), a grassroots consortium. In addition to providing suggestions for programming activities and marketing materials, the CSLP also gives librarians information on how to plan programs and services for specific populations. Of particular interest to libraries serving rainbow families is the page of the CSLP Web site dedicated to alternative families, especially the section on GLBT Family Resources (http://www.cslpreads.org/alternative-families.html). This site gives links to associations serving rainbow families and lists recommended LGBTQ children's books for library programming.

Other ideas for library programs that include parents and children from rainbow families are:

* Events in conjunction with Gay Pride (held in June)
* Outreach at LGBTQ events: Rainbow family picnics, PFLAG meetings/ events, etc.
* Adoption workshops that include information for LGBTQ parents
* Inclusive programming for rainbow families in general library programs
* Family films series that includes gay-friendly films

Figure 2.2   Promotional material created by Albert Afan, San Francisco State University, for "Dragons & Dresses & Ducklings — Oh My!" Directed by Amy Kilgard.

Figure 2.3   Rainbow Families Council poster: Developed by the Rainbow Families Council, Victoria, Australia, http://rainbowfamilies.org.au/

✳ Book discussion groups on issues of interest to all parents including LGBTQ parents

✳ Author visits from gay-friendly children's authors and illustrators such as Todd Parr, Patricia Polacco, and Henry Cole who have written a variety of children's books.

Creating Welcoming Environments and Inclusive Displays

It is important to remember that many rainbow families are "closeted," meaning that they want to keep the sexual orientation of children and/or parents or other relatives a secret rather than making their status public knowledge. Librarians should respect rainbow families' need for privacy and not "out" them during a program or in the library. However, the problem with rainbow families being closeted is that librarians and other educators often have a difficult time identifying this population and often assume that they do not have any rainbow families in their community. A study of U.S. public libraries situated in communities with a large concentration of same-sex families with children (Naidoo 2009) discovered that many of the librarians were not aware of gay families in the neighborhoods served by their branch libraries. In addition, many of these libraries did not offer inclusive programs and services for rainbow families because they could not identify them in community analyses conducted by the library.

However, librarians can create welcoming environments that are accepting of rainbow families and represent the accomplishments of LGBTQ individuals even if they are unable to identify specific rainbow families in their community. Inclusive environments benefit everyone, not just the children and caregivers in rainbow families. If librarians do know of LGBTQ parents in the community, they may want to consult with them about creating an inclusive and welcoming children's department and library setting and about developing programs and services specifically for rainbow families. According to Kosciw and Diaz (2008), LGBTQ parents are more likely to be involved in their child's education than other parents. This is great news for school and public librarians who need assistance in making the library a place where rainbow families feel a sense of belonging. Librarians can also consider contacting local LGBTQ organizations such as PFLAG to identify "out" parents in their neighborhood.

Displaying posters that are inclusive of rainbow families helps to normalize their presence in society and suggest that the library is a safe haven for them. A wonderful resource for librarians looking for suitable posters or for suggestions on including rainbow families in early childhood programs is the Rainbow Families Council, a volunteer community organization based in Victoria, Australia. Their Web site (http://rainbowfamilies.org.au/) contains beautiful information sheets and posters (see, for example, Figure 2.3) that can be printed and used in the library. The information sheets can be placed in LGBTQ-friendly displays in the parenting and/or picture book section of the library and the posters can be used in library programming rooms.

The American Library Association has created a toolkit with helpful information for libraries interested in creating welcoming environments for LGBTQ individuals.

Included in "Out in the Library: Materials, Displays and Services for the Gay, Lesbian, Bisexual, and Transgender Community" is information about LGBTQ materials in school libraries as well as LGBTQ children's books (available at http://www.ala.org/ala/aboutala/offices/oif/iftoolkits/glbttoolkit/glbttoolkit.cfm).

Figure 2.4 contains additional considerations for making the children's department welcoming and inclusive. These suggestions have been adapted from Janmohamed and Campbell's *Building Bridges: Queer Families in Early Childhood Education* (2009).

Librarians wanting information from the front lines of library service will also want to consult Figure 2.5 for Nancy Silverrod's advice about developing services and

---

Creating Welcoming Library Spaces for Rainbow Families

✳ Ensure open communication among library staff, parents, and children to promote mutual understanding when differences in opinion arise around queer topics.

✳ Recognize and address personal prejudices and fears among library staff working with adults and children in rainbow families.

✳ Commit to professional development opportunities for children's and service library staff that promote openness and respect for rainbow families.

✳ Adopt a children's department philosophy that communicates an explicit commitment to sexual/gender diversity.

✳ Ensure the library staff maintains respectful verbal and nonverbal language when interacting with adults and children in rainbow families. This includes interactions during programming and reader's advisory but also when discussing rainbow families. Do not assume that rainbow families are "out" or comfortable sharing their queer status.

✳ Take advantage of teachable moments to address children's inquiries relating to queer issues and rainbow families.

✳ Confront any observed instances of teasing and bullying relating to diversity in sexual or gender identity. These could be interactions among children, among parents, or even among library staff.

✳ Encourage LGBTQ parents and caregivers to volunteer and participate in library programs for young children.

✳ Collaborate with community agencies that serve children and/or adults in rainbow families.

✳ Create positive, safe, and welcoming library spaces in which rainbow families feel supported. This includes the use of inclusive language in all marketing and promotional materials (program schedules and descriptions, parent newsletters, posters, etc.) as well as library forms (library card applications, volunteer forms, etc.).

Figure 2.4   Creating Welcoming Library Spaces for Rainbow Families. Adapted from Janmohamed and Campbell (2009).

✳ Display safe zone or rainbow stickers to symbolize a welcoming environment for families using visual cues. Note: These should not be displayed on library materials as such labeling can deter children and adults in rainbow families from using the material, particularly if they are not "out."

✳ Create visual displays and bulletin boards that include all families, introducing rainbow families along with single-parent families, grandparent-headed families, stepfamilies, multiracial families, foster families, etc.

✳ Integrate LGBTQ children's books into regular storytimes and library programs, and display them on bookshelves alongside other children's books.

✳ Examine library materials for stereotypes and biases such as gender stereotypes, sex role stereotypes, homophobia, etc.

✳ Create programming materials that ensure non-stereotypical representations of LGBTQ children and adults and rainbow families.

✳ Avoid tokenism or the tourist approach in exploring LGBTQ topics with children and their families. For example, don't limit your exploration of LGBTQ topics to the month of June for Gay Pride month. Rather, incorporate LGBTQ representation in regular children's programming.

Nancy Silverrod: Serving Rainbow Families in the Library

As an adult reference librarian and former youth services librarian at the San Francisco Public Library, Nancy Silverrod has had numerous opportunities to work with both children and adults in rainbow families. She emphasizes the importance of having high quality fiction and nonfiction library materials available to all children and families (whether rainbow or not) as a way to normalize the rainbow family within the community. Silverrod also notes that parents and caregivers in rainbow families have very specialized needs and seek resources that will advocate for their children at school, in society, and in the medical community. However, she believes that the single most important informational need of LGBTQ families is to see themselves positively reflected in library materials and to feel welcome in the library.

WELCOMING LIBRARIES

Silverrod suggests that librarians be welcoming and helpful to all families, regardless of their informational needs or family makeup. Rainbow families should receive the same treatment as other families. Is there the same warmth in your voice and bounce in your step when you help them as when you are working with heterosexual families? Librarians should know the reading interests of both the children and caregivers in LGBTQ families and offer library programming that acknowledges these families. Relevant programming could consist of a craft activity with Marcus Ewert's *10,000 Dresses* where children make dresses they fantasize about. This type of program would be relevant to gender-variant and other children as well. Having Gay Pride displays or displays that are

Figure 2.5   Nancy Silverrod: Serving Rainbow Families in the Library (continued on page 28).

inclusive of LGBTQ families are another way to make rainbow families feel welcome in the library.

COLLECTION CONSIDERATIONS

While high-quality collections of LGBTQ materials for children and their parents should be a staple for libraries serving rainbow families, Silverrod points out there is a dilemma in managing these collections. Should librarians label queer children's materials with rainbow stickers to make them easier to find? Some advocates say these stickers make it easier for those who are closeted to find LGBTQ materials, but at the same time they also clearly announce to library staff and other patrons that the material is "queer." Silverrod notes that she leans toward labeling the books. Interestingly, the rainbow sticker confuses some parents and children as they think the materials are ones featured on the children's television program Reading Rainbow, which has nothing to do with LGBTQ children's materials.

Silverrod also suggests that children's librarians include a small parenting section in the youth department in addition to the larger parenting collection in the adult nonfiction section. This section would include all types of parenting books, with LGBTQ titles filed alongside the others. Silverrod further comments that a parenting brochure that includes LGBTQ and other parenting titles would be useful to caregivers in rainbow families.

HANDLING CENSORSHIP ATTEMPTS

Censorship attempts seem to be inevitable for libraries with a collection of LGBTQ materials. Silverrod advises librarians to make sure their library has a strong collection development policy that conforms with the ALA Bill of Rights and that they have the administration's support of services and collections to rainbow families.

She also encourages librarians to know their community demographics and identify community organizations that serve LGBTQ families. With their support, librarians can identify the number of rainbow families in the community and can use this information to support the inclusion of LGBTQ materials. Taxpayers — including LGBTQ members of this community — support the library, and we are here to serve everybody.

Silverrod also points librarians to library director Jamie LaRue's response to the censorship attack on Sarah Brannen's Uncle Bobby's Wedding as the model for a respectful and responsible response to censorship attempts on queer materials. Available at http://jaslarue.blogspot.com/2008/07/uncle-bobbys-wedding.html.

JOYS AND CHALLENGES

One of the biggest joys of serving rainbow families, according to Silverrod, is giving the right book to the right people at the right time. She quickly adds that having an environment where rainbow families feel comfortable approaching the reference desk is also rewarding.

Perhaps the biggest challenge of serving rainbow families is educating librarians about the needs of this community. Silverrod observes that many librarians believe that "those people" exist somewhere else but not in their city or neighborhoods. As a result, librarians don't plan collections, programs, and services that are inclusive of rainbow families. She believes that sensitivity to the informational needs of LGBTQ families should be emphasized both in library school and in staff training. Once librarians understand that LGBTQ families are present in 96 percent of all counties nationwide and realize that their needs are just as important as any other patrons, rainbow families will feel a warm sense of welcome in the library.

programs for rainbow families and how to handle challenges to LGBTQ children's material.

Distributing Relevant Bibliographies and Pamphlets

As suggested in the programming section, librarians can create bibliographies of recommended LGBTQ parenting books or children's picture books, chapter books, and informational books that are inclusive of LGBTQ-themes. These can be offered in print format or made available online (or both). For instance, the San Francisco Public Library offers a specific online bibliography of recommended LGBTQ-themed children's books entitled "A Rainbow Celebration: Gays and Lesbians in Books for Children" (http://sfpl.org/index.php?pg=2000154901), the Wilmette (Illinois) Public Library offers "Gay and Lesbian Books for Young People" (http://www.wilmette. lib.il.us/kids/lists/bib.php?bib_title_id=167), and the Allen County (Indiana) Public Library provides "Parents' Primer: Families: Same-Sex Parents" (http://www.acpl.lib. in.us/children/family_samesex.html). The advantage of offering bibliographies online is that rainbow families can access the lists in the privacy of their own homes and then go to the library to find the materials.

Libraries can also offer relevant information in the form of electronic publications on their Web sites. The Oak Park (Illinois) Public Library provides a very useful Transgender Resource Collection that includes webstreams, readings lists, and a library toolkit (http://www.oppl.org/media/trc.htm), and the London (Ontario) Public Library offers a useful Web page on Gay and Lesbian Parenting (http://www. londonpubliclibrary.ca/node/75). Similarly, the Burbank (California) Public Library publishes the Burbank Library Blog and in August 2011 posted "New Children's Books About Children with Gay Parents" in which they talk about gay-themed picture books and profile two of the newest titles available in the children's department (http://burbanklibrary.blogspot.com/2011/08/what-were-reading.html).

These are only a few of the ways in which libraries provide information about services to rainbow families using print and online bibliographies and webographies. However, these samples can give librarians ideas about how to publicize their own collections and services to children and their caregivers.

Overcoming Barriers to Library Services to Rainbow Families

In an ideal world, librarians would not experience any problems when planning services and programs or developing collections for children and adults in rainbow families. Unfortunately, the reality is that many librarians have good intentions and work hard to plan services but meet resistance from their administrators or local community. Alternatively, librarians may plan creative and dynamic programs for rainbow families only to discover that these families in their community are not "out" and will not attend an exclusive program celebrating rainbow families.

What follows are common problems or barriers identified by public children's librarians, accompanied by suggested solutions. Many of these problems were identified during an examination of U.S. public libraries situated in communities with significant same-sex parent adoptions (Naidoo 2009).

> **Problem A:** Some librarians have complained that LGBTQ parents are hard to identify and the library cannot ask a person about their sexuality. As a result, it is difficult to plan programs and services for LGBTQ parents and their children.
>
> **Solution:** Librarians can work with local adoption agencies and LGBTQ community groups to identify and locate LGBTQ parents. Once these parents are identified, librarians can devise focus groups of LGBTQ parents to determine their needs and strategize how the library can best meet those needs via materials, programs, and services.
>
> **Problem B:** The library does not have the desire — or the resources — to offer services to segregated groups of children or populations, and would not want to have an LGBTQ-themed storytime that would bring attention to rainbow families. (Or this barrier could simply be that librarians assume that rainbow families are not using their library or requesting services for their children.)
>
> **Solution:** Librarians can be proactive and inclusive, incorporating books and other materials about all types of families in the library's regular children's programming. Because parents may feel uncomfortable outing themselves to the librarian, specific requests for LGBTQ-themed materials in storytimes are not likely to surface.
>
> **Problem C:** The library has planned special programs and services for rainbow families but the programs have been poorly attended and the services are rarely used.
>
> **Solution:** There are multiple solutions here. Children's librarians can work with local agencies serving LGBTQ parents to advertise programs, collections, and services. For instance, the library can distribute recommended bibliographies of children's books and parenting books to adoption agencies serving LGBTQ parents or to pediatrician offices serving children in rainbow families. Librarians can also include numerous types of gay-friendly resources on these lists so that they are useful to all families and not seen as only for "those" types of families. Examples would be general parenting books that include information for LGBT parents or family picture books such as those by Todd Parr that include same-sex parents. These bibliographies can be distributed to neighborhood preschools and displayed in the parenting section of the library.

Problem D: The library does not have money to purchase LGBTQ-themed children's books or parenting titles.

Solution: Librarians can apply for special grants from various local and national LGBTQ organizations that offer educational funding. Another option is to incorporate LGBTQ-themed titles in regular book orders for children's and parenting materials. Librarians can justify these purchases as evidence of inclusive collection development practices that round out the library collection with materials about all types of families and parents and for all types of families and parents. A final solution would be to take advantage of free online LGBTQ children's books such as those found on the Rainbow Rumpus Web site (http://rainbowrumpus.org/htm/printable.htm) and the Spanish Web site ONG por la No Discriminación (http://www.trabajemosporelmundo.org/ong-nd/editorial_nd_conjunto_ingles.html).

Problem E: A particular library is located in a conservative area and cannot jeopardize its funding by incorporating LGBTQ content into regular children's programs or by offering specialized booklists that would include LGBTQ children's or parenting titles.

Solution: Library staff can undergo sensitivity training to learn how to serve rainbow families discreetly, outside special programs. Librarians can tell parents where LGBTQ children's/parenting books are located or how to use the catalog to find these books (assuming these books have been cataloged using consistent terminology). Then again, librarians can incorporate said books into displays about all types of families rather than using them in specialized programs. Many books about rainbow families do not outwardly look "gay" and would not attract the ire of would-be censors.

Although these are only a few of the many possible barriers to serving rainbow families, librarians can use these examples to spur creative "out-of-the-box" solutions for meeting the needs of rainbow families. With ingenuity and sensitivity, children's librarians can offer services and collections to children and adults in rainbow families. And what children's librarian doesn't have a good dose of ingenuity and creativity ready to help a child?

References

Baker, Jean M. *How Homophobia Hurts Children: Nurturing Diversity at Home, at School, and in the Community*. Binghamton, NY: Harrington Park Press, 2002.

Casper, Virginia, and Steven B. Schultz. *Gay Parents/Straight Schools: Building Communication and Trust*. New York, NY: Teachers College Press, 1999.

Derman-Sparks, Louise, and Julie Olsen Edwards. *Anti-Bias Education for Young Children and Ourselves*. Washington, DC: National Association for the Education of Young Children, 2010.

Gelnaw, Aimee, and Margie Brickley. "Supporting Children in Lesbian/Gay-Headed Families." In *Anti-Bias Education for Young Children and Ourselves*, by Louise Derman-Sparks and Julie Olsen Edwards, pp. 122–124. Washington, DC: National Association for the Education of Young Children, 2010.

Harding, Vicki. *Learn to Include Teacher's Manual: Teaching and Learning About Diverse Families in a Primary School Setting*. Dulwich Hill, New South Wales (Australia): Learn to Include, 2005. Accessed on Jan. 10, 2011, at http://www.hotkey.net. au/~learn_to_include/pdf/revised%20manual%20Sept%2005.pdf.

Janmohamed, Zeenat, and Ryan Campbell. *Building Bridges: Queer Families in Early Childhood Education*. Toronto, ON: Atkinson Centre for Society and Child Development, 2009.

Kosciw, Joseph, and Elizabeth M. Diaz. *Involved, Invisible, Ignored: The Experiences of Lesbian, Gay, Bisexual, and Transgender Parents and Their Children in Our Nation's K–12 Schools*. New York, NY: Gay, Lesbian, and Straight Education Network, 2008.

Naidoo, Jamie Campbell. *Focus on My Family: An Analysis of Gay-Themed Picturebooks and Public Library Services for LGBTQ Children and Children with Same-Sex Parents*. Paper presented at the annual conference of the American Library Association, Chicago, IL, July 2009.

Rowell, Elizabeth. "Missing! Picture Books Reflecting Gay and Lesbian Families: Make the Curriculum Inclusive for All Children." *Young Children* 62, no. 3 (2007): 24–30.

Tunks, Karyn Wellhousen, and Jessica McGee. "Embracing William, Oliver Button, and Tough Boris: Learning Acceptance from Characters in Children's Literature." *Childhood Education* 82, no. 4 (Summer 2006): 213–218.

Wolf, Virginia L. "The Gay Family in Literature for Young People." *Children's Literature in Education* 20, no. 1 (1989): 51–58.

PART 2

✳

LGBTQ Content in Children's Literature

CHAPTER 3

Overview of LGBTQ *Children's* Literature

Books for young children often interpret their world, and, considering the size of the homosexual population, it is perhaps surprising that references to homosexuality do not occur more frequently and naturally in books which expand and explain the child's world. (Clyde and Lobban 1992, p. xvi)

Most of this volume focuses on locating, evaluating, and developing collections of LGBTQ children's literature to better serve the various literacy needs of rainbow families. From picture books to novels to informational books, LGBTQ children's literature can take a variety of formats and encompass a wide range of topics such as family composition, identity development, artificial insemination, AIDS, and social activism. In order for librarians, teachers, parents, and other educators to better understand the literature highlighted throughout this book, a review of the history, current trends, and future of LGBTQ children's publishing is worthwhile, along with information about intellectual freedom and the censorship of LGBTQ children's literature.

Critical Overview of LGBTQ Children's Literature

When compared with their younger counterparts, adolescents have no shortage of high-quality books representing LGBTQ perspectives and families. Considerable research has been conducted in the area of young adult LGBTQ literature, and a growing body of critical work highlights scholars' analyses of these works as well as how to use these books in libraries and classrooms (Cart and Jenkins 2006; Whelan 2006; Alexander and Miselis 2007; Martin and Murdock 2007; Duke 2011; Webber 2010). However, children's literature representing LGBTQ perspectives and families has been scarce. In addition, the research, critical insights, and practical suggestions relating to young adult LGBTQ materials are virtually nonexistent in the children's literature realm. Abate and Kidd (2011) acknowledge,

> While the LGBTQ teenager can be imagined and even brought into the light of day, not yet so for the lesbian/gay first-grader. The bulk of LGBTQ literature for younger readers has focused on lesbian/gay parents or uncles. The children's picture book has been more resistant to LGBTQ theming, in large measure because of the prohibition against the representation of any sexuality, much less queer sexuality, especially in childhood. . . . [M]ost lesbian/gay-affirmative picture books evacuate sexuality from the family portrait, and refer only obliquely to HIV and AIDS. Persistent is the belief that sexuality, and especially homosexuality, threatens the essence of childhood. (pp. 5–6)

The avoidance of homosexuality in children's literature is a plight that the field has suffered for quite some time and that still continues today. For the most part, the children's books that do present LGBTQ characters are either self-published or published by small or independent presses that have a feminist or queer focus. McRuer (2011) suggests that, "the exclusion of gay men and lesbians from mainstream children's literature is still an unspoken imperative" (p. 184). Certainly the same can be said for children's books representing transgender and bisexual characters. Naidoo (2012) notes that relatively few children's picture books and early chapter books present transgender characters and even fewer depict bisexual characters. Of the children's books that do represent LGBTQ characters "most focus on parental sexuality and family structure rather than families engaged in day-to-day activities. Rarely do books portray LGBT characters as normal people living everyday lives" (Emfinger 2007, p. 25).

Within the scant body of queer children's literature (for ages 11 and under) there is a predilection for depicting predominantly middle-class white households with two lesbian mothers. A growing number of books depict middle-class gay fathers, but books that represent mixed-race or culturally diverse couples are virtually nonexistent. LGBTQ characters that are differently able (have varying abilities) as well as elderly LGBTQ characters are even scarcer. Similarly, queer family members beyond parents generally focus on gay uncles, ignoring lesbian aunts, lesbian grandmothers, gay grandfathers, and other queer relatives (Naidoo 2012).

The absence of queer characters in children's literature is partially related to commercial viability. Previous research on publishing statistics and trends indicates that children's books about culturally diverse populations do not sell as well as culturally generic or mainstream topics (Norton 2008; Taxel 2002). Librarians, teachers, parents, and other consumers are less likely to purchase books that are different from their own or mainstream culture for a variety of reasons. First, librarians and teachers are concerned about purchasing titles written about a culture that they do not understand for fear of acquiring books that are stereotypical or derogatory toward that particular culture. Second, parents often purchase books for their children that they remember from childhood or that mirror their own situations, hobbies, passions, and so forth. Also, purchasing books for classrooms and libraries that do not reflect the beliefs, values, or lives of mainstream society can almost guarantee that social conservatives will oppose the books and try to censor them from collections.

Playing It Safe

Ford (2011) and Garden (1994) suggest that children's book authors choose "safe" options for depicting LGBTQ characters, often requiring readers to read between the lines to identify queer content. Whether the omission of clearly described, concrete queer behavior is the author's doing or evidence of the editor's influence, many children's books with would-be queer content do require astute children and adults to pointedly impute certain elements. Books such as *Rosa Bonheur* (Turner 1991) and *Families* (Tax 1981) mention homosexual relationships in a roundabout fashion. When describing the relationship between Rosa Bonheur and her partner, Turner uses the phrase "lifetime friend" to describe Nathalie Mica. Similarly, Tax uses mother and "godmother" to refer to a child's two moms. In both instances, children and parents, particularly those in rainbow families, often recognize the lesbian relationship, but this relationship must be imputed.

Lester (2007) also believes that authors play it safe by failing to address the developing sexual identity of children, thereby ignoring the feelings of LGBTQ children. Although numerous accounts and interviews with LGBTQ adults confirm that they began to realize their otherness and sexuality as young as five or six years of age, children's books tend to stay far away from identifying children who have same-sex feelings and desires. Unfortunately, this reinforces the "wrongness" and "otherness" that these children feel in their heteronormative environments. Harding (2005) suggests, "Ignoring gay and lesbian existence is dishonest. It also does little to encourage a strong sense of self-identity in children who have LGBT people in their lives, or who may grow up to be LGBT, to not see their world reflected in [their] books" (p. 532).

By writing "safe" books, authors are not as likely to be the targets of censors as authors who clearly delineate queer content. If a reader has to infer a relationship, sexual orientation, or gender in children's literature, there is always the chance that would-be censors will not notice the queer content. Unfortunately, this presumes that children in rainbow families will be able to read between the lines to identify particular content that mirrors their own lives and situations. Whether or not these children are successful in this venture depends largely on their own deductive abilities.

Picture-Perfect Families

Esposito (2009) further suggests that lesbian-themed children's books do not fully capture the experience of running a lesbian household with children. In her analysis of five children's picture books depicting lesbian families, Esposito surmises that lesbian families are "de-queered" in an attempt to make them more accessible to mainstream children, parents, and educators. In doing so, the complexity of issues facing lesbian parents is not completely conveyed and lesbian families are portrayed as happy and without problems. These inauthentic books deny "the very real and very painful political and social struggles lesbians face" (Esposito 2009, p. 75). As a result, lesbian mothers and their children who read these picture books may have a difficult time identifying with the characters and situations presented.

This sentiment is mirrored by Bronski (1993) in his examination of LGBTQ children's books published in the early 1990s. He notes,

> Most of the books produced for children of lesbian and gay families are overwhelmingly "positive." And although this is clearly an attempt to offset cultural and homophobic assumptions about the parenting abilities of lesbians and gay men, the problem is that almost all of these books are *simply* (emphasis in original) positive. They seem, to some degree, to be knee-jerk responses to mainstream cultural assumptions and have no complexity, edge or wit to them. They are purely reactive and purely imitative. (Bronski 1993, p. 64)

Bronski goes on to describe the stereotypical images of gay men in *Uncle What-Is-It Is Coming to Visit!!* (Willhoite 1993), pointing out that drag queens and leather daddies are used by the working class to define gay men as "grotesque" while it is the middle-class, preppy gay uncle who assuages children's fears about homosexuals and indicates that some "gay men do dress like women and some do wear black leather, but that's all right too" (1993, p. 67). Ostensibly, the underlying message of the book is that "normal" gay men are okay but eccentricities in the gay community are not acceptable.

Portrayals of Cross-Dressing and Transgender Children

The idea of cross-dressing males is certainly one that is not agreeable to numerous parents and educators. They believe the notion that a boy would voluntarily dress as a woman and suppress his masculinity is beyond the realm of acceptable subjects in books for young children. Various children's books have attempted to address cross-dressing males by ridiculing them. Flanagan (2007) mentions *Another Perfect Day* (MacDonald 2002) and *Marvin Redpost: Is He a Girl?* (Sachar 1993) as two examples of books in which femininity and cross-dressing take away male power. However, Flanagan also mentions books such as *Princess Max* (Stiller 2001) as titles that introduce children to the idea that cross-dressing is wrong — something they pick up easily from the social messages around them — and then reinterpret that message as an expression of individuality and normalcy. This is also clearly evident in the picture book *Jesse's Dream Skirt* (Mack 1979) in which a preschool boy wants to wear a skirt to school, is ridiculed by his classmates, and then eventually embraced for his individuality. Likewise, *What a Year!* (dePaola 2002), part of children's author and illustrator Tomie dePaola's early chapter book series, follows his childhood exploits including dressing up as Snow White for Halloween and being a bride at his brother's birthday party. In the book, young Tomie is never admonished for cross-dressing and his behavior is treated as a non-issue.

While male cross-dressing is taboo, female cross-dressing is not regarded with the same level of concern. The topic of cross-dressing among females is covered in several historical children's books including *Rough, Tough Charley* (Kay 2007), *No Girls Allowed: Tales of Daring Women Dressed as Men for Love, Freedom and Adventure* (Hughes 2008), and *Sarah Emma Edmonds Was a Great Pretender: The True Story of a Civil War Spy* (Jones 2011). In these instances, females dress and masquerade as men for a variety of reasons but for the most part are not condemned or ridiculed for the act. In books such as *Rough, Tough Charley* the female character spends her entire adult life as a man and is a successful entrepreneur. When her cross-dressing is discovered, condemnation is not as forthcoming as it would have been if she were a man dressed as a woman. Similarly, Tunks and McGee (2006) point out that children and educators embrace the female character in *Amazing Grace* (Hoffman 1991) for taking on the role of Peter Pan in a school play; however, these same educators and children, because of social conditioning, would balk at the idea of a male character dressing up as Tinkerbell or Wendy in the same school play.

Although books such as *Princess Max; Rough, Tough Charley; Jesse's Dream Skirt*; and *What a Year!* avoid the topic of the transgender child, they could easily be embraced by transgender or gender-nonconforming children searching for books that present characters that shed or mask their gender. One of the most vivid portrayals of a transgender/gender-nonconforming boy can be seen not in a book but in the French family film *Ma vie en rose* (translated as *My Life in Pink*) (Berlinder 1997). In this film, seven-year-old Ludovic clearly believes and feels that he is a girl, particularly because he enjoys wearing makeup, dressing in girls' clothing, and playing with dolls. When his family moves to a new neighborhood, Ludovic becomes infatuated with the boy next door and declares that they will marry someday once he becomes a girl. Ludovic clearly believes that in time he will change into a girl and that the reason he is physically a boy is purely scientific — that his extra X chromosome fell into the garbage on its way from heaven. Berlinder's clear depiction of a transgender child is unfortunately never encountered by the childhood audience that could benefit from it most because of the movie's "Restricted" rating.

Children's books and materials that feature positive portrayals of transgender characters are needed to support the positive identity development of transgender children. Unfortunately, children's picture books and chapter books that present transgender children in such a matter-of-fact manner are virtually invisible in contemporary classrooms and libraries. Only a few are available from small presses and they rarely make their way into classrooms and onto library shelves.

History of LGBTQ Children's Literature

In addition to a critical overview of the politics of publishing LGBTQ children's literature, a historical look at this genre of literature can assist librarians, teachers, and other educators in their understanding of contemporary LGBTQ children's books.

By looking at the past along with the key works of pioneer authors and illustrators, we can see influences on the groundbreaking works being published today.

Pre-1980s

Prior to the 1980s, very few U.S. books or books published outside the United States for younger children mentioned lesbian and gay characters, much less those that were bisexual or transgender. Jane Severance's *When Megan Went Away* (1979) is considered by many children's literature scholars to be the first U.S. children's picture book to depict a lesbian relationship as well as a separation (divorce) between lesbian partners. However, the book was published by the small feminist press Lollipop Power and was not readily available to rainbow families.

In 1983 Goodman (1983) conducted a survey of LGBTQ children's and young adult literature to ascertain the quality of these titles. Of the thousands of picture books published between 1969 and 1983, she could only identify three books that depicted same-sex relationships, and all of these represented lesbians whose relationships were so sketchily described that children would not be able to understand them. Consequently, she surmised "Lesbian and gay characters are as good as invisible in books for preschool and early elementary-age children" (Goodman 1983, p. 15).

However, representations of gender diversity and gender-nonconforming characters did appear in children's books prior to the 1980s. Munro Leaf's *The Story of Ferdinand* (1936) is considered one of the first U.S. children's books to depict gender nonconformity, albeit a nonconforming bull that prefers smelling flowers to fighting. Gender nonconformity among human characters was scarce in children's books during this time period. Some children's books, such as *Tomboy's Doll* (Steiner 1969), presented girls who were "tomboys" and boys who were considered "sissies," but for the most part these representations did not seek to normalize these behaviors. Rather, gender nonconformity was regarded as a problem for boys and girls that needed to be "fixed."

It was not until the 1970s that positive depictions of gender nonconformity among human characters became more prevalent in children's literature. Feminist presses such as Daughters Publishing and Lollipop Power produced books that illustrated girls in active and traditionally male roles, males in nurturing roles, and boys and girls defying gender roles altogether. Herzog (2009) notes that this era saw the publication of 83 gender-non-normative books for young children. One of the best-known books during this period was the seminal picture book *William's Doll* (Zolotow 1972), which normalized a boy's desire to play with dolls and engage in gender-variant activities. The book was an instant hit in the educational and library communities and was adapted the same year into a song for the successful children's album *Free to Be . . . You and Me* (Thomas 1972), which also presented positive depictions of girls and boys engaged in gender-nonconforming activities. Just a few years later *X: A Fabulous Child's Story* (Gould 1978) was a groundbreaking U.S. picture book, in which a child is raised as both male and female, exhibiting feminine and masculine characteristics. This book was ostensibly written to confront sex-role stereotyping in children; however, Gould's treatment of the subject is executed in such a way that the book could be considered a precursor to transgender picture books. A year later, as part of its series of picture books confronting gender stereotyping, the small press Lollipop Power published *Jesse's Dream Skirt* (Mack 1979). Although the book was much more blatant in its treatment of gender nonconformity in young boys, it was overshadowed by the success of another highly popular children's picture book published the same year by Tomie dePaola: *Oliver Button Is a Sissy.* Much like *William's Doll,* Oliver was published by a larger press than *Jesse's Dream Skirt,* was written by an established children's author, and was less deliberate in its attempts to subjugate gender stereotypes and negative attitudes toward childhood gender variance.

1980s

Throughout the 1980s, children's books dealing with family composition became more common with the increase in divorce and single-parent households. Sometimes these books included a family with two mothers, such as *Your Family, My Family* (Drescher 1980) and *Families* (Tax 1981). During the early 1980s, the first picture book with gay male characters appeared. Published in Denmark in 1981 as *Mette bor hos Morten og Erik* and translated into English in 1983, *Jenny Lives with Eric and Martin* (Bösche 1983) is a photographic picture book that profiles a young girl's life with her dad and his boyfriend. The book attempts to normalize her experience of having a gay father and a single mother while also addressing the topic of homophobia. Regrettably, in one spread the photographer chose to depict the young girl in bed with her naked father and his boyfriend. Nudity is avoided by the strategic positioning of the girl between her father's legs; however, numerous educators have made an issue of the close encounter of nakedness and the unintentional implications of pedophilia that could be suggested.

The same year that English-speaking children read about Jenny living with her dad and his boyfriend, a young girl named Emily and her loving lesbian family were introduced to readers. Severance's *Lots of Mommies* (1983) was one of the first U.S. picture books to represent a nontraditional lesbian family, albeit an implicit one, that included several women raising one daughter. Horning (2008) notes that subtleties in the text and illustrations of the book mirror the lives of lesbians in Michigan at the time, particularly the characters' dress and the name of one of the characters. Severance further explains that the book was indeed modeled after lesbian families during this decade (Crisp 2010).

Just a few years after Severance's book, Lesléa Newman self-published the LGBTQ picture book *Heather Has Two Mommies* (1989). Although previous children's books had featured lesbian characters, this was the first to clearly delineate a lesbian couple planning the birth of their child. The book included several pages that discussed artificial insemination as the means by which Heather came to be. Of course, the inclusion of insemination made the book very controversial and is perhaps why it overshadowed previous lesbian picture books.

In the same year *Heather* was published, the first children's book about AIDS appeared, *Losing Uncle Tim* (Jordan 1989). While the book did not explicitly say that the uncle with AIDS was gay, the suggestion of his sexuality can be implied, particularly because most identified AIDS cases during this period were among gay men.

As in the 1970s, more books appeared depicting gender nonconformity in children. Books portraying females in "nontraditional" roles and as equals to boys

---

Moving Beyond Heather and Her Mommies

Author Lesléa Newman has been immortalized for writing one of the earliest and most controversial lesbian-themed picture books in the United States. For years, *Heather Has Two Mommies* has been stolen, burned, banned, and otherwise defiled to keep it out of the hands of children who might be interested in reading about a rainbow family.

HEATHER IS BORN

According to Newman, her inspiration for *Heather* arrived one day in North Hampton, Massachusetts, when she was stopped by a lesbian mother who was looking for lesbian-themed children's books that she could read to her children. The author understood this woman's desperation to find books that mirrored her children's experiences. As a Jewish child growing up in the 1950s, Newman rarely saw reflections of her life in books. As a child she couldn't articulate the importance of seeing her family in books, but as an adult she could see that it was very important for children to encounter families like theirs in literature. She believed that as an author she could help children with two moms have a place in the world and see families just like theirs.

Unfortunately, Newman could not find any established presses interested in publishing *Heather Has Two Mommies*. After several rejection letters, Newman and her friend Tzivia Gover, a lesbian mom, decided to self-publish the book with the backing of In Other Words, Gover's publishing business. They asked for donations and collected prepayments of $10 from potential buyers. After raising $4,000, they hired an illustrator and brought the book out in December 1989. Six months later, Sasha Alyson of Alyson Books approached Newman and Gover about purchasing the rights for *Heather*. He was already publishing Michael Willhoite's gay-themed picture book *Daddy's Roommate* for his new children's imprint Alyson Wonderland. In 1990, Alyson published the second edition of Newman's book.

Looking back, Newman says that if she could change anything about *Heather*, she would delete the famous insemination scene. It was not in the original manuscript, but when she was first shopping for a publisher she was told that kids are smart and will know that two moms can't make a baby and the topic should be addressed. Newman heeded the advice and even though that publisher did not publish the book, the infamous insemination scene made it into the first edition. After receiving letters of complaint from parents who said they couldn't share the book with their children, Newman decided to omit the section from the 10th anniversary edition.

BEYOND HEATHER

Since the publication of *Heather*, Newman has had fairly good success in publishing her children's books and has seen progress in the industry in terms of publishing LGBTQ picture books. She recalls that she was very surprised when Tricycle Press asked her to

---

Figure 3.1   Moving Beyond Heather and Her Mommies.

write board books *Daddy, Papa, and Me* and *Mommy, Mama, and Me* — only twenty years before she had been forced to beg for donations to publish *Heather*. Newman also says that editors of her non-queer children's books — such as *Remember That* and *Cats, Cats, Cats!* — did not initially want to note that Newman was the author of *Heather* because of the negative association with queer-themed children's literature. However, more recently editors have been proud to note that Newman is the author of *Mommy, Mama, and Me* — so progress is being made.

Newman also says that several presses have asked if she has other manuscripts about rainbow families in her back pocket. Newman sees this as a positive sign — in the past it was believed that only brave librarians and LGBTQ families would purchase such books. She laments that there are still very few high-quality books with queer content available in the United States and cites Arthur A. Levine's *Monday Is One Day* as an exceptional picture book that just happens to feature a gay family along with other types of families. Newman remarks, "There is no fanfare, no issue with the gay family in the book. LGBTQ families are a part of the fabric of society and this book captures that."

The author suggests that her picture book *Donovan's Big Day* (2011) is another book that encapsulates the rainbow family in a non-issue-driven way. It is purely a joyful story about two mothers getting married and their son helping prepare for the big day. No one is upset, no one has to justify their relationship, and the child is not bullied for having two mothers.

IMPORTANCE OF QUEER CHILDREN'S LITERATURE

Newman remarks that queer children's books normalize the experiences of children in rainbow families. These books make their own experiences and those of their friends and family as normal as those of others. She notes the importance of children in rainbow families feeling validated and celebrated, and of other children seeing normalized representations that can stop the problems with teasing, bullying, violence, and terror that often afflict queer children.

She says: "Kids need to see themselves in books, movies, and television to feel good about themselves. When I write books, I try to remember what I felt like as a child. I want to tap into the universal feelings of all children — joy, anger, fear, and loneliness — then the circumstances such as an LGBTQ family are layered on top of that."

Newman also confirms that she tries to infiltrate the mainstream of children's literature by creating non-issue books that have one mom or one dad of any sexuality. This allows rainbow families to "read in" their queer experiences. And children do try very hard to see themselves in books. The author recalls that years ago she received a note from a girl named Tasha saying that she knew Newman wrote *Heather Has Two Mommies* just for her. Although Tasha was black, she still inserted herself into the book.

Children see what they want to see in their books and without high-quality books depicting rainbow families, children in these families will search for any glimpses they can find on the pages. It is time for more authors to follow Newman's lead and create high-quality board books and picture books representing the daily experiences of rainbow families. The children in these families have certainly been searching long enough!

became more common. The classic picture books *The Paper Bag Princess* (Munsch 1980) and *Princess Smartypants* (Cole 1986) as well as *White Dynamite and Curly Kidd* (Martin and Archambault 1986) and *In Christina's Toolbox* (Homan and Heine 1981) are just a few of the feminist children's books that were published during the 1980s.

1990s

In the 1990s children's books with LGBTQ content generally contained one of the following themes: understanding AIDS, conceptualizing family, or normalizing gay parents. The children's imprint of Alyson Publications, Alyson Wonderland, was established during this period and they published the majority of the LGBTQ children's picture books. Clyde and Lobban (2001) note that by early 1999, 53 percent of all LGBTQ picture books were published by Alyson Wonderland.

Bubon, quoted in Op de Beeck (2005), observes that publishers at this time had the best intentions, but the LGBTQ children's books were not written or illustrated by people who understood the development of children or the "culture of children's literature" (p. 32). She explains that the quality of these books could not compare with those published by larger publishing houses. Bruhm and Hurley (2004) have also criticized the quality of children's books in the 1990s, noting that the children have very few desires and concerns of their own and certainly do not question their own sexuality. The scholars note, "We find sanitized middle-class worlds where the children are evacuated of any desires but those of creature comforts — Who will pick me up from my politically correct day care? or Why do I have to eat Brussels sprouts? These children do express some anxiety about their queer domestic configurations . . . but these anxieties are quelled by the assurance that they are just like everyone else" (Bruhm and Hurley 2004, p. xii).

At the same time, children's books were trying to dispel the myth that AIDS was "the gay cancer" and to place a human face on the disease. Several children's books presented gay or presumed-gay uncles and/or neighbors with HIV/AIDS and attempted to demonstrate the love the children in their lives had for them. Nonetheless, the majority of the 1990s LGBTQ children's books were extremely didactic, written for the sole purpose of filling a void in the literature. Whether the stories were actually interesting or ones that children wanted to hear seemed to be less important than normalizing and humanizing the experiences of rainbow families — albeit only same-sex families and their children.

However, Cristina Salat's *Living in Secret* (1993) is one notable exception — a realistic chapter book for elementary children that depicts real-life problems faced by LGBTQ families. Although the book was written almost twenty years ago, the topic and sentiment remain relevant today. The main character, eleven-year-old Amelia, draws readers in as she explains how she ran away to San Francisco with her mother and her mother's partner rather than stay with her father and his girl-friend. Amelia's parents are divorced and a homophobic judge gave full custody of the girl to her father and his girlfriend because he thought the mother's "lifestyle" would be a bad influence. Throughout the book upper elementary children experience firsthand some of the discriminations faced by rainbow families. Although there are elements that require the reader to suspend disbelief, this book still serves as a viable mirror for children in rainbow families and as a window for other children and their families.

2000s

While depictions of rainbow families at the turn of the 21st century became less didactic and began to focus on aspects of family relationships aside from overcoming bias, little diversity was presented in terms of race, ethnicity, religion, and family arrangement. Chick (2008) observes that the majority of the picture books published throughout the 2000s depicted same-sex parents with one child. Rarely were families with more than one child or families with a divorced lesbian or gay character presented.

However, things began to change in the mid to latter part of the decade. Novels for children depicted multiple siblings as well as other gay family members. Nancy Garden's *The Case of the Stolen Scarab* (2004) is an upper elementary mystery novel that features multiple siblings in a lesbian-headed household; refreshingly, their mothers' sexuality is a non-issue. Similarly, Christian Burch's *The Manny Files* (2006) is a light-hearted romp with a gay nanny and his charges. Readers catch glimpses of the Manny's sexuality and blooming relationship with the Uncle but these aspects are not fully explored until the equally funny sequel, *Hit the Road, Manny* (2008).

Another breakthrough toward the end of this decade was the publication of the first transgender picture book for children — *10,000 Dresses* (Ewert 2008) — in which a young child named Bailey dreams about the dresses that she would like to wear and each morning describes these wonderful dresses to a family member. Bailey's mother, father, and brother all tell her that she is a boy and that boys don't wear dresses. The book's success in portraying a child who identifies as transgender rests in the author's switching of pronouns to indicate how Bailey describes herself and how his family describes him.

It was also during this decade that both U.S. and non-U.S. publishers began recognizing the importance of gay-positive literature for very young children. In 2006 Spanish publisher Topka published *Manu se va a la cama/Manu's Bedtime* (Moreno) as the first title in the Manu board book series that follows a little boy with two lesbian mothers. Three years later, the first board books with gay fathers and gay mothers appeared in the United States: *Mommy, Mama, and Me* (Newman 2009) and *Daddy, Papa, and Me* (Newman 2009).

A final breakthrough worthy of note during the 2000s was the increase in self-published children's books with LGBTQ themes. While authors often self-published LGBTQ picture books and short chapter books for children prior to this decade, a significant increase in titles was noticeable because of the rising popularity of print-on-demand systems that allowed authors to print books only after they were sold. This significantly decreased the overhead for self-publishing, allowing virtually anyone to publish a book, and resulted in a mixed-bag of children's titles ranging from very poor and amateurish to high-quality and professional. From 2000 to 2010, more than thirty LGBTQ children's picture books were self-published. Considering that typically less than five LGBTQ children's picture books are published by mainstream publishers each year, self-published literature plays an important role in the body of available children's books on these topics.

2010 to the Present

Although this decade has barely started, trends in LGBTQ children's publishing are already emerging, with more titles addressing the topic of transgender and gender identity. *Gender Now Coloring Book: A Learning Adventure for Children and Adults* (Gonzalez 2010) was the first U.S. children's informational and activity book to introduce young children to famous two-spirit and transgender people throughout history. The children's book also covers topics such as intersex, which has rarely, if ever, been covered in literature for young children.

Exploring *Gender Now* with Maya Christina Gonzalez

Author-artist Maya Christina Gonzalez is dedicated to helping transgender, intersex, and two-spirit children feel empowered through creativity and art. With the help of her partner, Matthew, she created Reflection Press to support educators who want to bring books and creativity into the learning environments as tools to help children understand their identity. Reflection Press's motto — "A people should not long for their own image" — is evident in their work, which supports educators and children as they explore identity. Maya has worked with children of color and gender-nonconforming youth using self-portraiture to empower them to see their own faces, which are usually absent in dominant culture and media.

GENDER NOW BOOK

The first book published by Reflection Press was the professional book *Claiming Face*, aimed at classroom teachers interested in using art to help children explore identity. *Gender Now*, the press's second book, creates an "engaged reflection" for children with multiple gender expressions — two-spirit, transgender, intersex, etc. According to Maya, this community is incredibly ignored in children's literature, educational settings, and the media at large. She observes that multiple gender expression in books is very scarce and there are few resources for these children who do not fit into society's definitions of gender. In fact, Maya confesses that she feels limited by language when talking about *Gender Now* because the term "transgender" doesn't fully convey the spectrum of gender diversity.

Gender Now is partly a coloring book, which may discourage librarians at first glance, but the book is chock-full of information about the history of transgender, intersex, and two-spirit individuals around the world. Maya chose this format because she sees coloring books as a way for children to engage with creativity and know themselves better. Coloring books were important to her as a child and she believes they allow children more opportunity to interact than traditional books. Developed for an audience aged two and up, *Gender Now* contains a section for adults to read to children as well as games and activities just for children.

Figure 3.2   Exploring *Gender Now: Transgender, Two-Spirit, and Intersex Children.*

GENDER SPECTRUM

Maya believes that many people do not fully understand gender diversity and that transgender represents a huge spectrum of gender identities. She suggests that gender is like a wheel that moves and travels, defined not by anatomical parts but by how a person feels inside. The author-artist explains that she is "a huge Fem — a total drag queen" with parts of her that are more boyish and others that are very girly. She explains that she likes to chop a block of wood for her artwork while wearing a dress. Maya believes transgender is the fluidity of how we understand and define our own gender.

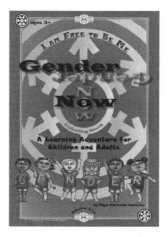

On the other hand, intersex describes how we were born anatomically. Society has a rigid perception of reality with very defined male and female parts. Maya cites the statistic that "2 in 100 babies are born with a gender that can't easily be identified as boy or girl." *Gender Now* includes naked children to show that there are many different ways to feel inside and to normalize the experience of intersex children. Maya believes this part of the book is for parents to use one-on-one with children, noting that children as young as age two start understanding gender and how they do or don't fit in with society's rigid definitions.

While some may balk at the idea of unclothed children, this book provides a binary format that will help very young children better understand the gender spectrum in simple terms. Maya understands that the constraints of public education may keep her book out of regular classrooms because of the

Written and illustrated by Maya Christina Gonzalez, published by Reflection Press 2010

nudity. In fall 2011 she created a classroom version of *Gender Now* with clothes on the children, more text for classroom educators, and specific educational activities that are developmentally appropriate for supporting work with the "littles" (children ages three to eight). This version is one that public libraries will want to adopt for their collections.

POTENTIAL OF *GENDER NOW*

Maya believes there is a lack of insight and understanding about how culture is influencing our children and notes that "transgender children suffer greatly from bullying and the general lack of understanding in the community." She sees leadership as the key to helping educators understand that we as adults need to be active in supporting children across the gender spectrum. Her book, particularly the school edition, is one that will significantly help adults educate children about gender diversity and hopefully end the violence and hate towards LGBTQ children.

(continued on page 48)

Gender Now has been adopted by the organization Gender Spectrum, which has an annual conference for caregivers of children who are gender-variant, transgender, two-spirit, and intersex. The director of Gender Spectrum has been using the book in public schools, and finds it particularly successful because it uses nature to help children explain and understand gender. The author-artist cites examples of creatures that are "male" or "female" but take on the characteristics of the opposite gender, such as seahorses.

Gender Spectrum worked with Maya to create a series of print and audiovisual resource materials that educators can use to support gender diversity and shift the classroom paradigm to include transgender children. According to Maya, "transgender kids are the canary in the classroom and I want to normalize their experiences through education that will end harmful, close-minded attitudes in the classroom."

GENDER DIVERSITY IN THE LIBRARY

The author-artist suggests that librarians can be leaders in their communities just by having a section of Gender Spectrum materials for children and parents in the library's collection. She emphasizes the importance of providing these resources in the library and making them available to children. She warns that as adults we should not project to kids that they are too young to fully grasp the concepts of gender diversity. If children as young as two can understand that their bodies are different, then educators and librarians have to allow them opportunities to explore and understand gender. Maya points to Disney's *Finding Nemo* as an example of an opportunity to discuss gender diversity with young children using nature. She explains that if Nemo's father had been left alone to be the only parent, then the fish would have transformed into a female to take care of Nemo. This is instinctive and a part of the natural world around us.

Maya comments that parents with transgender children are starving for peer connections and are looking for support, which comes naturally in the form of the public library. Having a librarian who is understanding and supportive of gender diversity can be transformational for these families. Librarians hold the key to information and information is certainly powerful. Maya concludes, "We hide this information from ourselves and our children. There is so much ignorance around the topic of gender. There are cultural overlays that are fearful of what can't be controlled and fit into little boxes. In my life this information is completely normal and I want it to be that way for children, educators, and parents too."

Self-published titles through print on demand are on the rise with more than 15 LGBTQ children's picture books being published from 2010 to 2011. Two of these titles positively portray transgender characters: *Be Who You Are!* (Carr 2010) and *All I Want to Be Is Me* (Rothblatt 2011). Queer e-books for children are also beginning to appear. Some of these books are digital interactive books for electronic readers such as iPads, Kindles, and Nooks while other titles are simply static PDFs of book pages. Some of these books are available for free on Web sites such as the Rainbow Rumpus children's magazine; others must be purchased.

For additional information on milestones in U.S. and non-U.S. LGBTQ children's publishing and materials, consult Figure 3.3.

Milestones in LGBTQ Children's Publishing and Production

1936	Publication of Munro Leaf's *The Story of Ferdinand*, the first U.S. children's book to depict gender nonconformity.
1970	North Carolina-based feminist publisher Lollipop Power Press begins publishing a series of children's picture books relating to gender identity and gender nonconformity.
1972	Publication of *William's Doll* (by Charlotte Zolotow), a landmark picture book demonstrating that it is okay for boys to play with dolls. Marlo Thomas's *Free to Be . . . You and Me* is a groundbreaking children's recording (album) that specifically addresses gender nonconformity, gender stereotypes, sex roles, and individuality among children.
1974	Elizabeth Levy's picture book *Nice Little Girls* dabbles with the topic of gender identity by describing a young girl who looks like a boy, prefers "boy" activities, wants to use the boys' restroom, and decides she is a boy.
1978	Lois Gould's *X: A Fabulous Child's Story* is a U.S. picture book in which a child is raised as both male and female. This book is considered a precursor to transgender picture books.
1979	Jane Severance's *When Megan Went Away* is the first U.S. children's picture book to depict a lesbian relationship as well as a separation (divorce) of lesbian partners. Bruce Mack's *Jesse's Dream Skirt* is one of the first U.S. children's picture books to attempt normalization of boys cross-dressing. This is also considered a precursor to transgender picture books Tomie dePaola's *Oliver Button Is a Sissy*, a widely popular picture book, addresses gender nonconformity and bullying among boys.
1980	Joan Drescher's *Your Family, My Family* is one of the first U.S. informational picture books to represent a same-sex family in its lineup of diverse families.
1981	One of the first children's picture books featuring gay dads is published in Denmark as *Mette bor hos Morten og Erik* (Susanne Bösche). English translation in 1983: *Jenny Lives with Eric and Martin*.
1989	MaryKate Jordan's *Losing Uncle Tim* is the first U.S. picture book with a presumed gay character with AIDS.
1989	Lesléa Newman self-publishes *Heather Has Two Mommies*, the first U.S. picture book to portray a lesbian couple using artificial insemination.
1990	Alyson Publications launches Alyson Wonderland, an imprint that publishes gay-themed children's books. Alyson Wonderland publishes *Daddy's Roommate* (by Michael Willhoite), the first U.S. children's picture book featuring a gay male couple. Alyson Wonderland buys the publishing rights for *Heather Has Two Mommies* (Newman) and the book is mass-produced.

Figure 3.3   Historical Milestones in LGBTQ Children's Publishing and Production (continued on page 50).

Milestones in LGBTQ Children's Publishing and Production	
1993	*Alfie's Home* (Richard Cohen) is the first anti-gay U.S. children's picture book, promoting ex-gay ministries and equating homosexuality to pedophilia.
1996	Deborah Prihoda's *"Mommy, Why Are They Holding Hands?"* is the first anti-gay children's novel published in the United States.
1998	Two Lives Publishing begins publishing LGBTQ children's books as well as distributing them in the United States for other publishers and authors.
2000	The number of self-published children's books with LGBTQ content begins to increase with the creation of on-demand publishing companies such as BookSurge (2000), LuLu (2002), and CreateSpace (2009). Twelve years later, more and more self-published books with LGBTQ content are available each year. *Note:* While AuthorHouse print-on-demand was launched in 1997, the surge in self-publishing LGBTQ literature for children was not evident until other strong competitors were established.
2002	Australian author and educator Vicki Harding, along with her elementary school daughter Brenna, publish the first of four titles in the Learn to Include easy-to-read series, which is one of the first books for beginning readers featuring lesbian parents.
2005	Suzi Nash's *Rainbow Sprinkles* is the first children's CD that specifically celebrates LGBTQ families. *Rainbow Rumpus* is developed and produced by Laura Matanah, the first online magazine for children of LGBTQ parents
2006	Sheila Butt's *Does God Love Michael's Two Daddies?* is the first overtly anti-gay picture book in the United States. Moreno's *Manu* series offers the first Spanish board books with lesbian mothers.
2007	The first two children's programs (films) featuring gay and lesbian main characters were produced: "Dottie's Magic Pockets" (Maxwell & Stoner) and "Buddy G, My Two Moms and Me" (Towne-Colley & Edwards). Both of these programs are for a preschool and early childhood audience.
2008	Marcus Ewert's *10,000 Dresses* is the first U.S. children's picture book to clearly depict a transgender child.
2009	Lesléa Newman's *Daddy, Papa, and Me* and *Mommy, Mama, and Me* are the first U.S. board books featuring children with gay parents.
2010	Maya Christina Gonzalez's *Gender Now Coloring Book: A Learning Adventure for Children and Adults* is the first U.S. children's informational and activity book to introduce young children to famous two-spirit and transgender people throughout history. Growth in children's e-books with LGBTQ content both in interactive and static formats.

Publishers and Distributors of LGBTQ Children's Books

Although LGBTQ children's publishing is still a relatively young field, two publishers have made a significant contribution to the publication and distribution of children's picture books and chapter books. Alyson Wonderland and Two Lives Publishing are no longer publishing new LGBTQ children's titles, but many of their older titles are still in print and both publishers plan to move to either an e-book or print-on-demand system that will still ensure the availability of their books. The following section profiles each of these publishers along and their titles for rainbow families.

Alyson Wonderland

Established in 1990 by Sasha Alyson as the children's imprint of the gay-owned Alyson Publications, Alyson Wonderland was designed to highlight the experiences of children in LGBTQ families, to promote acceptance of LGBTQ families, and to counteract heterosexual stereotypes in children's literature (Yampell 1999). The first two picture books published by Alyson Wonderland were *Heather Has Two Mommies* (Newman) and *Daddy's Roommate* (Willhoite). (*Heather* was self-published by Newman in 1989 and Alyson purchased the rights to the book in 1990 to begin his imprint and to accompany *Daddy's Roommate*.) In the 1990s the imprint published around 20 coloring books, picture books, fairytale collections, and nonfiction books for children, including a sequel to *Daddy's Roommate* and other books by Newman and Willhoite. Sasha Alyson penned some of the picture books and fairytale collections under the pseudonym Johnny Valentine.

The company was sold to Liberation Publications in 1995 and then to Here! Media/Regent Media in 2008. No new children's titles were published after the 1990s, but Alyson Wonderland did issue paperback and anniversary editions of its titles up until 2009. In 2010, coinciding with the dip in the U.S. economy and with restructuring in many U.S. publishing houses, Alyson Books turned to e-publishing and a print-on-demand system (Umbach 2010).

Two Lives Publishing

Launched in 1998 by Bobbie Combs and Sally Lindsay, Two Lives Publishing originated as a publisher of books for children with LGBTQ parents. It grew out of the need for books to share with the children that the couple planned to have. Bobbie and Sally both worked for Koen book distributors at the time and knew that very few books were available for children with LGBTQ parents. They, like many other authors of LGBTQ children's books, decided to create the books they wanted to share with their children. When they could not find a publisher to accept their books, Bobbie and Sally created Two Lives.

Two Lives: Rainbow Family Publishing and Distribution

During its prime, Two Lives Publishing filled a significant niche in the children's publishing field. Bobbie Combs and Sally Lindsay started the publishing house as a way to distribute Bobbie's books about rainbow families, but they soon began acquiring manuscripts of well-known, award-winning authors such as Lesléa Newman and Nancy Garden.

ON THE FAST TRACK

Almost as soon as they published their first two books, Bobbie recalls that they made a Web site, marketing themselves as the only publisher focusing on rainbow family children's books. Soon Two Lives became a distributor of other gay children's titles and began marketing itself as a place where rainbow families and their supporters could find everything they wanted — gay children's books from around the world, LGBTQ parenting titles, classroom sets, and more. It had an extensive catalog that served as a resource for librarians, parents, and educators looking for rainbow family materials.

Bobbie remembers that the distribution side of Two Lives was the company's bread and butter for a while but soon online megastores such as Amazon started to cut into their profits. She points out that this trend mirrors everything that happens in the book world and says Two Lives is not as viable as it was even a few years ago. Bobbie also suggests, "We grew a little too quickly. I'm not making any money now and I'm still in debt." However, she doesn't regret creating Two Lives as she sees it as her and Sally's offering to the world — like working at a soup kitchen.

FUTURE OF RAINBOW FAMILY PUBLISHING

Bobbie agrees that there is still a great need for queer children's books, particularly gay dad books and she admits that it was she who suggested to Tricycle Press that they contract Lesléa Newman to write her queer board books *Daddy, Papa, and Me* and *Mommy, Mama, and Me*. There are too few books for young children in rainbow families and while Newman's board books fill a gap, Bobbie notes there is plenty of room for more.

She has talked to several publishers about buying Two Lives as a queer children's imprint, but the interested publishers decided the economy is too tight. Bobbie notes that it is the economy, not a bias against gay books, that is preventing more children's books from being published. Like many other children's books about diverse cultures, queer children's books do not always turn a profit for publishers.

One way in which authors are overcoming the problem is by going digital. Bobbie says that Two Lives has started using Amazon's Create Space to produce another print run of Jennifer Bryan's *The Different Dragon*, which has been very successful. The print-on-demand digital system is much cheaper than self-publishing. She suggests that digital publishing may have been best all along for Two Lives because of the low overhead needed to publish a book. However, Bobbie does worry that with digital self-publishing we'll see more queer children's books but a lot of them will be of poor quality. Certainly time will tell!

Figure 3.4   Examining the Dual Lives of Rainbow Family Publishing and Distribution.

Ostensibly the mission of Two Lives was to "publish books of integrity, depicting [LGBTQ] children, . . . families and . . . friends in positive, loving ways in picture books and stories" (Two Lives 2010, par. 1). In 2000 the publishing house's first two LGBTQ picture books rolled off the presses: *ABC: A Family Alphabet Book* and *123: A Family Counting Book*. Written by Bobbie Combs and illustrated by friends, each of these books presents young readers with a diverse array of LGBTQ families and children from various ethnic groups and of varying abilities. Soon after these books were published, Two Lives published two children's books by established lesbian writers: a picture book by Lesléa Newman, *Felicia's Favorite Story* (2002) and a chapter book by Nancy Garden, *The Case of the Stolen Scarab* (2004).

In 2004 Two Lives expanded its mission and became a distributor of LGBTQ children's, young adult, and parenting literature, creating a mail-order catalog offering works from a vast array of publishers. For several years Two Lives was the heart of the LGBTQ children's publishing world, offering books from around the globe. Its Web site was a resource for librarians and other educators looking for materials for rainbow families. However, when the U.S. economy dipped in 2008 and publishers began downsizing, Two Lives returned to its original roots, offering only its published titles. By this time, a few of the titles were out of print but became available again in 2011 when the company began using the print-on-demand system that became popular around 2000. See Figure 3.4 for an interview with Bobbie Combs about Two Lives Publishing.

Censorship and LGBTQ Children's Literature and Materials

Books and other materials that include LGBTQ content for any audience have been the target of would-be censors from the very beginning. However, materials and literature for children that include LGBTQ topics are particular targets of conservative individuals and concerned citizens. Each year the American Library Association (ALA) compiles lists of frequently challenged or banned books in the United States. Children's books that represent gay families or characters are often among the top ten challenged books. For instance, the children's picture book *And Tango Makes Three* (Richardson and Parnell 2005), which depicts two gay penguins at the Central Park Zoo, was the most-challenged book in 2006, 2007, 2008, and 2010. It held second place in 2009.

ALA also publishes a list of the one hundred most-challenged books of the decade. From 1990 to 1999, four of these were books for children (11 and under) that presented LGBTQ topics. Two of these books *Daddy's Roommate* (Willhoite 1990) and *Heather Has Two Mommies* (Newman 1989), were among the top ten most-challenged books of the decade (ALA 2000). Similarly, from 2000 to 2009, four of the top one hundred were also gay-themed children's books.

As an author of one of the most-challenged picture books in the 1990s, Lesléa Newman received numerous letters from concerned parents and other citizens, insisting that she was promoting a homosexual agenda. Copies of her books, along with copies of other gay children's books, disappeared from public library shelves in the 1990s as would-be censors tried to limit public access to her picture book.

In an article in *Horn Book Magazine*, Newman explained her frustrations over these censorship attempts and described why many parents dislike her book:

> It seems to me that a disproportionate number of parents live in fear of their child reading just one book with a gay character in it, for such exposure will, in these parents' minds, cause their child to grow up to be lesbian or gay. It is usually useless to point out that the vast majority of lesbians and gay men were brought up by heterosexual parents and spent countless hours of their childhood reading books with heterosexual characters. . . . I have no problem with parents deciding their child cannot read *Heather Has Two Mommies*. I do have a problem with these same parents deciding that nobody can have access to it — or to any other book, for that matter. (Newman 1997, p. 153)

One of the best-known controversies surrounding the use of gay-themed children's literature in schools began in 1992 when opponents of the New York City Board of Education's *Children of the Rainbow* first-grade curriculum waged a war to have three picture books removed from the curriculum (Agard-Jones 1994; Casper and Schultz 1999). *Children of the Rainbow* was developed as a multicultural curriculum to teach young children about our culturally pluralistic world. Multiple teaching units included one on families and encouraged educators to teach children about *all* types of families. The books *Daddy's Roommate* (Willhoite 1990), *Heather Has Two Mommies* (Newman 1989), and *Gloria Goes to Gay Pride* (Newman 1991) were selected to present same-sex families to first-graders. Conservative parents thought this was highly inappropriate and initially sought to have this part of the curriculum removed. After a long battle that lasted more than a year, the entire curriculum was deemed inappropriate and in need of revision. Throughout the 1990s other school districts in the United States and Canada were engaged in similar battles to remove gay-themed children's books from classrooms and schools (Casper and Schultz 1999).

In January 2005 a similar controversy arose when Education Secretary Margaret Spellings objected to an episode of the children's program *Postcards from Buster* that depicted a family with two mothers. In the brief episode "Buster's Sugartime" the cartoon rabbit, Buster, and his dad visit a maple farm in Vermont that is run by two lesbians and their children. Spellings opposed the "lifestyle" that was being promoted by the show and threatened to pull funding from public-supported children's programming if "Buster's Sugartime" was aired (Oldenburg 2005). Her reaction caused a stir among supporters of the LGBTQ community and special screenings of the program were later aired at LGBTQ family events in places such as Provincetown, Massachusetts. In essence, Spellings's reaction confirmed that rainbow families were still not accepted in the United States and that the educational needs of their children were clearly being ignored. Various responses decrying her view were published and are best summarized by Debra Chasnoff's editorial in *Social Education:*

> The truth is that today, millions of children have a parent, uncle, aunt, cousin, sibling, or grandparent who is gay. Thousands of dedicated

teachers, school administrators and coaches are gays or lesbians. What kind of message are we sending to our youth when we say that their loved ones and trusted mentors aren't safe for children to meet on TV? . . . we say, "Sorry, your family has been censored today." Even if we keep Buster the bunny from visiting children whose parents aren't gay, we can't put the rabbit back in the hat. Gay people and gay issues are part of everyone's world now, including that of our children. Our only choice is whether we step up and give kids the skills and opportunities to treat everyone respectfully, or whether we try to perpetuate a false silence around the real lives of millions of Americans, a silence that is damaging to all young people. (2005, p. M3)

Chasnoff is no stranger to censorship herself; her work has also seen its fair share of challenges. In 1999 the educational film *It's Elementary: Talking About Gay Issues in School* that she created with Helene Cohen received religious and political opposition from Christian groups claiming Cohen and Chasnoff were promoting a homosexual agenda and attempting to brainwash young children to the "homosexual lifestyle" (Schenden 1999). Idaho conservatives protested against public broadcasting of *It's Elementary* and placed billboards around the state in opposition to the film (Advocate 1999). In addition, the American Family Association (AFA) produced and aired their response to *It's Elementary* in the form of a film entitled *Suffer the Children: Answering the Homosexual Agenda in Public Schools*. This film takes comments and quotes out of context from *It's Elementary* and frames them in a way to convince parents that children are taught to be homosexual in the classroom. *Suffer the Children* provides parents with information on how to protest against the use of *It's Elementary* and other gay-positive materials in public schools.

Homophobia and censorship attempts and controversies surrounding gay-positive materials for children are found in other countries as well. In 1986 *Jenny Lives with Eric and Martin* (Bösche 1983) was discovered in the library at the Inner London Education Authority (ILEA), where it was presumably used with preschool children. As a result, Kenneth Baker, the education secretary, wrote a letter to the ILEA calling the book "blatant homosexual propaganda" and demanding its removal from library shelves. Eventually, the controversy led to the "introduction of Section 28 of the Local Government Act, 1988, which made it illegal for local authorities to promote homosexuality. As a result, many teachers were afraid to discuss the subject at all" (Bloom 2006, p. 3).

Harding (2005) also describes political protests in Australia against the use of her Learn to Include series of easy-reader books in classroom curricula. Harding's series was written with her young daughter in response to her daughter's need to see a lesbian-headed household in children's literature. While the easy-readers do not focus on the two-mom aspect, some Australian school officials and parents did not approve of the gay-positive message. Similarly, in 1997 the Surrey School Board in British Columbia, Canada, began what would be a six-year battle to keep three picture books about same-sex families out of the kindergarten-grade one curriculum. Conservative religious groups did not approve of *Asha's Mums*

(Elwin and Paulse 1990), *Belinda's Bouquet* (Newman 1991), and *One Dad, Two Dads, Brown Dad, Blue Dads* (Valentine 1994) being part of a diversity curriculum for young children because of their positive depiction of LGBTQ families (Collins 2006).

With all of these censorship challenges and banning attempts, librarians and educators might become despondent. However, through the years librarians in particular have fought for intellectual freedom and to protect the Library Bill of Rights, which guarantees access of information to all people on all topics. As mentioned in another chapter, a special interpretation of the Library Bill of Rights "Access to Library Resources and Services Regardless of Sex, Gender Identity, or Sexual Orientation" (http://www.ala.org/ala/issuesadvocacy/intfreedom/librarybill/interpretations/accesslibrary.cfm) relates to LGBTQ materials and could be useful when fighting challenges. Another highly useful resource is the American Library Association's Challenges to Library Materials Web page (http://www.ala.org/ala/issuesadvocacy/banned/challengeslibrarymaterials/index.cfm), which explains what to do if a book is challenged.

Summary

The field of LGBTQ children's literature is still in its infancy. When compared with other genres of children's literature, very few children's picture books, informational books, and chapter books relating to queer themes and topics have been published in the United States or other countries. While there are distinct titles that stand out, many LGBTQ children's books suffer from an agenda that tries to normalize the experience of rainbow families to such an extent that storylines are didactic and characters are not multidimensional. The end results are books that neither young children nor their families find interesting. However, on the other end of the spectrum are anti-gay titles that attempt to demonize children and parents in rainbow families, perpetuating hate and homophobia that is harmful to all children and families. Like their counterparts that show positive aspects of rainbow families, these hate-mongering books contain stale characters and didactic storylines that hold little appeal for young readers.

Over the years more well-known children's authors have begun writing LGBTQ children's books and larger publishing houses have increasingly published more titles, although the average is still less than five a year. At the same time a variety of formats have appeared including board books and interactive digital books. Self-publishing has become more popular within the past ten or so years with more and more titles available about same-sex parents, transgender parents and children, and gay animals.

Unfortunately, there are still aspects of LGBTQ families and culture that are not covered in children's literature such as bisexual parents, elderly LGBTQ characters, and mainstream transgender characters. Additionally, small presses that have specialized in LGBTQ children's publishing have stopped publishing new titles and many would-be LGBTQ children's authors have few venues other than print-on-demand self-publishing to make their works available to the public.

Finally, LGBTQ children's literature remains the target of censors, and many libraries and schools struggle to keep titles on their shelves. Resources are available to assist with censorship attempts, and specific interpretations of the Library Bill of Rights exist for LGBTQ materials.

References

Abate, Michelle Ann, and Kenneth Kidd. "Introduction." In *Over the Rainbow: Queer Children's and Young Adult Literature,* ed. by Michelle Ann Abate and Kenneth Kidd, pp. 1–11. Ann Arbor, MI: University of Michigan Press, 2011.

Advocate Editors. "School-Yard Rumble." *The Advocate* (September 14, 1999): 16.

Agard-Jones, Leslie. "Going Over the 'Rainbow' Curriculum for Multicultural Education." *Education Digest* 59, no. 7 (1994): 12–16.

Alexander, Linda B., and Sarah D. Miselis. "Barriers to GLBTQ Collection Development and Strategies for Overcoming Them." *Young Adult Library Services* 5, no. 3 (2007): 43–49.

American Library Association. "OIF Lists 100 Most Challenged Books of the Decade," June 6, 2000. Accessed August 14, 2011, at http://www.ala.org/ala/alonline/currentnews/newsarchive/2000/june2000/oiflists100most.cfm.

Berliner, Alain, and Chris Vander Stappen. *Ma vie en rose* (My Life in Pink). Culver City, CA: Sony Pictures, 1997.

Bloom, Adi. "Jenny Is Still an Outcast After 20 Years." *Times Educational Supplement* 4703 (Sept. 15, 2006): 3.

Bronski, Michael. "Positive Images and the Stupid Family: Queer Books for Kids?" *Radical America* 25, no. 1 (January/March 1993): 61–70.

Bruhm, Steve, and Natasha Hurley. *Curiouser: On the Queerness of Children.* Minneapolis, MN: University of Minnesota Press, 2004.

Cart, Michael, and Christine A. Jenkins. *The Heart Has Its Reasons: Young Adult Literature with Gay/Lesbian/Queer Content, 1969–2004.* Lanham, MD: Scarecrow Press, 2006.

Casper, Virginia, and Steven B. Schultz. *Gay Parents, Straight Schools: Building Communication and Trust.* New York, NY: Teachers College Press, 1999.

Chasnoff, Debra. "Gay Parents Do Exist: Letting the Rabbit Out of the Hat." *Social Education* 69, no. 4 (May-June 2005): M2–M3.

Chick, Kay. "Fostering an Appreciation for All Kinds of Families: Picturebooks with Gay and Lesbian Themes." *Bookbird* 46, no. 1 (2008): 15–22.

Clyde, Laurel, and Marjorie Lobban. "A Door Half Open: Young People's Access to Fiction Related to Homosexuality." *School Libraries Worldwide* 7, no. 2 (2001): 17–30.

Clyde, Laurel, and Marjorie Lobban. *Out of the Closet and Into the Classroom: Homosexuality in Books for Young People.* Deakin, ACT, Australia: ALIA ; Melbourne, Vic., Australia: Thorpe, 1992.

Collins, Damian. "Culture, Religion and Curriculum: Lessons from the 'Three Books' Controversy in Surrey, BC." *Canadian Geographer* 50, no. 3 (2006): 342–357.

Crisp, Thomas. "Setting the Record 'Straight': An Interview with Jane Severance." *Children's Literature Association* 35, no. 1 (2010): 87–96.

Duke, Thomas Scott. "Lesbian, Gay, Bisexual, and Transgender Youth with Disabilities: A Meta-Synthesis." *Journal of LGBT Youth* 8, no. 1 (2011): 1–52.

Emfinger, Kay. "Rethinking Welcoming Literacy Environments for LGBT Families." *Childhood Education* 84, no. 1 (2007): 24–28.

Esposito, Jennifer. "We're Here, We're Queer, But We're Just Like Heterosexuals: A Cultural Studies Analysis of Lesbian Themed Children's Books." *Educational Foundations* 23, no. 3/4 (2009): 61–78.

Flanagan, Victoria. *Into the Closet: Cross-Dressing and the Gendered Body in Children's Literature and Film.* New York, NY: Routledge, 2007.

Ford, Elizabeth. "Why Lesléa Newman Makes Heather into Zoe." In *Over the Rainbow: Queer Children's and Young Adult Literature,* ed. by Michelle Ann Abate and Kenneth Kidd, pp. 201–214. Ann Arbor, MI: University of Michigan Press, 2011.

Garden, Nancy. "Lesbian and Gay Kids' Books Under Fire." *Lambda Book Report* 4 (1994): 11–13.

Goodman, Jan. "Out of the Closet, But Paying the Price: Lesbian and Gay Characters in Children's Literature." *Interracial Books for Children Bulletin* 14, no. 3/4 (1983): 13–15.

Harding, Vicki. "Literature, Early Childhood." In *Youth, Education, and Sexualities: An International Encyclopedia,* ed. by J. Sears, pp. 532–535. Westport, CT: Greenwood, 2005.

Herzog, Ricky. "Sissies, Dolls, and Dancing: Children's Literature and Gender Deviance in the Seventies." *The Lion and the Unicorn* 33, no. 1 (January 2009): 60–76.

Horning, K. T. "Retro Reads: Before Heather." *Worth the Trip: Queer Books for Kids and Teens* (February 1, 2008). Accessed September 19, 2009, at http://www.worththetrip.wordpress.com.

Lester, Neal. "(Un)Happily Ever After: Fairy Tale Morals, Moralities, and Hetero-sexism in Children's Texts. *Journal of Gay and Lesbian Issues in Education* 4, no. 2 (2007): 55–74.

McRuer, Robert. "Reading and Writing 'Immunity': Children and the Anti-Body." In *Over the Rainbow: Queer Children's and Young Adult Literature,* ed. by Michelle Ann Abate and Kenneth Kidd, pp. 183–200. Ann Arbor, MI: University of Michigan Press, 2011.

Martin, Hillias, and James Murdock. *Serving Lesbian, Gay, Bisexual, Transgender, and Questioning Teens: A How-To-Do-It Manual for Librarians.* New York, NY: Neal-Schuman, 2007.

Naidoo, Jamie Campbell. "Representation in Queer Children's Books: Who's In and Who's Out," In *Diversity in Youth Literature: Opening Doors Through Reading,* ed. by Jamie Campbell Naidoo and Sarah Park. Chicago, IL: American Library Association, 2012.

Newman, Lesléa. "Heather and Her Critics." *Horn Book Magazine* 73, no. 2 (1997): 149–154.

Norton, Donna. *Multicultural Children's Literature: Through the Eyes of Many Children* (3rd ed.). Englewood Cliffs, NJ: Prentice Hall, 2008.

Oldenburg, Ann. "Children's TV Fears a Funding Flap After 'Buster.'" *USA Today,* January 31, 2005: 1D.

op de Beeck, Nathalie. "Diversity Breeds Controversy." *Publishers Weekly* 252, no. 17 (2005): 32–33.

Schenden, Laurie. "School's 'out' for Summer." *The Advocate* (June 8, 1999): 63–64.

Taxel, Joel. "Children's Literature at the Turn of the Century: Toward a Political Economy of the Publishing Industry." *Research in the Teaching of English* 37, no. 2 (2002): 145–197.

Tunks, Karyn Wellhousen, and Jessica McGee. "Embracing William, Oliver Button, and Tough Boris: Learning Acceptance from Characters in Children's Literature." *Childhood Education* 82, no. 4 (Summer 2006): 213–218.

Two Lives. "About Two Lives," September 19, 2010. Accessed July 12, 2011, at http://www.twolives.com/about.html.

Umbach, Mark. "Alyson Books Reorganizes to Focus on E-book Publishing," Alyson Books, October 1, 2010. Accessed August 14, 2011, at http://www.alyson.com/press.html.

Webber, Carlisle. *Gay, Lesbian, Bisexual, Transgender and Questioning Teen Literature: A Guide to Reading Interests.* Santa Barbara, CA: Libraries Unlimited, 2010.

Whelan, Debra Lau. "Out and Ignored: Why Are So Many School Libraries Reluctant to Embrace Gay Teens?" *School Library Journal* 52, no. 1 (2006): 46–50.

Wittlinger, Ellen. "Too Gay or Not Gay Enough?" *Horn Book Magazine* 86, no. 4 (2010): 146–151.

Yampell, Cat. "Alyson Wonderland Publishing." *Bookbird* 37, no. 3 (1999): 31–33.

Children's Literature

Bösche, Susanne. *Jenny Lives with Eric and Martin.* Illus. by Andreas Hansen. Translation by Louis Mackay. London, UK: Gay Men's Press, 1983.

Bryan, Jennifer. *The Different Dragon.* Illus. by Danamarie Hosler. Ridley Park, PA: Two Lives, 2006.

Burch, Christian. *Hit the Road, Manny.* New York, NY: Atheneum, 2008.

Burch, Christian. *The Manny Files.* New York, NY: Atheneum, 2006.

Carr, Jennifer. *Be Who You Are.* Illus. by Ben Rumback. Bloomington, IN: Author-House, 2010.

Cole, Babette. *Princess Smartypants.* London, UK: Hamish Hamilton, 1986.

Combs, Bobbie. *ABC: A Family Alphabet Book.* Illus. by Desiree Keane and Brian Rappa. Ridley Park, PA: Two Lives Publishing, 2000.

Combs, Bobbie. *123: A Family Counting Book.* Illus. by Danamarie Hosler. Ridley Park, PA: Two Lives Publishing, 2000.

dePaola, Tomie. *Oliver Button Is a Sissy.* New York, NY: Harcourt Brace Jovanovich, 1979.

dePaola, Tomie. *What a Year!* New York, NY: Putnam, 2002.

Drescher, Joan. *Your Family, My Family*. New York, NY: Walker, 1980.

Elwin, Rosamund, and Michele Paulse. *Asha's Mums*. Illus. by Dawn Lee. Toronto, ON: Women's Press, 1990.

Ewert, Marcus. *10,000 Dresses*. Illus. by Rex Ray. New York, NY: Seven Stories Press, 2008.

Garden, Nancy. *The Case of the Stolen Scarab*. Illus. by Danamarie Hosler. Ridley Park, PA: Two Lives Publishing, 2004.

Gonzalez, Maya Christina. *Gender Now Coloring Book: A Learning Adventure for Children and Adults*. San Francisco, CA: Reflection Press, 2010.

Gould, Lois. *X: A Fabulous Child's Story*. Illus. by Jacqueline Chwast. New York, NY: Daughters Publishing, 1978.

Hoffman, Mary. *Amazing Grace*. Illus. by Caroline Birch. New York, NY: Dial, 1991.

Homan, Dianne. *In Christina's Toolbox*. Illus. by Mary Heine. Chapel Hill, NC: Lollipop Power, 1981.

Hughes, Susan. *No Girls Allowed: Tales of Daring Women Dressed as Men for Love, Freedom and Adventure*. Illus. by Willow Dawson. Toronto, ON: Kids Can Press, 2008.

Jones, Carrie. *Sarah Emma Edmonds Was a Great Pretender: The True Story of a Civil War Spy*. Illus. by Mark Oldroyd. Minneapolis, MN: Carolrhoda Books, 2011.

Jordan, MaryKate. *Losing Uncle Tim*. Illus. by Judith Friedman. Niles, IL: Whitman, 1989.

Kay, Verla. *Rough, Tough Charley*. Illus. by Adam Gustavson. Berkeley, CA: Tricycle Press, 2007.

Leaf, Munro. *The Story of Ferdinand*. Illus. by Robert Lawson. New York, NY: Viking, 1936.

Levine, Arthur A. *Monday Is One Day*. Illus. by Julian Hector. New York, NY: Scholastic, 2011.

Levy, Elizabeth. *Nice Little Girls*. Illus. by Mordicai Gerstein. New York, NY: Delacorte, 1974.

MacDonald, Ross. *Another Perfect Day*. Brookfield, CT: Roaring Brook, 2002.

Mack, Bruce. *Jesse's Dream Skirt*. Illus. by Marian Buchanan. Chapel Hill, NC: Lollipop Power, 1979.

Martin, Jr., Bill, and John Archambault. *White Dynamite and Curly Kidd*. Illus. by Ted Rand. New York, NY: Holt, Rinehart and Winston, 1986.

Moreno Velo, Lucía. *Manu se va a la cama/Manu's Bedtime*. Illus. by Javier Termenón Delgado. Translation by Gwyneth Box. Madrid, Spain: Topka, 2006.

Munsch, Robert. *The Paper Bag Princess*. Illus. by Michael Martchenko. Toronto, ON: Annick Press, 1980.

Newman, Lesléa. *Belinda's Bouquet*. Illus. by Michael Willhoite. Boston, MA: Alyson Wonderland, 1991.

Newman, Lesléa. *Daddy, Papa, and Me*. Illus. by Carol Thompson. Berkeley, CA: Tricycle Press, 2009.

Newman, Lesléa. *Donovan's Big Day*. Illus. by Mike Dutton. Berkeley, CA: Tricycle Press, 2011.

Newman, Lesléa. *Felicia's Favorite Story*. Illus. by Adriana Romo. Ridley Park, PA: Two Lives, 2002.

Newman, Lesléa. *Gloria Goes to Gay Pride*. Illus. by Russell Crocker. Boston, MA: Alyson Wonderland, 1991.

Newman, Lesléa. *Heather Has Two Mommies*. Illus. by Diana Souza. Northhampton, MA: In Other Words Press, 1989.

Newman, Lesléa. *Mommy, Mama, and Me*. Illus. by Carol Thompson. Berkeley, CA: Tricycle Press, 2009.

Richardson, Justin, and Peter Parnell. *And Tango Makes Three*. Illus. by Henry Cole. New York, NY: Simon & Schuster, 2005.

Rothblatt, Phyllis. *All I Want to Be Is Me*. Lexington, KY: CreateSpace, 2011.

Sachar, Louis. *Marvin Redpost: Is He a Girl?* New York, NY: Random House, 1993.

Salat, Cristina. *Living in Secret*. New York, NY: Bantam Skylark, 1993.

Severance, Jane. *Lots of Mommies*. Illus. by Jan Jones. Chapel Hill, NC: Lollipop Power, 1983.

Severance, Jane. *When Megan Went Away*. Illus. by Tea Schook. Chapel Hill, NC: Lollipop Power, 1979.

Steiner, Charlotte. *Tomboy's Doll*. New York, NY: Lothrop, Lee & Shepard, 1969.

Stiller, Laurie. *Princess Max*. Illus. by Gregory Rogers. Milsons Point, NSW: Random House Australia, 2001.

Tax, Meredith. *Families*. Illus. by Marilyn Hafner. Boston, MA: Little, Brown, 1981.

Turner, Robyn. *Rosa Bonheur*. Boston, MA: Little, Brown, 1991.

Valentine, Johnny. *One Dad, Two Dads, Brown Dads, Blue Dads*. Illus. by Melody Sarecky. Boston, MA: Alyson Wonderland, 1994.

Willhoite, Michael. *Daddy's Roommate*. Boston, MA: Alyson Wonderland, 1990.

Willhoite, Michael. *Uncle What-Is-It Is Coming to Visit*. Boston, MA: Alyson Wonderland, 1993.

Zolotow, Charlotte. *William's Doll*. Illus. by William Péne Du Bois. New York, NY: Harper & Row, 1972.

CHAPTER 4

Book Awards for
LGBTQ
Children's Literature

Children's books regarding the GLBT experience are critical tools in teaching tolerance, acceptance and the importance of diversity . . . Our nation is one of diverse cultures and lifestyles and it is important for parents, educators and librarians to have access to quality children's books that represent a spectrum of cultures. (ALA President Roberta Stevens quoted in *ALA News* 2010)

Award-winning children's books always find their way into library and classroom collections, and librarians and educators often use award-winning books in library programs and classroom lessons. Children's books that have received honors, awards, or designations from LGBTQ or related organizations can be helpful to librarians and educators who are not knowledgeable about LGBTQ topics, or who may not understand the experiences of children and adults in rainbow families. Although the field of LGBTQ children's books is relatively young, a number of awards recognizing the literature have been established. This chapter profiles the major awards for this genre and, in some instances, details significant changes in the award's criteria.

Lambda Literary Awards

First presented by the Lambda Literary Foundation in 1989, the Lambda Literary Awards identify, celebrate, and promote the best in literary fiction and nonfiction books that represent the LGBT experience. There are several categories of annual awards for adults and one for children's and young adult (YA) titles. The Young Adult/ Children's Book Award was not presented until the second annual awards in 1990. Children's book titles are sometimes also found in categories such as "small press."

Prior to 2009 candidates for the Lambda Literary Awards did not have to identify as LGBT; however, in an effort to increase the number of books written by LGBT authors, the foundation decided that only individuals identifying as LGBT were eligible for the award. This caused quite a stir in the literary community (both LGBT and straight), and YA author Ellen Wittlinger (2010), a former winner of a Lambda Literary Award, wrote a scathing article in the *Horn Book Magazine* criticizing the foundation. She described how she was often "too gay" to attend author visits at schools because of the subject of her LGBT youth books. Yet, according to the new stipulations of the Lambda Literary Foundation, she was "not gay enough." The author went on to describe how she writes books for kids both straight and LGBT to show them the commonalities of their lives. Wittlinger also asserted, "I'm disappointed that an organization like Lambda has decided to judge people on the basis of who they are rather than what they do. Isn't this what LGBT organizations have been fighting against for decades?" (2010, p. 151). In 2011 Lambda retracted its statement about the sexual orientation of a book's author but added a clause that the author awards were given for two genders: male and female, ignoring intersex, trans, two-spirit, and other genders.

Although the issue of eligibility remains a point of contention, children's books that win the award make worthy additions to library and classroom collections. Further information about the Lambda Literary Awards can be found on the award's Web site (http://www.lambdaliterary.org/awards/awards-history/); children's book award winners can be found in the lists of previous winners (http://www.lambdaliterary. org/category/winners-finalists/).

Amelia Bloomer List

Established in 2002 by the Feminist Task Force of the Social Responsibilities Round Table (SRRT) of the American Library Association (ALA), the Amelia Bloomer Project identifies children's and YA books for ages birth to 18 that have strong feminist content. The annual Amelia Bloomer List, produced as part of the project, recommends high-quality fiction and nonfiction titles that are age-appropriate and that present factually accurate content. While the project does not necessarily address LGBTQ characters and content, many of the titles chosen for elementary students are appropriate for gender-variant or gender-nonconforming children. Additionally, some of the books on the lists present characters that impersonated or seemingly identified as males their entire lives, making these specific titles suitable for transgender children. Finally, some of the books include characters that could be identified as lesbians, making these specific texts good for sharing with lesbian girls or children in lesbian-headed households. Additional information about the Amelia Bloomer Project can be found on the project's Web site (http://ameliabloomer.wordpress.com/); children's titles can be found in the bibliographies of previous commended titles (http://libr.org/ftf/bloomer.html).

Rainbow Books

Originally an initiative of ALA's SRRT, the Rainbow Project was developed in 2007 to provide youth with materials that accurately reflect LGBTQ individuals and experiences. In 2009 SRRT joined with ALA's Gay, Lesbian, Bisexual, and Transgender Round Table (GLBTRT) to create an annual annotated booklist of commendable titles for children and young adults (ages birth to 18). This booklist, called Rainbow Books, includes fiction and nonfiction titles that authentically portray children and adults in rainbow families. The first booklist included a retroactive list of recommended titles; each subsequent list has covered the previous publication year. Rainbow Books lists generally include a smattering of picture books and chapter books for elementary children, but the list is heavy on YA titles simply because more YA titles are published than children's titles in this genre each year. Additional information about the Rainbow Books project and lists can be found on the award's Web site (http://www.ala.org/ala/mgrps/rts/glbtrt/rainbow/bibliographies.cfm) or on the Rainbow Books Blog (http://glbtrt.ala.org/rainbowbooks/rainbow-books-lists).

Stonewall Children's and Young Adult Literature Awards

In 2010 the Gay, Lesbian, Bisexual, and Transgender Round Table (GLBTRT) presented the first Stonewall Book Awards in the category of Children's and Young Adult Literature. The Stonewall Book Awards began in 1971 with awards for various works intended for adult audiences. By 2010 the award expanded to include books for youth. A year later, the award was added as part of the ALA Youth Media Awards press conference that announces such prestigious awards as the Caldecott, Newbery, Coretta Scott King, Pura Belpré, and Printz. Carolyn Plocher (2010), writing for the NewsBusters blog (a project of the Media Research Center), lambasted ALA's decision to include the children's and YA literature recipients of Stonewall Book Award, stating:

> If past awards are any indication, parents can look forward to the ALA guiding them to dozens of books with themes about "coming out," pedophilia, trans-gender issues, and sodomy laws. The ALA does not exist simply to provide good, wholesome literature to children. . . . The ALA is a liberal organization that relentlessly pursues a homosexual agenda, and it relies heavily on "authentic literature" to drive that agenda. (Plocher 2010, par. 5)

Comments such as Plocher's became viral, with numerous people complaining that the Stonewall Book Awards in the children's and YA category should not be placed alongside other literary awards for diversity, such as the Coretta Scott King and Pura Belpré. Other objections to the award were that it was yet another way in which ALA was "sexualizing kids in general" (Segelstein 2010, par. 15). Regrettably, many of the complaints were by people who had obviously not read the award-winning books. The board books *Daddy, Papa, and Me* (Newman 2009) and *Mommy, Mama, and Me* (Newman 2009) were among the 2010 Stonewall Honor Books in Children's and Young Adult Literature. Both of these books, intended for very young children, include bouncy text and bright illustrations that celebrate either gay fatherhood or lesbian motherhood. Neither of the books mentions sex, sodomy, or pedophilia.

Controversies aside, the Stonewall Children's and Young Adult Literature Awards provide librarians and other educators with a source of children's (and YA) books that positively and accurately represent the experiences of children and adults in rainbow families. Additional information about the awards is available on the official award Web site: http://www.ala.org/ala/mgrps/rts/glbtrt/stonewall/index.cfm.

Summary

The books receiving the awards profiled here provide librarians and educators with a vast array of fiction and nonfiction as well as picture books and chapter books representing the diverse experiences of children and adults in rainbow families as well as other members of the LGBTQ community. The subjects covered in these books and specific awards criteria make these awards vulnerable to harsh criticism from literary and professional communities as well as from the general public. Nonetheless, these awards provide professionals developing LGBTQ children's collections with a solid starting point. Additional sources of recommended titles will be profiled in subsequent chapters.

References

ALA News. "ALA Adds GLBT Youth Literature Award to Prestigious Youth Media Award Announcements." *American Libraries* Online (November 1, 2010). Accessed August 17, 2011, at http://americanlibrariesmagazine.org/news/ala/ala-adds-glbt-youth-literature-award-prestigious-youth-media-award-announcements.

Plocher, Carolyn. "American Library Association's Not-So-Hidden Gay Agenda." *NewsBusters* Online (January 5, 2010). Accessed January 9, 2010, at http://www.newsbusters.org/blogs/carolyn-plocher/2010/01/05/american-library-association-s-not-so-hidden-gay-agenda.

Segelstein, Marcia. "Award for Gay Kids' Books." *OneNewsNow* Online (November 16, 2010). Accessed July 31, 2011, at http://www.onenewsnow.com/Perspectives/Default.aspx?id=1233520.

Wittlinger, Ellen. "Too Gay or Not Gay Enough?" *Horn Book Magazine* 86, no. 4 (2010): 146–151.

Children's Books

Newman, Lesléa. *Daddy, Papa, and Me.* Illus. by Carol Thompson. Berkeley, CA: Tricycle Press, 2009.

Newman, Lesléa. *Mommy, Mama, and Me.* Illus. by Carol Thompson. Berkeley, CA: Tricycle Press, 2009.

CHAPTER 5

Building a Collection of Children's Materials Reflecting LGBTQ Content

Homophobia . . . still keeps most gay families hidden and accounts for the absence of information about them. It also keeps what information there is out of the library, especially the children's room, and makes it difficult to locate through conventional research strategies. (Wolf 1989, p. 52)

Even though more [children's] books with lesbian and gay themes are finally being written and published, omission continues to be one of the biggest problems in the field. Exclusion is one of the most insidious and painful forms of bias — lesbian and gay titles are often excluded from an entire [library] collection. (Day 2000, p. xxiv)

Wolf's comment is just as relevant today as it was more than twenty years ago. Rainbow families are still virtually unrepresented in library collections, at least according to public libraries' online catalogs. While searching for the children's materials to include in this book, it was extremely difficult to identify LGBTQ content using WorldCat, online catalogs, and Amazon.com. The term *homosexuality* will not retrieve all the holdings in a particular catalog, nor will the terms *children of gay parents, same-sex families, lesbian mothers, gay fathers, bisexual, gay, queer,* or *transgender.* Sometimes research articles and bibliographies relating to LGBTQ children's literature identify titles of children's materials, but most of these are in English. Rainbow families looking for bilingual books or materials in Spanish, French, German, and so forth, will find it very hard to locate materials in WorldCat, Amazon.com, or library catalogs simply because many materials in other languages do not contain subject headings or keywords identifying queer topics.

The materials presented in this book are the result of years of efforts to locate LGBTQ children's materials. Researchers and librarians are often relentless when trying to find the answer to a question or information on a topic, but what about children or parents in rainbow families? They probably will not exhaust an inordinate amount of time trying to locate materials at the library or bookstore. If a few searches are unsuccessful, they may well give up.

As a librarian or educator building a collection of LGBTQ children's materials, your time is wasted if you purchase rows, stacks, and piles of materials that rainbow and other families cannot locate. One of your professional roles is to catalog or organize materials in such a way that interested children and their families can find them easily. This organization pertains to the physical layout of the collection and to catalog subject access that provides useful keywords and tags.

Subject Access

The frustration of being unable to find needed children's books or information in library catalogs is described by school librarian Patricia Sarles (Mendell and Sarles 2010). Sarles and her partner began searching for children's books on assisted reproductive technology (ART) or artificial insemination. Unfortunately, their library searches were unsuccessful; when they did find one book, they tried using the Library of Congress cataloging information to find additional books only to discover that the subject headings did not exist. Keyword searches were not helpful either because information about ART, particularly relating to same-sex couples, was not provided in the book descriptions.

Sarles's experience is one that many rainbow families and those who support them face daily as they search for materials in the library. As mentioned above, public library catalogs often do not use keywords or subject headings such as *children of gay parents* or *lesbian parents* or even simply *gay, lesbian, bisexual,* and *transgender.* Without any such signifiers, children's books with queer content are effectively invisible in the collection.

Another problem is that some books are cataloged using subject headings with negative connotations. For instance, the Library of Congress and World-Cat cataloging information for the informational picture book *Celebrating Families* (Hausherr 1997) includes the subject headings *problem families* and *dysfunctional families.* These classifications imply that there is something wrong with rainbow, divorced, multiracial, and single-parent families. If you were a child in a family mirrored in this picture book, how would you feel if your family was labeled as *dysfunctional?*

Arrangement of Physical Collections

Once a library patron has searched the library catalog and determined that a particular book on rainbow families is available, the next step is locating the book. Regrettably, librarians are not quite sure where to place children's books with LGBTQ content, and the task of locating them can be quite complex. Should they be in the children's section, interfiled with other picture books and chapter books? Do they go in a special section in the children's department, such as a parenting section? Or should they be placed outside the children's department in the adult section? If they are put in the adult section, where do they go?

Chapman and Birdi (2008) surveyed 33 libraries in the United Kingdom to determine their holdings and placement of LGBTQ children's and youth materials. Some librarians indicated that children's picture books with LGBTQ content should be placed in a separate section of the collection, while others believed that this strategy would bring negative feedback. A portion of the librarians surveyed believed that interfiling these picture books with other picture books would increase access to materials; yet some librarians expressed concern that doing so would lead to complaints from parents and other caregivers.

Similarly, a study of U.S. public libraries situated in communities with a large concentration of same-sex families with children discovered that many of these libraries do interfile their picture books with LGBTQ content alongside other picture books (Naidoo 2009). However, many of the libraries that engage in this practice also place spine labels on the book such as rainbows or pink triangles. In one instance, a library used the label "Broken Homes" to denote books with queer content. This last practice has significant ramifications as it clearly conveys to children in rainbow families that this particular library believes that something is wrong with their family.

Regardless where a library decides to place children's materials with LGBTQ content, the most important criterion to remember is that children and parents in rainbow families must have open and private access to these materials as well as to parenting materials for rainbow families. The Naidoo (2009) study showcases additional biases of public librarians based upon where they placed LGBTQ parenting and adoption materials. One library placed LGBTQ parenting books in a "special" section that required interested parties to ask the librarian at the desk for access to the materials, which were located in the library office. The problem with such a placement is that it requires library patrons to identify themselves as either LGBTQ or interested in LGBTQ parenting materials. Clearly this is an invasion of privacy; straight parents take for granted in this particular library that they are able to go to the regular collection and find parenting manuals and other materials. Naidoo also discovered that some libraries interfile their LGBTQ parenting and adoption books with parenting/adoption books on "illnesses" such as Tourette syndrome and Asperger's syndrome. Libraries that engage in this practice send a resounding message to rainbow families that the public library believes someone in their family has an "illness," namely the LGBTQ caregiver.

Another type of physical arrangement that can deter rainbow families from using LGBTQ children's materials is the placement of these books in a section with a label such as "LGBTQ Picture Books," "Gay-Themed Children's Books," or "Gay Parenting." Although librarians may have the best intentions of making their collections freely accessible to rainbow families, placing queer-themed materials in labeled sections calls attention to these materials. If a lesbian mother is not out and wants to browse parenting books with LGBTQ topics or locate gay-themed picture books to read to her twin daughters, then she will have to risk identification as a lesbian parent by browsing books in this section or decide to forgo these materials. At the same time, such labeling also calls would-be censors' attention to these materials.

You may be asking yourself what to do; where to put these books. The decision is up to your library system, but the important thing to consider is how your placement and labeling of LGBTQ children's and parenting materials influence the access, availability, and privacy of rainbow and other families wanting to use them.

Criteria for Evaluating and Selecting Children's Materials with LGBTQ Content

Given the dearth of LGBTQ children's materials in comparison with other types of children's materials, librarians and educators might be tempted to use any materials they can locate. However, as with any other genre, children's materials with LGBTQ content range in quality of text and illustrations, developmental appropriateness, and appeal to children. They can include stereotypical depictions of LGBTQ individuals, sanitized versions of reality, and one-dimensional characters. Chapter 3 of this book highlights children's scholars' critical reactions to queer-themed children's materials. However, Huskey (2002) perhaps best summarizes the problems that have plagued LGBTQ children's materials, particularly picture books, for decades. She notes:

> Produced under financial constraints that favor undistinguished illustra-
> tions and unimpressive book design, gay-themed picture books embrace
> their limitations, allowing the book to support the ideological message,
> "Nothing overly appetizing or fun here." Rigorously separating the plea-
> sures of the eye from the gay-themed picture book keeps the text as
> free from seduction as possible, as if the book itself were the mythic
> pedophile who haunts any discursive connection of "gay" and "child."
> (Huskey 2002, p. 68)

Librarians searching for "appetizing" LGBTQ children's books to use in programs and collections often need assistance sifting through the relatively small piles of potential options to find the one or two delectable titles that will reach out to children and adults in rainbow families. Fortunately, a few resources are available.

The American Library Association's Gay, Lesbian, Bisexual, and Transgen-der Round Table (GLBTRT) provides suggestions for "Evaluating the Treatment of Gay Themes in Books for Children and Younger Adults: What to Do Until Utopia Arrives" that can be helpful (ALA 2011). According to GLBTRT (1976), librarians should consider:

✳ *How a child reacts when he/she learns that an important person in his/her life is LGBTQ.* Children should see positive acceptance of LGBTQ individuals and, if a negative response to the sexuality of an individual is present in the book, librarians and educators should counter that response with a positive example.

✳ *How the sexual orientation of an LGBTQ character is explained.* Children's books that portray heterosexual characters do not go into great detail about the sexuality of the individual, and the same treatment should be available for LGBTQ individuals. Books for young children do not need to explain why a person is straight or gay.

✳ *How the book's narrative presents the lives of LGBTQ characters and families.* Many books for young children that describe rainbow families go to great lengths to prove that the family is "normal" like other families. While this could be helpful to children who struggle with the question of the normalcy of their family, it could also make children in rainbow families and other children stop and question *why* a rainbow family wouldn't be normal.

✳ *What role LGBTQ characters play in the book's narrative.* Are LGBTQ characters given major or minor roles? Are they naturally integrated into the story or are they the token queer characters whose sexuality is the "situation" in the book to be explored?

✳ *How LGBTQ characters are portrayed in the illustrations.* Are LGBTQ characters and rainbow families depicted as ordinary people or are they portrayed differently from other characters? Do the illustrations portray a variety of LGBTQ characters — caregivers, other relatives, children, diverse races and ethnicities, multiple ages, and so forth?

Similar to those of GLBTRT, Frances Ann Day (2000) provides librarians and educators with "Guidelines for Evaluating Books with Lesbian and Gay Content" in her book *Lesbian and Gay Voices: An Annotated Bibliography and Guide to Literature for Children and Young Adults.* While some of her suggestions overlap with those of GLBTRT, she does include many additional helpful points. First, she asks librarians to consider how the book will influence the self-esteem of children in rainbow families. If a child has LGBTQ parents or family members, does he/she see a positive and accurate representation of adults in rainbow families or is the representation contrived and oversimplified? If a child identifies as LGBTQ, does she/he see authentic depictions of other LGBTQ children who live average lives and overcome obstacles? Day also suggests that librarians and educators consider whether a book contains any overt or subtle homophobic or heterosexist messages. Sometimes books are written for the specific purpose of guiding young minds to hate those who are different. For instance, the picture book *Seth and Sara Ask . . . Does God Love Michael's Two Daddies?* (2006) encourages young children to tell children in rainbow families that their parents are bad and that they should divorce. It goes without saying that books such as this one can have damaging effects for all children.

Day further recommends that queer-themed children's books should portray LGBTQ characters as multidimensional individuals who change and grow throughout

(continued on page 78)

Evaluation Sheet for Selecting Children's Books with Lesbian, Gay, Bisexual, Transgender, or Queer/Questioning (LGBTQ) Characters

Title of Book:				U.S. Publication Date:		Publisher:	
Non-U.S. Book: Yes No			**Non-U.S. Publication Date:**		**Non-U.S. Title & Publisher:**		
Small Press Publisher: Yes No **Self Published:** Yes No					**Country of Origin:**		
Author:				**Illustrator:**			
Format of the Book:				**Intended Age/Grade Level:**			
Book Characteristics:	**Please Circle ONE Answer**						
1. What is the genre of the book?	Fiction				Nonfiction/Informational		
2. If the genre of the book is fiction, is it realistic, historical, or fantasy/make-believe?	Realistic	Historical		Fantasy/Make-Believe			N/A
3. Is the author of the book LGBTQ?	Yes: Lesbian	Yes: Gay	Yes: Bi-sexual	Yes: Trans/Other	No: Straight		Not Provided
4. Is the illustrator of the book LGBTQ?	Yes: Lesbian	Yes: Gay	Yes: Bi-sexual	Yes: Trans/Other	No: Straight		Not Provided
5. What is the language of the book?	English Only		Bilingual or Single Non-English Language. What language:				
6. Has the book received any awards?	No	Yes Please list:					Don't Know
7. Has the book been challenged in the U.S.?	No	Yes Please detail if known:					Don't Know
Characterization in Narrative & Illustrations:	**Please Circle ONE Answer**						
1. Overall, are female characters depicted in minor or major roles in the narrative (text)?	Minor Roles		Major Roles		No Female Characters		
2. Overall, are male characters depicted in minor or major roles in the narrative?	Minor Roles		Major Roles		No Male Characters		
3. Which gender of character appears more often in the narrative?	Female		Male		Equal Representation		
4. Which gender of character appears more often in the illustrations?	Female		Male		Equal Representation		
5. Overall, are female characters portrayed in gender-stereotyped roles such as submissive housewives?	Yes		No		N/A		
6. Overall, are male characters portrayed in gender-stereotyped roles such as breadwinners or macho tough-guys?	Yes		No		N/A		
7. Are the major characters in the book children or adults?	Children		Adults		Both		
8. Are only nuclear families represented in the narrative and illustrations?	Yes		No		N/A No Families Rep.		

Figure 5.1   Evaluation Sheet for Selecting Children's Books with Lesbian, Gay, Bisexual, Transgender, or Queer/Questioning (LGBTQ) Characters, copyright Jamie Campbell Naidoo, 2012.

Evaluation Sheet for Selecting Children's Books with Lesbian, Gay, Bisexual, Transgender, or Queer/Questioning (LGBTQ) Characters

9. Are the LGBTQ characters in the book children or adults? Queer or questioning characters can include gender-variant children (sissies and tomboys).	Children		Adults		Both
10. Do LGBTQ characters have a primary or secondary role in the narrative?	Primary Role			Secondary Role	
11. Overall, are LESBIAN characters portrayed stereotypically as dykes, masculine, or extremely butch?	Yes		No		N/A
12. Overall, are GAY characters portrayed stereotypically as extremely effeminate, weak, overly flamboyant, or in drag?	Yes		No		N/A
13. Overall, are TRANSGENDER or BISEXUAL characters portrayed as confused?	Yes		No		N/A
14. Are LGBTQ characters with disabilities represented in the story or illustrations?	Yes			No	
15. Are LGBTQ or gender-variant characters portrayed as pedophiles, child molesters, etc.? It is a common misconception that homosexuals try to hurt or "recruit" children to join the homosexual community.	Yes			No	
16. Are the LGBTQ characters humans or animals?	Humans		Animals		Both
17. If LGBTQ characters are human, what is their implied ethnicity in the illustrations? **Select all that apply, placing the number of characters representing each ethnicity in the corresponding boxes.**	Black / White	Latino	Asian	Native Amer./ Indian	Other (Please specify)
18. Are any of the characters described as being of mixed race?	Yes			No	
19. Are there *any* elderly characters in the story or illustrations?	Yes			No	
20. If elderly characters are present, are they depicted as frail and feeble-minded?	Yes		No		N/A
21. Are LGBTQ characters or gender-variant characters (sissies or tomboys) portrayed as acting or behaving unnaturally?	Yes			No	
22. Do any of the LGBTQ characters have a role as a community leader?	Yes			No	

(continued on page 76)

Evaluation Sheet for Selecting Children's Books with Lesbian, Gay, Bisexual, Transgender, or Queer/Questioning (LGBTQ) Characters

23. Are lesbian or gay characters' sexual identities the only defining feature of their character? LGBTQ characters should be portrayed as multidimensional with various interests, problems, etc.	Yes		No	N/A No LGBTQ Characters
24. Are LGBTQ households or characters depicted as living in lower-, middle-, or upper-class neighborhoods?	Lower	Middle	Upper	N/A Not enough information provided

Setting & Plot:	**Please Circle ONE Answer**		
1. Does the story have a contemporary or historical setting?	Contemporary Setting (2000–Present)	Historical Setting (Pre-2000)	Both
2. Is the story set in the United States or in another country?	U.S. Setting	Non-U.S. Setting	Not Addressed in Narrative
3. Is the overall mood of the story upbeat and positive or negative?	Positive Mood		Negative Mood
4. Are LGBTQ characters portrayed positively or negatively?	Positively		Negatively
5. Does the book portray LGBTQ couples in healthy, loving relationships?	Yes	No	N/A (no couple relationships described)
6. Does the plot of the book focus on LGBTQ characters/content or does it just happen to include LGBTQ content?	LGBTQ Content Central		LGBTQ Content Not Central
7. Are characters that are LGBT or queer/questioning (sissies and tomboys) ridiculed or bullied for being "different"?	Yes	No	N/A
8. Do LGBT characters in the narrative have HIV or AIDS?	Yes	No	N/A
9. Are characters embarrassed by their or their family members' sexuality or gender-variant behavior?	Yes	No	N/A
10. If the book is about a child of LGBTQ parents or who has an LGBTQ family member, does he/she face issues at school because of the sexuality of his/her relative?	Yes	No	N/A
11. Does the book's narrative imply that homosexuality or bisexuality is a choice? Sometimes homosexuality is referred to as a preference (sexual preference). Preference suggests people CHOOSE to be homosexual.	Yes	No	N/A
12. Does the book have a didactic or overly moralistic tone?	Yes		No
13. Does the narrative use anti-gay slurs such as "dyke," "queer," or "faggot"?	Yes		No

Evaluation Sheet for Selecting Children's Books with Lesbian, Gay, Bisexual, Transgender, or Queer/Questioning (LGBTQ) Characters

14. Does the narrative use negative, gender-related terms such as "sissy" or "tomboy" to describe characters whose actions defy "typical" behaviors of their sex?	Yes		No
15. If characters are portrayed as queer, questioning, or gender variant (sissy or tomboy), do they ultimately accept themselves as unique individuals?	Yes	No	N/A
16. Does the book use terms such as homosexual *lifestyle* to refer to homosexuality? LGBTQ people have varying lifestyles just as heterosexual people do. There is not a single homosexual lifestyle.	Yes		No

Theme:	Please Circle ONE Answer		
1. Which *one* of the following best represents the theme of the book?	Adoptions/Births/Parent-Child Relations	Social Tolerance	Celebrating Individuality
	Illness/Sick Family Member	First Love/Same-Sex Relationships / Learning About Sexuality	Marriages/Celebrations
	Antigay Sentiments	Diverse Family Compositions/Accepting New Partner	Important LGBTQ Leader/Advocate
	Other, please specify:		

Illustrations (if illustrations are absent, skip this section):	Please Circle ONE Answer		
1. Are the illustrations in color or black-and-white?	Color	Black-and-White	Both Color & B/W
2. Are the illustrations photographs or media-based (drawings, paintings, computer-generated, etc.)?	Photographs	Media-Based	Both Photos & Media-Based
3. Do the illustrations extend the story, adding further information?	Yes		No
4. Are "props" such as rainbow flags and pink triangles <u>avoided</u>? Pink triangles should only be used in historical settings. Not every member of the LGBTQ community displays rainbow flags and pink triangles in their houses, on their cars, etc.	Yes		No
5. Do the illustrations depict LGBTQ or gender-variant characters as ordinary or exotic?	Ordinary		Exotic
6. Do any of the illustrations contain nudity or suggested nudity?	Yes		No

(continued on page 78)

Evaluation Sheet for Selecting Children's Books with Lesbian, Gay, Bisexual, Transgender, or Queer/Questioning (LGBTQ) Characters			
Overall Quality of the Book:	**Please Circle ONE Answer**		
1. Do the illustrations exemplify the same high quality that would be found in other types of children's literature?	Yes	No	N/A
2. Does the narrative exemplify the same high quality that would be found in other types of children's literature?	Yes		No
3. Is the book developmentally appropriate for the intended child audience?	Yes		No
Additional Observations or Comments about the book:			

the narrative. As noted in other areas of this book, LGBTQ characters and situations are often portrayed as both idealistic and unrealistic. While every single book in a collection should not portray LGBTQ characters dealing with problems, the idea that queer characters never face dilemmas, are always good (or bad depending on the intent of the book), and lead uneventful lives is flawed. Day also warns about the erasure of sexual identity in informational books and biographies. Although it is perfectly acceptable to list the name of a significant other when profiling a famous and/or notable heterosexual subject, almost all children's books seem to avoid the mention of significant others/partners of homosexual inventors, authors, poets, political leaders, and so forth. There are a few exceptions to this unwritten rule, but children in rainbow families — like all children — deserve to see representations of themselves and their families in all types of library materials.

For an extensive list of criteria for evaluating LGBTQ children's books, see Figure 5.1. This is an evaluation sheet that can be reproduced by librarians and educators who want to evaluate seriously the content of this genre of literature. LGBTQ stereotypes, as well as common themes in LGBTQ children's literature, are also described.

Children and adults in rainbow families include transgender, questioning, intersex, two-spirit, or gender-variant individuals. Unfortunately, very few children's books cover these topics specifically. However, books that challenge gender roles can be helpful for children who identify as transgender, gender-variant, two-spirit, or intersex. These books hold appeal for heterosexual children too because they open the door for discussion of gender and sex role topics. These discussions can promote acceptance of other children who are trans, gender-variant, and so forth, and support the identity development of heterosexual children who do not want to be locked into gender-defined roles. Figure 5.2 provides guidelines for evaluating the treatment of gender in children's books.

Evaluating Gender Roles in Children's Books

EXAMINE THE PERSONAL TRAITS OF THE CHARACTERS:

* Are female characters portrayed as very emotional and dependent?
* Are male characters portrayed as independent and unemotional? **OR**
* Are female characters shown as courageous, independent, and competent individuals?
* Are male characters depicted as sensitive and nurturing?
* What brings about disapproval for the various genders?
* Are boys shown playing with dolls and/or are girls shown playing outside or with trucks?
* Are words such as "sissy" and "tomboy" avoided?
* Are characters only portrayed as male and female? Are transgender or intersex characters portrayed?

EXAMINE THE ROLE OF VARIOUS CHARACTERS:

* Do females have a secondary or passive role in the book while males brave the challenges and issues?
* Are females portrayed as subservient to males? **OR**
* Are females depicted in nontraditional roles such as construction workers, business women, inventors, explorers, etc.?
* Are males depicted in nontraditional roles such as nurses, nannies, elementary school teachers, librarians, etc.?
* What are the roles of transgender or intersex characters?

EXAMINE THE ILLUSTRATIONS FOR SIGNS OF GENDER STEREOTYPES:

* Are females always wearing dresses?
* Do most of the illustrations depict females cooking, cleaning, or caring for the children?
* How do fathers interact with children in the illustrations? Are they busy reading papers or working **OR** are they changing diapers, cooking, etc.?
* Are females shown outdoors and active?
* Do girls typically play with dolls and jump rope while boys play with trucks, balls, and play tag?
* How are transgender or intersex characters depicted in the illustrations?

EXAMINE CULTURAL DIVERSITY IN TEXT AND ILLUSTRATIONS:

* Are white characters portrayed as having power over characters from other cultural and ethnic groups?
* Are certain cultures depicted as having particular gender stereotypes? For instance, are all Latino males full of machismo while Latinas are only depicted as housewives?

Many of the ideas for these evaluation criteria are my own; others are adapted from:
Heine, P., and Inkster, C. "Talking About Books: Strong Female Characters in Recent Children's Literature." *Language Arts* 76 (1998–99).
Mitchell, D. *Children's Literature: An Invitation to the World.* Boston: Allyn & Bacon, 2003.

Figure 5.2   Evaluating Gender Roles in Children's Books.

Creating a Rumpus for Rainbow Families

Rainbow Rumpus (http://www.rainbowrumpus.org/) is one of the only online literary magazines for children in rainbow families. This resource includes free downloadable children's books about rainbow families, comic strips, reviews of LGBTQ children's books, short stories and artwork created by children in rainbow families, and suggestions for hands-on activities to promote literacy.

According to Laura Matanah, the publisher and executive director of Rainbow Rumpus, the seed for the literary magazine was first planted by her daughter in 2005 when they were sitting in the dining room flipping through the pages of a Human Rights Campaign magazine. The girl saw a picture of a lesbian mother and her daughters and became very excited because the family mirrored her own. It was at that point that Laura realized the importance of children in LGBTQ families seeing reflections of their families.

At the time, Laura could find few children's resources for rainbow families, and because LGBTQ families are geographically dispersed throughout the United States, her daughter had little exposure to other children in rainbow families and resources celebrating these families. Realizing that public libraries carried few books about LGBTQ families, Laura began to dream up the idea of a free online community where LGBTQ stories and rainbow family children could intersect.

A former elementary school educator, Laura understood the importance of high-quality literature for children in rainbow families and decided to create an advisory board of well-known LGBTQ authors to review short stories and digital books before they were posted on the Web site. This board consists of Jacqueline Woodson, Nancy Garden, Marion Dane Bauer, and Gregory Maguire. The authors and illustrators of most of the LGBTQ children's books and stories available on Rainbow Rumpus are hired through the Society of Children's Book Writers and Illustrators (http://www.scbwi.org/) and represent countries from around the world including Spain, Australia, and Canada as well as the United States. Similarly, the literacy and hands-on activities on Rainbow Rumpus are developed by professional educators who understand child psychology and development.

Laura's planning and development have been well received by parents and children in both LGBTQ and heterosexual families, as well as by librarians and educators. Laura receives letters and e-mails from children and young people who are happy to finally find a place that normalizes their family experiences and allows them to connect with other children in rainbow families. Parents, librarians, and educators also share experiences of how Rainbow Rumpus has been used to affirm and celebrate rainbow families. For instance, one mother shared her positive experience of printing Rainbow Rumpus's online books about LGBTQ families and taking them to school to share with the teachers and school library because of the absence of LGBTQ literature for her child.

Rainbow Rumpus is supported by individual donations, foundation support in the form of grants, and advertising. Many of the Web developers and copy editors are volunteers who have a strong commitment to providing this important resource not only to children in rainbow families but to all children in order to foster acceptance and understanding of LGBTQ families.

Figure 5.3   Creating a Rumpus for Rainbow Families.

Laura notes that the best thing that librarians and educators can do for LGBTQ families is to provide plenty of resources and a supportive, welcoming environment. She states that it is important to let all children know about the site as a resource as it is hard to identify LGBTQ families. Laura further suggests that librarians and educators work on the assumption that LGBTQ families are present in classrooms and libraries and make a concerted effort to reflect *all* types of families: LGBTQ, culturally diverse, those with various abilities and religious preferences, and so forth.

If educators and librarians are at a loss as to where to find positive materials featuring LGBTQ families, Laura suggests that they use the downloadable picture books on Rainbow Rumpus. These can be printed out and shared with children, giving them the opportunity to illustrate and personalize the books to represent their family structures. Finally, she remarks: "A lot of what we want to do as teachers and librarians is support the curiosity and creativity in children, encouraging them to think for themselves, to learn about others and families, and to explore diversity." Rainbow Rumpus is certainly one resource that facilitates this exploration.

Sadly, very few of the mainstream children's review sources — such as *School Library Journal*, *Kirkus*, *Booklist*, and *Horn Book* — review LGBTQ-themed materials. This is problematic for librarians developing rainbow family collections because some library systems require a certain number of positive reviews before a title can be purchased. Positive reviews also come in handy when an item is challenged by would-be censors. A considerable number of LGBTQ children's books are self-published and never receive the attention of *any* review resource. At the same time, many of these books are either in paperback format or have poor bindings that will not circulate well in public or school libraries. Chapters 6 to 8 of this book identify reviews of specific LGBTQ children's materials and include suggestions for librarians and educators considering the purchase of these materials for their collections. Self-published titles that are recommended for library collections can be strengthened using paperback reinforcement or rebinding systems offered by vendors such as Brodart and Demco.

Chapter 9 provides an extensive list of resources including recommended booklists of LGBTQ children's materials and blogs and Web sites devoted to the topic. These suggestions will help librarians starting brand-new collections for rainbow families. One innovative and useful resource for children of LGBTQ parents and for librarians and educators is Rainbow Rumpus (http://www.rainbowrumpus.org/), which features the writing of children in LGBTQ families along with e-books and book reviews of LGBTQ books for children. The content of the Web site is approved by an advisory board of notable children's authors who write books with LGBTQ content. Figure 5.3 is an interview with the creator of Rainbow Rumpus and profiles some of the Web site's content.

References

ALA Gay, Lesbian, Bisexual, and Transgender Round Table. "Evaluating the Treatment of Gay Themes in Books for Children and Younger Adults: What to Do Until Utopia Arrives." *Wilson Library Bulletin* 50, no. 7 (March 1976): 532–533. Accessed May 14, 2011, at http://isd.usc.edu/~trimmer/glbtrt/bibthemeslit.htm.

Chapman, Elizabeth, and Briony Birdi. "Fiction for All." *Public Library Journal* (Spring 2008): 8–11.

Day, Frances Ann. *Lesbian and Gay Voices: An Annotated Bibliography and Guide to Literature for Children and Young Adults.* Westport, CT: Greenwood Press, 2000.

Huskey, Melynda. "Queering the Picture Book." *The Lion and the Unicorn* 26, no. 1 (2002): 66–77.

Mendell, Patricia, and Patricia Sarles. "'Where Did I Really Come From?' Assisted Reproductive Technology in Self-Published Children's Picture Books." *Children and Libraries* 8, no. 2 (Summer/Fall 2010): 18–29.

Naidoo, Jamie Campbell. *Focus on My Family: An Analysis of Gay-Themed Picturebooks and Public Library Services for LGBTQ Children and Children with Same-Sex Parents.* Paper presented at the annual conference of the American Library Association, Chicago, IL, July 2009.

Wolf, Virginia L. "The Gay Family in Literature for Young People." *Children's Literature in Education* 20, no. 1 (1989): 51–58.

Children's Books

Butt, Shelia K. *Seth and Sara Ask . . . Does God Love Michael's Two Daddies?* Illus. by Ken Perkins. Montgomery, AL: Apologetics Press, 2006.

Hausherr, Rosemarie. *Celebrating Families.* New York, NY: Scholastic Press, 1997.

PART 3

✳

Materials with LGBTQ Content for Children

Introduction

*A*S MANY LIBRARIES DO NOT READILY IDENTIFY THEIR children's materials as having queer content, it can be difficult for librarians, educators, and caregivers to locate them. Chapters 6, 7, and 8 cover picture books, chapter books, informational books, and other children's media with LGBTQ content. Entries are arranged alphabetically by author. Chapter 8 is further divided by media type (films, coloring books, music recordings, magazines, and e-books). These chapters present more than 175 picture books, 30 chapter books, and 40 informational books, concept books, and biographies that depict same-sex parents, queer relatives, rainbow families, gender-variant children, and other queer characters and situations. The materials include titles published in the United States as well as in Australia, Canada, Denmark, France, Germany, Italy, Mexico, the Netherlands, New Zealand, Spain, Sweden, and the United Kingdom. Books for older children and young adults in grades six and up are not included, as numerous other resources recommend LGBTQ books for these age groups. A few titles were on the cusp of this demarcation and it was decided to omit books that deal with dating, children in sixth grade or above, or that do not have child characters.

As discussed in Chapter 5, problems with subject access and collection organization can make children's materials with LGBTQ or queer content very hard to locate. For this reason, both recommended and non-recommended materials are presented in these chapters to provide the broadest picture possible of materials with queer content for children up to the age of eleven. Some books might be the only titles available on a particular subject and are recommended for larger collections or for libraries in communities with a growing presence of rainbow families. Also, by providing a listing of both recommended and non-recommended titles, *Rainbow Family Collections* is able to present a historical record of readily available children's materials with LGBTQ content. Out-of-print titles have been included in some cases with the idea that librarians and educators can obtain these from used bookstores, or that the titles may later become available again.

Each entry provides information about book awards and a list of keywords that could be useful for information retrieval. As children's materials with LGBTQ content are often the targets of censors, sources of available professional reviews are listed. The abbreviations for these review sources are listed below.

Review Source Abbreviations:

BKLST = Booklist   LBR = Lambda Book Report
BL = Book Links   LMC = Library Media Connection
BCCB = Bulletin of the Center   PW = Publishers Weekly
        for Children's Books   SLJ = School Library Journal
HB = Horn Book   WOW = World of Words
KS = Kirkus   VOYA = Voice of Youth Advocates

A rating scale makes collection development decisions easy. Books that are highly recommended are identified in the title index with an asterisk.

The ratings are as follows:

HIGHLY RECOMMENDED – This rating indicates that the title should be seriously considered for any collections in libraries and classrooms. Entries receiving this designation have been found to be distinctive in quality and to authentically present the experiences of children and/or adults in rainbow families.

RECOMMENDED – This rating suggests that the title be considered for medium- to larger-size collections in libraries and classrooms. Entries receiving this designation represent high-quality materials or those covering a topic that fills a gap in the body of LGBTQ literature. While these materials would be appropriate for any library, it is understood that some libraries will only be able to purchase titles that are highly recommended.

ADDITIONAL SELECTION – This rating indicates that the title be considered for collections in libraries and classrooms serving a specific rainbow family population. Entries receiving this designation may have one or more flaws but a specific need of a child or adult in a rainbow family may dictate purchase of this title.

NOT RECOMMENDED – This rating suggests that the title not be considered for any collection in a library or classroom. Entries receiving this designation have numerous flaws and may contain harmful stereotypes and messages that denigrate children and/or adults in rainbow families.

CHAPTER 6

Picture Books

*T*his chapter includes more than 175 picture books that depict same-sex parents, queer relatives, rainbow families, gender-variant children, and other queer characters and situations. For additional information on these entries, see p. 85.

ABRAMCHIK, LOIS. *Is Your Family Like Mine?* Illus. by Alaiyo Bradshaw. Brooklyn, NY: Open Heart, Open Mind, 1993. Unpaged. ISBN: 9780964714502. OCLC #: 36147738. Ages 4–8. FORMAT: Paperback. AWARDS: None. REVIEWS: None.

As five-year-old Armetha, the daughter of a lesbian couple, walks to school she asks her friends and classmates to describe their families and learns that families come in all shapes and sizes. She also learns that her family is different because she does not have a dad. When she returns from school, Armetha has her mothers explain how she came to be. At times the text is didactic and forced, although the detailed black-and-white charcoal illustrations depict a loving family in a multicultural neighborhood. The lesbian couple in the family appears to be a mixed race couple with one being Latino and the other being African American, although their ethnicity is difficult to determine conclusively from the illustrations. Considering the lack of picture books depicting multiracial rainbow families, libraries may want to consider adding this book to their collections. ADDITIONAL SELECTION.

Keywords: Lesbian Mothers, Children of Gay Parents, Family Relations, School Relations, Family Composition, Self-Published Literature.

ALDEN, JOAN. *A Boy's Best Friend.* Illus. by Catherine Hopkins. Boston, MA: Alyson Wonderland, 1992. Unpaged. ISBN: 9781555832032. OCLC #: 25510052.

Ages 3–8. FORMAT: Hardcover. AWARDS: Lambda Literary Award Finalist, LGBT Children's/YA Category, 1993. REVIEWS: None.

Six-year-old Will lives just outside Montreal with his two mothers. It's almost time for his seventh birthday and he wants nothing more than a dog. Sadly, he has asthma and the family can't have pets. His mothers buy him a stuffed toy dog that looks similar to the real dog that Will wants, and Will totes the dog around with him everywhere. At school, his male classmates bully Will for having a stuffed dog, eventually taking it away from him and throwing it into a tree that he can't climb because of his illness. By a stroke of luck or magic, the toy dog jumps down into Will's open arms and he takes him home to his mothers. Illustrated with color photographs that extend but also date the text, this important book will be helpful to children with asthma or other physical illnesses. While the text borders on didacticism, its depiction of an asthmatic boy with lesbian mothers is not mirrored in any other piece of literature and may be useful for library collections. ADDITIONAL SELECTION.

Keywords: Children of Gay Parents, Lesbian Mothers, Bullying, Teasing, Asthma, Dogs, Toys, Canadians.

ALDRICH, ANDREW. *How My Family Came to Be — Daddy, Papa and Me.* Illus. by Mike Motz. Oakland, CA: New Family Press, 2003. Unpaged. ISBN: 9780974200804. OCLC #: 60647841. Ages 4–8. FORMAT: Hardcover. AWARDS: None. REVIEWS: None.

A young African American boy explains to readers in a straightforward manner how his two dads adopted him and created the happy home they share. Children learn that the gay dads have created a "forever" family for the boy and that the boy is surrounded by people who love him such as his dads, godmother, and granny. The caricature-style illustrations add a light-hearted touch but are distracting at times. ADDITIONAL SELECTION.

Keywords: Adoption, Family Relations, Gay Fathers, Children of Gay Parents, African Americans, Mixed Race Families, Self-Published Literature.

ALEXANDER, EARL, SHELIA RUDIN, AND PAM SEJKORA. *My Dad Has HIV.* Illus. by Ronnie Walter Shipman. Minneapolis, MN: Fairview Press, 1996. 28p. ISBN: 9780925190994. OCLC #: 33947930. Ages 5–8. FORMAT: Hardcover. AWARDS: Lambda Literary Award Finalist, LGBT Children's/YA Category, 1997. REVIEWS: None.

Seven-year-old Lindsey explains how her dad helps out at school by telling stories, playing his guitar, and substitute teaching. She is proud of all that he does but she's afraid to tell her classmates and teachers that he has HIV. To help her, Lindsey's dad goes to school and talks to the guidance counselor and teachers. Then they help Lindsey tell her classmates and explain what the HIV virus is and how it can and can't be contracted. The book ends with the girl hoping that there will one day be a cure for HIV because she wants her dad around. The informational text is simple and the bright illustrations are appropriate for young children. Although the book never states that the dad is gay and his wife or partner is never mentioned, the likelihood of him being gay is high considering that many books during this time period depicted HIV-infected characters as gay men. The nebulous sexuality of the character allows the book to work for both rainbow and traditional families. ADDITIONAL SELECTION.

Keywords: Family Relations, AIDS, HIV, Gay Fathers, Children of Gay Parents.

ARC-DEKKER, TAMARA. *Bedtime for Baby Teddy.* Illus. by Jenni Boettcher. Malvern, Vic., Australia: Rainbow Babies Books, 2002. Unpaged. ISBN: 9780958134903. OCLC #: 57300502. Ages 1–4. FORMAT: Paperback. AWARDS: None. REVIEWS: LBR.

Baby Teddy and his two Mummy Teddies do a variety of activities together such as making a salad for dinner, getting ready for bed, and reading a bedtime story. The easy-to-read text is appropriate for young children, although some of the non-American English spellings may be confusing for young readers. Boettcher's bright, simple watercolor illustrations are on target for the intended audience. While the book's plot is virtually nonexistent, libraries looking for LGBTQ books for babies and toddlers may want to consider this for their collection. Librarians may also want to know that the book promises to be the first in a series about Teddy; unfortunately, the author never published the remaining books. ADDITIONAL SELECTION.

Keywords: Lesbian Mothers, Children of Gay Parents, Australian Literature, Self-Published Literature, Teddy Bears.

ARGENT, HEDI. *Josh and Jaz Have Three Mums.* Illus. by Amanda Wood. London, UK: British Association for Adoption and Fostering, 2007. 22p. ISBN: 9781905664122. OCLC #: 166315517. Ages 4–8. FORMAT: Paperback. AWARDS: None. REVIEWS: None. Positive review included in the UK review publication *Books for Keeps.*

Twins Josh and Jaz are nervous when their first-grade teacher Mr. Shah asks the class to create family trees. Since they have two moms, the brother and sister are worried that their classmates will laugh at them. To make matters worse, they learn that they really have three moms if you count their birth mom! Eventually, with the encouragement of their loving mothers, the twins learn that families come in all shapes and sizes. The soothing illustrations add warmth to the text-heavy narrative and extend the book's audience. Although somewhat didactic, the story accurately conveys the fears of elementary children and could lead to deeper discussions about family composition. ADDITIONAL SELECTION.

Keywords: Adoption, Family Composition, Family Relations, Lesbian Mothers, Children of Gay Parents, British Literature, Great Britain, School Relations, Twins, Family Tree.

ARNOLD, JEANNE. *Amy Asks a Question . . . Grandma — What's a Lesbian?* Illus. by Barbara Lindquist. Racine, WI: Mother Courage Press, 1996. 51p.

ISBN: 9780941300285. OCLC #: 35096011. Ages 8–12. FORMAT: Hardcover. AWARDS: Lambda Literary Award Finalist, LGBT Children's/YA Category, 1998. REVIEWS: None.

A young girl named Amy explains how she enjoys spending time with her family at her grandmothers' house doing wonderful things like crafting and reading adventure stories. She loves both Grandma Bonnie and Grandma Jo but has never stopped to consider their relationship. One day at school, Amy is teased for hugging another girl and called a lesbian. When she questions her mother about the word, Amy is taken to her lesbian grandmothers for an answer. The girl learns about her grandmothers' relationship, gay pride, and the importance of being true to oneself. At times the text is long and overly didactic and the pencil illustrations add little to the overall package. However, very few children's books include lesbian grandmothers and libraries may want to carefully consider whether this book would fill a specific void in their collection. ADDITIONAL SELECTION.

Keywords: Family Relations, Gay Relatives, Gay Uncles, AIDS, Lesbian Grandmothers, Gay Pride, Anti-Gay Sentiment.

ATKINS, JEANNINE. *A Name on the Quilt: A Story of Remembrance.* Illus. by Tad Hills. New York, NY: Atheneum, 1999. Unpaged. ISBN: 9780689815928. OCLC #: 37801413. Ages 5–9. FORMAT: Hardcover. AWARDS: Best Children's Books of the Year, 2000, Bank Street College of Education. REVIEWS: BKLST, BL, KS, PW, SLJ.

Lauren misses her Uncle Ron, who recently died, but is excited to help her parents, younger brother, grandma, and Ron's partner create a remembrance panel for the AIDS Memorial Quilt (*The NAMES Project*). As each family member stitches letters from Ron's name onto the panel, they share warm memories of the beloved uncle. Readers also understand that Lauren's grandfather is unhappy with Uncle Ron's sexuality, which is an all-too-common problem. Told in a sensitive style that will resonate with young children who have experienced the death of a loved one, the gentle narrative accompanied by soft watercolor and colored pencil illustrations could lead readers to share their own stories of deceased relatives. This would be a perfect book to pair with the informational book *The NAMES Project* (Brimner), which includes photographs and facts about the real AIDS Memorial Quilt. RECOMMENDED.

Keywords: Family Relations, Gay Uncles, Gay Relatives, Death, AIDS, NAMES Project, AIDS Memorial Quilt.

BAKER, DAVE. *The Roos: A Home for Baby.* Illus. by Randy Jennings. Raleigh, NC: Lulu.com, 2005. Unpaged. ISBN: 9781411691223. OCLC #: n.a. Ages 4–8. FORMAT: Hardcover. AWARDS: None. REVIEWS: None.

Daddyroo and Dadyroo-two are excited to adopt a Babyroo of their own. However, they have one problem — female kangaroos have pouches for their babies but male kangaroos do not. How will the dads carry their new baby? The duo travels around asking various other animals how they carry their babies only to discover that none of the options will work for a kangaroo. Finally, the dads find a human mother who gives them a baby sling to use to carry Babyroo. Readers learn how beavers, swans, crocodiles, and lions carry their young. The simple text is easy for beginning readers and the cartoon illustrations should add appeal, although the book would be more attractive with full-page illustrations rather than half pages surrounded by text. Available for purchase at http://www.theroos.com. RECOMMENDED.

Keywords: Gay Fathers, Children of Gay Parents, Adoption, Self-Published Literature, Kangaroos, Animal Babies.

BAKER, DAVE, AND SAGE KALMUS. *The Roos: Baby's New Friend.* Illus. by Timothy Au. Raleigh, NC: Lulu.com, 2006. Unpaged. ISBN: 9781411691247. OCLC #: n.a. Ages 4–8. FORMAT: Hardcover. AWARDS: None. REVIEWS: None.

The second book in The Roos series about two gay kangaroo dads follows Babyroo as he explains to his friend Babypotamus (baby hippopotamus) the many nurturing things that his dads do for him. Babypotamus is confused because he's never heard of a family with two dads, but the two Daddyroos set things straight by explaining various types of animal families with single parents and multiple caregivers. The didactic text is heavy-handed and the disjointed cartoon illustrations lack appeal for young readers. NOT RECOMMENDED.

Keywords: Gay Fathers, Children of Gay Parents, Self-Published Literature, Kangaroos, Animal Babies, Animal Families, Family Composition.

BANSCH, HELGA. *Odd Bird Out.* Translation by Monika Smith. Wellington, New Zealand: Gecko Press, 2008. Unpaged. ISBN: 9781877467080. OCLC #: 220875863. Ages 4–9. FORMAT: Hardcover. AWARDS: None. REVIEWS: None. (Originally published in German as *Ein schräger Vogel.* ISBN: 9783407793560.)

Robert is not like the other ravens. While everyone else in his family and flock prefers to dress in black, sing dull songs, and spend the day being gloomy, Robert belts out raucous songs and chirps along in drag — orange wig, bright dresses, and dazzling heels. Eventually the other ravens have had enough of Robert's outlandish behavior and make him leave. Not one to wallow in sadness, Robert packs his gowns and heads off to entertain other birds. In his absence, the ravens are quite bored and long for excitement, which eventually comes in a brightly feathered, orange-wigged raven named Bobby who sings and dances much like the long-lost Robert. Soon all the birds are dressing in bright colors and having a lark of a time. Bansch's bright illustrations add life and dimension to an otherwise banal text, extending the reach of the story to attract children who are gender-nonconformist. ADDITIONAL SELECTION.

Keywords: Family Relations, Cross-Dressing, Gender Nonconformity, Gender Identity, Individuality, Teasing, Bullying, New Zealand Literature, New Zealand.

BEECH, KIP. *When I'm Big.* Illus. by Stephanie Fizer. Raleigh, NC: Lulu.com, 2010. Unpaged. ISBN: 9780557584000. OCLC #: n.a. Ages 3–8. FORMAT: Paperback. AWARDS: None. REVIEWS: None.

From the first two-page spread, children learn that Kelsey's two dads have told her that when she grows up she can do anything that she wants as long as she tries her best. Like most young children, the girl has a long list of potential occupations: ballerina, rock star, teacher, firefighter, and so forth. The subsequent pages provide a forced rhyming description of an occupation and then a picture depicting Kelsey in that role. Although the soft illustrations add charm, the narrative contains words such as "innate" that are well above the reading level of the intended audience. In addition, the two fathers look almost identical, with very few distinguishing characteristics. NOT RECOMMENDED.

Keywords: Family Relations, Gay Fathers, Children of Gay Parents, Occupations, Self-Published Literature.

BENJAMIN, JUDITH. *And Baby Makes Four.* Illus. by Judith Freeman. Charleston, SC: Motek Press, 2009. Unpaged. ISBN: 9780615316826. OCLC #: 489374495. Ages 3–8. FORMAT: Paperback. AWARDS: None. REVIEWS: None.

In this self-published title, a preschool girl is both excited and anxious about the birth of her new brother. How will life with her two moms change when the baby makes four? Using Photoshop and family photos along with fairly simple text, this picture book covers typical emotions that children experience when they discover that a new sibling is on the way. Although the book exudes an amateurish quality, it successfully introduces the topic of sibling rivalry in a rainbow family rather than focusing on the gay parent aspect. ADDITIONAL SELECTION.

Keywords: Family Relations, Lesbian Mothers, Children of Gay Parents, Sibling Rivalry, Self-Published Literature, School Relations.

BEY-CLARKE, MONICA, AND CHERIL CLARKE. *Keesha and Her Two Moms Go Swimming.* Illus. by Aiswarya Mukherjee. Sicklerville, NJ: My Family!/ Dodi Press, 2010. Unpaged. ISBN: 9780976727354. OCLC #: n.a. Ages 4–7. FORMAT: Hardcover. AWARDS: None. REVIEWS: None.

A young African American girl named Keesha and her two mothers go to the local pool for an exciting water-filled day with other rainbow families. Beginning readers are introduced to a family with two moms, a biracial family with two dads, and a traditional family with a mom and a dad. The simple narrative is appropriate for early readers but may be difficult to decode in a few instances where the illustrations interfere with the text. Colorful, computer-generated illustrations complement this upbeat story adding to the overall quality, and librarians will appreciate the surprisingly strong binding of this self-published title. Considering the lack of early-reader books for rainbow families, particularly those depicting biracial families, this title is recommended for both public and school library collections. A coloring and activity book entitled *My Family! ABCs with Keesha* (ISBN 9780976727392) is also available. RECOMMENDED.

Keywords: Family Relations, Gay Fathers, Lesbian Mothers, Children of Gay Parents, Self-Published Literature, Swimming, African Americans, Mixed Race Families, Friendship.

BEY-CLARKE, MONICA, AND CHERIL CLARKE. *The Lopez Family: Science Fair Day.* Illus. by Aiswarya Mukherjee. Sicklerville, NJ: My Family!/Dodi

Press, 2011. Unpaged. ISBN: 9780976727361. OCLC #: n.a. Ages 5–8. FORMAT: Hardcover. AWARDS: None. REVIEWS: None. Also available in Spanish as *La Familia Lopez: La Feria de Ciencia* with a translation by Cristina Rosado.

A young Latino boy named Felix explains how his two dads helped him create an airplane for his science fair project. Readers follow Felix as he builds his plane, encounters a school bully, and eventually wins first place at the science fair. The straightforward narrative is appropriate for level two early readers but may be difficult to decode in a few instances where the illustrations interfere with the text. Colorful, computer-generated illustrations generally complement the story adding to the overall quality, although the illustrations are not as strong as in the first book in the My Family! Series — *Keesha and Her Two Moms Go Swimming*. Considering the lack of levelized-readers featuring rainbow families, particularly those depicting Latino families, this title should be considered for both public and school library collections. ADDITIONAL SELECTION.

Keywords: Family Relations, Gay Fathers, Children of Gay Parents, Self-Published Literature, Latinos, School Relations, Bullying.

BIXLER, DEB. *My Two Aunts.* Bloomington, IN: AuthorHouse, 2007. 17p. ISBN: 9781434311160. OCLC #: 644530211. Ages 3–5. FORMAT: Paperback. AWARDS: None. REVIEWS: None.

A young boy describes his two aunts who live together and all the fun things that he likes to do when he visits them. Readers learn that the aunts are called lesbians because they are "two girls in love" and that they enjoy spending time with the little boy. The crayon, child-like illustrations do little to extend the text, which is lackluster at best. With so few books about lesbian aunts, it is a disappointment that this offering is of such poor quality. NOT RECOMMENDED.

Keywords: Lesbian Aunts, Gay Relatives, Family Relations, Self-Published Literature.

BOENKE, MARY. *Carly: She's Still My Daddy.* Illus. by Dolores Dudley. Greensboro, NC: Transgender Network of Parents, Families, and Friends of Lesbians and Gays, 2004. 20p. ISBN: n.a. OCLC #: 70687168. Ages 6–10. FORMAT: Paperback. AWARDS: None. REVIEWS: None.

In this first children's picture book to address the topic of transsexual parents, Tommy explains to readers that his dad, Carly, is transitioning into a woman. The boy goes on to describe how this makes him and his mother feel, as well as how much happier Carly is now that he's become a woman. The writing, although informative, is didactic and stilted at times. Dudley's line drawings are inconsistent, with Tommy appearing older and younger in various spreads. The binding of the book is stapled and folded papers and will not withstand many library circulations. If a library has a significant transgender population, then it might consider adding this book, otherwise *My Mommy Is a Boy* (Martinez) might be a slightly better choice. ADDITIONAL SELECTION.

Keywords: Gender Nonconformity, Gender Identity, Individuality, Transgender, Children of Transsexuals, Transsexual Parents, Sex Change, Self-Published Literature, Intersex, Cross-Dressing.

BÖSCHE, SUSANNE. *Jenny Lives with Eric and Martin.* Illus. by Andreas Hansen. Translation by Louis Mackay. London, UK: Gay Men's Press, 1983. 51p. ISBN: 9780907040224. OCLC #: 466630317. Ages 6–9. FORMAT: Paperback. AWARDS: None. REVIEWS: None. (Originally published in 1981 in Denmark as *Mette bor hos Morten og Erik.* ISBN: 9788755710351.)

Five-year-old Jenny lives with her dad and his partner Eric in Denmark. In this lengthy picture book, children experience a weekend with Jenny and her dads. There is a birthday for Eric, routine chores such as laundry and cooking, and an unhappy encounter with a homophobic neighbor. Black-and-white photos chronicle the various events and the narrative is written in a style that would be best read and discussed with children. One of the first picture books to depict gay fathers, its illustrations are slightly dated, and in two photos Jenny is strategically placed to cover up her nude father as he lies in bed. While not the most accessible book for current children, it would work in libraries with a historical collection of rainbow family books. ADDITIONAL SELECTION.

Keywords: Gay Fathers, Children of Gay Parents, Family Relations, Danish Literature, Denmark, Homophobia.

BRADLEY, KIMBERLY BRUBAKER. *Ballerino Nate.* Illus. by R. W. Alley. New York, NY: Dial, 2006. Unpaged. ISBN: 9780803729544. OCLC #: 56194857. Ages 4–8. FORMAT: Hardcover. AWARDS: Best Children's Books of the Year, 2007, Bank Street College of Education. REVIEWS: BKLST, KS, PW, SLJ.

When his class takes a trip to see a ballet school performance, Nate knows that he wants to be a ballerina. His older brother, Ben, tells Nate that only girls can be ballerinas. But this does not deter Nate, particularly when his mother tells him that he can enroll in ballet classes when school starts in the fall. For the entire summer, Nate dances everywhere. But just before he is to begin his ballet classes, Ben warns Nate that ballerinas have to wear pink shoes and dresses. Nate is terrified about his new class and is convinced that his brother is right — only girls can be ballerinas. With the help of his caring parents, Nate eventually learns that boys can be dancers too. Bradley's text successfully captures the fears of young children and clearly conveys a gender-nonconforming child in his element. However, it is Alley's humorous illustrations that steal the show, bursting with movement and emotion. This is an excellent book to pair with *The Only Boy in Ballet Class* (Gruska) or *Dogs Don't Do Ballet* (Kemp) for a storytime program on ballet for boys. HIGHLY RECOMMENDED.

Keywords: Dance, Dogs, Gender Nonconformity, Gender Identity, Individuality, Ballet, Sex Roles.

BRANNEN, SARAH. *Uncle Bobby's Wedding.* New York, NY: Putnam, 2008. Unpaged. ISBN: 9780399247125. OCLC #: 132581114. Ages 4–8. FORMAT:

Hardcover. AWARDS: Rainbow List 2009. REVIEWS: BKLST, BCCB, KS, LBR, PW, SLJ.

A young guinea pig named Chloe loves spending time with her Uncle Bobby but she's worried! He has just announced that he is getting married to his boyfriend, Jamie, and Chloe is despondent that Uncle Bobby will then forget all about her. After spending time with Jamie, Chloe realizes he's actually a nice guy and looks forward to gaining another uncle. Although the book has been one of the most challenged books in the United States for its depiction of gay marriage, the actual focus of the book is not on the marriage but on the betrayal and sadness that a young girl feels when she thinks she's losing the attention of her beloved uncle. Brannen's treatment of the topic is right on target, and her soft illustrations complement the story, extending the title to a younger audience. Pair this book with *Mini Mia and Her Darling Uncle* (Lindenbaum) for a program on gay uncles and jealous nieces. Rainbow families will also delight in the author's follow-up title, which is currently in the works and follows Uncle Bobby and Uncle Jamie as they start their own family of guinea pigs. RECOMMENDED.

Keywords: Gay Uncles, Gay Relatives, Family Relations, Jealousy, Guinea Pigs, Gay Marriage, Weddings.

BROWN, MARC. *Buster's Sugartime.* New York, NY: Little, Brown, 2006. Unpaged. ISBN: 9780316159159. OCLC #: 60245825. Ages 4–8. FORMAT: Hardcover. AWARDS: None. REVIEWS: None.

Based on the PBS show *Postcards from Buster,* this levelized reader takes scenes from the episode entitled "Sugartime!" and combines them into a simple narrative imbued with information about Vermont and the process of making syrup. Stills from the television show along with cartoon illustrations provide beginning readers with contextual clues to better understand the text. In this particular episode, the family that Buster the rabbit visits includes two mothers and their three children. While the book is not very sophisticated, beginning readers in rainbow families might appreciate a book with two mothers. ADDITIONAL SELECTION.

Keywords: Lesbian Mothers, Children of Gay Parents, Vermont, Rabbits.

BRYAN, JENNIFER. *The Different Dragon.* Illus. by Danamarie Hosler. Ridley Park, PA: Two Lives Publishing, 2006. 32p. ISBN: 9780967446868. OCLC #: 71822789. Ages 4–8. FORMAT: Paperback. AWARDS: None. REVIEWS: KS.

As a little boy named Noah is readying for bed, he asks one of his mothers, Go-Ma, to tell him a bedtime story. The magical story she tells is about a brave not-so-little Noah and his cat setting sail under a moonlit sky. They travel to Dragon Cove where Noah meets a dragon that does not like breathing fire and scaring creatures away. Noah tells the dragon that it's okay to be different and they spend the night playing badminton. Bryan's narrative, while lengthy at times, successfully captures children interrupting during the bedtime story routine. Hosler's soothing illustrations depict a typical child-friendly household where the parents just happen to be lesbians. Pair this story with *Interrupting Chicken* (Stein) for a library program about bedtime stories. ADDITIONAL SELECTION.

Keywords: Individuality, Lesbian Mothers, Children of Gay Parents, Dragons, Cats, Pets, Storytelling.

BURKS, STEPHANIE. *While You Were Sleeping.* Illus. by Kelli Bienvenu. Victoria, British Columbia, Canada: Burks Publishing/Trafford, 2004. Unpaged. ISBN: 9781412028530. OCLC #: 55596723. Ages Birth–4. FORMAT: Paperback. AWARDS: None. REVIEWS: None.

In this gentle picture book two mothers explain to their adopted child what they were doing just after he was born and while he was sleeping. The repetitive text will hold the attention of young children and the bright cartoon illustrations successfully capture the love the mothers have for each other and for their newborn child. The only shortcoming of the book is that it is only available in paperback, which may limit its appropriateness for libraries. RECOMMENDED.

Keywords: Adoption, Lesbian Mothers, Family Relations, Children of Gay Parents, Canadian Literature, Canadians.

BUTT, SHELIA K. *Seth and Sara Ask . . . Does God Love Michael's Two Daddies?* Illus. by Ken Perkins. Montgomery, AL: Apologetics Press, 2006. 16p. ISBN: 9780932859945. OCLC #: 71203739. Ages 5–9. FORMAT: Hardcover. AWARDS: None. REVIEWS: None.

On their first day of school, twins Seth and Sara meet a classmate named Michael who has two daddies. Michael tells the twins that his dads are considering marriage. Sara and Seth are confused because they don't think men can marry each other and they also aren't sure if men are supposed to live together. Over dinner that night the twins ask their parents if God loves Michael's two daddies as they are gay. Their parents explain that God wants the dads to break up their family and each marry a woman. Of course, the narrative doesn't quite explain which dad poor Michael is supposed to live with and if the other dad should have visitation rights. The didactic text is accompanied by forced illustrations resembling Dick and Jane readers from the 1950s. Also included are a list of Bible verses about homosexuality and sodomy. Although it is important for librarians to balance their collections with materials that present both sides of a topic, this book leaves many questions unanswered and encourages the dissolution of gay families. NOT RECOMMENDED.

Keywords: Anti-Gay Sentiment, Homosexuality and Religion, Homosexuality and Christianity, Homosexuality and the Bible, Twins.

CARR, JENNIFER. *Be Who You Are!* Illus. by Ben Rumback. Bloomington, IN: AuthorHouse, 2010. 32p. ISBN: 9781452087252. OCLC #: 702678859. Ages 6–9. FORMAT: Paperback. AWARDS: Rainbow List 2012. REVIEWS: None.

Little Nick is different from other boys his age. He feels like a girl inside, and this sensitive picture book describes his budding awareness of his gender-nonconformity. Through the support and love of his parents and a child psychologist, the young boy begins the transition from Nick to a young girl named Hope. Along the way, Hope helps her younger brother understand the change and the book ends on a hopeful note that other children and adults will understand and respect her too. Based upon the author's own experiences with her young son, who transitioned to a girl before the age of six, the narrative is uneven at times, fluctuating from a voice that children will understand to one above the targeted developmental age group. Rumback's soothing illustrations complement the text but also display an imbalanced quality throughout as the younger brother is represented as a very small child in some illustrations and as much older in others. Nonetheless, the lack of picture books on the topic of transgender children marks this as a title for consideration for larger library systems. Smaller libraries may want to consider *My Princess Boy* (Kilodavis), which is more age-appropriate for young children. ADDITIONAL SELECTION.

Keywords: Family Relations, Cross-Dressing, Gender Nonconformity, Gender Identity, Individuality, Transgender, Self-Published Literature, School Relations.

CARTER, VANDA. *If I Had a Hundred Mummies.* London, UK: Onlywomen Press, 2007. Unpaged. ISBN: 9780906500910. OCLC #: 271310366. Ages 4–8. FORMAT: Paperback. AWARDS: None. REVIEWS: None.

Before falling asleep, a girl wonders what it would be like to have one hundred mothers. Her dreams are filled with female characters from her favorite books — would-be mothers — as she explores the advantages and disadvantages of having lots of mommies. In the end, she decides that the two she has are just enough for her. Although the cartoon illustrations vary in quality, children will enjoy searching for storybook characters in them as well as encountering women from various cultural backgrounds. The writing is accessible to U.S. children except for a few Britishisms. The particular strength of the book is the non-issue of the same-sex family. ADDITIONAL SELECTION.

Keywords: Family Composition, Family Relations, Lesbian Mothers, Children of Gay Parents, British Literature, Great Britain, Mixed Race Families.

CINQUETTI, NICOLA. *Salverò la principessa!* Illus. by Silvia Vignale. Rome, Italy: Edizioni Lapis, 2008. Unpaged. ISBN: 9788878741119. OCLC #: n.a. Ages 4–8. FORMAT: Hardcover. AWARDS: None. REVIEWS: None.

A young knight fights tirelessly, braving an evil dragon to save the princess from the castle. This is a classic story known all too well in traditional literature. However, the twist in Cinquetti's version is that the brave knight is actually a girl who saves the princess and then they run off together. But, just when readers think they've figured this out it turns out the entire story has all been make-believe and the dragon is simply the janitor outside the courtyard where one of the two girls live. Written entirely in Italian, the light-hearted narrative, accompanied by bright, cartoon illustrations, is a perfect companion to *The Princess Knight* (Funke) and would serve gender-variant children well. Full text of the book is available from the publisher at www.edizionilapis.eu/PDF_Quadrati/laprincipessa.pdf. RECOMMENDED.

Keywords: Princesses, Dragons, Gender Identity, Gender Nonconformity, Gender Roles, Sex Roles, Italian Literature, Italy, Individuality, Knights, Friendship.

CODELL, ESMÉ RAJI. *The Basket Ball.* Illus. by Jennifer Plecas. New York, NY: Abrams, 2011. Unpaged. ISBN: 9781419700071. OCLC #: 707968776. Ages 4–8. FORMAT: Hardcover. AWARDS: None. REVIEWS: PW.

Basketball puns abound in this alternative look at female sports. When the local boys won't let her play on their team, Lulu forms her own basketball team by hosting a "basket ball" complete with sequined jerseys. Girls from around the world compete at a game of basketball to determine who will be on Lulu's team. At times the rhymes become forced as Codell tries to entertain readers with yet another basketball pun. The whimsical illustrations complement but do little to extend the narrative. Gender-variant children who prefer balls to dolls may be attracted to the book, which is recommended for larger library collections. ADDITIONAL SELECTION.

   Keywords: Tomboys, Gender Nonconformity, Sex Roles, Individuality, Basketball.

COHEN, RICHARD A. *Alfie's Home.* Illus. by Elizabeth Sherman. Washington, DC: International Healing Foundation, 1993. 30p. ISBN: 9780963705808. OCLC #: 30446213. Ages 7–11. FORMAT: Hardcover. AWARDS: None. REVIEWS: None.

The overly didactic, disturbing book depicts a boy named Alfie who feels excluded by his parents who are always fighting. His mother makes him sit in her lap while she cries about her husband's rage and their wrecked marriage. Alfie doesn't feel loved by his dad and longs for his affection. The broken home gets worse when Alfie's uncle comes to live with them and ends up molesting the boy. When Alfie gets into high school he is confused by his gay tendencies and visits a guidance counselor who helps Alfie see that he needs to be touched and loved by his dad and that he is not gay, just in need of his dad's affection. The teen eventually reconciles with his dad who caresses the teen and holds him in his lap. A few pages later, Alfie meets a girl and is married. While at first glance the narrative seems appropriate for young children, there are numerous troubling undertones in the book that could be harmful to all children (not just those in rainbow families), such as the assumption that people are gay because they are molested as children or that gay people are pedophiles. NOT RECOMMENDED.

   Keywords: Anti-Gay Sentiment, Pedophilia, Child Sexual Abuse, Ex-Gay Ministries, Homophobia, Family Relations, Emotional Problems.

COLE, BABETTE. *Mummy Never Told Me.* London, UK: Jonathan Cape/Random House, 2003. Unpaged. ISBN: 9780224047364. OCLC #: 155947424. Ages 4–9. FORMAT: Hardcover. AWARDS: None. REVIEWS: None. Positive review included in the UK review publication *Books for Keeps.*

In this delightful, tongue-in-cheek look at life questions that children ask, readers follow a young boy as he lists a series of things that his mummy never told him, such as where belly buttons come from, why adults have hair in their ears, what mommy and daddy do behind locked doors, and why "some women prefer to fall in love with other women . . . and some men with other men?" Cole's droll illustrations are the perfect complement to the text; however more conservative parents may object to the boy peeing in the tub and two glimpses of breasts. Also, mummy never answers the boy's numerous questions. However, parents will be able to use this book to answer the burning questions from little ones that will arise in the reading. ADDITIONAL SELECTION.

Keywords: Family Relations, Lesbians, Gay Men, British Literature, Great Britain, Mixed Race Families, Life Questions.

CONSIDINE, KAITLYN. *Emma and Meesha My Boy: A Two Mom Story.* Illus. by Binny Hobbs. West Hartford, CT: Two Mom Books, 2005. Unpaged. ISBN: 9781413416008. OCLC #: 123912246. Ages 3–5. FORMAT: Paperback. AWARDS: Rainbow List 2008. REVIEWS: None.

Little Emma has a pet cat that she calls Meesha My Boy and her two mothers constantly scold her for treating him like a toy. Eventually she learns to treat her cat with care and is rewarded with a purr. Told in simple rhyming verse, the text is forced at times although the message is one that young children will easily understand. The bright, computer-generated illustrations extend the narrative and add to the appeal of the story. Not an essential purchase but it does have redeeming qualities. ADDITIONAL SELECTION.

Keywords: Cats, Family Relations, Lesbian Mothers, Children of Gay Parents, Pets, Self-Published Literature.

COOKE, TRISH. *Mr. Pam Pam and the Hullabazoo.* Illus. by Patrice Aggs. Cambridge, MA: Candlewick Press, 1994. Unpaged. ISBN: 9781564024114. OCLC #: 28890870. Ages 3–7. FORMAT: Hardcover. AWARDS: None. REVIEWS: BCCB, HB, SLJ. Other non-U.S. reviews included in the UK review publication *Books for Keeps.* (Originally published in the United Kingdom in 1994.)

With his baby in tow, Mr. Pam Pam regularly visits a little boy and his mother, regaling them with tales about an outlandish man called Hullabazoo who dances around the neighborhood. The boy wants to see Hullabazoo but always manages to miss him until the day the Hullabazoo bounds right in the door of the boy's house, bouncing and "twizzling." The boy and his mother share a loving embrace as Mr. Pam Pam and Hullabazoo walk arm in arm down the street pushing the baby stroller. The repetitive text may engage more imaginative children but is average at best. Aggs's cheerful watercolor illustrations steal the show, marking this picture book as one to be considered by public libraries searching for queer-friendly picture books with African American characters. ADDITIONAL SELECTION.

Keywords: Gay Men, British Literature, Great Britain, African Americans, Single Parents.

CRAWFORD, GEORGINA. *The Tales of Zebedy-Do-Dah.* Illus. by Emily McCann. London, UK: Onlywomen Press, 2009. 28p. ISBN: 9780906500927. OCLC #: 619959982. Ages 5–7. FORMAT: Paperback. AWARDS: None. REVIEWS: None.

In this collection of five stories, Zebedy-Do-Dah the Jack Russell terrier has various adventures with her family — twins Piers and Sofia and their two mothers Nora Zloti and Hester. Readers follow the adventurous pup as she celebrates the twins' birthday, receives a bath, finds herself lost in the park, spends a bored day at home, and saves a family of drowning ducklings. While the lackluster text does feature a household with two mothers and their well-adjusted children, the trite stories do little to hold the interest of young children. Additionally, in three instances the illustrations contradict the text by depicting the wrong mother involved in the action or the wrong color of an object distinctly described in the text. With the number of high-quality titles available, librarians can give this title a miss. NOT RECOMMENDED.

Keywords: Lesbian Mothers, Children of Gay Parents, Family Relations, Pets, Dogs, British Literature, Great Britain, Twins.

CROWTHER, KITTY. *Jack and Jim.* New York, NY: Hyperion, 2000. Unpaged. ISBN: 9780786825271. OCLC #: 44045752. Ages 4–8. FORMAT: Hardcover. AWARDS: None. REVIEWS: PW, WOW. (Originally published in French as *Mon ami Jim.* Paris, France: Pastel/l'École des loisirs, 1996. ISBN: 9782211039338.)

Jack the crow has always wanted to explore the world beyond his forest home. One day he flies past the forest to the sea where he meets a seagull named Jim. The guys become instant friends, spending the day and eventually the night together. Jim takes Jack back to his house in the seagull village but the other birds don't like Jack because he's black. Later the newly formed couple visits Jack's house but decide they like Jim's better. While at Jim's house, Jack discovers a box of books. Each night before they go to bed, Jack reads Jim a story. None of the seagulls can read and soon word spreads that Jack tells wonderful stories (from books). Before long the entire town is in love with Jack and his stories. The accessible text and simple cartoon illustrations appeal to a wide range of children and the book's positive messages about the importance of literacy and the normalcy of interracial, same-sex relationships is powerful. Fortunately, the message is simple enough not to ruffle the feathers of even the most conservative family. Perfect for school and public libraries. HIGHLY RECOMMENDED.

Keywords: Birds, Gay Men, French Literature, France, Mixed Race Families, Interracial Dating.

DANISH, BARBARA. *The Dragon and the Doctor.* New York, NY: The Feminist Press/University of New York, 1995. 2nd rev. ed. Unpaged. ISBN: 9780967446868. OCLC #: 71822789. Ages 3–8. FORMAT: Paperback. AWARDS: None. REVIEWS: None. First edition, published in 1971, did not include the lesbian mothers.

Poor Dragon! Her tail is very sore and she doesn't know what to do. She visits Dr. Judy and Nurse Benjamin, who discover that Dragon's tail is full of unusual objects like roller blades, a peach pit, and a photograph. They find a zipper on Dragon's tail and unzip it. Then the trio goes to a party filled with Dragon's animal friends. One of the friends is Lucy, who develops chicken pox and has to be taken home to her two moms. The nonsensical narrative might appeal to some children but it is hard to follow at times and the cartoon illustrations add little to the story. NOT RECOMMENDED.

Keywords: Individuality, Lesbian Mothers, Children of Gay Parents, Dragons, Doctors.

DE HAAN, LINDA, AND STERN NIJLAND. *King and King.* Berkeley, CA: Tricycle Press, 2002. Unpaged. ISBN: 9781582460611. OCLC #: 48038589. Ages 5–8. FORMAT: Hardcover. AWARDS: Best Children's Books of the Year, 2003, Bank Street College of Education; Lambda Literary Award Finalist, LGBT Children's/YA Category, 2003. REVIEWS: BKLST, BL, BCCB, HB, KS, LBR, PW, SLJ. (Originally published in Dutch as *Koning & Koning.* Haarlem, Netherlands: J. H. Gottmer, 2000. ISBN: 9789025732738.)

Once upon a time on a tall mountain in a large castle there lived a tired and demanding old queen, her fabulous unwed son, and the curious crown kitty. One day the queen decides that she no longer wants to rule the land and it is high time for her fickle son to get married so he can become king. Reluctantly the prince agrees, stating he's never cared for princesses. The next day, after the prince deems a stream of eligible princesses unsuitable, he finally meets his long-awaited true love — not a princess but another prince. Promptly the two are married and become King and King. The busy collage illustrations are appealing and include hidden words from other languages that children will enjoy identifying along with the hi-jinks of the crown kitty that are found on every page. The simple text introduces readers to a contemporary and long-overdue fairy tale, but it does ridicule a princess with long arms from Mumbai, which would need to be addressed when shared with young children. Nonetheless, the book does present gay marriage in a positive light and rainbow families will appreciate the lack of didacticism when presenting a same-sex relationship. RECOMMENDED.

Keywords: Gay Men, Gay Marriage, Kings, Fairy Tales, Family Relations, Dutch Literature, Netherlands, Weddings.

DE HAAN, LINDA, AND STERN NIJLAND. *King and King and Family.* Berkeley, CA: Tricycle Press, 2004. Unpaged. ISBN: 9781582461137. OCLC #: 53138924. Ages 5–8. FORMAT: Hardcover. AWARDS: None. REVIEWS: BCCB, HB, KS, PW, SLJ.

In this sequel to *King and King,* King Lee and King Bertie honeymoon in the jungle. As they travel, King Bertie has the feeling that they are being followed. They meet many wild animals, but the mystery of who is trailing them isn't solved until they return to their kingdom. In their suitcase, they find a stowaway — a young jungle girl who has decided she wants to have two dads. The kings fill out the proper paperwork and officially adopt Princess Daisy. There are several obvious plot flaws, but the vibrant collage illustrations will appeal to young readers and the positive portrayal of a gay couple may lead families to overlook the obvious dilemma of children hiding in luggage! ADDITIONAL SELECTION.

Keywords: Children of Gay Parents, Gay Fathers, Kings, Fairy Tales, Family Relations, Dutch Literature, Netherlands, Adoption.

DE LA TIERRA, TATIANA. *Xía y las mil sirenas.* Illus. by Anna Cooke. Guadalajara, Mexico: Editorial Patlatonalli, 2009. Unpaged. ISBN: 9786079511005. OCLC #: 535220501. Ages 3–7. FORMAT: Hardcover. AWARDS: None. REVIEWS: None.

Written entirely in Spanish, this magical tale follows young Xía who is born by the sea without a mother or father. She longs for a family until the day a woman with perfume takes Xía on a plane to meet her new *familia.* From the plane, the girl sees thousands of mermaids calling out to her and singing. When she arrives at her new home — which is complete with two loving mothers (one brown and one white), a brother, a puppy, and a pony — Xía longs to see the mermaids rather than engage the family. During a dream her pony takes her to the mermaids, who help her understand that she has a beautiful family of her own and that they (the magical mermaids) will always live within her heart. Bright, child-like illustrations capture the magic of the girl, her multiracial family, and her thousand mermaids. Both male and female mermaids are depicted, some in various stages of undress, which may raise the ire of more conservative parents uncomfortable with the female anatomy. The story exudes elements of magical realism and may be beneficial in libraries in need of Spanish-language materials. ADDITIONAL SELECTION.

Keywords: Adoption, Lesbian Mothers, Children of Gay Parents, Family Relations, Spanish Literature, Mexico, Mermaids.

DEPAOLA, TOMIE. *Bonjour, Mr. Satie.* New York, NY: Putnam, 1991. Unpaged. ISBN: 9780399217821. OCLC #: 21904721. Ages 4–8. FORMAT: Hardcover. AWARDS: Bulletin Blue Ribbons, 1991, Bulletin of the Center for Children's Books; Lasting Connections, 1991, American Library Association. REVIEWS: BCCB, KS, PW, SLJ. Also known as *Mr. Satie and the Great Art Contest.*

Chock-full of innuendos that will be lost on most children, this delightful look at the Paris art scene follows Uncle Satie and his "traveling companion" as they visit Satie's niece and nephew in the States. Satie tells his young relatives about his fortuitous opportunity to judge an art contest between Henri Matisse and Pablo Picasso in the salon of Gertrude Stein and Alice B. Toklas. Of course, Satie is not one to name-drop so all the last names are missing, but astute adults will pick up on all the references and will also note that some of those on the guest list include a lesbian couple and that Uncle Satie's traveling companion is more like his life partner. DePaola's picture book offers many classroom and library extensions and his replicas of famous paintings will delight art lovers. HIGHLY RECOMMENDED.

Keywords: Artists, Erik Satie, Gay Relatives, Gay Uncles, France, Pablo Picasso, Henri Matisse, Gertrude Stein, Alice B. Toklas, Cats, Mice, Gay Men, Lesbians.

DEPAOLA, TOMIE. *Oliver Button Is a Sissy.* New York, NY: Harcourt Brace Jovanovich, 1979. Unpaged. ISBN: 9780881033571. OCLC #: 4194907. Ages 3–8. FORMAT: Hardcover. AWARDS: None. REVIEWS: BL, KS, PW, SLJ.

Based on the author's childhood experiences, this sensitive book follows Oliver, who, unlike other boys, enjoys jumping rope, dressing up, drawing, playing with paper dolls, and dancing. His father encourages him to play ball with the other boys but Oliver is teased and called a "sissy." Eventually, his parents relent and allow him to take dance lessons to get his needed exercise. Even though his male classmates tease him, Oliver excels at tap dancing and participates in a talent show. Although he does not win, he proves to everyone that he is still a star! As relevant today as it was more than thirty years ago, dePaola's picture book provides both a mirror and a window for children to see the world of a gender-nonconforming child. Appropriate for both school and public libraries. HIGHLY RECOMMENDED.

Keywords: Dance, Gender Identity, Gender Nonconformity, Individuality, Family Relations, Sex Roles, Teasing.

DEPAOLA, TOMIE. *Stagestruck.* New York, NY: Putnam, 2005. Unpaged. ISBN: 9780399243387. OCLC #: 55106298. Ages 3–8. FORMAT: Hardcover. AWARDS: Best Children's Books of the Year, 2005, Bank Street College of Education. REVIEWS: BL, KS, LMC, SLJ.

Based on the author's childhood experiences in kindergarten, this charming picture book follows a young Tomie and his classmates as they prepare for a school play of *Peter Rabbit.* When Tomie doesn't get the part he wanted (Peter Rabbit) because he was talking in class, he decides to take his dance teacher's advice and ham it up whenever the character of Peter Rabbit is saying his lines. Tomie's performance inevitably steals the show and he's the star of the play. Much like Oliver Button, Tomie in this story loves dancing, but unlike Oliver, he is not ridiculed because of this interest. Pair this book with *Oliver Button Is a Sissy* to show the reactions that boys can receive from their classmates when they engage in gender-nonconforming behaviors. Appropriate for both school and public libraries. RECOMMENDED.

Keywords: Dance, Gender Nonconformity, Individuality, School Relations.

DE VEAUX, ALEXIS. *An Enchanted Hair Tale.* Illus. by Cheryl Hanna. New York, NY: HarperCollins, 1987. 41p. ISBN: 9780060216245. OCLC #: 13125168. Ages 5–8. FORMAT: Hardcover. AWARDS: Cooperative Children's Book Center Choices 1987; Coretta Scott King Book Award, Author Honor 1988; American Library Association Notable Children's Book 1988. REVIEWS: PW, SLJ.

A young African American boy named Sudan looks like his dad but has long, magical dreads like his mother. The hair giggles when he talks, roars when he walks, and sprouts wings! The grown-ups and other children in his neighborhood tease Sudan and call him "queer" because he looks different from other boys with his long hair. Sudan is sad and angry all the time, and one rainy day he has had enough. Taking to the streets, he meets a magical circus that has other people with magical dreads like his. The circus crew encourages him to be proud of his "pretty self" and instills in Sudan a sense of personal pride. Imbued with magical realism and detailed charcoal illustrations, this book could be welcoming to gender-variant children. However, at times the rhyme is a little hard to follow and may be confusing for some children. ADDITIONAL SELECTION.

Keywords: Gender Nonconformity, Individuality, Family Relations, Teasing, Hair, African Americans.

DE WITTE VAN LEEUWEN, JARKO. *Arwen and Her Daddies.* Dordrecht, Netherlands: De Witte van Leeuwen (Self-Published), 2009. 56p. ISBN: 9789081485425. OCLC #: 496229747. Ages 4–7. FORMAT: Hardcover. AWARDS: None. REVIEWS: None. (Originally published in Dutch as *Arwen en haar papa's.* ISBN: 9789081485418.)

Arwen is an African American preschooler who lives in the Netherlands with her two daddies and their dog Tox. Through bold, clean cartoon illustrations and simple text, young children learn how her mother in the United States gave Arwen up for adoption and chose her two daddies to be her parents. The illustrations clearly communicate the love among the biracial family and make a non-issue of the fact that Arwen's parents are both men. With few picture books representing biracial rainbow families, public libraries may want to consider adding this title to their collection; however, the price may preclude smaller libraries from purchasing the book. ADDITIONAL SELECTION.

　　Keywords: Adoption, African Americans, Mixed Race Families, Gay Fathers, Children of Gay Parents, Family Relations, Dutch Literature, Self-Published Literature, Netherlands.

DYKSTRA, LAUREL. *Uncle Aiden.* Vancouver, BC: BabyBloc Publishing, 2005. Unpaged. ISBN: 9780973819106. OCLC #: 60739483. Ages 4–8. FORMAT: Paperback. AWARDS: None. REVIEWS: None.

Anna is a Mexican Irish girl who loves spending time with her Uncle Aiden because he takes time to play with her (dress-up, tea parties, baseball), attend her school concerts, introduce her to his boyfriends, and listen to what she has to say. The simple text is accessible to beginning readers and the child-like illustrations clearly convey the love between these two family members. This charming title is appropriate for both public and school libraries, although the paperback format may limit its practicality for some libraries. Available at http://babybloc.org/Uncle%20Aiden.html. RECOMMENDED.

　　Keywords: Gay Uncles, Gay Relatives, Gay Pride, Family Relations, School Relations, Canada, Canadian Literature, Latinos, Mixed Race Families, Self-Published Literature.

EDMONDS, BARBARA LYNN. *Mama Eat Ant, Yuck.* Illus. by Matthew Daniele. Eugene, OR: Hundredth Munchy Publications, 2000. Unpaged. ISBN: 9780965670029. OCLC #: 47045709. Ages 4–8. FORMAT: Paperback. AWARDS: None. REVIEWS: None.

Mama eat ant, yuck! These are not the first words a mother expects her child to say but in this rhyming picture book a mother accidentally eats an ant along with her raisins. When she causes a commotion at the table, her daughter shouts, "Mama eat ant, yuck!" as her first words. Throughout the rest of the story, the girl will not stop saying this phrase. When the girl grows up and has her own baby, her lesbian mothers are surprised that their granddaughter's first words are "Grandmama eat ant, yuck." While young children may delight in the silly story, the telling is forced and the illustrations do little to extend the narrative. NOT RECOMMENDED.

Keywords: Lesbian Mothers, Children of Gay Parents, Family Relations, First Words, Babies.

ELWIN, ROSAMUND, AND MICHELE PAULSE. *Asha's Mums.* Illus. by Dawn Lee. Toronto, ON: Women's Press, 1990. Unpaged. ISBN: 9780889611436. OCLC #: 26503744. Ages 4–8. FORMAT: Paperback. AWARDS: None. REVIEWS: None.

Asha's class is about to take a school trip to the Science Center but they must have permission forms signed by their parents. Both her mothers sign the form and send it to school. Asha's teacher pulls her aside and accuses her of not filling out the form correctly because she can't have two mothers. Asha's mothers speak to the teacher the next day but the class is still confused about Asha having two mothers. Eventually, the teacher relents and allows Asha on the field trip with one of her mothers. Although the purpose of the book is to demonstrate that lesbian parents exist, the conflict of the story is not fully addressed. The teacher never tries to explain to the class about Asha's family composition nor does she correct children who tell Asha it is wrong to have two mothers. While this is an all-too-common reality, rainbow families reading this story will be left with conflicting feelings about their families' place in public classrooms. **NOT RECOMMENDED.**

Keywords: Anti-Gay Sentiment, Lesbian Mothers, Children of Gay Parents, Family Relations, School Relations, Canada, Canadian Literature, African Canadians.

EWERT, MARCUS. *10,000 Dresses.* Illus. by Rex Ray. New York, NY: Seven Stories Press, 2008. Unpaged. ISBN: 9781583228500. OCLC #: 216939889. Ages 4–8. FORMAT: Hardcover. AWARDS: Stonewall Book Awards 2010, Children's and Young Adult Honor Book; Rainbow List 2009. REVIEWS: None.

Each night Bailey dreams about the dresses that she would like to wear and each morning she tells a family member about these wonderful dresses. Bailey's mother, father, and brother all tell her that she is a boy and that boys don't wear dresses. She is heartbroken until she finds a girl at the end of her street making dresses. The girl sees Bailey for who she really is and asks her to help. One of the first picture books to clearly depict a transgender character, this groundbreaking title could be useful to gender-variant and transgender children. The strength of the book is its use of pronouns to clearly delineate Bailey as a girl although the illustrations depict her as a boy. The effect is a window into the struggle of gender-variant and transgender children to make the world understand them. With few picture books representing transgender children, libraries might want to consider adding this title to the collection. However, the pages are laden with text at times and the illustrations fail to reflect the dazzling beauty of the story. **ADDITIONAL SELECTION.**

Keywords: Gender Nonconformity, Gender Identity, Individuality, Transgender, Sex Roles, Cross-Dressing, Family Relations.

FALLENS, BRONNY. *My Two Super Dads.* Illus. by Muntsa Vicente. Elwood, Victoria (Australia): Bronny & Muntsa, 2011. Unpaged. ISBN: 97809871070. OCLC #: n.a. Ages 4–8. FORMAT: Hardcover. Awards: None. REVIEWS: None.

A young girl explains that she is adopted and then describes the many wonderful activities that she and her two dads tackle together. The fact that she has gay dads is a refreshing non-issue in the book. Unfortunately, the rhyming text is forced at times and the lack of punctuation makes it difficult for readers to decode sentence structures. A few regionalisms will be lost on a U.S. audience. However, Vicente's cheerful mixed-media illustrations take on a life of their own, propelling the text and extending the book's reach. The non-didactic message and beautiful illustrations make this a book worthy of consideration for larger public libraries that may want to use it in library programs where children write their own stories to accompany the illustrations. Available for purchase from http://www.bronnyandmuntsa. com/. RECOMMENDED.

Keywords: Adoption, Gay Fathers, Children of Gay Parents, Self-Published Literature, Family Relations, Australian Literature, Australia.

FARRELL, JOHN. *Dear Child.* Illus. by Maurie J. Manning. Honesdale, PA: Boyds Mills Press, 2008. Unpaged. ISBN: 9781590784952. OCLC #: 137331352. Ages 4–7. FORMAT: Hardcover. AWARDS: None. REVIEWS: KS, LMC.

Three diverse families are depicted in this ode from parents to their children. The lyrical text and cheerful illustrations depict a biracial lesbian couple and their adopted daughter, a straight African American couple and their son, and a single father and his son. In the various spreads, the three families are shown on the beach, at a carnival, in their homes, at the library, and in the woods camping. The special bond between caregiver and child is clearly conveyed in both the text and illustrations, although the narrative may be aimed more at adults than children. A potential resource for parenting programs or family storytimes, this selection would be good for larger library systems. ADDITIONAL SELECTION.

Keywords: Adoption, Family Composition, Lesbian Mothers, Children of Gay Parents, Family Relations, Asian Americans, African Americans, Single Parents, Mixed Race Families.

FERREIRA, JEANNELLE. *City Life.* Illus. by J. Cecelia Haytko. Rockville, MD: Books for All Families, 2010. Unpaged. ISBN: 9781607012993. OCLC #: n.a. Ages 3–7. FORMAT: Paperback. AWARDS: None. REVIEWS: None.

A young girl describes the entertaining things that she and her moms do in the city — riding bikes, going to the zoo, feeding pigeons in the park, and visiting a museum. The book focuses on the options for fun in the city and not the two-mom aspect. Unfortunately, the narrative is not engaging and the line illustrations are difficult to interpret at times. NOT RECOMMENDED.

Keywords: Lesbian Mothers, Children of Gay Parents, Family Relations.

FIERSTEIN, HARVEY. *The Sissy Duckling.* Illus. by Henry Cole. New York, NY: Simon & Schuster, 2002. Unpaged. ISBN: 9780689835667. OCLC #: 44934197. Ages 3–8. FORMAT: Hardcover. AWARDS: Lambda Literary Award Finalist, LGBT Children's/YA Category, 2003. REVIEWS: BKLST, BL, BCCB, KS, LBR, PW, SLJ.

Although other boy ducks like to build forts and play ball, Elmer prefers to bake, put on puppet shows, and make sandcastles. Although he is teased by Drake duckling for being weak, Elmer makes no excuses for his gender nonconformity. He is quite content being his happy jovial self; that is until he overhears his father calling him a "sissy" and saying that Elmer is no son of his. Not wanting to shame his parents, Elmer runs away to make his home in a hollowed-out tree. As the flock is about to leave for the winter, a hunter shoots Elmer's father and Elmer saves him while all the other "brave" ducks fly away. Similar in scope to *Oliver Button Is a Sissy* (dePaola), this refreshing tale presents a boy who is "a big sissy and proud of it." Appropriate for both school and public libraries, the picture book will resonate with gender-variant and possibly transgender children. RECOMMENDED.

Keywords: Gender Identity, Gender Nonconformity, Individuality, Family Relations, School Relations, Sex Roles, Teasing, Ducks.

FLORIDI, PICO. ***Quante Famiglie.*** Illus. by Amelia Gatacre. Milan, Italy: Il Castoro, 2010. Unpaged. ISBN: 9788880335269. OCLC #: 735980267. Ages 4–8. FORMAT: Hardcover. AWARDS: None. REVIEWS: None.

The best type of family is a happy family, regardless how it is formed. This positive, uplifting message is the theme of Floridi's Italian picture book, which profiles eight children's vignettes about a day in the life of their family. Readers meet extended families, single parents, lesbian grandmothers, gay fathers, grandparent caregivers, and traditional nuclear families, to name a few. Gatacre's bright, cheerful illustrations are filled with details that will capture and hold the attention of young children. Although the text is entirely in Italian, the illustrations clearly convey the love of the profiled families and would be appropriate for any library. RECOMMENDED.

Keywords: Adoption, Divorced Parents, Gay Fathers, Lesbian Grandmothers, Children of Gay Parents, Family Composition, Family Relations, Single Parents, Stepparents, Mixed Race Families, Extended Families, Grandparent Caregivers, Family Tree, Italian Literature, Italy.

FOX-LEE, KYME, AND SUSAN FOX-LEE. ***What Are Parents?*** Illus. by Randy Jennings. Antelope, CA: StoryTyme Publishing, 2004. Unpaged. ISBN: 9780975369906. OCLC #: 57717034. Ages 3–7. FORMAT: Hardcover. AWARDS: None. REVIEWS: None.

A newborn baby wonders "What are parents?" as the nurse takes her to meet her two mothers. While riding in a hospital bassinet, the infant passes rooms with single parents, biracial families, and adoptees. She also sees a christening ceremony and a girl playing peek-a-boo with her new sibling. At the end of the hallway, she is presented to her mothers. In the last spread of the book, readers can follow the illustrations to see how the girl matures, goes to school, marries, and has her own child. While the concept is admirable, the execution and end-product are not age-appropriate. The text contains words and concepts unfamiliar to young children, and the graphic-novel style illustrations are not simple enough for the target audience. Also, the newborns in the book are shown sitting up, holding their own bottles, etc., which is obviously not factually accurate. NOT RECOMMENDED.

Keywords: Adoption, Children of Gay Parents, Family Composition, Family Relations, Single Parents, Mixed Race Families, Extended Families, Lesbian Mothers, Self-Published Literature, Babies.

FUNKE, CORNELIA. *The Princess Knight.* Illus. by Kerstin Meyer. Translation by Anthea Bell. New York, NY: Chicken House/Scholastic, 2004. Unpaged. ISBN: 9780439536301. OCLC #: 54464077. Ages 4–8. FORMAT: Hardcover. AWARDS: Amelia Bloomer List 2005; Best Children's Books of the Year, 2004, Bank Street College of Education. REVIEWS: BKLST, BCCB, KS, LMC, PW, SLJ. (Originally published in German as *Der geheimnisvolle Ritter Namenlos.* Frankfurt, Germany: Fischer Taschenbuch Verlag, 2001; ISBN: 9783596850945.)

Princess Violetta was born the only girl with three older brothers. The king teaches each of his children how to fight like a knight. And after many long hours of practicing, Violetta is faster than her brothers and can beat any other knight in the kingdom. On her sixteenth birthday, she is surprised to discover that her father plans to have a jousting tournament with her as the prize. When she tells him she will not be the prize of some dimwitted knight who can't read, the king locks Violetta in the tower. Eventually she concedes to his plans but has her own ideas about how to win. She dresses her nursemaid as herself and she goes undercover as a knight in the tournament. She beats all the other knights, winning her own hand in marriage and eventually the right to marry whomever she chooses. Funke's contemporary fairy tale is accented with Meyer's humorous illustrations and would pair well with *The Paper Bag Princess* (Munsch). Gender-variant females in particular will appreciate Funke's strong female character, although the fact that she does eventually marry a man may be off-putting for some. RECOMMENDED.

Keywords: Princesses, Knights, Gender Identity, Gender Nonconformity, Gender Roles, Sex Roles, German Literature, Germany.

GARDEN, NANCY. *Molly's Family.* Illus. by Sharon Wooding. New York, NY: Farrar, Straus & Giroux, 2004. Unpaged. ISBN: 9780374350024. OCLC #: 50417337. Ages 4–8. FORMAT: Hardcover. AWARDS: None. REVIEWS: BKLST, BL, HB, KS, LMC, SLJ, PW.

In preparation for her kindergarten class's Open School Night, Molly draws a picture of her family, which includes her Mommy, Mama Lu, and her puppy. One of Molly's classmates sees the picture and loudly tells her and the rest of the class that a family can't have two mommies. Molly is sad and her teacher tries to comfort her, but it takes reassurance from her mothers and several days before Molly is finally convinced that her family is "okay" with its two mommies. Mirroring a situation that is all too common in the lives of rainbow families, the book's gentle, accessible narrative and soft, colored pencil illustrations create a story appropriate for both school and public library collections. RECOMMENDED.

Keywords: Adoption, Lesbian Mothers, Children of Gay Parents, Family Composition, School Relations, Single Parents.

GONZÁLEZ, RIGOBERTO. *Antonio's Card/La tarjeta de Antonio.* Illus. by Cecilia Concepción Álvarez. San Francisco, CA: Children's Book Press, 2005. 32p. ISBN: 9780892392049. OCLC #: 56096467. Ages 4–8. FORMAT: Hardcover. AWARDS: Lambda Literary Award Finalist, LGBT Children's/YA Category, 2006; Independent Publisher Book Award (IPPY), 2006 Honorable Mention Multicultural Fiction Children's — United States; Rainbow List 2008. REVIEWS: KS, LMC, SLJ.

Antonio loves his mami and her partner Leslie, but when some of his classmates ridicule Leslie's appearance, the young boy struggles with the embarrassment of having a nontraditional family. With Mother's Day approaching, Antonio's class creates cards to be displayed around the classroom. Antonio draws a picture of his family — Mami, Leslie, and himself — reading under a tree. Later he is worried that his classmates will tease him or Leslie when they see the picture. Eventually, he decides his love for his mothers is stronger than the desire to avoid the taunts of his classmates. The sensitive narrative, written in English and Spanish, is easily accessible to young children and captures the emotions of children with queer parents. Álvarez's vibrant illustrations complement the story and include many embedded words about family and love. HIGHLY RECOMMENDED.

    Keywords: Lesbian Mothers, Children of Gay Parents, Family Relations, Bilingual Literature — English and Spanish, Latinos, Mixed Race Families, Mother's Day, Teasing, School Relations.

GOULD, LOIS. *X: A Fabulous Child's Story.* Illus. by Jacqueline Chwast. New York, NY: Daughters Publishing, 1978. 52p. ISBN: 9780913780213. OCLC #: 4499675. Ages 10 and up. FORMAT: Hardcover. AWARDS: None. REVIEWS: PW. (Originally published as a short story for *Ms.* Magazine in 1972 and later as a full-length picture book in 1978.)

X and its parents are part of a top-secret scientific experiment. X's parents have agreed to raise the child as both male and female and to refer to it as X, rather than he or she. They buy X both girl and boy clothes and toys and teach the child all types of hobbies. When the child goes to school, the other parents and children have a huge problem with X's gender nonconformity. The parent association forces the principal to have a team of impartial experts examine X because their children are learning gender-nonconforming behaviors. The experts decide that X is the best-adjusted, least mixed-up child they've ever met. Later, when X's friends come to its house, they see that X's family has a new gender-variant baby called Y. This picture book is hard to find, but it is perfect for librarians to share with all children, particularly transgender and gender-variant children who will see reflections of themselves in X. A copy of the book's text and selected illustrations can be found in *Tales for Little Rebels: A Collection of Radical Children's Literature* (Mickenberg and Nel, 2008). HIGHLY RECOMMENDED.

    Keywords: Gender Nonconformity, Gender Identity, Individuality, Transgender, Self-Published Literature, Sex Roles, Cross-Dressing, School Relations, Babies.

GREENBERG, MELANIE HOPE. *Mermaids on Parade.* New York, NY: Putnam, 2008. Unpaged. ISBN: 9780399247088. OCLC #: 132681408. Ages 4–7. FORMAT: Hardcover. AWARDS: Best Children's Books of the Year, 2009, Bank Street College of Education. REVIEWS: BKLST, KS, LMC, PW, SLJ.

Mermaids, sea creatures, and gods of the sea abound in this colorful and loving tribute to the Mermaid Parade that is held annually on Coney Island during the summer solstice. Readers follow a young girl, her family, and a menagerie of costumed people as they participate in the festivities. Greenberg's vibrant gouache pen and pencil illustrations are the perfect addition to the bouncy text and add many details, including a host of drag queens scattered throughout the pages. Although the text never mentions the cross-dressers, children of rainbow families will delight in locating the dazzling men and women who may represent members of their own families. RECOMMENDED.

Keywords: Cross-Dressing, Gender Identity, Gender Nonconformity, Individuality, Mermaids, Family Relations, Parades.

GREGG, JENNIFER C. *Flying Free.* Illus. by Janna Richards. North Charleston, SC: BookSurge, 2004. 29p. ISBN: 9781594579721. OCLC #: 60407022. Ages 4–7. FORMAT: Paperback. AWARDS: None. REVIEWS: None.

Firefly is enjoying the night air when she is captured by five-year-old Violet. Readers soon learn that Violet is scared of the dark and she hopes to use the firefly as a nightlight. Although her mothers don't think this is a good idea, Violet is allowed to keep the firefly as long as she puts air holes and grass in the jar that she used to capture the bug. Firefly tries to escape several times but to no avail. She then decides that she will not shine her light for Violet and that the girl will then release her. Her plan works and the girl allows Firefly to fly free. The fact that Violet has two mothers is a non-issue in the story, a refreshing approach to rainbow families. Unfortunately, both the text and the illustrations have problems. The illustrations lack expression, with the human characters often appearing very stiff, and the overall narrative lacks the necessary impetus to keep young children engaged. NOT RECOMMENDED.

Keywords: Lesbian Mothers, Children of Gay Parents, Family Relations, Fear of the Dark.

GRIFFITHS, JOE, AND TONY PILGRIM. *Picnic in the Park.* Illus. by Lucy Pearce. London, UK: British Association for Adoption and Fostering, 2007. 21p. ISBN: 9781905664085. OCLC #: 159696690. Ages 4–8. FORMAT: Paperback. AWARDS: None. REVIEWS: None. Positive review included in the UK review publication *Books for Keeps.*

Today is Jason's fifth birthday and he is having a big celebration in the park with all of his friends and their families. Readers are introduced to various types of families and the food they bring. Almost every type of family, from single parent to rainbow to foster to biracial, is represented as are children of different races and abilities. The simple text is perfect for beginning readers and the bright, cheerful illustrations will hold their attention, particularly the final spread with all the families, foods, and presents. RECOMMENDED.

Keywords: Adoption, Mixed Race Families, Family Composition, Gay Fathers, Lesbian Mothers, Children of Gay Parents, Family Relations, Foster Parents, British Literature, Great Britain, Divorced Parents, Single Parents, Birthdays, Indians, African Americans.

GRUSKA, DENISE. *The Only Boy in Ballet Class.* Illus. by Amy Wummer. Layton, UT: Gibbs Smith, 2007. Unpaged. ISBN: 9781423602200. OCLC #: 83603298. Ages 4–8. FORMAT: Hardcover. AWARDS: None. REVIEWS: PW, SLJ.

Tucker doesn't just like to dance — he *loves* to dance and spends most of his day doing various ballet moves. Unfortunately his male classmates and his opinionated uncle all think that dancing is for girls. The boys constantly tease him and Tucker's uncle is always saying he should be playing football instead of dancing. One day after a recital, Tucker is snagged by a group of boys to play football because they are a player short. He surprises himself and the team by using various ballet moves to win the game, thereby proving that ballet may be useful for boys. Wummer's colorful cartoon illustrations exude Tucker's passion for dancing and Gruska's narrative successfully captures the emotions of gender-variant boys. Unfortunately, the happy ending is somewhat contrived and may not resonate with the target audience. ADDITIONAL SELECTION.

Keywords: Dance, Football, Gender Nonconformity, Individuality, Ballet, Sex Roles, Single Parents, Teasing.

HARDING, BRENNA, AND VICKI HARDING. *Going to Fair Day.* Illus. by Chris Bray-Cotton. Dulwich Hills, New South Wales (Australia): Learn to Include, 2002. 12p. ISBN: 9780958129015. OCLC #: 223414144. Ages 4–7. FORMAT: Paperback. AWARDS: None. REVIEWS: None. Positive reviews are included in Australian publications such as *Reading Time: The Journal of the Children's Book Council of Australia* and *Family Matters.*

The second title in the Learn to Include Easy-to-Read series follows a girl and her two mothers as they enjoy a day at the fair. Bright cartoon illustrations accompany the age-appropriate text that describes how the girl meets one of her friends who has two dads, enjoys playing at the fair, and leaves with a new pet dog. Part of one of the few beginning reader series to include rainbow families, this title is recommended for both school and public libraries. It should be noted that certain words are spelled using British English, such as "colour" instead of "color." RECOMMENDED.

Keywords: Gay Fathers, Lesbian Mothers, Children of Gay Parents, Family Relations, Australian Literature, Australia, Easy-to-Read Books, Self-Published Literature, Pets, Dogs, Fairs.

HARDING, BRENNA, AND VICKI HARDING. *Koalas on Parade.* Illus. by Chris Bray-Cotton. Dulwich Hills, New South Wales (Australia): Learn to Include, 2005. 12p. ISBN: 9780958129039. OCLC #: 60460747. Ages 6–8. FORMAT: Paperback. AWARDS: None. REVIEWS: None.

In this fourth title in the Learn to Include Easy-to-Read series, a girl and her two mothers prepare for the costume parade at the girl's school. Bright cartoon illustrations accompany the age-appropriate text that is written at a more difficult level than the first two books in the series. This title includes Australian cultural references such as a children's television program that American audiences may find unfamiliar, and, readers may need assistance with British spellings although this is not a reason to avoid purchase. RECOMMENDED.

Keywords: Lesbian Mothers, Children of Gay Parents, Family Relations, Australian Literature, Australia, Easy-to-Read Books, Self-Published Literature, School Relations.

HARDING, BRENNA, AND VICKI HARDING. *My House.* Illus. by Chris Bray-Cotton. Dulwich Hills, New South Wales (Australia): Learn to Include, 2002. 12p. ISBN: 9780958129008. OCLC #: 57341288. Ages 4–7. FORMAT: Paperback. AWARDS: None. REVIEWS: None.

The first title in the Learn to Include Easy-to-Read series introduces young readers to a girl who has two mothers, a cat, and two dogs. Bright cartoon illustrations accompany the age-appropriate text that describes how the girl's cat and dogs do not get along. Part of one of the few beginning reader series to include rainbow families, this title is recommended for both school and public libraries. A teaching guide for the series is available at http://www.hotkey.net.au/~learn_to_include/. RECOMMENDED.

Keywords: Lesbian Mothers, Children of Gay Parents, Family Relations, Australian Literature, Australia, Easy-to-Read Books, Self-Published Literature, Pets, Dogs, Cats.

HARDING, BRENNA, AND VICKI HARDING. *The Rainbow Cubby House.* Illus. by Chris Bray-Cotton. Dulwich Hills, New South Wales (Australia): Learn to Include, 2005. 12p. ISBN: 9780958129022. OCLC #: 60460745. Ages 6–8. FORMAT: Paperback. AWARDS: None. REVIEWS: None.

The third title in the Learn to Include Easy-to-Read series describes how a young girl, her two moms, her friend Jed, and his two dads all work together (with the help of their dogs) to build a cubby house (club house/tree house). Bright cartoon illustrations accompany the age-appropriate text that is slightly more difficult than the first two books in the series. Part of one of the few beginning reader series to include rainbow families, this title is recommended for both school and public libraries. The use of British English terms will allow for intercultural connections with the text. RECOMMENDED.

Keywords: Gay Fathers, Lesbian Mothers, Children of Gay Parents, Family Relations, Australian Literature, Australia, Easy-to-Read Books, Self-Published Literature, Pets, Dogs, Cooperation.

HILTON, PEREZ. *The Boy with Pink Hair.* Illus. by Jen Hill. New York, NY: Celebra Children's Books/Penguin, 2011. Unpaged. ISBN: 9780451234209.

OCLC #: 697264991. Ages 5–8. FORMAT: Hardcover. AWARDS: None. REVIEWS: KS, PW.

Life is not rosy if you have pink hair — especially if you are a boy! But the protagonist of this cheerfully illustrated picture book is not bothered by stares and jeers; instead he uses his energy to concoct delicious pink creations. Although he is teased because of his pink tresses, The Boy with Pink Hair becomes a local celebrity after saving parent-teacher day by cooking up pink mounds of food when the school's stove stalls. Written in a similar vein to *The Sissy Duckling* (Fierstein), the trite narrative attempts to showcase individuality at the expense of literary quality. Characters are never given real names and the plot is not compelling. Readers will enjoy the bright illustrations, but only the most determined will reach the end merely to be rewarded with a dollop of didacticism. NOT RECOMMENDED.

Keywords: Gender Nonconformity, Individuality, School Relations, Teasing, Cooking, Celebrity Fiction.

HOFFMAN, ERIC. *Best Best Colors/Los mejores colores.* Illus. by Celeste Henriquez. Translation by Eida de la Vega. St. Paul, MN: Redleaf Press, 1999. Unpaged. ISBN: 9781884834691. OCLC #: 41439489. Ages 4–8. FORMAT: Paperback. AWARDS: None. REVIEWS: BL.

Nate loves colors and has a hard time picking just one to be his "best, best color." As readers follow the preschool boy through his day, they are introduced to a variety of colors as well as to Nate's vibrant imagination. Eventually, with the help of his two mothers and a rainbow flag, Nate learns that he can love a rainbow of colors instead of just one. The predictable English/Spanish text captures the emotions of preschool children who believe they can only have one best friend and one favorite color. The soft watercolor illustrations are uneven at times and do little to hold the attention of younger children. While not the best book, libraries needing materials for Spanish-speaking rainbow families may want to consider this title. ADDITIONAL SELECTION.

Keywords: Lesbian Mothers, Children of Gay Parents, Family Relations, Bilingual Literature — English and Spanish, Latinos, African Americans, Mixed Race Families.

HOWE, JAMES. *Horace and Morris But Mostly Dolores.* Illus. by Amy Walrod. New York, NY: Atheneum, 1999. Unpaged. ISBN: 9780689856754. OCLC #: 34553554. Ages 4–8. FORMAT: Hardcover. AWARDS: Best Children's Books of the Year, 2000, Bank Street College of Education. REVIEWS: BKLST, BCCB, KS, PW, SLJ.

Horace, Morris, and Dolores are the best of friends and do everything together until the day the boy mice decide to join the Mega-Mice club, which does not allow girls. In turn, Dolores decides to join the Cheese Puffs club, which does not allow boys. Collectively the friends are miserable in their respective clubs and, with the urging of Dolores, decide to form a new club along with a few new friends. The inaugural Frisky Whisker club is open to everyone regardless of gender. With bouncy accessible text and energetic collage illustrations, this picture book demonstrates the importance of individuality and gender nonconformity. RECOMMENDED.

Keywords: Gender Identity, Gender Nonconformity, Sex Roles, Individuality.

ISAACK, SANDRO. *Stork M.I.A.* Raleigh, NC: Lulu.com, 2009. Unpaged. ISBN: 9780557167241. OCLC #: n.a. Ages 4–8. FORMAT: Paperback. AWARDS: None. REVIEWS: None.

Dad and Dad love each other but are very sad because the stork brings babies to other houses but not theirs. Tired of waiting for a baby to arrive, the duo searches the city, phonebook, and the Internet for the stork. Eventually their neighbors Mom and Mom call from Guatemala, where they are visiting, to say the stork just left them baby Paco and is heading for China. The Dads fly to China and catch the stork just in time to receive baby Ava, who they take home with them to the United States. Together, the gay dads, lesbian moms, and two babies create a happy extended family. The cartoon illustrations and simple text make this an appropriate read-aloud for young children, although it is never explained why the dads want to invite the stork before they get married and why they don't marry and wait for the stork. The narrative would have been stronger without this portion of the plot. Nevertheless, libraries may want to consider this book for their collections, especially if they serve rainbow families that have participated in international adoptions. This is the first in a proposed book series following Dad and Dad and Mom and Mom. ADDITIONAL SELECTION.

Keywords: Mixed Race Families, Latinos, Guatemala, Babies, Lesbian Mothers, Gay Fathers, Children of Gay Parents, Adoption, Self-Published Literature, Chinese Americans, International Adoption.

ISHIGUCHI, PAUL. *Crabbing at High Tide.* Illus. by Carl Stahlmann. Broome, Western Australia: Magabala Books, 2001. Unpaged. ISBN: 9781875641215. OCLC #: 155596997. Ages 5–9. FORMAT: Paperback. AWARDS: None. REVIEWS: None.

Focusing on the indigenous culture in Derby, Australia, and told from the point of a view of a young boy, this is an adventure story about a family trapping mud crabs (crab potting) in the mangroves. Uncle Paul and Uncle Carl (the creators of the story) accompany the boy and his father on the crabbing trip. The straightforward storyline and folk art style illustrations complement each other and provide readers with a glimpse into a culture not often covered in children's literature. The gay uncle aspect is a non-issue, which rainbow families will appreciate. The book has also been adapted to the stage with a touring production for schools in Australia. ADDITIONAL SELECTION.

Keywords: Gay Uncles, Gay Relatives, Australian Literature, Australia, Crabs, Indigenous People.

JACOBSON, KRISTINA. *Renee's Family.* Raleigh, NC: Lulu.com, 2010. 32p. ISBN: n.a. OCLC #: n.a. Ages 4–8. FORMAT: Paperback. AWARDS: None. REVIEWS: None.

Renee is a little girl who lives in the country with her two mommies, a cat, two dogs, and a few horses. In this didactic picture book she describes her extended family, friends, church, and school along with other ordinary elements of her life. Poorly executed cartoon illustrations do not always complement a text that is rife with grammatical errors. NOT RECOMMENDED.

Keywords: Family Composition, Lesbian Mothers, Children of Gay Parents, Family Relations, Self-Published Literature.

JIMÉNEZ, KARLEEN PENDLETON. *Are You a Boy or a Girl?* Toronto, ON: Green Dragon Press, 2000. 16p. ISBN: 9781896781143. OCLC #: 46843269. Ages 4–8. FORMAT: Paperback. AWARDS: None. REVIEWS: None.

Karleen is different from other girls — she does not like dolls, make-up, or dresses. She keeps her hair short and often wears boys' clothing. At school and around her neighborhood, people tease her and ask, "Are you a boy or a girl?" This makes Karleen very sad but her mother reassures her daughter that she will eventually find her place in the world and be happy. Based on the author's own childhood experience, the text is didactic at best but might start a discussion with children about gender nonconformity. Unfortunately, the black-and-white photos and sketches do little to enhance the story. With so many other high-quality titles available on this topic, libraries may want to give this one a pass. NOT RECOMMENDED.

Keywords: Gender Nonconformity, Gender Identity, Individuality, Transgender, Self-Published Literature, Sex Roles, Cross-Dressing, Canadian Literature, Canada, School Relations.

JOHNSON, DAVID. *Evan's Beard.* Raleigh, NC: Lulu.com, 2006. Unpaged. ISBN: n.a. OCLC #: n.a. Ages 3–6. FORMAT: Paperback. AWARDS: None. REVIEWS: None.

Two-year-old Evan asks his Uncle Mark about the beard on his face, noting that his two mothers do not have beards. His uncle then tells Evan all about facial hair on men, highlighting various men in the neighborhood and their mustaches, beards, side burns, goatees, and so forth. The text is simple and young children would appreciate the photos of Evan; however, some of the photos are pixilated and the overall quality of the book is marginal for libraries. NOT RECOMMENDED.

Keywords: Beards, Facial Hair, Lesbian Mothers, Children of Gay Parents, Self-Published Literature.

JOHNSON, PHYLLIS HACKEN. *The Boy Toy.* Illus. by Lena Shiffman. Durham, NC: Lollipop Power, 1988. 29p. ISBN: 9780914996262. OCLC #: 18259224. Ages 4–8. FORMAT: Paperback. AWARDS: None. REVIEWS: None.

Chad's grandmother made him a doll, Dan, that looks just like him. Chad loves to play with Dan, cooking him dinner, reading him stories, and driving the doll in his toy car. When Chad starts school a classmate named Sam, tells him that dolls are for girls and that girls can't be doctors. Chad wants to be friends with Sam but is worried the boy will discover that he has a doll. A few weeks before he goes into the hospital for surgery, Chad gives Dan to his sister in hopes that Sam will not discover Chad's doll. When Chad is in the hospital he asks his parents to bring Dan to keep him company. Eventually, he learns that women can be doctors and that it is okay for boys to play with dolls. The two-tone illustrations do little to extend the narrative, but this levelized reader is still perfect for gender-variant boys who worry about peer acceptance. RECOMMENDED.

Keywords: Gender Identity, Gender Nonconformity, Sex Roles, Individuality, Dolls, School Relations, Doctors.

JOPLING, HEATHER. *Monicka's Papa Is Tall.* Illus. by Allyson Demoe. Cobourg, ON: Nickname Press, 2006. Unpaged. ISBN: 9780978073916. OCLC #: 154320400. Ages 4–8. FORMAT: Paperback. AWARDS: Rainbow List 2008. REVIEWS: None. Positive review included in the Canadian publication *CM: Canadian Review of Materials,* published by the Manitoba Library Association.

Comparing a family with a puzzle whose unique pieces create a whole, this simple picture book compares and contrasts a young girl's papa and daddy. Readers learn about the varied interests of Monicka's two dads and are reassured that although the men are different they both love the girl very much. The text is appropriate for young children while the watercolor illustrations are composed of puzzle pieces that add small visual details. The paperback format of the book is limiting for some libraries and the overall quality of the book marks it as a supplemental purchase. ADDITIONAL SELECTION.

Keywords: Gay Fathers, Children of Gay Parents, Family Relations, Self-Published Literature, Canada, Canadian Literature.

JOPLING, HEATHER. *The Not-So-Only Child.* Illus. by Lauren Page Russell. Cobourg, ON: Nickname Press, 2006. Unpaged. ISBN: 9780978073947. OCLC #: 77556872. Ages 5–9. FORMAT: Hardcover. AWARDS: None. REVIEWS: None. Positive review included in the Canadian publication *CM: Canadian Review of Materials,* published by the Manitoba Library Association.

Told from the point of view of an only child named Larissa, this book uses a scrapbook style with various hand-drawn illustrations of family members. Some of the illustrations are meant to appear like that of a child and others are supposed to be more realistic photos. Throughout the simple story, Larissa introduces readers to her vast extended family, which includes traditional grandparents, aunts and uncles, cousins, lesbian grandmothers, and half-siblings who are the results of Larissa's parents participating in surrogacy. As the family tree progressively branches out, it becomes hard for readers to keep track of the relations, and the half-siblings will take considerable explaining for younger children to understand. Nonetheless, the topic is handled in a way that makes it accessible for older children and particularly useful to rainbow families that want to broach the subject of surrogacy. ADDITIONAL SELECTION.

Keywords: Gay Fathers, Children of Gay Parents, Lesbian Mothers, Lesbian Grandmothers, Family Composition, Surrogacy, Grandparents, Aunts, Uncles, Self-Published Literature, Canada, Canadian Literature.

JOPLING, HEATHER. *Ryan's Mom Is Tall.* Illus. by Allyson Demoe. Cobourg, ON: Nickname Press, 2006. Unpaged. ISBN: 9780978073909. OCLC #: 77556877.

Ages 4–8. FORMAT: Paperback. AWARDS: Rainbow List 2008. REVIEWS: None. Positive review included in the Canadian publication *CM: Canadian Review of Materials,* published by the Manitoba Library Association.

Associating the concept of family with a puzzle whose unique pieces create a whole, this simple picture book compares and contrasts a young boy's mom and mummy. Readers learn about the varied interests of Ryan's two mothers and are reassured that although the women are quite dissimilar they both love the boy very much. The text is appropriate for young children and the watercolor, colored pencil, and ink illustrations are composed of puzzle pieces that add small details. The paperback format is limiting for some libraries and the overall quality of the book marks it as a supplemental purchase. ADDITIONAL SELECTION.

Keywords: Lesbian Mothers, Children of Gay Parents, Family Relations, Self-Published Literature, Canada, Canadian Literature.

JORDAN, MARYKATE. *Losing Uncle Tim.* Illus. by Judith Friedman. Niles, IL: Albert Whitman, 1989. Unpaged. ISBN: 9780807547564. OCLC #: 19129337. Ages 5–9. FORMAT: Hardcover. AWARDS: Cooperative Children's Book Center Choices 1989; Lambda Literary Award Finalist, LGBT Children's/YA Category, 1990. REVIEWS: BKLST, BCCB, KS, HB, LBR, PW, SLJ, VOYA.

Daniel loves spending time with his Uncle Tim. He's the most exciting adult that Daniel knows and together they play checkers, go sledding, and make quilt tents in the woods. Daniel spends many hours with Uncle Tim in his antiques store, but lately he has noticed that his uncle sometimes falls asleep while they are talking. Daniel later learns from his mother that Uncle Tim has AIDS and is getting progressively sicker. Daniel is both sad and angry about his uncle's situation but spends time with him up until Tim's death. Although the text is lengthy at times, the narrative captures a child's grief over the illness and eventual death of a relative. Friedman's muted illustrations match the tone of the book, adding to the overall quality. While Uncle Tim is never said to be gay in the text, adults and older readers will likely assume that he is as most young men with AIDS during this time period were gay. RECOMMENDED.

Keywords: Family Relations, Gay Uncles, Gay Relatives, Death, AIDS.

JUDES, MARIE-ODILE. *Max the Stubborn Little Wolf.* Illus. by Martine Bourre. Translation by Joan Robins. New York, NY: HarperCollins, 2001. Unpaged. ISBN: 9780060294175. OCLC #: 44502201. Ages 4–7. FORMAT: Hardcover. AWARDS: None. REVIEWS: BKLST, BCCB, KS, SLJ, PW. (Originally published in French as *Maxime Loupiot.* Paris, France: Flammarion, 1996. ISBN: 9782081628397.)

Max wants to be a florist when he grows up but his father has different ideas; he wants his son to be a hunter as male wolves are supposed to be. After a series of unsuccessful attempts to get Max to enjoy hunting and ditch the florist notion, father has had enough. He goes to a department store and buys three strong bottles of perfume and douses Max's room with them. He thinks Max will detest the smell and decide on a different career. But his plan backfires and Max announces he would rather make perfume than become a florist. Judes's text is a perfect read-aloud accompanied by Bourre's droll illustrations that are sure to entice children, especially gender-variant boys. RECOMMENDED.

Keywords: Wolves, Gender Nonconformity, Individuality, Family Relations, French Literature, France, Occupations, Sex Roles.

KEMP, ANNA. ***Dogs Don't Do Ballet.*** Illus. by Sara Ogilvie. London, UK: Simon & Schuster, 2010. Unpaged. ISBN: 9781416998396. OCLC #: 614193737. Ages 4–8. FORMAT: Hardcover. AWARDS: Best Children's Books of the Year, 2011, Bank Street College of Education; Rainbow List 2011. REVIEWS: None.

Poor Biff! He's not like other dogs. While other dogs pee on fire hydrants, scratch fleas, and drink out of toilets, this persistent little pug dreams of donning a tutu and practicing ballet. His owner, a young girl, sees his potential, but time and again she is told by her father and other adults that "Dogs Don't Do Ballet." Eventually Biff sneaks off to the Royal Ballet and takes over after the prima ballerina has an unfortunate accident. Soon everyone learns that some dogs actually *do* perform ballet. The humorous illustrations of Biff will remind readers of another spritely dog named Gloria — in *Officer Buckle and Gloria* (Rathmann). This whimsical title with its affirming message of individuality and gender nonconformity is a perfect addition to all library collections. HIGHLY RECOMMENDED.

Keywords: Dogs, Cross-Dressing, Gender Nonconformity, Individuality, Pets, Ballet, British Literature, Great Britain.

KENNEDY, JOSEPH. ***Lucy Goes to the Country.*** Illus. by John Canemaker. Los Angeles, CA: Alyson Wonderland, 1998. Unpaged. ISBN: 9781555834289. OCLC #: 37987174. Ages 4–8. FORMAT: Hardcover. AWARDS: Lambda Literary Award Finalist, LGBT Children's/YA Category, 1999. REVIEWS: PW, LBR.

Lucy is a city cat and a country cat. Although she lives in the city with a gay couple that she calls her "Big Guys," Lucy spends the weekends having adventures with them at their country home in Peckerwood. One particular weekend, the Big Guys are having a garden party with their gay and lesbian friends. One lesbian couple shows up with a yippy blue dog that Lucy dislikes instantly. As the cat is chasing the dog around the yard, they unleash a hive of bees on the guests and end up stuck in a tree. The day is saved when a handsome, gay fire-fighter rescues the pets. Kennedy's droll text may appeal more to adults than young children but the cheerful, cartoon style illustrations hit the mark and extend the narrative. Unfortunately, a few inaccuracies in the illustrations and the town's name of Peckerwood may limit the circulation of this title. ADDITIONAL SELECTION.

Keywords: Cats, Family Relations, Pets, Gay Men, Lesbian Mothers, Children of Gay Parents, Mixed Race Families.

KILODAVIS, CHERYL. ***My Princess Boy.*** Illus. by Suzanne DeSimone. New York, NY: Aladdin/Simon & Schuster, 2011. Unpaged. ISBN: 9781442429888. OCLC #: 681503510. Ages 3–8. FORMAT: Paperback. AWARDS: None. REVIEWS: None. (Originally self-published by KD Talent LLC, 2009. ISBN: 9780615395944.)

Based on the author's own experiences with her young son, this simple picture book describes all the things that a mother's Princess Boy likes to do, such as wearing sparkly jewelry and tiaras, waving magic wands, and dressing in girls' clothing. The watercolor illustrations depict faceless characters, which allows children to project their own faces and situations into the story. The story would be much stronger if it were told from the point of view of the Princess Boy herself and not that of her mother, but while this is not the most engaging read, it could assuage the fears of transgender children or enlighten their classmates if shared one-on-one and followed by discussion. With the lack of picture books on the topics of gender-variant and transgender children, libraries may want to consider this title. ADDITIONAL SELECTION.

Keywords: Family Relations, Cross-Dressing, Gender Nonconformity, Gender Identity, Individuality, Transgender, School Relations.

KING, THOMAS. *A Coyote Columbus Story.* Illus. by William Kent Monkman. Toronto, ON: Groundwood Books, 1992. Unpaged. ISBN: 9780888991553. OCLC #: 27677745. Ages 9–12. FORMAT: Hardcover. AWARDS: None. REVIEWS: HB, SLJ.

Coyote is the woman behind the world! She created rainbows, flowers, rivers, toenail polish, TV commercials, and baseball. Unfortunately, she can't find anyone to play ball with her — not the animals that prefer lounging around in the pond, not the Native Americans who prefer sky-diving and Caribbean cruises, and certainly not Christopher Columbus, who has material greed on his mind. While Coyote attempts to coax Columbus and his lackey drag queens into a game of ball, the explorers are rounding up the Native people to sell as slaves back in Spain. King's tongue-in-cheek text is sure to generate hours of discussion with older children and Monkman's garish but droll illustrations carry their own social messages. The fact that Columbus's entourage is portrayed as machine-gun-toting drag queens carries its own message that will need sorting out as well. ADDITIONAL SELECTION.

Keywords: Cross-Dressing, Gender Nonconformity, Canada, Canadian Literature, Christopher Columbus, Coyotes, Native Americans, Creation Stories, Explorers.

KRESSLEY, CARSON. *You're Different and That's Super.* Illus. by Jared Lee. New York, NY: Simon & Schuster, 2005. Unpaged. ISBN: 9781416900702. OCLC #: 62119840. Ages 4–8. FORMAT: Hardcover. AWARDS: None. REVIEWS: PW, SLJ.

When Trumpet is born he isn't like the other ponies in the farmer's pasture. At first he's just a different color and is shepherded in with rest of the ponies. However, after his first birthday, things begin to change as Trumpet sprouts a horn, which gets in the way when he plays with the other ponies. Eventually the others don't want anything to do with Trumpet because he's different. Then one day Trumpet's uniqueness comes in handy and he uses his horn to rescue everyone from a burning barn. Afterward, everyone appreciates Trumpet's fabulous self and he travels around the world enjoying stardom as a unicorn. Bordering on didacticism, this fable with simple line illustrations mirrors the lives of many gender-variant, queer, and gay children, and most likely is a nod toward Kressley's own childhood when he felt different as a gay boy. ADDITIONAL SELECTION.

Keywords: Individuality, Unicorns, Horses.

LaCroce, James. *Chimpy Discovers His Family.* Lexington, KY: CreateSpace, 2010. Unpaged. ISBN: 9781456309671. OCLC #: n.a. Ages 6–9. FORMAT: Paperback. AWARDS: None. REVIEWS: None.

With a penchant for flower picking and green banana facials, Chimpy is not like the other chimpanzees on his island. He has a few friends who accept him, but he feels out of place. One day he discovers a gay human couple and decides he wants them to be his parents. Unfortunately, the adoption agency does not allow gay adoption. When the couple heads to Italy to continue their honeymoon, Chimpy and one of his friends hatch a plan to find his would-be dads. The issue-driven plot tries to tackle too many topics and the slapstick humor seems misplaced. Similarly, the cartoon illustrations are uneven, exhibiting an amateurish quality. NOT RECOMMENDED.

Keywords: Adoption, Mixed Race Families, Gay Marriage, Anti-Gay Sentiment, Gay Fathers, Children of Gay Parents, Self-Published Literature, Chimpanzees, Individuality, Gender Nonconformity.

Leaf, Munro. *The Story of Ferdinand.* Illus. by Robert Lawson. New York, NY: Viking Press, 1936. Unpaged. ISBN: 9780670013234. OCLC #: 659768069. Ages 3–8. FORMAT: Hardcover. AWARDS: None. REVIEWS: BKLST, SLJ.

Ferdinand is not like the other bulls in the pasture. They like to butt heads, run, jump, and fight, but Ferdinand prefers to sit under the cork tree and smell flowers day in and day out. When he is taken to the arena in Madrid for a bullfight, no amount of teasing or poking can anger Ferdinand or distract him from his flowers. As relevant today as it was more than seventy-five years ago, this heartwarming picture book provides gender-variant children with an opportunity to see their experiences reflected as Ferdinand bucks stereotypes. HIGHLY RECOMMENDED.

Keywords: Gender Nonconformity, Individuality, Bulls.

Levine, Arthur A. *Monday Is One Day.* Illus. by Julian Hector. New York, NY: Scholastic, 2011. Unpaged. ISBN: 9780439789240. OCLC #: 317697827. Ages 2–5. FORMAT: Hardcover. AWARDS: None. REVIEWS: BKLST, KS, PW, SLJ.

Caregivers must work and are often away from the children they love. This heartwarming picture book puts a positive spin on the separation by encouraging young readers to count their way through special moments Monday to Friday that draw children and their caregivers closer together. Levine's gentle text provides opportunities for caregivers to bring the text to life while reading one-on-one with the child. Hector's timeless illustrations depict a variety of caregivers from single mothers and fathers to grandparents to a gay couple. The broad appeal of this book to all types of rainbow families makes it a staple for public and school library collections. HIGHLY RECOMMENDED.

Keywords: Family Composition, Gay Fathers, Children of Gay Parents, Family Relations, Single Parents, African Americans.

LEVY, ELIZABETH. *Nice Little Girls.* Illus. by Mordicai Gerstein. New York, NY: Delacorte Press, 1974. Unpaged. ISBN: 9780440062073. OCLC #: 737046. Ages 4–8. FORMAT: Hardcover. AWARDS: None. REVIEWS: BCCB, KS, PW, SLJ.

On Jackie's first day at a new school her teacher mistakenly calls her a boy because Jackie is wearing overalls instead of a dress. Initially embarrassed by the teacher's mistake, Jackie then decides she's much happier being a boy than a girl. Unfortunately, the teacher and Jackie's classmates don't agree and try to force her to subscribe to their narrow definition of gender roles. Eventually, Jackie meets another classmate, Susie, who accepts her gender nonconformity and helps the rest of the class and the teacher to break free from their gender molds. One of the first books to play freely with the gender identity of children, this picture book could be useful to gender-variant children today. Gerstein's expressive illustrations, although dated, add just the right amount of humor to counter the slightly didactic text. While numerous other children's books include tomboy characters, this title's approach is certain to spark discussions among contemporary children and educators. RECOMMENDED.

Keywords: Gender Nonconformity, Gender Identity, Individuality, Transgender, Sex Roles, Cross-Dressing, School Relations, Teasing.

LINDENBAUM, PIJA. *Mini Mia and Her Darling Uncle.* Translation by Elisabeth Kallick Dyssegaard. New York, NY: R&S Book (distributed by Farrar, Straus and Giroux), 2007. Unpaged. ISBN: 9789129667349. OCLC #: 154670921. Ages 4–8. FORMAT: Hardcover. AWARDS: Cooperative Children's Book Center Choices 2007; Outstanding International Booklist 2008, United States Board on Books for Young People; Rainbow List 2008. REVIEWS: BCCB, KS, PW, SLJ. (Originally published in Swedish as *Lill-Zlatan och morbror raring.* Stockholm, Sweden: Rabén & Sjögren Bokförlag, 2006. ISBN: 9789129664850.)

Mini Mia has four uncles — three of whom are b-o-r-i-n-g. But not Uncle Tommy! He travels all the time and brings Mia wonderful presents like dead snakes in a jar. Mia loves spending time with Uncle Tommy as he does all kinds of cool things with his young niece: coloring her hair a different color everyday, jumping with two feet down the street, and people-watching at the coffee shop. However, Mia's glorious days with her darling uncle are short-lived when he shows up with a Scottish boyfriend named Fergus. The girl does not like sharing her uncle with Fergus and finds innumerable ways to insult him. Eventually, though, Uncle Tommy is sick one afternoon and Fergus spends the day with Mia playing soccer, which is her favorite sport. Maybe Fergus isn't so bad after all! Lindenbaum's droll illustrations perfectly capture the seething emotions of a fickle jealous niece, and her simple text makes for a perfect read-aloud. HIGHLY RECOMMENDED.

Keywords: Gay Uncles, Gay Relatives, Family Relations, Swedish Literature, Sweden, Jealousy.

McAllister, Angela. *Yuck! That's Not a Monster.* Illus. by Alison Edgson. Intercourse, PA: Good Books, 2010. Unpaged. ISBN: 9781561486830. OCLC #: 438052806. Ages 3–8. FORMAT: Hardcover. AWARDS: None. REVIEWS: BKLST, KS, PW SLJ.

As Mr. and Mrs. Monster eagerly watch their three eggs hatch, they are delighted with the arrival of Frightful — their first little monster, who has ugly spikes and snarly fangs — and of Horrid — their second little monster, who has horny spikes and bristly warts. However, the couple is more than a little shocked when their final monster hatchling appears — Little Shock is pink, soft, cuddly, and sweet! At first instinct Mr. Monster wants to throw the pink hatchling into the trash; but when a thunder crash sends the bundle into Mrs. Monster's arms, she decides that "he may look different but inside he is a monster, just like us." The two "normal" scary monsters despise having Little Shock around, but one day when he kisses another monster and protects his ghastly, growling siblings, they decide he might not be so bad after all. A fresh twist on the typical individuality story, this beautifully and brightly illustrated picture book makes for a great read-aloud and is sure to appeal to gender-variant children who are their own "little shocks" to their parents. **HIGHLY RECOMMENDED.**

Keywords: Gender Identity, Gender Nonconformity, Individuality, Family Relations, Monsters.

MacDonald, Ross. *Another Perfect Day.* Brookfield, CT: Roaring Brook Press, 2002. Unpaged. ISBN: 9780761326595. OCLC #: 49002041. Ages 3–7. FORMAT: Hardcover. AWARDS: International Reading Association Children's and Young Adult's Book Award, 2003; Our Choice 2003, Canadian Children's Book Centre. REVIEWS: BKLST, KS, PW, SLJ.

As Jack wakes up, this Clark Kent look-alike prepares for his stupendous workday. His regimen includes wrestling crocodiles, destroying space aliens and robots, and catching a derailed train that is about to crash. After his day of work as an ice cream tester, Jack has started for home when his perfect day suddenly changes and he finds himself in a pink dress, clown shoes, and bonnet. Now in drag, Jack is mysteriously being chased by cops and an angry mob of people. When he wonders what happened to his perfect day, a boy tells him that he's still asleep. Jack tries to follow numerous suggestions from the boy and eventually wakes up in bed, yawning, stretching and in the form of the real Jack (the little boy from his dream). While children of all ages are sure to delight in MacDonald's skillful rendering of 1940s cartoon characters, particularly Superman, the book does perpetuate the weakness of cross-dressing men. With so many other negative social influences telling gender-variant children they're bad, libraries do not need another book that reinforces the ridicule of cross-dressing or being gender nonconforming. **NOT RECOMMENDED.**

Keywords: Cross-Dressing, Dreams, Superheroes.

MACK, BRUCE. *Jesse's Dream Skirt.* Illus. by Marian Buchanan. Chapel Hill, NC: Lollipop Power, 1979. 35p. ISBN: 9780914996200. OCLC #: 6048831. Ages 3–7. FORMAT: Paperback. AWARDS: None. REVIEWS: None.

Jesse likes dressing up in his mother's clothes, especially her dresses and skirts. Unfortunately, her dresses are too long and her heels make him trip. One night he dreams about having a skirt of his own that is full of bright beautiful colors and is just the right size. With the help of his mother, the next day he makes a skirt that is perfect. When he wears the skirt to preschool to show his classmates, many of the young boys and girls ridicule him. His savvy teacher comforts Jesse and then has the children discuss why some of them do not like his skirt. Through this dialog, readers understand that some girls like to wear pants and some boys like to wear skirts and that it is perfectly okay to be your true self. This sensitive, out-of-print picture book is one of the early attempts to address gender nonconformity among boys. RECOMMENDED.

Keywords: Family Relations, Cross-Dressing, Gender Nonconformity, Gender Identity, Teasing, Individuality, School Relations.

MAGORIAN, MICHELLE. *Jump!* Illus. by Jan Ormerod. London, UK: Walker Books, 1992. Unpaged. ISBN: 9780744520736. OCLC #: 24712654. Ages 4–8. FORMAT: Paperback. AWARDS: None. REVIEWS: None. Positive review included in the UK review publication *Books for Keeps.*

Each week Steven and his father watch his sister Theresa at her ballet class and he longs to join his sister and the other dancers as they twirl and jump. Unfortunately, when he expresses interest in learning ballet, Steven's mother tells him that ballet is not for real boys. Real boys are supposed to play basketball. Steven is confused as there are other boys in Theresa's class, and one day he can sit still no longer and joins them in practice. The teacher allows him to stay, and a bit later he surprises his mother by taking part in a performance in which the dancers are dressed as basketball players. Ormerod's gentle illustrations clearly convey the mood of the story and complement Magorian's somewhat didactic narrative about gender nonconformity. This would be a good book to pair with *Ballerino Nate* (Bradley), *The Only Boy in Ballet Class* (Gruska), and *Dogs Don't Do Ballet* (Kemp) for a storytime program on ballet for boys. RECOMMENDED.

Keywords: Dance, Gender Nonconformity, Gender Identity, Individuality, Ballet, British Literature, Great Britain, Sex Roles.

MARTIN JR., BILL, AND JOHN ARCHAMBAULT. *White Dynamite and Curly Kidd.* Illus. by Ted Rand. New York, NY: Holt, Rinehart and Winston, 1986. Unpaged. ISBN: 9780030083990. OCLC #: 12946110. Ages 4–8. FORMAT: Hardcover. AWARDS: None. REVIEWS: BKLST, KS, SLJ.

Lucky Kidd is helping his dad, Curly Kidd, prepare for the rodeo, and the two banter back and forth about how great Curly Kidd is at bull riding. Lucky decides he would like to be a bull rider just like his dad. Children will delight in the "cowboy" jargon and may want their own chance in the saddle. However, it is Rand who is the winner here as he keeps readers thinking that Lucky is a boy up until the very last page when Curly Kidd takes off Lucky's hat to reveal a girl! This book is exceptional for gender-variant and transgender children, particularly those interested in cowboys, bull riding, or the rodeo. RECOMMENDED.

Keywords: Family Relations, Cross-Dressing, Gender Nonconformity, Gender Identity, Individuality, Tomboys, Rodeos, Cowboys.

MARTINEZ, JASON. *My Mommy Is a Boy.* Illus. by Karen Winchester. Raleigh, NC: Lulu.com, 2008. Unpaged. ISBN: n.a. OCLC #: n.a. Ages 4–8. FORMAT: Paperback. AWARDS: None. REVIEWS: None.

Written for the author's daughter to explain his transition from female to male, this straightforward book uses a young girl's perspective to describe how her mommy decided to become a "boy." The text is printed in large font and the vocabulary is age-appropriate for young children. Brightly colored, amateurish illustrations detract from the overall quality of the book with little consistency of character depictions between spreads. While the paperback format of the book may limit its addition to library collections, the dearth of books on this topic warrants its serious consideration. Children with transgender parents could be encouraged to draw their own pictures! RECOMMENDED.

Keywords: Gender Nonconformity, Gender Identity, Individuality, Transgender, Children of Transsexuals, Children of Gay Parents, Lesbian Mothers, Transsexual Parents, Sex Change, Self-Published Literature.

MARTINEZ JOVER, CARMEN. *The Baby Kangaroo Treasure Hunt: A Gay Parenting Story.* Illus. by Rosemary Martinez. Mexico City, Mexico: Carmen Martinez Jover Books, 2009. Unpaged. ISBN: 9786070008468467. OCLC #: n.a. Ages 4–8. FORMAT: Paperback. AWARDS: None. REVIEWS: None.

Jack and Sam are a gay kangaroo couple who would like to have a child of their own. They visit Wise William, who gives them a scroll from his treasure chest entitled "The Baby Kangaroo Treasure Hunt." By following the three steps on the treasure hunt — find a sperm, find an egg, and find a womb — the duo are well on their way to surrogacy and their very own daughter. Martinez's bright cartoon illustrations add a cheerful air to the slightly stilted text, extending the appeal of the book to younger children. While the book does suffer from the flaws common in self-published literature, the topic is covered in a more age-appropriate fashion than other rainbow family books about surrogacy. ADDITIONAL SELECTION.

Keywords: Children of Gay Parents, Gay Fathers, Mexican Literature, Mexico, Self-Published Literature, Surrogacy.

MENDIETA, MARÍA JOSÉ. *Aitor tiene dos mamás.* Illus. by Mabel Piérola. Barcelona, Spain: Bellaterra Edicions, 2006. 36p. ISBN: 9788472903098. OCLC #: 77072549. Ages 5–9. FORMAT: Hardcover. AWARDS: None. REVIEWS: None. (Originally published in Euskara as *Aitorrek bi ama ditu.* Donostia [Basque]: Erein, 2004.)

Aitor is a little boy who has two mothers. When a new boy moves to town and learns about Aitor's family composition he embarrasses Aitor and makes him ashamed of having two mothers. Later at school, a classmate calls Aitor "queer," which makes him feel even worse. Aitor's teacher decides it's time for diversity education and takes the class on a field trip to the capital to see an art exhibit about diversity. One of the pieces features a two-mom family like Aitor's, which makes him feel better. When he explains all of this to his mothers, they decide that Aitor should visit the capital more often and that he should meet the children of their lesbian friends. Eventually, the family decides to move to the capital where their family will be accepted without contention. This would be a great book to pair with *Paula tiene dos mamas* (Newman), which is also illustrated by Piérola and is about a child who has two mothers. RECOMMENDED.

Keywords: Spanish Literature, Spain, Children of Gay Parents, Lesbian Mothers, Homophobia, School Relations, Teasing, Diversity Education.

MERCHANT, ED. *Dad David, Baba Chris, and Me.* Illus. by Rachel Fuller. London, UK: British Association for Adoption and Fostering, 2010. 19p. ISBN: 9781905664894. OCLC #: 551430782. Ages 6–9. FORMAT: Paperback. AWARDS: None. REVIEWS: None. Positive review included in the UK review publication *Books for Keeps.*

Eight-year-old Ben used to live with his mom and dad, but they could not care for him properly so he was sent into foster care. He was eventually adopted by two new dads, a biracial couple (one Caucasian and one from Africa) who love him very much. Throughout the book, Ben tries to convince young readers he is just like everyone else. When bullies at school call him gay for having gay dads, the boy begins to wonder if he isn't so ordinary after all. With the encouragement of his schoolteacher, Ben learns that he is special because he has two dads that love him. Although there are very few picture books with biracial rainbow families and this book fills that void, the didactic, stilted text tries too hard to convince the reader that Ben and his family are normal. NOT RECOMMENDED.

Keywords: Adoption, Mixed Race Families, Family Composition, Teasing, Gay Fathers, Children of Gay Parents, Family Relations, Foster Parents, School Relations, British Literature, Great Britain.

MEYERS, SUSAN. *Everywhere Babies.* Illus. by Marla Frazee. New York, NY: Harcourt, 2001. Unpaged. ISBN: 9780152022266. OCLC #: 41070603. Ages 1–5. FORMAT: Hardcover. AWARDS: ABC Children's Booksellers Choices Award, 2002; Best Children's Books of the Year, 2002, Bank Street College of Education. REVIEWS: BKLST, BCCB, HB, KS, SLJ, PW.

Babies of all shapes, ethnicities, races, and sizes fill the pages of this tender, rhyming picture book. Muted, detailed illustrations depict a variety of babies, family compositions, and lifestyles. Almost every family will find at least one of the vastly diverse families that mirrors their own situation. Appropriate for all families as well as for young children, this delightful book is an easy way to include rainbow family diversity within library collections. Multiple formats of the book are available including an oversized board book edition. RECOMMENDED.

Keywords: Gay Fathers, Lesbian Mothers, Children of Gay Parents, Family Composition, Family Relations, Asian Americans, African Americans, Latinos, Native Americans, Single Parents, Mixed Race Families, Extended Families, Grandparent Caregivers.

MILGRIM, DAVID. *Time to Get Up, Time to Go.* New York, NY: Clarion, 2006. 32p. ISBN: 9780618519989. OCLC #: 59756126. Ages 1–5. FORMAT: Hardcover. AWARDS: Best Children's Books of the Year, 2007, Bank Street College of Education; Cooperative Children's Book Center Choices 2007. REVIEWS: HB, KS, PW, SLJ.

A young boy has a very busy day ahead with a list of things he must do with his doll. From feeding his baby breakfast to cuddling with a book to cooking meals and cleaning house, the boy enjoys a fun-filled day with his doll, his parents, and several of his friends. The cheerful, cartoon illustrations appropriately complement the gentle rhyming text and will appeal to young children. Written in a similar style to *William's Doll* (Zolotow), the book's strength is that the boy's nurturing demeanor and participation in traditional "female" activities is a non-issue. This is a refreshing addition to library collections. RECOMMENDED.

Keywords: Gender Identity, Gender Nonconformity, Sex Roles, Individuality, Dolls.

MILLER, JENIFER INGERMAN. *The Turklebees of Turkledorf.* Lexington, KY: CreateSpace, 2008. 44p. ISBN: 9781440466328. OCLC #: n.a. Ages 7–11. FORMAT: Paperback. AWARDS: None. REVIEWS: None.

Written in the style of Dr. Seuss classics such as *The Sneetches* and *The Lorax*, Miller's nonsensical rhyme for contemporary times tackles such topics as prejudice, racism, and homophobia. Initially the Turklebees of Turkledorf declare that only Turklebees of the same color can go to the same schools; then school integration is approved. Soon the Turklebees are in an uproar because Turklebees of different colors want to marry. After interracial marriages are approved, Turklebees try to ban gay marriages until one lone voice and then a chorus proclaim, "We will share the same rights." While many authors try to imitate Seuss's style and fail, Miller succeeds in both illustration and text and creates a book that will lead to hours of discussion, particularly for older children. The only drawback for libraries is its paperback format. HIGHLY RECOMMENDED.

Keywords: Family Composition, Family Relations, Gay Marriage, Self-Published Literature, Homophobia, Gay Rights, Equality.

MORENO VELO, LUCÍA. *El amor de todos los colores/The Many-Colored Love.* Illus. by Javier Termenón Delgado. Translation by Gwyneth Box. Madrid, Spain: Topka, 2007. Unpaged. ISBN: 9788493523954. OCLC #: 137315986. Ages 2–6. FORMAT: Hardcover. AWARDS: None. REVIEWS: None.

Imbued with magical realism, this delightfully accessible story follows young Maite as she tracks the many-colored (rainbow) love that overflows from their apartment into the neighborhood. Maite explains that the many-colored love was conceived when Mama met Mami and they had her. Now that Mama is pregnant again, the girl wants to be the first to enjoy all the many-colored love that accompanies a new baby. Perfect for parents who are expecting new additions to their family, this picture book sensitively portrays the bountiful love in a rainbow family. HIGHLY RECOMMENDED.

Keywords: Lesbian Mothers, Children of Gay Parents, Family Relations, Bilingual Literature — English and Spanish, Spanish Literature, Spain, Pregnancy, Love, New Siblings.

MORENO VELO, LUCÍA. *¡Manu, no!/No, Manu.* Illus. by Javier Termenón Delgado. Translation by Gwyneth Box. Madrid, Spain: Topka, 2006. Unpaged. ISBN: 9788493523909. OCLC #: 216733368. Ages Birth–3. FORMAT: Board Book. AWARDS: None. REVIEWS: None.

In the second title in the Manu board book series, the young preschooler wants another cookie but his mothers tell him no. He makes multiple attempts to get the cookie on his own and is put in time-out for misbehaving. But, after time-out ends, his two mothers reassure him that they still love him. Like the other books in this series, the simple, age-appropriate text in Spanish and English, along with sparse illustrations on a white background, makes this title perfect for sharing with young children. This is a solid addition to board book collections. RECOMMENDED.

Keywords: Lesbian Mothers, Children of Gay Parents, Family Relations, Bilingual Literature — English and Spanish, Spanish Literature, Spain, Board Books.

MORENO VELO, LUCÍA. *Manu pone la mesa/Manu Sets the Table.* Illus. by Javier Termenón Delgado. Translation by Gwyneth Box. Madrid, Spain: Topka, 2006. Unpaged. ISBN: 9788493523923. OCLC #: 213514228. Ages Birth–3. FORMAT: Board Book. AWARDS: None. REVIEWS: None.

The third title in the Manu board book series follows our very young protagonist as he helps his two mommies prepare the table for dinner. The simplistic, bilingual (Spanish/English) text depicts a preschool-aged boy, Manu, who tries to help with dinner preparations but accidentally drops the basket of bread, which lands him in the loving arms of his parents. Readers understand that Manu has two mommies but the text is not overly didactic and would work well as a one-on-one read-aloud for very young children. The bright, cartoon-style characters pop against the white background of the pages, an appropriate stylistic feature for young children. Considering the lack of board books with LGBTQ families, this is a good addition to a library's collection. The presence of Spanish text extends the audience. RECOMMENDED.

Keywords: Lesbian Mothers, Children of Gay Parents, Family Relations, Bilingual Literature — English and Spanish, Spanish Literature, Spain, Board Books.

MORENO VELO, LUCÍA. *Manu se va a la cama/Manu's Bedtime.* Illus. by Javier Termenón Delgado. Translation by Gwyneth Box. Madrid, Spain: Topka, 2006.

Unpaged. ISBN: 9788493523916. OCLC #: 216782228. Ages Birth–3. FORMAT: Board Book. AWARDS: None. REVIEWS: None.

This first title in the Manu board book series depicts a very young child as he readies for bed. The simplistic, bilingual (Spanish/English) text shows preschooler Manu fighting off sleep until he is finally coaxed to bed by sharing a bottle of milk with his two mothers. Readers understand that Manu has two mommies but the text is not overly didactic and would work well as a bedtime story for very young children. The bright, cartoon-style illustrations of the characters pop against the white background of the page and are appropriate for babies. Considering the lack of board books with LGBTQ families, this is a sound addition to library collections, particularly those serving very young children. The presence of Spanish text is an added bonus and extends the audience of the book. RECOMMENDED.

Keywords: Lesbian Mothers, Children of Gay Parents, Family Relations, Bilingual Literature — English and Spanish, Spanish Literature, Spain, Board Books.

MUNSCH, ROBERT. *The Paper Bag Princess.* Illus. by Michael Martchenko. Toronto, ON: Annick Press, 1980. Unpaged. ISBN: 9780920236826. OCLC #: 11926922. Ages 4–8. FORMAT: Hardcover. AWARDS: Amelia Bloomer List 2007; Our Choice 2005, Canadian Children's Book Centre. REVIEWS: KS, SLJ. Positive review included in the Canadian publication *CM: Canadian Review of Materials,* published by the Manitoba Library Association.

A beautiful princess named Elizabeth is supposed to marry Prince Ronald one day. Unfortunately, a horrible dragon kidnaps Prince Ronald and destroys Elizabeth's castle and everything she owns. The only thing she has to wear is a paper bag, which she quickly dons before setting off to outsmart the dragon. When she frees Ronald, he tells Elizabeth that she is dirty and smells bad and that she should come back and rescue him when she looks like a real princess. Nonplussed, Elizabeth tells Ronald he has pretty clothes and hair but he isn't the one for her. She then skips off happily into the sunset. For more than twenty years, Princess Elizabeth has been empowering girls to think for themselves and inspiring all children to embrace their individuality. Perfect for children in both school and public libraries. HIGHLY RECOMMENDED.

Keywords: Princesses, Dragons, Gender Identity, Gender Nonconformity, Gender Roles, Sex Roles, Canadian Literature, Canada, Individuality.

NEWMAN, LESLÉA. *Belinda's Bouquet.* Illus. by Michael Willhoite. Boston, MA: Alyson Wonderland, 1991. Unpaged. ISBN: 9781555831547. OCLC #: 26224143. Ages 4–8. FORMAT: Paperback. AWARDS: None. REVIEWS: None.

Daniel and his friend Belinda like to do everything together — play dress-up, swim, ride bikes, and attend summer camp. On their first day of this year's camp, the bus driver comments on how much weight Belinda has gained since the previous summer. The girl feels self-conscious and decides to stop eating. Daniel's two mothers convince Belinda that she is unique and her own special person by comparing her with flowers, particularly short fat marigolds. The book ends with Belinda walking away with a "fat yellow bouquet," which seems to imply that Belinda is fat too — not exactly a positive comparison. The tone of the story is didactic and the watercolor illustrations do little to extend the text. NOT RECOMMENDED.

Keywords: Lesbian Mothers, Children of Gay Parents, Family Relations, Friendship, Individuality, Weight Control, Self-Perception.

NEWMAN, LESLÉA. *The Boy Who Cried Fabulous.* Illus. by Peter Ferguson. Berkeley, CA: Tricycle Press, 2004. Unpaged. ISBN: 9781582461014. OCLC #: 53006684. Ages 4–8. FORMAT: Hardcover. AWARDS: None. REVIEWS: LBR, LMC, PW, SLJ.

Roger is a splendid boy who has a slight attention problem — he thinks everything is fabulous and he would much rather look at all the wonderful things in the world than make it to school on time or arrive home before dark. His parents worry about his tardy and hyperactive behavior and ban him from using the word "fabulous." This works fine for Roger who thinks his neighborhood is filled with "marvelous" things. As he spends a day out on the town with his parents, he teaches them how to enjoy the simply marvelous (and fabulous) things in life. Although the text never states that Roger is gay, his overuse of the word fabulous and his excitement over things such as fine clothes and purses could lead readers to believe that Roger will one day embrace his fabulously, marvelously gay self. Ferguson's jewel-tone illustrations capture the exuberance of this story set in a time long past, and the rhyming text would work well as a read-aloud. ADDITIONAL SELECTION.

Keywords: Gender Nonconformity, Individuality.

NEWMAN, LESLÉA. *Daddy, Papa, and Me.* Illus. by Carol Thompson. Berkeley, CA: Tricycle Press, 2009. Unpaged. ISBN: 9781582462622. OCLC #: 244065722. Ages Birth–3. FORMAT: Board Book. AWARDS: Stonewall Book Awards 2010, Children's and Young Adult Honor Book; Rainbow List 2010; American Library Association Notable Children's Book 2010; Cooperative Children's Book Center Choices 2010. REVIEWS: HB, KS, PW, SLJ.

Lively, rhythmic verse describes a series of activities undertaken by a young child and his two fathers. The simple text, appropriate for read-alouds, is perfectly complemented by cheerful, mixed-media illustrations that depict the child helping around the house, playing musical instruments, and simply enjoying time with his dads. Newman clearly conveys the abundance of love in the family without being didactic or solely focusing on the same-sex parent aspect. The story is purely about a young child and his adventures with his family. One of the few board books depicting LGBTQ families, this upbeat title is a strong choice for public libraries. HIGHLY RECOMMENDED.

Keywords: Gay Fathers, Children of Gay Parents, Family Relations, Board Books.

NEWMAN, LESLÉA. *Donovan's Big Day.* Illus. by Mike Dutton. Berkeley, CA: Tricycle Press, 2011. Unpaged. ISBN: 9781582463322. OCLC #: 471237509. Ages 4–8. FORMAT: Hardcover. AWARDS: Rainbow List 2012. REVIEWS: BKLST, KS, PW, SLJ.

Today is a big day for Donovan! He has many important jobs to do such as getting up early without a fuss, dressing up in a suit, staying clean, meeting lots of relatives and grown-ups who insist on giving him kisses, and showing up on time to serve as the ring bearer for his two mothers' wedding. Warmly told in a fashion that children will easily understand and relate to, Newman's text carefully focuses on all the things Donovan needs to do for his big day. Although his mothers are getting married, little Donovan is the key feature as he prepares for his important role and it is only at the very end of the story that the two-mom aspect is revealed. The normalization of the wedding is the strength of this timely book and the colorful gouache illustrations subtly hint at the story's ending. Whereas many books about gay marriages and same-sex parents are didactic, this charming book is simply a story about a boy preparing for an important task. HIGHLY RECOMMENDED.

Keywords: Family Relations, Gay Marriage, Lesbian Mothers, Children of Gay Parents, Weddings.

NEWMAN, LESLÉA. *Felicia's Favorite Story.* Illus. by Adriana Romo. Ridley Park, PA: Two Lives Publishing, 2002. 24p. ISBN: 9780967446851. OCLC #: 51273798. Ages 3–8. FORMAT: Paperback. AWARDS: Lambda Literary Award Finalist, LGBT Children's/YA Category, 2003. REVIEWS: BL, PW, SLJ.

Before Felicia will go to sleep she must hear her favorite story about how her two mothers boarded a plane for Guatemala and adopted her. As her Mama Linda is telling the story, Felicia interrupts with comments and additions. At the close of the gentle story, readers learn that the little girl's name means "happy" in Spanish and "happy" describes her mothers' lives now that they have Felicia to love. The narrative is accessible to young children and captures their need to hear stories about how they joined a family, but the watercolor illustrations are uneven in quality with characters that often appear unnatural and stiff. However, this would be a good book for parents to read aloud to their children to encourage sharing of their own family histories. RECOMMENDED.

Keywords: Adoption, Mixed Race Families, Family Relations, Lesbian Mothers, Children of Gay Parents, Latinos, Guatemalans, Puerto Ricans, Storytelling, International Adoption.

NEWMAN, LESLÉA. *A Fire Engine for Ruthie.* Illus. by Cyd Moore. New York, NY: Clarion Books, 2004. 32p. ISBN: 9780618159895. OCLC #: 54046788. Ages 3–8. FORMAT: Hardcover. AWARDS: Amelia Bloomer List 2006. REVIEWS: BKLST, BCCB, KS, PW, SLJ.

Although she loves visiting her Nana, Ruthie does not always enjoy the activities that her grandmother chooses — playing with dolls, performing fashion shows, and hosting tea parties. The young girl would rather be playing with the trains, fire engines, and cars owned by Brian, the boy who lives in her Nana's neighborhood. Moore's vibrant watercolor illustrations and Newman's upbeat text collectively demonstrate that it is perfectly okay for little girls to like toys typically associated with boys. Similar in scope to *William's Doll* (Zolotow), this gentle read is a solid choice for school and public libraries. RECOMMENDED.

Keywords: Tomboys, Gender Identity, Gender Nonconformity, Sex Roles, Individuality.

NEWMAN, LESLÉA. *Gloria Goes to Gay Pride.* Illus. by Russell Crocker. Boston, MA: Alyson Wonderland, 1991. 35p. ISBN: 9781555831851. OCLC #: 23991416. Ages 5–8. FORMAT: Paperback. AWARDS: Lambda Literary Award Finalist, LGBT Children's/YA Category, 1992. REVIEWS: None.

A young girl named Gloria describes the various holidays that she celebrates with her mothers and then details how the family is preparing for the Gay Pride Parade. Readers are introduced to rainbow families, dancing, music, balloons, and pride merchandise (t-shirts, caps, etc.), as well as a crowd of anti-gay protesters. Newman's straightforward text clearly communicates the special day for Gloria and her family; however, Crocker's illustrations are lackluster, uneven, and often distracting. The illustrations depict Gloria as a toddler, preschooler, and older child — despite the fact that she never ages in the narrative. This book may be helpful to families who want to describe Gay Pride Parades to their children but children may want to create their own colorful illustrations to remember Gay Pride. ADDITIONAL SELECTION.

Keywords: Gay Pride, Children of Gay Parents, Gay Fathers, Lesbian Mothers, Anti-Gay Sentiment, Holidays, Jews.

NEWMAN, LESLÉA. *Heather Has Two Mommies.* Illus. by Diana Souza. New York, NY: Alyson Books, 2009. 3rd rev. ed., 20th anniversary ed. Unpaged. ISBN: 9781593501365. OCLC #: 318876910. Ages 3–8. FORMAT: Paperback. AWARDS: Lambda Literary Award Finalist, LGBT Children's/YA Category, 1990. REVIEWS: BL, HB, PW. Originally self-published in 1989 by In Other Words Publishing. The Spanish version is *Paula tiene dos mamas.* Illus. by Mabel Piérola. Barcelona, Spain: Bellaterra Ediciones, 2003. ISBN: 9788472902206. Incidentally the illustrations in this version are more attractive and kid-friendly than the English version.

Heather, a young preschool girl with two mothers, visits a playgroup where she meets other children with various family compositions. The children create illustrations of their families and then describe how much they are loved. In this updated version of the classic and highly controversial picture book, readers are treated to full-color illustrations as well as a narrative that is more age–appropriate. Discussion of artificial insemination and use of words such as "womb" and "vagina" were removed in the 10th Anniversary Edition. Libraries will want to update their original editions with this kid-friendly version. RECOMMENDED.

Keywords: Lesbian Mothers, Children of Gay Parents, Gay Fathers, Family Relations, School Relations, Family Composition, Single Parents, Divorced Parents.

NEWMAN, LESLÉA. *Mommy, Mama, and Me.* Illus. by Carol Thompson. Berkeley, CA: Tricycle Press, 2009. Unpaged. ISBN: 9781582462639. OCLC #: 244065723. Ages Birth–3. FORMAT: Board Book. AWARDS: Stonewall Book Awards 2010, Children's and Young Adult Honor Book; Rainbow List 2010; American

Library Association Notable Children's Book 2010; Cooperative Children's Book Center Choices 2010. REVIEWS: HB, PW, SLJ.

Bouncy, rhythmic text describes the various activities of a young child and her two mothers. The simple text is appropriate for reading aloud and is perfectly complemented by cheerful, mixed-media illustrations that depict the child getting her juice, taking a nap, reading books, and playing with her mothers. Newman clearly conveys the abundance of love in the family without being didactic or focusing solely on the two-mommy aspect. The story is simply about a young child and her adventures with her family. One of the few board books depicting LGBTQ families, this upbeat title is a strong choice for public libraries. HIGHLY RECOMMENDED.

Keywords: Lesbian Mothers, Children of Gay Parents, Family Relations, Board Books.

NEWMAN, LESLÉA. *Saturday Is Pattyday.* Illus. by Annette Hegel. Norwich, VT: New Victoria Publishers, 1993. Unpaged. ISBN: 9780934678520. OCLC #: 28149954. Ages 4–8. FORMAT: Hardcover. AWARDS: Lambda Literary Award Finalist, LGBT Children's/YA Category, 1994. REVIEWS: BKLST, BCCB.

Preschooler Frankie is very sad when his two mothers decide to get a divorce. He's not quite sure what that means except that his mothers Allie and Patty used to fight all the time and Patty moved out because of this. He now lives with his mother Allie but she tells him that he can visit Patty every Saturday; Frankie decides he will call these days Pattydays. On his first Pattyday, Frankie and Patty go to the park for a picnic but the boy is moody and doesn't want his apple. He gets into an argument with Patty and tells her that he doesn't want to get a divorce because they are fighting. Patty reassures him that only grownups can get a divorce and that he will always have two mothers who love him very much. Newman's text captures the confusion and anxiety that children feel during a divorce and is not overly didactic. Unfortunately, at times the text is lost in the illustrations and readers will struggle to decode the words. Hegel's watercolor illustrations, which alternate between full-color and black-and-white spreads, have a childlike quality that younger readers will appreciate. This picture book tackles a topic seldom covered in LGBTQ children's literature and is recommended for public libraries. RECOMMENDED.

Keywords: Lesbian Mothers, Children of Gay Parents, Family Relations, Divorce, Divorced Parents.

NEWMAN, LESLÉA. *Too Far Away to Touch.* Illus. by Catherine Stock. New York, NY: Clarion, 1995. 32p. ISBN: 9780395689684. OCLC #: 28798846. Ages 4–8. FORMAT: Hardcover. AWARDS: None. REVIEWS: BKLST, BCCB, HB, LBR, PW, SLJ.

Like several other books published in the 1990s, this book depicts a child whose favorite uncle is dying from AIDS. Unlike the other stories, however, Newman doesn't spend time explaining about the disease and the fact that it's not contagious. Rather, she develops a loving relationship between Zoe and Uncle Leonard as they spend special moments together at the planetarium and later on the beach with

Uncle Leonard's partner. Uncle Leonard does not die in the book, but his death is imminent and Zoe wants to talk about it. He tells her that after he dies, he'll be like the stars they saw at the beach and planetarium "too far away to touch, but close enough to see." This comforts the little girl as she sleeps every night under the stars pasted on her ceiling and thinks about Uncle Leonard. Stock's characteristic soft, expressive illustrations are the perfect complement to this touching tale, which is recommended for both public and school libraries. RECOMMENDED.

   Keywords: Family Relations, Gay Uncles, Gay Relatives, Death, AIDS.

NITE, KENDAL. *The Prince and Him: A Rainbow Bedtime Story.* Illus. by Y. Brassel. Raleigh, NC: Lulu.com, 2007. 12p. ISBN: 9781430325024. OCLC #: 492201493. Ages 6–8. FORMAT: Paperback. AWARDS: None. REVIEWS: None.

In this rainbow fairy tale, a king and queen tell their son, Prince Edmond, that it is time for him to marry. The prince kisses all the girls in the kingdom and in a nearby village but none of them are "the one" for Edmond. Eventually, he does find his true love — a naked man swimming in a nearby river. Upon seeing the naked man, the prince runs to him, gives him a kiss, and pronounces the man "the one." Edmond and his true love go back to the palace where they are married, becoming the first king and king of the land of Once Upon a Time. The writing and illustrations are of very poor quality, with grammatical errors in the text and images that are not appropriate for the target audience. For a better-quality rainbow fairy tale, libraries should consider *King and King* (de Haan and Nijland). NOT RECOMMENDED.

   Keywords: Gay Marriage, Fairy Tales, Self-Published Literature, Weddings, Kings.

NONES, ERIC JON. *Caleb's Friend.* New York, NY: Farrar, Straus & Giroux, 1993. Unpaged. ISBN: 9780374310172. OCLC #: 27728437. Ages 6–10. FORMAT: Hardcover. AWARDS: None. REVIEWS: KS, PW, SLJ.

In this bittersweet fairy tale Caleb is an orphaned boy who works on a fishing boat. The only thing besides the fishing trade that he has to remember his father by is the harmonica that his father taught him to play. One night Caleb accidentally drops the harmonica overboard but a merboy — a merman — saves it! To thank the merboy, Caleb brings him a rose the next day. Caleb is delighted with his new friend, who dances and shimmers in the water but doesn't want anyone else to find out about him. Unfortunately, the merboy is caught in a net of fish one day and sold to a local merchant as a freak show attraction. Caleb saves him and returns him to the water. The merboy later saves Caleb's life by directing his fishing ship away from rocks during a storm. A while afterward, Caleb is delighted — his heart jumps — when his merboy comes to visit him again in his fishing village. He has no rose to give the merboy to show him how much he loves and cares for him, so instead he gives him his father's harmonica. The merboy then disappears. And each year for the rest of Caleb's life, he returns to the fishing village and throws armfuls of roses out to sea for his beloved merboy. Nones's touching story and striking, detailed paintings create a surreal setting where almost anything magical can happen. Gay boys will certainly find the story endearing and may even seek their own merboys in the sea. RECOMMENDED.

Keywords: Fairy Tales, Friendship, Mermaids, Mermen, Gender Nonconformity, Homosexuality, Fishermen.

OELSCHLAGER, VANITA. *A Tale of Two Daddies.* Illus. by Kristin Blackwood and Mike Blanc. Akron, OH: VanitaBooks, 2010. Unpaged. ISBN: 9780981971452. OCLC #: 464593886. Ages 3–8. FORMAT: Hardcover. AWARDS: Cooperative Children's Book Center Choices 2011. REVIEWS: BKLST.

As a young girl and her friend are playing, he asks her which of her two daddies is responsible for various care-giving activities such as building tree houses, fixing boo-boos, cooking breakfast, and helping with homework. The straightforward, rhyming text explains Poppa's and Daddy's roles in the little girl's life and reinforces that both dads are around when she is sad and in need of love. Bold, computer-generated illustrations extend the text and give a retro feel that will attract young readers. Pair this book with *Monicka's Papa Is Tall* (Jopling and Demoe) to show children how daddies are different and have unique familial responsibilities. This is a particularly noteworthy self-published title. RECOMMENDED.

Keywords: Gay Fathers, Children of Gay Parents, Family Relations, Self-Published Literature.

OELSCHLAGER, VANITA. *A Tale of Two Mommies.* Illus. by Mike Blanc. Akron, OH: VanitaBooks, 2011. Unpaged. ISBN: 9780982636664. OCLC #: 711045801. Ages 3–8. FORMAT: Hardcover. AWARDS: None. REVIEWS: None.

In this companion to *A Tale of Two Daddies*, a young boy is playing with two friends at the beach when they begin to question him about which of his two mommies is responsible for various activities such as helping him find his missing cat, setting up his campsite, supplying him with fishing worms, coaching his T-ball team, and hugging away his bad dreams. The straightforward, rhyming text explains Mommy's and Momma's roles in the boy's life and reinforces that both mommies are around when he needs love and encouragement. Bold, computer-generated illustrations extend the text and give a retro feel that will attract readers. Pair this book with *Ryan's Mom Is Tall* (Jopling and Demoe) to show children how mothers are different and have unique familial responsibilities. RECOMMENDED.

Keywords: Mixed Race Families, Lesbian Mothers, Children of Gay Parents, Family Relations, Self-Published Literature, African Americans, Asian Americans.

OKIMOTO, JEAN DAVIES, AND ELAINE M. AOKI. *The White Swan Express: A Story About Adoption.* Illus. by Meilo So. New York, NY: Clarion, 2002. 32p. ISBN: 9780618164530. OCLC #: 49664276. Ages 6–10. FORMAT: Hardcover. AWARDS: Best Children's Books of the Year, 2003, Bank Street College of Education; Cooperative Children's Book Center Choices 2003; Charlotte Zolotow Award, 2003; Notable Social Studies Trade Books for Young People 2003. REVIEWS: BKLST, BCCB, KS, PW, SLJ, WOW.

Based on the international adoption experience of one of the authors, this endearing picture book follows four families (three from the United States and one from Canada) as they travel to China to adopt baby girls from an orphanage. One of the four couples consists of two women but their sexuality is not an issue. Throughout the informative text and cheerful, detailed illustrations readers can observe how each of the families is unique and prepares in its own way for the new addition to the family. A helpful afterword situates the story and provides additional information. This is a perfect story for both school and public library collections, particularly those that serve families who have participated in international adoptions. RECOMMENDED.

Keywords: Adoption, Mixed Race Families, Lesbian Mothers, Children of Gay Parents, International Adoption, Chinese Americans, Chinese Canadians, Single Parents.

PACKARD, ROBBI ANNE. *Two Daddies . . . and Me.* Illus. by Lori Ann McElroy. Bloomington, IN: AuthorHouse, 2009. Unpaged. ISBN: 9781438955582. OCLC #: 639873023. Ages 3–7. FORMAT: Paperback. AWARDS: None. REVIEWS: None.

In this didactic, rhyming picture book, a young girl explains some of the things she and her two gay fathers can do together. With forced rhymes and lackluster cartoon illustrations, the book may leave more questions than answers as some concepts are above the comprehension of the target audience. For instance, the text describes answered prayers and the illustrations depict the girl as a woman with a baby of her own — both concepts that young children will find difficult to understand. In addition, the back of the book provides a name for the girl that is never mentioned in the text. NOT RECOMMENDED.

Keywords: Gay Fathers, Children of Gay Parents, Family Relations, Self-Published Literature.

PASTOR, RAQUEL ESTECHA. *Isla Mágica.* Illus. by Ángel Domínguez. Bilbao, Spain: Editorial A Fortiori, 2005. Unpaged. ISBN: 9788493462727. OCLC #: 65461019. Ages 4–8. FORMAT: Hardcover. AWARDS: None. REVIEWS: None.

In this magical tale, two mothers tell their daughter a story about how they came to be a family. Mami and Mamá Ruth wanted a child but were unable to have one so they adopted Ana Ling from a magical island with sad and lonely children. Ana and her friends were unhappy because there were no flowers on the island. Ana explained their sadness to the heavens, which began to cry. The tears became rain and flowers began to grow. Ana's mothers explain that just as the flowers were a gift from heaven, she was heaven's gift to them. The storytelling is forced at times and the illustrations do little to capture the excitement that should be in the story. NOT RECOMMENDED.

Keywords: Adoption, Spanish Literature, Spain, Children of Gay Parents, Lesbian Mothers.

PATTISON, DARCY. *19 Girls and Me.* Illus. by Steven Salerno. New York, NY: Philomel /Penguin, 2006. Unpaged. ISBN: 9780399243363. OCLC #: 61240505. Ages 4–8. FORMAT: Hardcover. AWARDS: None. REVIEWS: KS, PW, SLJ.

John Hercules Po is the only boy in his kindergarten class. Each day he plays with his 19 female classmates at recess and each night his brother warns John that the girls will turn him into a sissy. Each day John is convinced he can turn the girls into tomboys but loses himself in the fun they have together. By the end of the school week, John decides that his female classmates are not tomboys and he's not a sissy. Rather, they are all friends. While the author attempts to break gender and sex role stereotypes, the fact that John, not the girls, is always the person to instigate the rambunctious play clearly shows female subjugation. Although the bright, retro illustrations might capture the attention of young readers, librarians would do better with books such as *The Paper Bag Princess* (Munsch). NOT RECOMMENDED.

   Keywords: Tomboys, Gender Identity, Gender Nonconformity, Sex Roles, School Relations, Individuality.

PENA, WIELAND. *¿De quién enamoraré?* Illus. by Roberto Maján. Badajoz, Spain: Eraseunavez.com y Fundación Triangulo, 2007. Unpaged. ISBN: 9788493059217. OCLC #: 433858319. Ages 6–11. FORMAT: Hardcover. AWARDS: None. REVIEWS: None.

One of the winners of a publishing contest in 2004 held by Eraseunavez.com and Fundación Triangulo to promote children's stories representing LGBTQ families, this simple, Spanish-language picture book follows a boy and girl as they explore what it means to fall in love with someone. Their teacher tells them that eventually everyone will fall in love. At first the boy and girl decide they'll just fall in love with each other but they soon realize that common interest and not gender determines love — in other words sexuality is fluid. With this in mind, bisexual and same-sex parents could use the book to explain their love relationships to their children. The stylized, abstract illustrations reminiscent of Picasso's work add interest to the story but would be more appealing to older children and tweens. ADDITIONAL SELECTION.

   Keywords: Spanish Literature, Spain, Relationships, Love, Heterosexuality, Homosexuality, Bisexuality.

PHILLIPS, LYNN. *Exactly Like Me.* Chapel Hill, NC: Lollipop Power, 1972. Unpaged. ISBN: n.a. OCLC #: 2145547. Ages 4–8. FORMAT: Paperback. AWARDS: None. REVIEWS: None.

An unnamed girl explains to the reader that she is happy just the way she is. No, she does not fit the gender and sex roles assigned to her but that's okay with her. Maybe the people around her find her choice of play and her aspirations unfitting for a girl but she is proud of being a strong girl who will grow into a strong woman. The simple text, while slightly didactic, is accompanied by sparse line illustrations. Gender-variant girls will appreciate this book, although some parents may have a problem with the page that shows the girl entirely naked. ADDITIONAL SELECTION.

Keywords: Gender Identity, Gender Nonconformity, Individuality, Sex Roles, Feminism.

PIÑÁN, BERTA. *Las cosas que le gustan a Fran.* Illus. by Antonia Santolaya Ruiz-Clavijo. Madrid, Spain: Hotelpapel Ediciones, 2007. Unpaged. ISBN: 9788493564513. OCLC #: 166391138. Ages 4–8. FORMAT: Hardcover. AWARDS: None. REVIEWS: None. The text is entirely in Spanish but includes an English translation by Simon Jennings in the back of the book.

There is more than meets the eye in this charming story about a young girl who describes all the things that Frankie likes to do and the many ways in which Frankie shows love to the girl and her mother. The author and illustrator work well together to keep Frankie's face hidden and not to use pronouns until the very end of the book. The intent is to show Frankie as a caring parent who does many of the same things that a dad would do. It is only on the next-to-last double-page spread that readers learn that Frankie is short for Francisca and the girl actually has two mothers rather than a mom and dad. This delightful deception is a wonderful way to help children understand that rainbow families are similar to other families. HIGHLY RECOMMENDED.

Keywords: Spanish Literature, Spanish Literature, Spain, Children of Gay Parents, Lesbian Mothers.

PITTAR, GILL. *Milly, Molly and Different Dads.* Illus. by Cris Morrell. Gisborne, New Zealand: Milly Molly Books, 2002. 25p. ISBN: 9781869720193. OCLC #: 56315998. Ages 4–6. FORMAT: Hardcover. AWARDS: None. REVIEWS: None. Positive review included in the UK review publication *Books for Keeps.*

Part of the Milly, Molly early-reader series, this volume addresses family compositions relating to male caregivers. When a tearful girl in Milly and Molly's classroom arrives late to school, the class learns that her father left home that morning. The teacher then asks children in the classroom to talk about their dads, who are quite diverse: one is in a wheelchair, one is deaf, two are gay, one is a single father, and so forth. Cheerful, cartoon-style illustrations accompany the simple text and are appropriate for young readers. Although slightly didactic, the book introduces gay fathers without being too overt. Considering the lack of beginning readers on this topic, this title is recommended for both school and public libraries. RECOMMENDED.

Keywords: Adoption, Gay Fathers, Children of Gay Parents, Family Relations, School Relations, Single Parents, Mixed Race Families, Uncles, Self-Published Literature, New Zealand Literature, New Zealand.

POLACCO, PATRICIA. *In Our Mothers' House.* New York, NY: Philomel Books, 2009. Unpaged. ISBN: 9780399250767. OCLC #: 244701973. Ages 6–10. FORMAT: Hardcover. AWARDS: Notable Social Studies Trade Books for Young People 2010; Rainbow List 2010. REVIEWS: BKLST, BCCB, KS, LMC, SLJ.

Marmee and Meema's house is always full of sunshine and love as the narrator recalls the happy life that her two mothers built for her and her adopted siblings. Readers are treated to a series of childhood memories ranging from block parties to new puppies to mother-daughter tea parties as the family's life is described from the children's adoption to the eventual death of the mothers. In an attempt to avoid sugarcoating the lives of same-sex families, Polacco also introduces readers to a homophobic neighbor who does not approve of the mothers' lifestyle. The gentle narrative and soothing, expressive illustrations perfectly complement each other to create a picture of a rainbow family whose home overflows with love. While the book is lengthy for the younger set, older children will appreciate a glowing reflection of their families. RECOMMENDED.

Keywords: Adoption, Lesbian Mothers, Children of Gay Parents, Family Composition, School Relations, Homophobia, Mixed Race Families, African Americans, Asian Americans, Italian Americans.

POLLACK, EILEEN. *Whisper Whisper Jesse, Whisper Whisper Josh: A Story About AIDS.* Illus. by Bruce Gilfoy. Cambridge, MA: Advantage/Aurora Publications, 1992. Unpaged. ISBN: 9780962482847. OCLC #: 28523905. Ages 5–9. FORMAT: Hardcover. AWARDS: None. REVIEWS: BKLST.

Jesse is tired of whispering! His mother and father seem to whisper all the time about him and sometimes about his Uncle Josh, whom he has not seen in a long time. When the family attends an ice skating show, Jesse's mom explains that the man dressed as Frosty the Snowman is Uncle Josh and that he will moving in with the family. Jesse is excited but picks up on his father's disdain for Uncle Josh. Soon the boy learns that Josh is very sick with the AIDS virus, and his cousin tells Jesse that Josh contracted AIDS because he is a "bad man." As time passes, Uncle Josh becomes sicker and eventually dies. The sensitive narrative perfectly captures the emotions of young children dealing with the terminal illness of a loved one and, while the ending is inevitable, Pollack's treatment is never didactic or overly verbose. Although the text never identifies Uncle Josh as gay, the implication is present. Slightly stronger than *Losing Uncle Tim* (Jordan), this picture book is appropriate for all library collections. RECOMMENDED.

Keywords: Family Relations, Gay Uncles, Gay Relatives, Death, AIDS.

QUINLAN, PATRICIA. *Tiger Flowers.* Illus. by Janet Wilson. New York, NY: Dial, 1994. Unpaged. ISBN: 9780803714076. OCLC #: 28425804. Ages 4–8. FORMAT: Hardcover. AWARDS: Lambda Literary Award Finalist, LGBT Children's/YA Category, 1995. REVIEWS: BKLST, BCCB, PW, SLJ.

Joel used to do fun things with his uncle Michael — building a tree house, gardening, and going to baseball games. For a while Michael even lived with Joel, his mother, and his little sister Tara. But now Michael is gone, having died from AIDS. Through simple text, readers learn that Michael used to have a partner named Peter, who also died of AIDS. After Peter's death Michael discovered he also had the disease and came to live with Joel's family until his death. Quinlan attempts to address the hole that Michael has left in Joel's life and includes a scene where the boy dreams that his uncle tells him he has been set free of his illness just like an escaped animal from the zoo. This concept may be a little too hard for the intended audience to grasp. Nonetheless, the book may be helpful as bibliotherapy for children dealing with the death of a relative. ADDITIONAL SELECTION.

Keywords: Family Relations, Gay Uncles, Gay Relatives, Death, AIDS, Canada, Canadian Literature.

QUINTIÁ, XERARDO. *Titiritesa.* Illus. by Maurizio A. C. Quarello. Translation by Xerardo Quintiá. Pontevedra (Galicia), Spain: OQO Editora, 2007. Unpaged. ISBN: 9788496788961. OCLC #: 156831573. Ages 6–9. FORMAT: Hardcover. AWARDS: None. REVIEWS: None. (Originally published in Galician.)

Princess Titiritesa lives in the land of The-Day-Before-Yesterday with her conventional parents who would like nothing more than to see her married off to a nice prince. But Titiritesa has other plans and decides to run away from the castle. She and her donkey set out on an adventure where she meets a monster, a word inventor, and a beautiful princess whom she decides to marry. Written entirely in Spanish, this charmingly surreal fairy tale features magical elements in both text and illustration and may be beneficial for libraries serving Spanish-speaking rainbow families. ADDITIONAL SELECTION.

Keywords: Lesbians, Family Relations, Spanish Literature, Spain, Princesses, Gay Marriage, Weddings.

RECIO, CARLES. *El príncipe enamorado.* Illus. by Enrique Hurtado Rodriguez. Barcelona, Spain: Ediciones de la Tempestad, 2001. Unpaged. ISBN: 9788479480448. OCLC #: 733561162. Ages 7–10. FORMAT: Hardcover. AWARDS: None. REVIEWS: None.

Based on true events and set during the reign of James II, Count of Barcelona, and King of Valencia, Aragón, Mallorca and Sicilia in the14th century, this tale follows Prince Jaime as he grows from a boy into a teen in line to be the next heir to the Spanish throne. Jaime's mother dies at a young age and an evil queen marries his father. Jaime has an arranged marriage when he comes of age, but before the marriage can occur, he meets a Muslim worker named Karim and falls in love. Jaime and Karim's relationship is taboo on many levels — Jaime is crossing gender, class, and religious lines. When the evil queen discovers the love affair, she attempts to have Karim taken away but Jaime thwarts her plans. The tale ends with Jaime and Karim living happily ever after. Whether or not the story has factual elements, it does provide a perspective missing in the annals of historical fiction. Older children would enjoy this, but unfortunately the illustrations, which are rendered in the style of stills from a cheap animated film, often feature stiff poses and out-of-place action. ADDITIONAL SELECTION.

Keywords: Family Relations, Spanish Literature, Spain, Princes, Gay Men, Muslims, Interracial Dating.

RELLA, TINA. *Daddy and Pop.* Illus. by Monica Meza. Glendale, CA: Love Makes a Family Books & Guess Who? Multimedia, 2011. Unpaged. ISBN: 9781450554114. OCLC #: n.a. Ages 4–8. FORMAT: Paperback. AWARDS: None. REVIEWS: None.

On the first day of school, first-grader Jessie is more than happy to tell her class about the fun things she does with her two dads. After she finishes her jaunty rhyme about her daddy and pop, a classmate asks Jessie if she has a mom. That afternoon, Jessie discovers that her dads wanted her enough to use surrogacy. Via rhyming text and computer-generated illustrations, readers learn a little about the surrogacy process and are reminded about the extensive love Jessie's two dads have for her. Part of the Love Makes a Family series, this picture book includes a musical CD that can be purchased separately. One unfortunate drawback is the illustrations, which are framed by a 2.5-inch top and bottom black margin that creates the overall effect of watching a movie rather than reading a book. ADDITIONAL SELECTION.

Keywords: Children of Gay Parents, Gay Fathers, Self-Published Literature, Surrogacy, School Relations.

RELLA, TINA. *Mom, Mama, and Me . . . and How I Came to Be!* Illus. by Monica Meza. Glendale, CA: Love Makes a Family Books & Guess Who? Multimedia, 2011. Unpaged. ISBN: 9781452875668. OCLC #: n.a. Ages 4–8. FORMAT: Paperback. AWARDS: None. REVIEWS: None.

Part of the Love Makes a Family series, this picture book follows a boy named Jonathan as he explains the special love that his two moms have for him and learns about how he came to be. Readers discover that his mothers used surrogacy to create their son and that they care for him very much. Unfortunately, Meza's computer-generated illustrations and Rella's forced rhyming text will do little to hold the attention of young children. NOT RECOMMENDED.

Keywords: Children of Gay Parents, Lesbian Mothers, Self-Published Literature, Surrogacy, School Relations.

RICHARDSON, JUSTIN, AND PETER PARNELL. *And Tango Makes Three.* Illus. by Henry Cole. New York, NY: Simon & Schuster, 2005. Unpaged. ISBN: 9780689878459. OCLC #: 55518633. Ages 4–8. FORMAT: Hardcover. AWARDS: American Library Association Notable Children's Books 2006; American Society for the Prevention of Cruelty to Animals Henry Bergh Children's Book Award, 2005; Best Children's Books of the Year, 2005, Bank Street College of Education; Cooperative Children's Book Center Choices 2006; Lambda Literary Award Finalist, LGBT Children's/YA Category, 2006; Notable Social Studies Trade Books for Young People 2006; Rainbow List 2008. REVIEWS: BLST, HB, KS, LMC, PW, SLJ.

Based on two chinstrap penguins at the Central Park Zoo in New York, Richardson and Parnell's narrative follows penguins Roy and Silo as they meet during mating season, take up cohabitation, and eventually work together to raise an abandoned egg that hatches to become a girl penguin named Tango. The text is straightforward and never graphic, with a simple storyline that provides readers with factual information about penguins. Cole's attractive watercolor illustrations capture the emotions of the birds and normalize their experience. One of the most frequently challenged and censored books in the United States, this accessible picture book has a place on both school and public library shelves as it demonstrates that same-sex attractions and rainbow families occur just as easily in the animal world as the human one. It would work well with lesson plans and programs relating to arctic animals, zoos, and rainbow families in nature. RECOMMENDED.

Keywords: Gay Fathers, Children of Gay Parents, Adoption, Homosexuality, Penguins, Wildlife, Friendship, Family Composition.

RICHARDSON, JUSTIN, AND PETER PARNELL. *Christian, the Hugging Lion.* Illus. by Amy June Bates. New York, NY: Simon & Schuster, 2010. Unpaged. ISBN: 9781416986621. OCLC #: 262428697. Ages 4–7. FORMAT: Hardcover. AWARDS: Lambda Literary Award Finalist, LGBT Children's/YA Category, 2010. REVIEWS: LMC, PW, SLJ.

Based on a true story, this picture book by the authors of *And Tango Makes Three* profiles the unusual family that was formed when two gay men purchased a three-month-old lion cub from the Harrods department store in London. On the first day at his new home, the lion, Christian, is so excited that he hugs his two new "dads." Readers follow the small family as Christian matures and is eventually released to the wild in Kenya. A few years later, the men are briefly reunited with their lion on a visit. Bates's warm illustrations portray their rambunctious but loving relationship, and an author's note provides additional factual information, mentioning an online video showing footage of the real Christian. RECOMMENDED.

Keywords: Pet Adoption, Gay Men, Lions, Wildlife, Friendship.

RICKARDS, LYNNE. *Pink!* Illus. by Margaret Chamberlain. New York, NY: Chicken House/Scholastic, 2009. Unpaged. ISBN: 9780545086080. OCLC #: 299752126. Ages 3–8. FORMAT: Hardcover. AWARDS: Rainbow List 2010; Royal Mail Award for Scottish Children's Books, 2009. REVIEWS: BKLST, BCCB, KS, LMC, PW, SLJ. Other non-U.S. reviews appeared in the UK review publication *Books for Keeps* and the Irish publication *Inis — The Magazine of Children's Books Ireland.* (Originally published in the United Kingdom in 2008.)

When he awakens one morning, suddenly bright pink, Patrick is appalled. No other penguin is pink, especially not a boy penguin! He visits his doctor but she can do nothing for Patrick. His dad reassures him that there are pink boy birds who live elsewhere in the world and his mother tries to convince Patrick that he and everyone else will get used to his new color. When he is ridiculed at school, Patrick takes his stuffed doll and travels all the way to Africa to visit pink boy flamingos. It takes seven days to get there and he soon discovers that he is nothing like a flamingo and is sorely out of place. Back home he finds that everyone has missed him (especially his friend Arthur) and wants to hear about his adventures and the other pink birds. The light-hearted text will certainly hit home with gender-variant children and the expressive cartoon illustrations complete this appealing read-aloud. For a program on gender-nonconforming penguins, librarians can pair this with *And Tango Makes Three* (Richardson and Parnell). RECOMMENDED.

Keywords: Gender Identity, Gender Nonconformity, Individuality, Family Relations, Penguins, British Literature.

RODRÍGUEZ, ISABEL CARMEN. *Y nosotros . . .¿de dónde venimos?* Illus. by Isabel Carmen Rodríguez and M. Luisa Guerrero. Alicante, Spain: ONG por la No Discriminación, 2008. Unpaged. ISBN: 9788493624408. OCLC #: 733659755. Ages 7–10. FORMAT: Paperback. AWARDS: None. REVIEWS: None.

A child asks her mother how she was conceived and her mother explains how she and the girl's other mother loved each other and wanted children. The mother then details how the couple used artificial insemination to get pregnant. At first they were unsuccessful but eventually they succeeded. The girl asks her mother why she never told her the story before and the mother explains that she thought the girl was too young to hear it. The book concludes with the girl deciding to draw the story and share it at school the next day. The descriptions of contraception are quite technical and not accessible to children. Oddly, the book contains dual identical Spanish texts that differ only in the font style. The illustrations are a combination of child-drawn illustrations and more realistic ones. Although many libraries need Spanish-language materials for the growing population of Latino rainbow families, this book adds little to the collection. NOT RECOMMENDED.

Keywords: Lesbian Mothers, Children of Gay Parents, Spanish Literature, Spain, Artificial Insemination.

RODRÍGUEZ MATUS, JUAN. *Las tres Sofías.* Illus. by Anna Cooke. Guadalajara, Mexico: Editorial Patlatonalli, 2008. Unpaged. ISBN: 9786079511012. OCLC #: 404026050. Ages 4–8. FORMAT: Hardcover. AWARDS: None. REVIEWS: None.

Written entirely in Spanish, this unique picture book is part of the Colección cuento infantil: Todas las Familias son Sagradas, which is a series intended to honor the sacredness of today's families, including transgender, lesbian, and gay parents. Set in Oaxaca, Mexico, the book describes young Sofía and her two mothers, who are part of the indigenous population of the region. Unknown to most of the world, this tribe does not condemn same-sex relationships. In this particular story, the girl's mother is sad but eventually decides that she wants to be happy and find someone that she loves. This new life companion also happens to be named Sofía just like the girl and her mother — so the family becomes the three Sofías. The text is simple and the illustrations pop against their bold backgrounds, highlighting the people and lush landscapes. Presenting a culture often not available to U.S. children, this book will be appreciated in public libraries, particularly those needing Spanish-language materials. RECOMMENDED.

Keywords: Lesbian Mothers, Children of Gay Parents, Family Relations, Spanish Literature, Mexico, Oaxaca, Indigenous People.

ROSS, ERIC. *My Uncle's Wedding.* Illus. by Tracy Greene. Lexington, KY: CreateSpace, 2011. Unpaged. ISBN: 9781456531034. OCLC #: 719451581. Ages 3–8. FORMAT: Paperback. AWARDS: None. REVIEWS: None.

A young boy named Andy is excited when he learns that his Uncle Mike is marrying his boyfriend Steve. Andy helps with the wedding planning by assisting with flower selection, food choices, and cake flavors. On the day of the wedding, he serves as the ring bearer and his sister is the flower girl. Told simply, this book is neither heavy-handed nor didactic regarding gay marriage. Rather, children meet a boy who is excited that his uncle is getting married. The fact that his uncle's partner is a man and not a woman is never discussed. The cartoon-style, computer-generated illustrations lend a light-hearted flair to the book but do little to extend the story. While not a staple for most collections, this title might be appropriate for larger library systems that can afford to circulate paperback picture books. ADDITIONAL SELECTION.

Keywords: Family Relations, Gay Marriage, Gay Uncles, Gay Relatives, Self-Published Literature, Weddings.

ROTHBLATT, PHYLLIS. *All I Want to Be Is Me.* Lexington, KY: CreateSpace, 2011. Unpaged. ISBN: 9781452818252. OCLC #: n.a. Ages 3–8. FORMAT: Paperback. AWARDS: None. REVIEWS: None.

"I want to be all of me, All I want to be is me" is the refrain in this self-published picture book that affirms that children can be whatever gender they choose to be. Several multicultural, gender-variant children — boys who feel like girls, girls who feel like boys, children who feel like neither gender — are introduced in gentle text and warm watercolor illustrations. Although the narrative borders on didactic, gender-variant children, their parents, and their educators will appreciate the book along with the accompanying song found on the author's Web site. Pair this book with *10,000 Dresses* (Ewert) for a program celebrating gender-variant children. ADDITIONAL SELECTION.

Keywords: Family Relations, Cross-Dressing, Gender Identity, Gender Nonconformity, Individuality, Transgender, School Relations, Self-Published Literature, Teasing.

SCAMELL, RAGNHILD. *Toby's Doll's House.* Illus. by Adrian Reynolds. London, UK: Levinson, 1998. Unpaged. ISBN: 9781862330269. OCLC #: 41450252. Ages 4–8. FORMAT: Hardcover. AWARDS: None. REVIEWS: PW, SLJ.

It's almost time for Toby's birthday and what he really wants is a dollhouse for his paper dolls. Unfortunately, his self-absorbed family thinks they know best, insisting that he'd rather have a fort, a farmyard, or a multi-story parking garage. As each family member gives Toby the gift they think he needs (and that they secretly want to play with), Toby resigns himself to using his own creativity to make a dollhouse from the birthday gift boxes. The straightforward text and bright cartoon illustrations captures an all-too-common occurrence when gender-variant children choose nontraditional toys. Librarians can pair this book with the classic *William's Doll* (Zolotow) for a storytime on boys and their dolls. RECOMMENDED.

Keywords: Gender Identity, Gender Nonconformity, Individuality, Dolls, Family Relations, British Literature, Sex Roles.

SCHIMEL, LAWRENCE. *Amigos y vecinos.* Illus. by Sara Rojo. Madrid, Spain: Ediciones La Librería, 2005. Unpaged. ISBN: 9788496470217. OCLC #: 389886567. Ages 6–10. FORMAT: Hardcover. AWARDS: None. REVIEWS: None.

Paco lives with his two fathers in Madrid and has a good friend and neighbor whose mother is dating a homophobic, macho man. The boyfriend doesn't like the fact that Paco's friend plays dolls with him and he becomes verbally abusive when he discovers that Paco has two fathers. However, since the boyfriend accepts Paco — who is Asian — he believes he is not a bigot. At school the children learn that there are many types of families and Paco's friend shares this information with his mother's boyfriend, who eventually tolerates Paco's two dads. The book concludes with information about the gay district in Madrid as well as definitions of homophobia, machismo, racism, and xenophobia. The book is borderline didactic, but it does address many forms of discrimination and would certainly be a discussion starter for older children. ADDITIONAL SELECTION.

Keywords: Spanish Literature, Spain, Gender Identity, Gender Nonconformity, Sex Roles, Individuality, Gay Fathers, Children of Gay Parents, Lesbians, Homophobia, Xenophobia, Machismo, Family Composition, Single Parents, Divorced Parents, Extended Families.

SCHIMEL, LAWRENCE. *La aventura de Cecilia y el dragón.* Illus. by Sara Rojo Pérez. Madrid, Spain: Candela Ediciones y Bibliopólis, 2005. Unpaged. ISBN: 9788496173255. OCLC #: 60373072. Ages 4–8. FORMAT: Hardcover. AWARDS: None. REVIEWS: None.

Cecilia loves to have adventures and most of all she wants to meet a dragon. She's read about them in books but she's never seen one. One day she decides to use her ingenuity to track down a dragon. When she finally finds one, she realizes that he's captured a girl. Cecilia must save her — but how? Relying on gender stereotypes, she tricks the dragon into thinking that she's a helpless female and insists he go fight brave men. When the dragon is gone, Cecilia rescues the girl (Miranda) and they become the best of friends and have many more adventures of their own. Schimel's witty text, accompanied by Pérez's bright cartoon illustrations, is a perfect complement to other nontraditional stories such as *The Princess Knight* (Funke) and *The Paper Bag Princess* (Munsch). RECOMMENDED.

Keywords: Spanish Literature, Spain, Princesses, Dragons, Gender Identity, Gender Nonconformity, Gender Roles, Individuality.

SCHLEIN, MIRIAM. *The Girl Who Would Rather Climb Trees.* Illus. by Judith Gwyn Brown. New York, NY: Harcourt Brace Jovanovich, 1975. Unpaged. ISBN: 9780152309787. OCLC #: 1322930. Ages 6–9. FORMAT: Hardcover. AWARDS: None. REVIEWS: SLJ.

Melissa loves to climb trees, play ball, roller skate, jump rope, and ride bikes. She pretty much likes to do anything — except play with dolls. Much to her chagrin, Melissa is presented with a brand new doll complete with extra clothes and buggy. Her mother, grandmother, and neighbor all try to teach her how to play with the doll. Melissa decides to put the doll to bed and go outside and play. Although the message of the book is important, the conflict is too easily and unrealistically resolved. Brown's pen-and-ink illustrations successfully capture the tomboy nature of Melissa but would do little to hold the attention of contemporary children. NOT RECOMMENDED.

Keywords: Family Relations, Gender Identity, Gender Nonconformity, Individuality, Sex Roles, Tomboys, Dolls.

SETTERINGTON, KEN. *Mom and Mum Are Getting Married.* Illus. by Alice Priestley. Toronto, ON: Second Story Press, 2004. Unpaged. ISBN: 9781896764849. OCLC #: 55596683. Ages 4–8. FORMAT: Hardcover. AWARDS: Cooperative Children's Book Center Choices 2005; Our Choice 2005, Canadian Children's Book Centre. REVIEWS: KS, SLJ. Positive review included in the Canadian publication *CM: Canadian Review of Materials,* published by the Manitoba Library Association.

Mom and Mum are getting married and Rosie is super-excited about the prospect of being a bridesmaid or flower girl. At first her Mom tells her that she and Mum want a small wedding with no flower girls. However, the girl eventually convinces Mom to let her scatter rose petals during the small ceremony at the family cottage. As the extended family arrives, the mothers are concerned about losing the wedding rings, but Rosie and her gay uncle develop an ingenious way for Rosie and her brother to keep track of them during the ceremony. Priestley's cheerful illustrations extend the text and demonstrate the diversity of Rosie's family. Librarians could pair this book with *Donovan's Big Day* (Newman) for a program about children of gay parents and their role in their parents' weddings. RECOMMENDED.

Keywords: Gay Marriage, Lesbian Mothers, Children of Gay Parents, Family Relations, Canada, Canadian Literature, Weddings, Gay Uncles, Gay Relatives.

SEVERANCE, JANE. *Lots of Mommies.* Illus. by Jan Jones. Chapel Hill, NC: Lollipop Power, 1983. 35p. ISBN: 9780914996248. OCLC #: 10428444. Ages 4–8. FORMAT: Paperback. AWARDS: None. REVIEWS: None.

Often hailed as one of the first U.S. picture books to represent a non-traditional lesbian family, this groundbreaking book describes young Emily's first day of school. Readers learn that Emily and her mother live in a house with three other women, all of whom Emily considers her mommy. At school the other children tease Emily for saying she has lots of mommies. It is only after she falls off the monkey bars and is cared for by all of her mommies that her classmates realize you can have more than one mommy. The book never explicitly states that Emily's mother or the other women are lesbians, but visual clues in the black-and-white line illustrations suggest that some of the women may be lesbians. While the book offers a positive message, it is out-of-print and was only published in paperback. RECOMMENDED.

Keywords: Family Composition, Family Relations, Lesbian Mothers, Individuality, Gender Nonconformity, Asian Americans, Teasing, School Relations.

SEVERANCE, JANE. *When Megan Went Away.* Illus. by Tea Schook. Chapel Hill, NC: Lollipop Power, Inc., 1979. 32p. ISBN: 9780914996224. OCLC #: 6734819. Ages 5–9. FORMAT: Paperback. AWARDS: None. REVIEWS: None.

A young girl named Shannon is sad when she comes home after her mother's part-ner Megan moves away. Shannon remembers both her good and not-so-good mo-ments with Megan. Her mother is depressed but reassures Shannon that Megan's absence is not her fault and that together she and Shannon will survive. The text is sometimes too long and the line art amateurish. The first U.S. children's picture book to depict a lesbian relationship as well as a separation (divorce) between les-bian partners, this picture book differs from *Saturday Is Pattyday* (Newman) in that the child is not expected to see her mother's partner again. Public libraries should consider this hard-to-find, out-of-print picture book for their collections. ADDI-TIONAL SELECTION.

Keywords: Lesbian Mothers, Children of Gay Parents, Family Relations, Divorce, Divorced Parents.

SHEEHAN, MONICA. *Love Is You and Me*. New York, NY: Little Simon/Simon & Schuster, 2010. Unpaged. ISBN: 9781442407657. OCLC #: 701412203. Ages 1–4. FORMAT: Board Book. AWARDS: None. REVIEWS: PW.

In this gentle exploration of the concept of love, young children follow a mouse and a dog as they describe the love they have for each other. Children learn that love allows you to be yourself and that it lasts through good and bad. While the nature of the love relationship is not explained (whether it is parent/child, friends, a couple relationship), the characters are both portrayed as males. With this in mind, depictions of them holding hands, sleeping next to each other in bed, and sharing romantic nights can certainly represent gay relationships. Libraries may want to acquire this title for its understated, positive gay relationship. The title would also work well for Valentine's Day programming. RECOMMENDED.

Keywords: Same-Sex Relationships, Dogs, Mice, Board Books, Love.

SHERIDAN, SARA. *I'm Me*. Illus. by Margaret Chamberlain. New York, NY: Scholastic, 2011. Unpaged. ISBN: 9780545282222. OCLC #: 662407724. Ages 3–8. FORMAT: Hardcover. AWARDS: None. REVIEWS: BKLST, KS, SLJ.

A young girl named Imogene visits her Aunt Sara for a day of fun and excitement. Throughout the day, Aunt Sara suggests things they can pretend to be. Some of the suggestions are gender-stereotypical, such as a beautiful princess, while others are less so, such as dragon-taming knight. After each suggestion, Imogene answers in the negative until her aunt asks her what she wants to be. Imogene suggests that she be herself and then spends the day playing in the park and eating ice cream with her rambunctious aunt. The strong message of individuality along with the depic-tion of gender-nonconformist behaviors extends the scope of the book to gender-variant children. ADDITIONAL SELECTION.

Keywords: Family Relations, Aunts, Individuality, Gender Nonconformity.

SIMON, NORMA. *All Families Are Special*. Illus. by Teresa Flavin. Morton Grove, IL: Albert Whitman, 2003. Unpaged. ISBN: 9780807521755. OCLC #: 51764497. Ages 4–8. FORMAT: Hardcover. AWARDS: None. REVIEWS: KS, SLJ.

After Robert's teacher announces she is going to be a grandmother, the children in his class are encouraged to talk about their families. They tell stories of many types of families — adopted families, stepfamilies, extended families, families with two parents, families with one parent, families with same-sex parents, and families with opposite-sex parents. This book doesn't cover any new ground, but the presentation is simple and suitable for young children, and the cheerful watercolor illustrations highlight the love in the various families. RECOMMENDED.

Keywords: Adoption, Family Composition, Lesbian Mothers, Children of Gay Parents, Family Relations, Asian Americans, African Americans, Single Parents, Divorced Parents, Mixed Race Families, Grandparent Caregivers, Extended Families, International Adoption, Chinese Americans, Pakistani Americans, Latinos.

SKEERS, LINDA. *Tutus Aren't My Style.* Illus. by Anne Wilsdorf. New York, NY: Dial, 2010. Unpaged. ISBN: 9780803732124. OCLC #: 319602617. Ages 4–8. FORMAT: Hardcover. AWARDS: Rainbow List 2011. REVIEWS: BKLST, KS, LMC, SLJ.

Emma loves to explore the jungle, catch frogs, dig for treasure, and chase the cat. When the rambunctious girl receives a pink ballerina outfit complete with tutu from her uncle, she doesn't know quite what to do with it. The mailman, a neighbor, and her brother all offer her advice on how to be a ballerina. Eventually, Emma decides she has her own style of ballet — loud, thumping, and free of tutus! The comical watercolor illustrations extend the story with the antics of Emma's cat, which dons the tutu and develops her own style of ballet too. Gender-nonconforming girls will particularly enjoy this story that will pair well with *A Fire Engine for Ruthie* (Newman). RECOMMENDED.

Keywords: Family Relations, Uncles, Individuality, Gender Identity, Gender Nonconformity, Ballet.

SOLLIE, ANDRÉ. *Hello, Sailor.* Illus. by Ingrid Godon. London, UK: Macmillan, 2003. Unpaged. ISBN: 9780333987353. OCLC #: 179192310. Ages 5–9. FORMAT: Hardcover. AWARDS: None. REVIEWS: PW. Other reviews included in the UK review publication *Books for Keeps* and the Irish publication *Inis — The Magazine of Children's Books Ireland*. (Originally published in Dutch as *Wachten op Matroos*. Amsterdam, Netherlands: Querido's Uitgeverij BV, 2000. ISBN: 9789021464039.)

This gentle story describes lighthouse keeper Matt's determination to keep the light burning so his Sailor (lover) will find his way home after a long voyage. Matt is sure that Sailor will return and take him away to sail the world. Two townspeople try to get Matt to stop worrying about Sailor's return and get on with his life. They convince Matt to leave the lighthouse long enough to enjoy his birthday party. After the party, Matt goes back to the lighthouse to shine the light and wait for Sailor, who finally returns that night and takes Matt away. The two townspeople come the following morning to find Matt missing, and they decide to keep the light burning in hopes that he will return home. The simply told story clearly communicates the loneliness and pining that a person feels when their friend has gone away. Godon's sparse illustrations convey the characters' emotions but also leave room for interpretation. Perfect for both school and public libraries. RECOMMENDED.

Keywords: Gay Men, Dutch Literature, Netherlands, Sailors, Lighthouses.

STARK, ULF. *Min Syster är en Ängel (My Sister Is an Angel).* Illus. by Anna Höglund. Stockholm, Sweden: Alfabeta Bokförlag, 1996. Unpaged. ISBN: 9789150100237. OCLC #: 49875708. Ages 5–9. FORMAT: Hardcover. AWARDS: 1996 Augustpriset (Sweden), Children's and Young Adult Category. REVIEWS: None. Also available in Dutch as *Mijn zusje is een engel*, Danish as *Min søster er en engel*, Faroese as *Systir min er ein eingil*, German as *Meine Schwester ist ein Engel*, and Russian as *Moia sestrënka angel*.

This sensitive title is told from the point of view of Ulf, a young boy who befriends the angel of his older sister who died at birth. Ulf enjoys playing with the angel and wants her to experience some of his earthly joys such as drinking chocolate and orange sodas and going to the movies. In order to do this, the boy has his mother buy him a wig of long golden curls, which he dons along with one his mother's old dresses and a pair of heels. Wearing this costume, Ulf embodies his sister and sets about town to introduce her to his friends, take her to the movies, and share candy and soda with her. He meets some resistance from his neighbors and family for dressing as a girl, but Ulf is unfazed; he would do anything for his sister. This gentle picture book ends with his sister telling him good-bye and returning to heaven. Although the topic may seem a little macabre to some American audiences, the book would be quite useful for children dealing with the death of a sibling or for gender-variant boys who enjoy cross-dressing. The only disadvantage of the book for most American libraries is the lack of an English translation. HIGHLY RECOMMENDED.

Keywords: Family Relations, Swedish Literature, Sweden, Cross-Dressing, Gender Identity, Gender Nonconformity.

STEINER, CHARLOTTE. *Tomboy's Doll.* New York, NY: Lothrop, Lee & Shepard, 1969. Unpaged. ISBN: 9780688510701. OCLC #: 12167. Ages 5–9. FORMAT: Hardcover. AWARDS: None. REVIEWS: None.

Marie Louise is a tomboy who prefers to play with boys. Most of her time is spent with Billy, her best friend and neighbor. Because she is such a tomboy, everyone gives Marie the nickname "Tommy." Tommy's mother tries unsuccessfully to get her daughter to be more like other girls but Tommy could care less. Eventually, her mother buys her a doll in hopes that the doll will encourage Tommy to act more like a girl. Tommy and Billy have many adventures with the doll, but not the docile, well-mannered type of play that her mother hopes for. In the last few pages of the book, Tommy gets lost in the woods and talks to her doll to keep her company. This teaches her "how to care for a doll" and miraculously changes her into a different type of girl. The entire story is moralistic and contrived. What is wrong with Tommy being herself? Why can't she have adventures with the doll rather than sitting quietly and changing the doll's clothes? NOT RECOMMENDED.

Keywords: Family Relations, Gender Identity, Gender Nonconformity, Individuality, Sex Roles, Tomboys, Dolls.

STILLER, LAURIE. *Princess Max.* Illus. by Gregory Rogers. Milsons Point, New South Wales (Australia): Random House Australia, 2001. Unpaged. ISBN: 9780091834739. OCLC #: 49655760. Ages 4–8. FORMAT: Hardcover. AWARDS: 2001 Australian Family Therapists' Award for Children's Literature for Picture Books and Younger Readers. REVIEWS: None.

Max loves swaltzing! The young boy is happy wearing his mother's dress and becoming a beautiful fairy tale princess with a flowing gown that "swaltzes" when he moves. Unfortunately, his favorite older cousin Marty thinks it is unusual for a boy to wear a dress and calls him a weirdo. With the help of his understanding mother, Max realizes that it is okay for him to wear a dress, swaltz, and be who he is. Based on the author's experience with his own son, this heartwarming picture book celebrates individuality and promotes understanding of gender-variant children. The book is difficult to locate in the United States, but it would be a perfect complement to storytimes featuring books such as *William's Doll* (Zolotow) and *Ballerino Nate* (Bradley). RECOMMENDED.

    Keywords: Family Relations, Australian Literature, Australia, Cross-Dressing, Gender Identity, Gender Nonconformity, Bullying, Individuality.

TERMENÓN DELGADO, JAVIER. *Vengo.* Badajoz, Spain: Eraseunavez.com y Fundación Triangulo, 2007. Unpaged. ISBN: 9788493059224. OCLC #: 433857963. Ages 4–7. FORMAT: Hardcover. AWARDS: None. REVIEWS: None.

One of the 2004 winners of a publishing contest by Eraseunavez.com and Fundación Triangulo to promote children's stories representing LGBTQ families, this charming, Spanish-language picture book follows a young girl as she explores the myths that grownups tell children about their birth. From storks to baked loaves of bread to seeds to packages in the mail, the girl examines why each of these myths don't work for her. Although her two mothers explain where she came from, the girl decides to believe she came from the sea because she likes the ocean very much. Perfect for sharing one-on-one with a child, this picture book with cut-paper and collage illustrations is recommended for public libraries, particularly those serving Spanish-speaking families. ADDITIONAL SELECTION.

    Keywords: Spain, Spanish Literature, Children of Gay Parents, Lesbian Mothers, Babies, Conception, Birth Myths.

TOMPKINS, CRYSTAL. *Oh the Things Mommies Do! What Could Be Better Than Having Two?* Illus. by Lindsey Evans. New York, NY: Oh the Things Mommies Do! Publishing, 2009. Unpaged. ISBN: 9780578027593. OCLC #: 501837767. Ages 3–7. FORMAT: Paperback. AWARDS: None. REVIEWS: None.

In this joyful celebration of motherhood, children learn all the wonderful things that mommies can do, particularly when a child has two! From making breakfast to kissing boo-boos to hiking and reading bedtime stories, mothers of multiple ethnicities are depicted in a variety of activities. The bright, child-like illustrations complement the rhyming text and the repeated lines of the narrative will attract young listeners. While not a staple for most collections, this refreshing coverage of lesbian parenthood might be appropriate for larger library systems that can afford to circulate paperback picture books. ADDITIONAL SELECTION.

   Keywords: Family Relations, Lesbian Mothers, Children of Gay Parents, Self-Published Literature.

U'REN, ANDREA. *Pugdog.* New York, NY: Farrar, Straus & Giroux, 2001. Unpaged. ISBN: 9780374361495. OCLC #: 44675964. Ages 4–8. FORMAT: Hardcover. AWARDS: Parents' Choice Award 2001. REVIEWS: BKLST, HB, KS, PW, SLJ.

Pugdog is the happiest dog in the world! His owner Mike lets him roll in the dirt, chase squirrels, dig holes, and chew knucklebones. However, his blissful days are numbered when he gets a splinter and has to go to the vet. There Mike discovers that Pugdog is not a he but a she. Pugdog's life instantly changes — Mike forbids her former activities and insists on making her wear a dress and act like a lady. After several weeks of this mistreatment, Pugdog has had enough and runs away to the park where she plays fetch with strangers, digs holes, and chases squirrels. Mike soon realizes that he's mixed up about gender behaviors, especially when he sees a beautiful white poodle in pink bows and discovers that the poodle is a boy! Cleverly challenging gender stereotypes, U'Ren's delightful text and expressive illustrations make this a perfect read-aloud. Gender-variant children in particular will identify with Pugdog and her clueless owner! RECOMMENDED.

   Keywords: Gender Identity, Dogs, Cross-Dressing, Gender Nonconformity, Individuality, Transgender, Pets.

VALENTINE, JOHNNY. *The Daddy Machine.* Illus. by Lynette Schmidt. Los Angeles, CA: Alyson Wonderland, 2004. 2nd rev. ed. Unpaged. ISBN: 9781555838874. OCLC #: 54373072. Ages 3–8. FORMAT: Hardcover. AWARDS: Lambda Literary Award Finalist, LGBT Children's/YA Category, 1993. REVIEWS: LBR. (Extensively revised and updated text and illustrations from the 1992 version.)

Just as their moms are about to run a few errands, Sue and her brother receive a large box full of gears and levers. Together the siblings develop the world's first Daddy Machine, which is supposed to give them a dad for the day. Unfortunately, the dynamic duo forget to set an off switch on the machine and the entire house becomes filled to overflowing with dads. With the help of dad one, Sue and her brother reverse the machine and all the dads disappear except for dads one and two, who decide to move next door. Written in a whimsical style reminiscent of *The Cat in the Hat* (Seuss), the rhyming text and colorful cartoon illustrations may attract curious readers. Unfortunately, the extensive updates between the first and second editions created a much wordier and less appealing text. ADDITIONAL SELECTION.

   Keywords: Family Relations, Gay Fathers, Lesbian Mothers, Children of Gay Parents.

VALENTINE, JOHNNY. *The Day They Put a Tax on Rainbows and Other Stories.* Illus. by Lynette Schmidt. Boston, MA: Alyson Wonderland, 1992. Unpaged. ISBN: 9781555832018. OCLC #: 27319560. Ages 6–9. FORMAT: Hardcover.

AWARDS: Lambda Literary Award Finalist, LGBT Children's/YA Category, 1993. REVIEWS: LBR.

Valentine's second fairy tale collection introduces readers to magic, treasure, and rainbow families in three stories. The first is about a girl with two fathers and a magic ring. Two fathers also appear in the second story, about three brothers who save a fairy and are led on a quest to find treasure. In the final story, a boy with two mothers outsmarts a vexing king and his tax on rainbows. The collection is lackluster at best and not as strong as Valentine's *The Duke Who Outlawed Jelly Beans and Other Stories,* but the dearth of rainbow families in the traditional literature genre may make this collection appealing to some families. ADDITIONAL SELECTION.

Keywords: Family Relations, Gay Fathers, Lesbian Mothers, Children of Gay Parents, Mermaids, Mermen, Fairy Tales, Dragons, Rainbows.

VALENTINE, JOHNNY. *The Duke Who Outlawed Jelly Beans and Other Stories.* Illus. by Lynette Schmidt. Boston, MA: Alyson Wonderland, 1991. Unpaged. ISBN: 9781555831998. OCLC #: 25059347. Ages 6–9. FORMAT: Hardcover. AWARDS: Lambda Literary Award Finalist, LGBT Children's/YA Category, 1992. REVIEWS: BKLST, HB, SLJ.

Turning traditional fairy tales on their heads and adding a big dose of lesbian mothers, gay fathers, and gender-nonconforming children, Valentine has crafted a collection of five magical tales that are sure to entertain children in rainbow families as well as their friends. The first story is about a frog prince who is kissed by another boy and later adopted by the boy's two fathers. In the second story, a young girl with two mothers wants to be an Eaglerider, which is traditionally a job for boys. With her mothers' help she disguises herself as a boy and becomes the best eagle rider, saving the kingdom from dangerous dragons. The third story follows a boy as he outwits a dragon and collects treasure for his two poor mothers. Lesbian mothers also appear in the fourth tale, in which a small girl is able to outsmart an ogre and save her mother from being his dinner. In the final story, an immature duke takes over a kingdom and makes up nonsensical decrees. One of the decrees is that children in nontraditional families will be thrown into the dungeon. All of the children in the previous stories band together and thwart the duke. This collection, which features detailed illustrations, varies in quality and is in need of tighter editing, but the dearth of rainbow families in the traditional literature genre merits consideration of this book. ADDITIONAL SELECTION.

Keywords: Family Relations, Gay Fathers, Lesbian Mothers, Children of Gay Parents, Fairy Tales, Dragons, Gender Nonconformity.

VALENTINE, JOHNNY. *One Dad, Two Dads, Brown Dad, Blue Dads.* Illus. by Melody Sarecky. Boston, MA: Alyson Wonderland, 1994. Unpaged. ISBN: 9781555832537. OCLC #: 32046745. Ages 3–8. FORMAT: Hardcover. AWARDS: None. REVIEWS: PW, SLJ.

Written in the style of *One Fish, Two Fish, Red Fish, Blue Fish* (Seuss), this short rhyming book features a young African American boy named Lou who describes the many things that his two blue dads can do. The focus is on the fact that they are an unusual color, not gay. Young children will delight in the silliness of the text and bright illustrations, which work well together to convey that whether dads are gay, straight, white, black, or blue they all love their children. Appropriate for rainbow families in both school and public libraries. RECOMMENDED.

Keywords: Family Relations, Gay Fathers, Children of Gay Parents, African Americans, Mixed Race Families.

VALENTINE, JOHNNY. *Two Moms, the Zark, and Me.* Illus. by Angelo Lopez. Boston, MA: Alyson Wonderland, 1993. Unpaged. ISBN: 9781555832360. OCLC #: 29328568. Ages 4–8. FORMAT: Hardcover. AWARDS: None. REVIEWS: BCCB, KS, PW, SLJ.

A young boy is separated from his two mothers at the local zoo and must rely on a magical dinosaur-like creature called a Zark to find his parents. Along the way, he meets a conservative, anti-gay couple that decides the boy should live in a normal family with a mom and dad rather than a two-mom home. The couple attempts to kidnap the boy but he escapes with the Zark's help. Eventually, a gay couple and the Zark assist the boy in locating his mothers. Filled with magical realism, the didactic rhyming text is heavy-handed and imbued with an anti-conservative message that is more appropriate for adults than children. The caricature-style illustrations in subdued tones detract from the text. NOT RECOMMENDED.

Keywords: Adoption, Family Relations, Gay Fathers, Children of Gay Parents, Lesbian Mothers, African Americans, Mixed Race Families, Anti-Gay Sentiment.

VAN DER BEEK, DEBORAH. *Melinda and the Class Photograph.* London, UK: Piccadilly Press, 1991. Unpaged. ISBN: 9781853400650. OCLC #: 22625041. Ages 4–8. FORMAT: Hardcover. AWARDS: None. REVIEWS: None.

Mel, or Melinda to her mother and teacher, prefers her tracksuit and mud to dresses and cleanliness. Then school picture day arrives and Mel's mother forces her to wear a dress. The little piglet will do anything to make sure she is her happy, dirty self — even if it means inviting her muddy, smelly dog into the class photograph. Readers will delight in the charming, bright illustrations that exude Mel's personality and complement the straightforward text, which is perfect for storytime read-alouds. Transgender and gender-variant children will easily identify with Mel's need for everyone to know his name and his true personality. RECOMMENDED.

Keywords: Tomboys, Gender Identity, Gender Nonconformity, Transgender, Individuality, School Relations, Family Relations, Pigs, British Literature, Great Britain.

VIGNA, JUDITH. *My Two Uncles.* Morton Grove, IL: Albert Whitman, 1995. Unpaged. ISBN: 9780807555071. OCLC #: 30783245. Ages 4–8. FORMAT: Hardcover. AWARDS: Cooperative Children's Book Center Choices 1995; Lambda Literary Award Finalist, LGBT Children's/YA Category, 1996. REVIEWS: BKLST, BCCB, SLJ.

Best shared one-on-one with children, this sensitive and realistic title is told from the point of view of Elly, a young girl who is helping her family prepare for her grandparents' 50th anniversary. As part of the festivities, Elly's uncle and his partner help her create a diorama of the grandparents' wedding. Readers learn that the grandfather is uncomfortable with the uncle's sexuality when he refuses to allow them to attend the celebration as a couple. Although things seem to work themselves out, the grandfather does not appear to fully embrace his son's sexuality. The book's message is clearly communicated without being overly didactic and children learn that it is okay to have gay relatives. The soft, watercolor illustrations add a gentleness that complements the narrative, rendering this a worthy choice. RECOMMENDED.

Keywords: Gay Uncles, Gay Relatives, Family Relations.

WALKER, TAMSIN. *Not Ready Yet.* London, UK: Onlywomen Press, 2009. Unpaged. ISBN: 9780906500996. OCLC #: 441632486. Ages 4–8. FORMAT: Paperback. AWARDS: None. REVIEWS: None.

Jay, his mother, and Fran are about to go on holiday to a gay-friendly campground. Every time his mother or Fran asks him to do something Jay is "not ready yet." He would rather be playing with his snails, chasing butterflies, or painting pictures. When it is time to go back home neither Jay, his mother, or Fran are "ready yet." Although the story introduces readers to a lesbian relationship, it is never clear if Fran is Jay's other mother or his mom's girlfriend. The sparse text will not engage young children and the illustrations do little to extend the narrative. NOT RECOMMENDED.

Keywords: Family Relations, Lesbian Mothers, Children of Gay Parents, British Literature, Great Britain, Camping.

WARHOLA, JAMES. *Uncle Andy's Cats.* New York, NY: Putnam, 2009. Unpaged. ISBN: 9780399251801. OCLC #: 245597066. Ages 4–8. FORMAT: Hardcover. AWARDS: Cooperative Children's Book Center Choices 2010. REVIEWS: BKLST, KS, LMC, SLJ.

What happens when your house is overflowing with 25 cats named Sam and one named Hester? This whimsical story describes just that when Uncle Andy (Warhol) and Grandma Bubba find themselves with a few too many cats. In an effort to give some of them away, the duo paint portraits of the cats, print them, and create two books: *25 Cats Name Sam and One Blue Pussy* and *Holy Cats.* The books' success brings a long line of people wanting their own Sams. Eventually, all the Sams are gone except for the original one, and Hester. Uncle Andy and Grandma finally have their house back. Although the book does not explicitly mention Uncle Andy's sexuality, it can still offer a gay role model for all children. ADDITIONAL SELECTION.

Keywords: Artists, Family Relations, Gay Role Models, Gay Uncles, Gay Relatives, Individuality, Andy Warhol.

WATSON, KATY. *Spacegirl Pukes.* Illus. by Vanda Carter. London, UK: Onlywomen Press, 2005. Unpaged. ISBN: 9780906500873. OCLC #: 156805455. Ages 4–8. FORMAT: Paperback. AWARDS: None. REVIEWS: None.

Just as Spacegirl is about to blast off in her rocket ship, she pukes all over her space-suit. Her two mothers clean her up and take her home for bed rest. Unfortunately, both Mummy Loula and Mummy Neenee become ill too and the entire family is confined to the bed. Eventually, Spacegirl and her moms feel better and she is able to soar into space. Although the narrative lacks development, children are likely to relish the gross factor. Likewise, Carter's uneven cartoon illustrations are filled with piles of puke and green-gilled characters that will attract readers but are poorly executed. With many high-quality titles about lesbian mothers available, libraries may want to leave this one orbiting. NOT RECOMMENDED.

Keywords: Family Relations, Lesbian Mothers, Children of Gay Parents, British Literature, Great Britain, Mixed Race Families.

WEEKS, SARAH. *Red Ribbon.* Illus. by Jeffrey Greene. New York, NY: Laura Geringer Book/HarperCollins, 1995. Unpaged. ISBN: 9780060254308. OCLC #: 33879715. Ages 5–8. FORMAT: Hardcover. AWARDS: None. REVIEWS: KS, PW, SLJ.

Eight-year-old Jenny has an upstairs neighbor who is infected with AIDS, which has made him "get so old so fast." Jenny's mother gives her a red ribbon and tells her that she should wear the ribbon to remember people with AIDS. Throughout the rhyming text, Jenny wonders about her neighbor and discovers from her mother that he is getting sicker and sicker. Although the character is never identified as gay, the fact that he is a young man and that the book was written in the 1990s suggests that he is probably meant to be a gay man. While the author had good intentions, the book leaves readers with more questions than answers about AIDS. NOT RECOMMENDED.

Keywords: Family Relations, Gay Neighbors, Death, AIDS, Red Ribbon.

WICKENS, ELAINE. *Anna Day and the O-Ring.* Boston, MA: Alyson Wonderland, 1994. Unpaged. ISBN: 9781555832520. OCLC #: 31525072. Ages 5–8. FORMAT: Paperback. AWARDS: None. REVIEWS: PW, SLJ.

It is almost time for Evan's fourth birthday and his mothers have bought him a tent. Mama Gee reads the directions and realizes the tent is missing the O-ring that is needed for support. Evan looks everywhere and finally finds it under the family's dog, Anna Day. He goes to school on Monday and tells everyone about the missing O-ring. Although the text is simple, it will not hold the attention of young children, and the photographs of the rainbow family are dated. NOT RECOMMENDED.

Keywords: Children of Gay Parents, Lesbian Mothers, Dogs, Birthdays.

WILD, MARGARET. *Mr. Moo.* Illus. by Jonathan Bentley. Sydney, New South Wales (Australia): ABC Books for the Australian Broadcasting Corporation, 2002. Unpaged. ISBN: 9780733307836. OCLC #: 223138367. Ages 3–7. FORMAT: Hardcover. AWARDS: None. REVIEWS: None.

Mr. Moo has a comfortable life with a nice house, kind neighbors, and even his own island. Unfortunately, Mr. Moo has no one to keep him company and he is very lonely. One day a duck named Jimmy Johnson appears and asks to borrow Mr.

Moo's boat so he can go see the world. Jimmy doesn't get too far before the boat sinks and he moves in with Mr. Moo to work on the boat. Finally Mr. Moo has the special companion and bond that he's always wanted. The easy-to-read text is perfect for beginning readers and the bright, cartoon illustrations are sure to hold the attention of the youngest children. The story is simple, but the positive same-sex relationship will not be lost on rainbow families. RECOMMENDED.

Keywords: Gay Men, Australian Literature, Australia, Easy-to-Read Books, Cows, Ducks.

WILLHOITE, MICHAEL. *Daddy's Roommate.* Boston, MA: Alyson Wonderland, 1990. Unpaged. ISBN: 9781555831783. OCLC #: 22274777. Ages 4–8. FORMAT: Hardcover. AWARDS: Lambda Literary Award Finalist, Gay Men's Small Press, 1991. REVIEWS: BL, BCCB, LBR, PW, SLJ.

One of the most challenged, burned, banned, defaced, and stolen children's books in the United States, this simple, well-meaning picture book, in the same way as *Heather Has Two Mommies* (Newman), is virtually synonymous with the term gay picture book for most teachers and librarians. The first U.S. children's storybook to profile a gay (male) family in a positive light, Willhoite's cult classic helped to blaze a trail in LGBTQ children's publishing. Using a simple, accessible narrative and cartoon illustrations, this unassuming book introduces a boy who tells readers that his parents divorced and then his daddy's roommate moved in. Readers understand that gay couples are normal and that gay parents love their children. While not the most captivating title, the book is uplifting and supportive of rainbow families. RECOMMENDED.

Keywords: Family Relations, Gay Fathers, Children of Gay Parents, Divorced Parents.

WILLHOITE, MICHAEL. *Daddy's Wedding.* Los Angeles, CA: Alyson Wonderland, 1996. Unpaged. ISBN: 9781555833503. OCLC #: 33441771. Ages 4–8. FORMAT: Hardcover. AWARDS: Lambda Literary Award Finalist, LGBT Children's/YA Category, 1997. REVIEWS: BCCB, BKLST, KS, PW.

It has taken six years but in this sequel to *Daddy's Roommate*, Nick's dad finally decides to marry his partner, Frank. He and Frank announce their intentions to Nick and Nick's mother and stepfather at a family picnic. They greet the news with joy, plus a trite comment by mother about June weddings being perfect. The wedding preparations are uneventful at best and the commitment ceremony is lackluster. The only action in the story is when Clancy the dog decides to take a bite out of the cake. Afterward, the reception ends, Dads go on honeymoon, and Nick goes to baseball camp. The cartoon illustrations, reminiscent of "Family Circus," add little to the story. In his attempt to normalize gay marriage, Willhoite has managed to create a snooze of a day that will elicit yawns before the rings have been exchanged. ADDITIONAL SELECTION.

Keywords: Family Relations, Gay Fathers, Children of Gay Parents, Gay Marriage, Weddings, Stepparents.

WILLHOITE, MICHAEL. *The Entertainer: A Story in Pictures.* Boston, MA: Alyson Wonderland, 1992. Unpaged. ISBN: 9781555832025. OCLC #: 26604678. Ages 4–8. FORMAT: Paperback. AWARDS: None. REVIEWS: None.

A boy says goodbye to his two mothers and goes to the park to juggle. A talent agent spots the boy and promises him fame and fortune. The boy does become a star, and his mothers make occasional visits to his performances, but he soon realizes that he misses being with his family and friends. Told completely without words, this graphic novel positively portrays a rainbow family and, considering the renewed interest in wordless books and graphic novels for children, would be a good addition to school and public library collections. RECOMMENDED.

 Keywords: Family Relations, Lesbian Mothers, Children of Gay Parents, Graphic Novels, Wordless Books, Juggling, Individuality.

WILLHOITE, MICHAEL. *Uncle What-Is-It Is Coming to Visit!!* Boston, MA: Alyson Wonderland, 1993. Unpaged. ISBN: 9781555832056. OCLC #: 28659191. Ages 5–8. FORMAT: Hardcover. AWARDS: Lambda Literary Award Finalist, LGBT Children's/YA Category, 1994. REVIEWS: KS, PW, SLJ.

Nine-year-old Igor and his younger sister Tiffany are in for a big surprise! Uncle Brett is coming to visit and they've just discovered from their mother that he's gay. The siblings aren't quite sure what "gay" means so they ask two neighborhood bullies, who explain that gay men are either drag queens or leathermen. The children are terrified about their uncle as they aren't sure "what" is going to come through the door. When Uncle Brett arrives, he's just a preppy gay man in a polo and khakis, but the children love him. Although the intent of the book is to promote acceptance and to dissolve gay stereotypes, the end result may actually be the perpetuation of homophobia. In addition, gender stereotyping abounds and the cartoon illustrations are sure to offend almost everyone. NOT RECOMMENDED.

 Keywords: Family Relations, Gay Uncles, Gay Relatives, Homophobia, Gay Stereotypes, Cross-Dressing, Leathermen, Drag Queens.

WILLIAMS, VERA B. *Three Days on a River in a Red Canoe.* New York, NY: William Morrow, 1981. Unpaged. ISBN: 9780688040727. OCLC #: 740521043. Ages 4–8. FORMAT: Hardcover. AWARDS: Reading Rainbow Feature Selection. REVIEWS: BKLST, HB, KS, SLJ.

In this journal-style picture book, a young girl describes a three-day canoeing and camping trip that she takes with her Mom, Aunt Rosie, and cousin Sam. The accessible text introduces readers to various elements of camping such as how to put up a tent, make a knot, and cook appropriate food. Interspersed throughout the text are safety instructions for canoeing and soft colored-pencil illustrations depicting the adventures of the close-knit family. The book does not explicitly denote that Mom and Aunt Rosie are a couple, but more astute readers such as lesbian mothers and children in rainbow families will read between the lines and identify with the family presented. Librarian K.T. Horning mentions that this book was a personal favorite of lesbian mothers in her library (personal communication). HIGHLY RECOMMENDED.

Keywords: Camping, Canoeing, Family Relations, Lesbian Mothers, Children of Gay Parents, Aunts.

WILSON, ANNA. *Want Toast.* Illus. by Vanda Carter. London, UK: Onlywomen Press, 2009. Unpaged. ISBN: 9780956105301. OCLC #: 619959990. Ages 4–8. FORMAT: Paperback. AWARDS: None. REVIEWS: None.

Ruth wakes up and wants breakfast. However, the young girl must first get her two mothers out of bed so they can fix her toast. After several unsuccessful attempts and promises of a tree house and chocolate biscuits for afternoon tea if the girl lets her mothers sleep, Ruth trudges downstairs by herself to get yogurt out of the fridge. As she reaches inside, her chair breaks and she falls to the floor along with the contents of the fridge. The story ends with her wondering what type of tree house her mothers will build her. While the text leaves many issues unresolved, the illustrations successfully convey the young girl's varied emotions. Unfortunately, the inadequate resolution and depictions of semi-nude mothers may limit the audience of the book. NOT RECOMMENDED.

Keywords: Family Relations, Lesbian Mothers, Children of Gay Parents, Asian Americans, British Literature, Great Britain.

WINTHROP, ELIZABETH. *Tough Eddie.* Illus. by Lillian Hoban. New York, NY: E. P. Dutton, 1985. Unpaged. ISBN: 9780525441649. OCLC #: 10997393. Ages 4–8. FORMAT: Hardcover. AWARDS: None. REVIEWS: SLJ.

Eddie loves playing with his group of friends, making spaceships out of blocks and playing cops and robbers. However, Eddie has a secret! At home he likes to play with his dollhouse, which is filled with furniture his father helped him make. One day when he is annoying his older sister, she tells Eddie's friends that he has a dollhouse in his closet. Embarrassed, Eddie hits his sister and his friends have to go home. The next day at school they tease him until he proves how tough he is by braving a bee that has landed on his nose. The book ends with Eddie thinking he might bring his dollhouse to school for show-and-tell. While the book sends the message that it's okay for boys to like dolls, it also muddles it by forcing Eddie to prove his toughness to his peers. A better choice for libraries would be *William's Doll* (Zolotow) or *Time to Get Up, Time to Go* (Milgrim). ADDITIONAL SELECTION.

Keywords: Gender Identity, Gender Nonconformity, Teasing, Individuality, Dolls, School Relations, Sex Roles.

WURST, THOMAS SCOTT. *Pearl's Christmas Present.* Seattle, WA: Pearl and Dotty Press, 2004. Unpaged. ISBN: 9780977244102. OCLC #: 224184198. Ages 9–13. FORMAT: Hardcover. AWARDS: None. REVIEWS: None.

Thomas, nicknamed Pearl by his brothers and sisters because he likes to dress up in girl's clothing, prefers Barbie dolls, makeup, and high heels to traditional boys' toys. In this slice-of-life picture book, the boy describes a Christmas when he dresses up in a tree skirt and wears his sister's heels. Later the family goes to visit "Santy Claus" and his parents tell Pearl not to embarrass them by asking for a doll. Instead, the boy tells Santa that he wants to grow up to be a clown driving an ice cream truck and throwing candy sprinkles — though he would really like to be a Rockette. Although packaged as a book for younger children, the writing style is more appropriate for older students and will spark discussion from the opening line: "When I was a little boy I wanted to be a girl." Gender-variant and transgender children will identify with Pearl but the book is not as successful at portraying a transgender character as *10,000 Dresses* (Ewert). ADDITIONAL SELECTION.

Keywords: Gender Nonconformity, Gender Identity, Individuality, Transgender, Sex Roles, Cross-Dressing, Family Relations, Christmas.

YOLEN, JANE, AND HEIDI E. Y. STEMPLE. *Not All Princesses Dress in Pink.* Illus. by Anne-Sophie Lanquetin. New York, NY: Simon & Schuster, 2010. Unpaged. ISBN: 9781416980186. OCLC #: 258767950. Ages 4–8. FORMAT: Hardcover. AWARDS: None. REVIEWS: KS, LMC, PW, SLJ.

Readers beware, these are not your mother's princesses — they are a hundred times better! Rather than sitting around in frilly pink dresses and expensive shoes, these princesses would rather be in pants or shorts playing ball, rolling in the mud, wielding power tools, driving dump trucks, riding bikes, and fighting knights. But of course, they are princesses and they do wear sparkly crowns! The accessible, rhyming narrative is accompanied by vibrant images that extend the text and depict contemporary princesses in a variety of hands-on activities. Perfect for school and public libraries and all girls. RECOMMENDED.

Keywords: Princesses, Gender Identity, Gender Roles, Sex Roles.

ZOLOTOW, CHARLOTTE. *William's Doll.* Illus. by William Pène du Bois. New York, NY: Harper and Row, 1972. 32p. ISBN: 9780060270476. OCLC #: 347798. Ages 3–8. FORMAT: Hardcover. AWARDS: Best Books of 1972, *School Library Journal*; American Library Association Notable Children's Books 1971–1975; Outstanding Children's Books of 1972, *New York Times.* REVIEWS: BCCB, HB, KS, SLJ.

In this children's literature classic, a little boy named William wants a doll of his very own to cradle and love. However, his brother and the next-door neighbor think he's a creep and a sissy for wanting a doll. William's father insists on buying him a basketball and a train, which William likes but not as much as he would a doll. Eventually, the boy's grandmother comes to visit and buys him a doll so he can practice being a father. The easy-to-read narrative and soft, soothing illustrations mark this as a suitable read-aloud for young children. This timely book is just as relevant today as it was more than forty years ago and provides both a mirror and window for children into the world of a gender-nonconforming child. Appropriate for both school and public libraries. HIGHLY RECOMMENDED.

Keywords: Gender Identity, Gender Nonconformity, Individuality, Dolls, Family Relations, Sex Roles.

CHAPTER 7

Chapter Books

$\mathcal{T}$his chapter includes more than thirty chapter books for elementary-aged children (up to fifth grade) that depict same-sex parents, queer relatives, nontraditional families, gender-variant children, and other queer characters and situations. These books include titles published in the United States as well as titles from Australia and the United Kingdom. Books for older children and young adults in grades 6 and up are not included, as numerous other resources recommend LGBTQ books for these age groups. A few titles were on the cusp of this demarcation and it was decided to omit those that dealt with dating or with children in sixth grade or above, and those did not have child characters. For additional information on these entries, see p. 85.

AGELL, CHARLOTTE. *The Accidental Adventures of India McAllister.* New York, NY: Henry Holt, 2010. 152p. ISBN: 9780805089028. OCLC #: 383808831. Ages 8–10. FORMAT: Hardcover. AWARDS: Rainbow List 2011. REVIEWS: BKLST, BCCB, KS, PW, SLJ.

Fourth-grader India McAllister longs for a life full of adventure in this first book in a promised series. Ranging from mildly interesting to exciting, India's adventures include a bout of best friend jealousy and betrayal and nearly seeing a UFO while lost in the Maine woods during a freak snowstorm. An adopted child from China, India lives with her recently divorced mother, a breast cancer survivor, and visits her father and his boyfriend on weekends. Her day-to-day life is peppered with her matter-of-fact musings about love and the pursuit of happiness that elementary-aged readers will easily understand. Line drawings accompany the accessible narrative and extend the book's reach to reluctant readers. India's initial uncertainties about her father's new boyfriend are handled realistically, exhibiting a young child's concern over her parents' divorce and the potential new parental figure in her life. Similar to realistic books with well-loved characters such as Judy Moody, Amber Brown, Junie B. Jones, and Ramona Quimby, India's slice-of-life stories will ring true with all children, particularly those from nontraditional families. RECOMMENDED.

Keywords: Adoption, Gay Fathers, Children of Gay Parents, Family Relations, Divorce, Cancer Survivors, Chinese Americans, Single Parents, Individuality, School Relations.

APPELT, KATHI. Keeper. Illus. by August Hall. New York, NY: Atheneum, 2010. 339p. ISBN: 9781416950608. OCLC #: 419813534. Ages 9–12. FORMAT: Hardcover. AWARDS: Cooperative Children's Book Center Choices 2011; Notable Children's Books in the English Language Arts 2011, National Council of Teachers of English Children's Literature Assembly, United States. REVIEWS: BKLST, HB, KS, LMC, PW, SLJ.

Ten-year-old Keeper is not your average girl. For one thing her mother is a mermaid, which means she can hear crabs talking. And it is those talking crabs that get Keeper (and her best dog ever, BD) into a world of trouble. Keeper sets off on a moonlit boat trip in search of her mother, who she hopes will make everything right again. Although this is the major plot of the story, Appelt weaves in several different narratives: one about the old fisherman next door and his long-lost love (a merman), one about the caregiver Signe who took over Keeper's care after the girl's mother deserted her as a toddler, one about a wayward seagull who has an unusual relationship with BD, and one about a war veteran named Dogie who is in love with Signe. While the stories may be a little too divergent for younger or reluctant readers, they are skillfully united in a satisfying conclusion that more-sophisticated readers will enjoy. Gay boys or children with gay fathers will particularly like the story about the romance between the fisherman and merman. Librarians might want to pair this book with *Caleb's Friend* (Nones) for another magical tale about a tender relationship between a boy and a young merman. RECOMMENDED.

Keywords: Adoption, Family Relations, Single Parents, Individuality, Friendship, Mermaids, Mermen, Homosexuality, Fishermen, Magic.

BAUER, A. C. E. *No Castles Here.* New York, NY: Yearling/Random House, 2007. 270p. ISBN: 9780375839214. OCLC #: 70836627. Ages 9–12. FORMAT: Hardcover. AWARDS: Rainbow List 2009. REVIEWS: BKLST, KS, SLJ.

Eleven-year-old Augie Boretski is invisible — at least he tries to be in order to escape the gangs, bullies, and drug dealings that surround the rundown apartment he shares with his hard-working mother in Camden, New Jersey. As one of the few white kids in his predominantly African American neighborhood, the sixth-grader often finds it hard to blend in. The fact that his mother sets him up with a Big Brother who is gay and drives a flashy truck does not improve his invisibility status or endear him to the classroom bullies. His luck changes the day he accidentally steals an old green book of fairy tales from a local book shop. Imbued with a little magic from the shopkeeper, the book's tales — along with the courage imparted by his gay Big Brother — empower Augie to take on his bullies and to initiate plans to save his school, which is condemned after a winter storm wreaks havoc on the building. Containing elements of both realistic fiction and fantasy, the timely narrative addresses many sensitive topics and is one of the few novels for middle elementary school children that portrays a gay male adult in an empowering relationship with a child. Suitable for both public and school libraries. RECOMMENDED.

Keywords: Family Relations, Bullying, Gay Role Models, Single Parents, School Relations.

BURCH, CHRISTIAN. *Hit the Road, Manny.* New York, NY: Atheneum, 2008. 233p. ISBN: 9781416928126. OCLC #: 181516693. Ages 8–12. FORMAT: Hardcover. AWARDS: Lambda Literary Award Finalist, LGBT Children's/YA Category, 2008. REVIEWS: BKLST, KS.

The entire Dalinger family — Mom, Dad, Keats, Lulu, India, Belly, Uncle Max, DecapiTina, and the manny — is back in full force in the sequel to *The Manny Files*, and they are about embark on one unforgettable road trip! From *Glamour* Dos and Don'ts to outlaw mothers to old lady décolletage and projectile pool puke, the novel is filled with just the right amount of humor to offset the serious secondary plot as the manny visits his parents and longs for acceptance of his new partner, Uncle Max. Told from Keats's point of view, the narrative includes a believable amount of childhood naiveté about adult situations and ends with a whizz-bang wedding in Las Vegas. Although the narrative is not quite as tight as the first book in the series, this latest offering does promote acceptance and understanding of individuality, homosexuality, and gay marriage. RECOMMENDED.

Keywords: Family Relations, Gay Role Models, Gay Uncles, Gender Identity, Gender Nonconformity, Sex Roles, Gay Marriage, Vacations, Parents of Gay Children, Nannies.

BURCH, CHRISTIAN. *The Manny Files.* New York, NY: Atheneum, 2006. 296p. ISBN: 9781416900399. OCLC #: 57193443. Ages 8–12. FORMAT: Hardcover. AWARDS: Best Children's Books of the Year, 1999, Bank Street College of Education, United States; Lambda Literary Award Finalist, LGBT Children's/ YA Category, 2006; Rainbow List 2008; Stonewall Book Award, Honor Book, 2007. REVIEWS: BKLST, KS, LMC, SLJ.

Third-grader Keats Dalinger's life is about to become interesting with the introduction of the family's new babysitter. In the past, Keats and his three sisters have had babysitters who were generally much more interested in Keats's sisters than in the witty, vertically challenged, lone boy of the family. However, the new babysitter is a man — a manny — and an extremely funny, creative, caring, and lively one at that! Readers follow the daily antics of the manny as he works his way into the hearts of each member of the family including Grandma and Uncle Max. Particularly powerful is the background development of a love interest between the manny and Uncle Max. As the story is from Keats's point of view, readers receive subtle hints about the relationship but suspicions are not confirmed until the final kiss on the last page. The storytelling is not didactic and Burch's portrayal of a child's fascination with a male caregiver is right on target. Libraries seeking a light-hearted portrayal of a rainbow family will find a winner here. HIGHLY RECOMMENDED.

Keywords: Family Relations, Bullying, Gay Role Models, Gay Uncles, School Relations, Gender Identity, Gender Nonconformity, Sex Roles, Nannies.

COVILLE, BRUCE. *The Skull of Truth.* Illus. by Gary A. Lippincott. Orlando, FL: Harcourt, 1997. 195p. ISBN: 9780152754570. OCLC #: 36511556. Ages 8–12. FORMAT: Hardcover. AWARDS: Society of School Librarians International Book Awards, 1998. REVIEWS: BKLST, SLJ. Note: This is the third book in the Magic Shop series.

A talking skull that casts truth spells on the unsuspecting — that is what sixth-grader Charlie stole from a magic shop during his effort to escape from a group of bullies. Unfortunately for the boy, the skull is that of Hamlet's cursed court jester and anyone who possesses it is also cursed to tell the truth. Soon not only is Charlie telling the truth but so is his entire family. Hilarity and drama ensue as Charlie's Uncle Bennie comes out of the closet, his father's previous marriage is discovered, and Gramma Ethel gives everyone a piece of her mind. However, Coville turns serious when Charlie makes a hurtful remark to a classmate with cancer. Action-packed and quick-witted, the narrative demonstrates the consequences of lying (and telling the absolute truth) and positively portrays a gay relative and his struggle to be out to his family. RECOMMENDED.

Keywords: Family Relations, Bullying, Gay Uncles, Gay Relatives, School Relations, Cancer, Honesty, Magic, Librarians, Storytelling.

COVILLE, BRUCE. *Thor's Wedding Day.* Illus. by Matthew Cogswell. Orlando, FL: Harcourt, 2005. 137p. ISBN: 9780152014551. OCLC #: 57465446. Ages 8–12. FORMAT: Hardcover. AWARDS: Best Children's Books of the Year, 2005, Bank Street College of Education, United States. REVIEWS: BKLST, BCCB, KS, SLJ, PW.

Like the Percy Jackson series, Coville's tale involves a quest, a stolen magical weapon, and numerous hi-jinks. Based on the Norse poem "Thrymskvitha," the humorous narrative, told from the point of view of Thialfi the goat-herder, describes how Thor's magic hammer is stolen and a quest must be made to find it before all heck breaks loose when god Thrym discovers that the goddess he thinks he is marrying is actually a man in drag. This book has several problems for both females and gender-variant children. First, comments in the book objectify women asserting that goddesses have nice "buzzums," which is the only reason anyone would want to marry them. Similarly, the gods Thor and Loki, along with Thialfi, must denigrate themselves by dressing in women's clothing. Neither of these situations supports females or gender-variant children, and each serves to perpetuate stereotypes persistent throughout society. NOT RECOMMENDED.

Keywords: Quests, Gods, Cross-Dressing, Norse Mythology.

DEPAOLA, TOMIE. *Here We All Are.* New York, NY: Putnam, 2000. 71p. ISBN: 9780399234965. OCLC #: 42641624. Ages 6–10. FORMAT: Hardcover. AWARDS:

Cooperative Children's Book Center Choices 2001. REVIEWS: BKLST, BCCB, HB, KS, PW, SLJ.

In the second book in the 26 Fairmount Avenue series, readers follow young Tomie's kindergarten exploits and his budding interest in performance as he begins Miss Leah's dancing school. Stagestruck Tomie loves dancing and acting and "steals the show" in a school play in which he plays the bunny Flopsy from *Peter Rabbit*. Readers also learn about various members of his family including his aunts, uncles, grandparents, and his new baby sister. As in the first book, there are elements of the story that will appeal to gender-variant children, particularly boys: Tomie's best friends are girls, he idolizes Mae West and Shirley Temple, and he loves dancing. HIGHLY RECOMMENDED.

Keywords: Artists, Tomie dePaola, Biographies, Gender Nonconformity, Dance, Family Relations, Individuality, School Relations.

DEPAOLA, TOMIE. *On My Way.* New York, NY: Putnam, 2001. 73p. ISBN: 9780399235832. OCLC #: 44267980. Ages 6–10. FORMAT: Hardcover. AWARDS: Notable Social Studies Trade Books for Young People 2002. REVIEWS: BKLST, BCCB, HB, KS, PW, SLJ.

In the third book in the 26 Fairmount Avenue series, Tomie finishes kindergarten and begins first grade, where he learns to read and gets his first library card. He performs in his first dance recital, attends the 1939 World's Fair, and goes with his family to the beach. As in the other books in the series, elements of the story will appeal to gender-variant children (particularly boys): he wants to be a dancing star like Shirley Temple, he dresses up as a bride in a Tiny Tot wedding, and his best friends are girls. HIGHLY RECOMMENDED.

Keywords: Artists, Tomie dePaola, Biographies, Gender Nonconformity, Dance, Family Relations, Individuality, School Relations.

DEPAOLA, TOMIE. *26 Fairmount Avenue.* New York, NY: Putnam, 1999. 56p. ISBN: 9780399232466. OCLC #: 38550527. Ages 6–10. FORMAT: Hardcover. AWARDS: American Library Association Notable Children's Book 2000; ABC Children's Booksellers Choices Award, 2000; Cooperative Children's Book Center Choices 2000; Best Children's Books of the Year, 2000, Bank Street College of Education, United States; Newbery Honor, 2000. REVIEWS: BKLST, BCCB, HB, KS, PW, SLJ. Note: Although this series of books is autobiographical, I am including them in the chapter book section as they are all beginning chapter books and are more accessible to readers in a chapter book collection. And many of dePaola's picture books, which cover some of the topics covered in this series, are classified as fiction.

In the first installment in the 26 Fairmount Avenue series, readers are introduced to precocious young kindergartner Tomie, who loves to draw and paint and really wants to learn to read. Upon discovering that he won't learn to read until first grade, he immediately leaves school, stating he'll be back in a year. Tomie also describes the dramatic process of building their family home at 26 Fairmount Avenue, and readers learn that he has a penchant for Shirley Temple and Miss Mae West. One of the most endearing scenes is when he goes to the theatre to see the debut of Walt Disney's *Snow White and the Seven Dwarves*, which he greatly dislikes because Mr. Disney mixed things up to create a film that was nothing like the book! Gender-variant children will appreciate that Tomie has "nontraditional" boy interests such as Shirley Temple and Snow White. HIGHLY RECOMMENDED.

   Keywords: Artists, Tomie dePaola, Biographies, Gender Nonconformity, Family Relations, Individuality, School Relations.

DEPAOLA, TOMIE. *What a Year!* New York, NY: Putnam, 2002. 75p. ISBN: 9780399237973. OCLC #: 46785132. Ages 6–10. FORMAT: Hardcover. AWARDS: Cooperative Children's Book Center Choices 2003. REVIEWS: BKLST, BCCB, HB, KS, SLJ.

Tomie has a very exciting and eventful year filled with birthday, Halloween, Thanksgiving, and Christmas surprises, not to mention a case of chicken pox, in this fourth volume in the 26 Fairmount Avenue series. All of his relatives are back in full force, radiating unconditional love for the bubbly boy. For Christmas, he receives his first diary, in which he captured many of the childhood moments that he relates in this series. DePaola's upbeat text and cheerful illustrations complement each other perfectly and give readers a window into an amazing year in the author's life. Elements that will appeal to gender-variant and gay children (particularly boys) include dressing up as Snow White for Halloween, being excited about receiving a Ginger Rogers token, and idolizing Shirley Temple. HIGHLY RECOMMENDED.

   Keywords: Artists, Tomie dePaola, Biographies, Gender Nonconformity, Dance, Family Relations, Individuality, School Relations.

DEPAOLA, TOMIE. *Why.* New York, NY: Putnam, 2007. 87p. ISBN: 9780399246920. OCLC #: 66527098. Ages 7–10. FORMAT: Hardcover. AWARDS: Best Children's Books of the Year, 2008, Bank Street College of Education, United States; Notable Social Studies Trade Books for Young People 2008. REVIEWS: BKLST, KS, SLJ.

In the seventh volume in the 26 Fairmount Avenue series and third in The War Years subseries, Tomie struggles with the ultimate question that children ask about war: why? Readers learn about the food rations and scarcity of various products during the war as well as the numerous ways in which the country showed patriotism. The ending of the book is a little more somber than others in the series because Tomie's cousin is killed. DePaola's attention to children's sensitivities when dealing with social topics is commendable, along with his ability to convey humor during this scary period of U.S. history. Tomie loves making and playing with paper dolls, is excited about receiving a hula skirt from his cousin, and enjoys looking at all the beautiful displays of dolls at the department store. Note: Although the fifth and sixth books of this series are not covered in this chapter, they continue to follow Tomie's exploits at schools as well as his budding dance and artistic abilities. They are not described here because they did not add anything extra for gender-variant children that was not already profiled. HIGHLY RECOMMENDED.

Keywords: Artists, Tomie dePaola, Biographies, Gender Nonconformity, Dance, Family Relations, Individuality, School Relations, World War II.

FERRO, URSULA. *Mother's Day on Martha's Vineyard.* Illus. by Ruth Adams. West Tisbury, MA: Marti Books, 2007. 88p. ISBN: 9780976600626. OCLC #: 173643211. Ages 6–9. FORMAT: Paperback. AWARDS: None. REVIEWS: None. Available at http://www.martibooks.com/.

Eight-year-old Rachel returns with her cats and rainbow family in this third book in the Kids and Families Together series that highlights a trip to Martha's Vineyard. Rachel and her brother purchase Mother's Day gifts for their grandmother and two mothers from a local thrift store. Then they join the rest of the family for several days of fun, including a visit from a skunk! Like the other books in this series, this title can stand alone. The narrative is straightforward and the cartoon illustrations add just the right amount of charm. Although there may not be enough action for this book to be a read-aloud, early readers will appreciate its simplicity. RECOMMENDED.

Keywords: Children of Gay Parents, Family Relations, Lesbian Mothers, Cats, Pets, Self-Published Literature, Mother's Day, Grandparents.

FERRO, URSULA. *A Pet of My Own.* Illus. by Ruth Adams. West Tisbury, MA: Marti Books, 2008. 119p. ISBN: 9780976600633. OCLC #: 648131457. Ages 6–9. FORMAT: Paperback. AWARDS: None. REVIEWS: None. Available at http://www.martibooks.com/.

Unlike other books in the Kids and Families Together series, this fourth install-ment focuses solely on Rachel's friend Gabe, his two dads, and his new baby sister. Gabe wants a pet of his own, but because his family's apartment is small, he is only allowed to pet-sit other people's animals. Soon his fathers adopt a new baby, Ruth. At first Gabe is excited to have Ruth around, but after her novelty wears off he wants a pet again. He resumes pet-sitting only to discover that Ruth is allergic to furry pets. His Uncle Mark saves the day by introducing Gabe to a pet snake. Slightly longer than the other books in the series, this title has a more developed plot and wide appeal for all children who have ever wanted a pet. The positive portrayal of rainbow families is certainly the selling point of this early chapter book series. RECOMMENDED.

Keywords: Children of Gay Parents, Family Relations, Gay Fathers, Adoption, Interracial Parents, Jews, Jewish Holidays, Babies, New Siblings, Pets, Pet Allergies, Snakes, Self-Published Literature.

FERRO, URSULA. *Tanny's Meow.* Illus. by Ariella Huff. West Tisbury, MA: Marti Books, 2005. 51p. ISBN: 9780976600602. OCLC #: 60460742. Ages 6–9. FORMAT: Paperback. AWARDS: None. REVIEWS: None. Available at http://www.martibooks.com/.

When she arrives home from her new school, first-grader Rachel is surprised to find a new addition to her family in the mudroom. While she was cleaning out the tool shed at their new house, Rachel's Mama Mariah had found a half-starved kitten. Rachel is excited about the new kitten, as are her younger brother Tim and her other mother Mommy Ginny. The family decides to keep the new kitten, which they name Tanny, and Rachel becomes responsible for caring for it. The main conflict of this beginning chapter book is that Tanny will not meow, although eventually the kitten does surprise Rachel with a meow on Christmas Day. Ferro's affection for felines shines through the simple narrative that is sure to attract early readers, particularly cat aficionados. This first title in the Kids and Families Together series would be a solid addition to a library collection and portrays not only lesbian mothers but also gay dads. One unfortunate drawback is the occasional crude pencil sketch that detracts from the overall quality of the book. This is the only book in the series to use this illustrator; the other three volumes have cheerful, kid-friendly illustrations by Ruth Adams and are much smaller in size, taking on the format of a typical early chapter book. RECOMMENDED.

Keywords: Children of Gay Parents, Family Relations, Gay Neighbors, Lesbian Mothers, Gay Fathers, Cats, Pets, Self-Published Literature.

FERRO, URSULA. *Wishing for Kittens.* Illus. by Ruth Adams. West Tisbury, MA: Marti Books, 2006. 89p. ISBN: 9780976600619. OCLC #: 232660488. Ages 7–10. FORMAT: Paperback. AWARDS: None. REVIEWS: None. Available at http://www.martibooks.com/.

In this second book in the Kids and Families Together series, Rachel really wants her cat Tanny to have kittens, although the vet suggests that Tanny be spayed. Together with her best friend Susie, Rachel devises a plan to allow Tanny to have one litter before being spayed. The girl gets helpful advice from the vet and a few library books on how to take care of a pregnant cat and her newborn kittens. The straightforward narrative is good for children transitioning into chapter books, although some parents may object to the detailed description of the kittens' birth. The fact that Rachel has two mothers and that two of her friends have two dads is naturally integrated into the narrative and a non-issue. Cat aficionados will appreciate the detailed information at the back of the book relating to cat care. RECOMMENDED.

Keywords: Children of Gay Parents, Family Relations, Lesbian Mothers, Gay Fathers, Cats, Pets, Self-Published Literature, Pregnancy.

FINE, ANNE. *Bill's New Frock.* Illus. by Philippe Dupasquier. London (UK): Methuen, 1989. 96p. ISBN: 9780416121520. OCLC #: 17981788. Ages 6–10. FORMAT: Hardcover. AWARDS: Smarties Award (UK), 1990; Nottinghamshire Book Award (UK), 1990; Highly Commended, Carnegie Medal (UK), 1990. REVIEWS: None. Positive review included in the UK review publication *Books for Keeps.*

When Bill wakes up on Monday morning, he discovers that he's a girl! Before this new revelation can sink in, Bill's mother rushes in and ushers him into a frilly pink dress and sends him to school. Bill quickly learns that expectations are quite different for girls, and he's not sure he agrees with them. Because of his frilly pink dress, he can't move furniture, has lame lines in a reader's theatre, and is expected to be nice, quiet, and pretty. Finally he's had enough of the unequal treatment and tries to speak up for girls but finds obstacles at every turn. When a bully whistles at him on his way home, Bill knocks him down, telling the bully to whistle at dogs, not people. Whereas *Marvin Redpost: Is He a Girl?* (Sachar) reinforces gender stereotypes and that boys and girls really do think and act differently, Fine's offering is much more liberating because Bill learns that society treats boys and girls differently but they really are capable of the same things. This book would be good for all children, particularly gender-variant children. RECOMMENDED.

Keywords: Cross-Dressing, Gender Identity, Gender Nonconformity, British Literature, Great Britain, Family Relations, Sex Role Stereotypes, Individuality, School Relations.

FREEMAN, MARTHA. *The Trouble with Babies.* Illus. by Cat Bowman Smith. New York, NY: Holiday House, 2002. 121p. ISBN: 9780823416981. OCLC #: 48100293. Ages 6–10. FORMAT: Hardcover. AWARDS: None. REVIEWS: BKLST, BCCB, KS, PW, SLJ.

In this sequel to *The Trouble with Cats*, nine-year-old Holly has just moved with her mother, stepfather, and their four cats to a new neighborhood in San Francisco. Her new neighbors include Annie, a girl of Jewish and Chinese heritage, and Xavier, a boy with two gay fathers. Xavier has created a machine that will take the "yucky" off anything — including one of Holly's cats and Annie's baby sister. Throughout this early chapter book, Holly experiences the typical adjustments of moving to a new neighborhood and makes several friends along the way. Although the gay dads receive very little attention in the overall narrative, their sheer presence in an early chapter book is welcome and Holly's reaction to Xavier's dads demonstrates that children really do not care how many mothers or fathers a child has as long as they care for them. The book is a sequel, but children do not have to read the first book in the series to follow the exploits of Holly and her friends. Note: *The Trouble with Cats* does not include Xavier and his gay fathers and is not listed in this chapter, although it would also be a welcome addition to early chapter book collections as a complement to *The Trouble with Babies*. RECOMMENDED.

Keywords: Family Relations, Children of Gay Parents, Gay Neighbors, Gay Fathers.

FREEMAN, MARTHA. *The Trouble with Twins.* Illus. by Cat Bowman Smith. New York, NY: Holiday House, 2007. 85p. ISBN: 9780823420254. OCLC #: 66527247. Ages 6–10. FORMAT: Hardcover. AWARDS: None. REVIEWS: BKLST, BCCB, KS, SLJ.

In this sequel to *The Trouble with Cats* and *The Trouble with Babies*, Holly and her friends Annie, a girl of Jewish and Chinese heritage, and Xavier, a boy with gay fathers, are planning a birthday party for Holly's toddler twin brothers. Holly thinks it will be easy peasy to host a party for the twins and all their little friends — after all, she only needs cake and entertainment. After mishaps with cats, cakes, crickets, and kiddies galore, Holly finally pulls off a perfect birthday party. The spot-on humor and levelized text are perfect for readers just working their way into chapter books. Unfortunately, Xavier's gay dads do not reappear in this third book in the series. There is mention of one dad but not the other. Only readers who have read *The Trouble with Babies* will be able to identify the dad as gay. However, a perk of the book for gender-variant or transgender children resides in the scene where all the toddlers end up with mixed-up nametags. Boys now have names like "Jessica" and girls have names like "Kelton." This may resonate with children who identify with a different gender. The book is a sequel, but children do not have to read the first book in the series to follow the exploits of Holly and her friends. RECOMMENDED.

Keywords: Family Relations, Children of Gay Parents, Gay Neighbors, Gay Fathers, Twins, Gender Identity.

GARDEN, NANCY. *The Case of the Stolen Scarab.* Illus. by Danamarie Hosler. Ridley Park, PA: Two Lives Publishing, 2004. 205p. ISBN: 9780967446875. OCLC #: 56728789. Ages 8–12. FORMAT: Paperback. AWARDS: None. REVIEWS: SLJ.

Twelve-year-old Nikki, her eleven-year-old brother Travis, and their two moms run the newly opened Candlestone Inn in rural Vermont. Although their moms have been renovating for some time, Nikki and Travis have just moved to the inn. Not long into their first day, the local sheriff asks them to be on the lookout for a thief who stole a valuable piece from an art museum in Boston. Soon the inn is packed with visitors and the children are determined to discover which one of them is the robber. At times the narrative becomes cumbersome and more-reluctant readers will not push through to the end. The book does exemplify two positive gay relationships: the one between the mothers of Nikki and Travis and the one between two gay men who run a local restaurant. ADDITIONAL SELECTION.

Keywords: Children of Gay Parents, Family Relations, Gay Neighbors, Lesbian Mothers, Mysteries.

GARDEN, NANCY. *The Case of the Vanishing Valuables.* Illus. by Danamarie Hosler. Ambler, PA: Two Lives Publishing, 2010. 208p. ISBN: 9780967446882. OCLC #: 697291246. Ages 8–12. FORMAT: Paperback. AWARDS: None. REVIEWS: SLJ.

The second book in the Candlestone Inn Mystery series, this follow-up to *The Case of the Stolen Scarab* follows twelve-year-old Nikki, her eleven-year-old brother, and their two moms a few weeks into their venture as owners of the Candlestone Inn. A new crop of guests have checked in and one of them just might be a thief, given the number of valuables that suddenly go missing. One of the guests is certain that the ghosts of the former owners are the pesky thieves, but Nikki and Travis aren't so sure. Written in a classic mystery style that will keep young readers guessing until the last moment, Garden's second offering is much stronger than the first and its positive representation of two rainbow families makes it a sound addition to library collections. RECOMMENDED.

Keywords: Children of Gay Parents, Family Relations, Gay Neighbors, Lesbian Mothers, Mysteries.

GLEITZMAN, MORRIS. *Two Weeks with the Queen.* New York, NY: Penguin Putnam, 1991. 141p. ISBN: 9780399222498. OCLC #: 22184154. Ages 9–12. FORMAT: Hardcover. AWARDS: None. REVIEWS: BCCB, HB, KS, PW, SLJ. (Originally published in Australia.)

On Christmas Day, twelve-year-old Colin's life changes drastically when his younger brother Luke collapses as the result of a rare form of cancer. Colin wants to help his brother, but before he gets a chance he is sent from his home in Australia to the United Kingdom to stay with his aunt and uncle until his brother's imminent death. Colin decides that the Queen of England would have the best cancer doctor to heal his brother and tries unsuccessfully to reach her. He eventually ends up at a cancer hospital in London where he seeks the best cancer doctor in the world. He chances upon Ted, a young man whose partner is dying of AIDS. Ted helps Colin work through his fears and, when Ted's partner dies, he encourages Colin to go back to Australia to be with his dying brother. The fast-moving plot balances the heavy topics with humor and James Bond-style elements for a quick read that will attract reluctant readers. The tender relationship of the gay couple is authentic as is Ted's gay bashing. At times elements of the plot are a little far-fetched but they do not detract from the overall quality of the book. RECOMMENDED.

Keywords: Death, Terminal Illnesses, Cancer, AIDS, Family Relations, Gay Men, Gay Friends, Australian Literature, Australia.

HOWE, JAMES. *Pinky and Rex and the Bully.* Illus. by Melissa Sweet. New York, NY: Atheneum/Simon & Schuster, 1996. 40p. ISBN: 9780689800214. OCLC #: 32821259. Ages 6–9. FORMAT: Hardcover. AWARDS: None. REVIEWS: BKLST, KS, SLJ.

Part of the Pinky and Rex early chapter series, this installment deals with bullying and individuality. Second-grader Billy is known to his family, friends, and neighbors as "Pinky" because of his penchant for pink. A third-grade boy who believes that pink is for girls begins bullying Pinky for having a pink bike, pink sneakers, and a girl as a best friend. The bully calls Pinky a sissy and tells him that he'll turn into a girl. Pinky tries to change but finds that he's not very happy. A helpful neighbor encourages Pinky to embrace his individuality and to ignore the bully. In the end, Pinky follows her advice and also stands up to the bully. An affirmation for boys who like nontraditional toys and activities, this sensitive text successfully addresses a topic all too common in elementary school. Sweet's watercolor illustrations lend a gentle quality to the story, making this an excellent choice for school and public libraries. HIGHLY RECOMMENDED.

Keywords: Bullying, Gender Identity, Gender Nonconformity, Family Relations, Individuality, School Relations.

IGNATOW, AMY. *The Popularity Papers: The Long-Distance Dispatch Between Lydia Goldblatt and Julie Graham-Chang.* New York, NY: Amulet Book/Abrams, 2011. 205p. ISBN: 9780810997240. OCLC #: 657596112. Ages 9–12. FORMAT: Hardcover. AWARDS: None. REVIEWS: BKLST, SLJ.

Lydia and Julie are back in full force in this second equally hilarious installment of The Popularity Papers. Armed with their insights about popularity and friendship from the first book in the series, the two are sure they are well on their way to school stardom. Unfortunately, their plans hit the toilet when Lydia's mom moves the family to London for six months. Not ones to wallow in their misfortunes, Lydia and Julie each navigate the choppy waters of junior high, dealing with cliques, bullies, and friendship woes on both sides of the Atlantic. Once again, Julie's dads play an active role in the narrative, making this an attractive read for children in rainbow families. Perfect for reluctant readers and fans of The Diary of a Wimpy Kid (Kinney) series, this novel is recommended for both school and public libraries. HIGHLY RECOMMENDED.

Keywords: Gay Fathers, Children of Gay Parents, Family Relations, Single Parents, Individuality, School Relations, Mixed Race Families, Friendship, London.

IGNATOW, AMY. *The Popularity Papers: Research for the Social Improvement and General Betterment of Lydia Goldblatt and Julie Graham-Chang.* New York, NY: Amulet Book/Abrams, 2010. 206p. ISBN: 9780810984219. OCLC #: 430838792. Ages 9–12. FORMAT: Hardcover. AWARDS: Cooperative Children's Book Center Choices 2011; Rainbow List 2011. REVIEWS: BKLST, BCCB, HB, KS, PW, SLJ, VOYA.

Fifth-graders Lydia and Julie really want to know what makes popular girls tick in hopes that they will become popular too. In this series opener, the dynamic duo decides to create a journal of drawings, observations, and musings about the popular girls in their school and then try to copy them. Chockfull of cartoon illustrations, playful banter, and spot-on humor, this delightful read successfully captures the drama of tween girls in a fashion that will attract even the most reluctant of readers. A boon for rainbow families is the natural, carefree integration of Julie's two dads throughout the narrative. Perfect for both school and public libraries. HIGHLY RECOMMENDED.

Keywords: Gay Fathers, Children of Gay Parents, Family Relations, Single Parents, Individuality, School Relations, Mixed Race Families, Friendship.

IGNATOW, AMY. *The Popularity Papers: Words of (Questionable) Wisdom from Lydia Goldblatt and Julie Graham-Chang.* New York, NY: Amulet Book/Abrams, 2011. 206p. ISBN: 9781419700637. OCLC #: 707968808. Ages 9–12. FORMAT: Hardcover. AWARDS: None. REVIEWS: KS.

In this third installment of the acclaimed series, tweens Julie and Lydia again tackle the unpredictable life of junior high. Lydia is ready to apply her international knowledge about friendship and bullies to the girls' current social situation at school when their friend's terminally ill mother takes a turn for the worse and dies of breast cancer. Are cliques and popularity really worth it in the end if we all end up dead? Julie and Lydia deal with a host of serious problems including academic integrity, life expectancy, gossip, and vandalism. Ignatow adds just the right amount of comic relief to her illustrations and glib narrative to keep the book from being too weighty. As with the other two books in the series, Julie's two dads add their own humorous punch, taking on even more memorable personalities. Appropriate for school and public libraries. HIGHLY RECOMMENDED.

Keywords: Gay Fathers, Children of Gay Parents, Family Relations, Single Parents, Individuality, School Relations, Mixed Race Families, Friendship, Death, Breast Cancer.

KING-SMITH, DICK. *Lady Daisy.* Illus. by Jan Naimo Jones. New York, NY: Delacorte, 1993. 131p. ISBN: 9780689800214. OCLC #: 32821259. Ages 6–9. FORMAT: Hardcover. AWARDS: None. REVIEWS: BKLST, BCCB, KS, PW, SLJ. (Originally published in the United Kingdom. Positive review included in the UK review publication *Books for Keeps*.)

When he finds an old doll in his grandmother's attic, nine-year-old Ned is surprised to discover that she can talk to him. The doll, Lady Daisy Chain, has been asleep for more than ninety years and it is up to Ned to give her a lesson in contemporary life. In return, the doll tells him about Victorian life and his family history. Ned enjoys typical "boy" activities like soccer and is worried that his family, friends, and classmates will ridicule him for playing with a doll, which he deems a "girl" toy. While his mother is accepting of her son's new playmate, his father prefers for his son to be manlier and only takes an interest in the doll when an antique dealer declares her worth. Ned is teased at school by the class bully, who takes the doll. But Ned stands his ground and gets her back. Lady Daisy Chain stops communicating with him when he gets too old and he packs her away. The book ends with his grandmother predicting the doll will talk again in 2010 when Ned has his own daughter. This scene is played in an epilogue. Appropriate for all children, particularly gender-variant boys, this early chapter book is a good complement to the picture book *William's Doll* (Zolotow). If readers skip the prologue it would be easy to consider that Ned might be a gay child. RECOMMENDED.

Keywords: Bullying, Gender Nonconformity, School Relations, Family Relations, Individuality, Dolls, Magic.

LANTZ, FRANCES. *The Day Joanie Frankenhauser Became a Boy.* New York, NY: Dutton, 2005. 160p. ISBN: 9780525474371. OCLC #: 56621900. Ages 8–11. FORMAT: Hardcover. AWARDS: None. REVIEWS: BKLST, KS, SLJ.

Ten-year-old Joan loves to play football and engage in many of the activities that her brothers enjoy; however, because she is a girl her behavior is met with disapproval on the part of her parents and teachers. When the family moves and Joan starts at a new school, she discovers that her name has been misspelled as John. As she already has short hair and dresses in t-shirts and skater shorts, she decides to take the hand that fate has dealt her and become John. This allows her to do all the things she likes without reproach. However, she soon learns that things as a boy aren't as good as she thought and perhaps she can have traits of both boys and girls. Appropriate for elementary children, particularly gender-variant girls or transgender kids, this chapter book raises many issues about the fluidity of gender. A discussion guide is available at http://www.multcolib.org/talk/guides-joanie. html. RECOMMENDED.

Keywords: Bullying, Gender Nonconformity, Gender Identity, Gender Roles, Sex Roles, Transgender, School Relations, Family Relations, Individuality, Football, Tomboys.

PRIHODA, DEBORAH. *"Mommy, Why Are They Holding Hands?"* Illus. by Julia Haverford. Souderton, PA: Cutting Edge Publications, 1996. 60p. ISBN:

9780966338003. OCLC #: 43987675. Ages 8–12. FORMAT: Paperback. AWARDS: None. REVIEWS: None.

Written with the intent to teach children that homosexuality is a sin, this didactic chapter book follows a young girl named Sarah as she disobeys her parents, over-hears her father lying to their pastor, and questions her mother about gay couples that she encounters at the mall and on television. The author attempts to make Sarah and her father multidimensional by showing their good and bad traits, but Sarah's mother is portrayed as overly self-righteous, ignoring her own little white lies. The line illustrations are static and do little to enhance the narrative. Although it is important for librarians to balance their collections with materials that present both sides of a topic, this book leaves many questions unanswered while also perpetuating gender stereotypes. NOT RECOMMENDED.

Keywords: Anti-Gay Sentiment, Homosexuality and Religion, Homosexuality and Christianity, Homosexuality and the Bible.

RYAN, PAM MUÑOZ. *Riding Freedom.* Illus. by Brian Selznick. New York, NY: Scholastic, 1998. 138p. ISBN: 9780590957663. OCLC #: 37245963. Ages 8–11. FORMAT: Hardcover. AWARDS: Best Children's Books of the Year, 1999, Bank Street College of Education, United States; Cooperative Children's Book Center Choices 1998, Teachers' Choices, 1999, International Reading Association. REVIEWS: BKLST, BCCB, KS, LMC (Book Report), PW, SLJ.

Based on the life of Charley (Charlotte) Parkhurst, this fictional chapter book tells the story of young Charlotte, who lives a life full of restrictions because of her sex. When she gets a chance, she runs away, posing as Charley the stable boy, and begins what will be a long career as a stagecoach driver. Charley lives his entire life impersonating a man and doing many things that women would never have been able to do during the 1800s. An author's note explains that Charley's true sex was not discovered until her death. Ryan's storytelling, sprinkled with historical facts, engages readers and Selznick's eye-catching, life-like sketches add sparkle. Pair this with the picture-book biography *Rough, Tough Charley* (Kay) for another look at Parkhurst's life. Appropriate for gender-variant and transgender children or children with transgender or gender-variant family members. HIGHLY RECOMMENDED.

Keywords: Cross-Dressing, Gay Role Models, Gender Identity, Gender Non-conformity, Sex Roles, Transgender, Individuality, Charley Parkhurst.

RYLANT, CYNTHIA. *The Van Gogh Cafe.* San Diego, CA: Harcourt Brace, 1995. 53p. ISBN: 9780152008437. OCLC #: 31657102. Ages 8–11. FORMAT: Hardcover. AWARDS: American Library Association Notable Children's Book 1996; ABC Children's Booksellers Choices Award, 1996; Cooperative Children's Book Center Choices 1995. REVIEWS: BKLST, BCCB, KS, PW, SLJ.

Flowers, Kansas, is not the kind of town that attracts attention. It sits just off I-70 and for the most part is uneventful and average — except for the Van Gogh Café. Situated in an old movie theatre, the walls of the charming café are filled with a sort of magic that seems to find its way into the lives of the customers as well as owner Marc and his ten-year-old daughter Clara. Magic just turns up in the café, from food that cooks itself or multiplies inside the fridge, to seagulls and possums that appear out of nowhere, to mysterious visitors with glamorous pasts. One of the visitors is an elderly movie star from the days of silent films. He's returned to the café (where his movies once were played) in an effort to reunite with his true love — another man. Rylant's storytelling is well crafted, giving only just enough details to allow children to fill in their own story elements. The audiobook, read by John McDonough, is particularly engaging and extends the book to an even younger audience. RECOMMENDED.

Keywords: Divorced Parents, Single Parents, Family Relations, Gay Men, Homosexuality, Elderly Gay Men, Magic, Cafes.

SACHAR, LOUIS. *Marvin Redpost: Is He a Girl?* Illus. by Barbara Sullivan. New York, NY: Random House, 1993. 71p. ISBN: 9780679919483. OCLC #: 27174495. Ages 7–10. FORMAT: Hardcover. AWARDS: None. REVIEWS: BKLST.

When third-grader Marvin is told by his classmate Casey that a boy can turn into a girl if he kisses his elbow, he *has* to try it — not because he wants to be a girl but because there is nothing that Marvin Redpost *can't* do! That night he kisses his elbow and is convinced that he's turned into a girl. When he arrives at school the next day, Marvin uses words such as "cute" and "gross" and admires the clothes of his female classmates. Apparently this is something that only a girl would do so Marvin must be a girl! After one day as a girl, Marvin kisses his elbow again and turns back into a boy. Children are sure to be attracted to this droll series, but this specific title is one that should be avoided unless an adult is around to discuss the many questions that it raises. In his attempts to show the real difference between boys and girls, Sachar reinforces stereotypes — girls are only interested in clothes, hair, and getting boys into trouble, for example. For gender-variant children, the book is harmful as it uses the label "weirdo" to describe a boy who is interested in traditional female activities. Educators trying to incorporate an anti-bias curriculum will find that this book promotes ridicule unless it is discussed appropriately. NOT RECOMMENDED.

Keywords: Gender Identity, Gender Nonconformity, Sex Role Stereotypes, Individuality, School Relations, Bullying.

SALAT, CRISTINA. *Living in Secret.* New York, NY: Bantam Skylark, 1993. 183p. ISBN: 9780553086706. OCLC #: 26215533. Ages 9–12. FORMAT: Hardcover. AWARDS: Lambda Literary Award Finalist, LGBT Children's/YA Category, 1993. REVIEWS: BKLST, BCCB, KS, PW, SLJ.

"In the middle of the night my mother comes to steal me away." With this opening line, eleven-year-old Amelia draws readers in as she explains how she ran away with her mother and her mother's partner to San Francisco instead of staying behind with her father and his girlfriend. Amelia's parents are divorced, and a homophobic judge gave full custody of the girl to her father and his girlfriend because he thought the mother's "lifestyle" would be a bad influence. Unfortunately, Amelia's dad is always at work and his girlfriend prefers spending time on the phone with her friends. Amelia loves her mother and will do anything to be with her. She lives with her mother and her mother's partner Janey for about nine months until a private investigator hired by her father discovers them. Forced to move back to New York, Amelia must decide whether to live with her dad and his now-pregnant girlfriend until she is eighteen or to reopen the custody case in hopes that her mother will gain full custody. Salat's writing is engaging and she does a commendable job of developing Amelia as a multidimensional character that tweens will find believable. The idea that the mother doesn't face kidnapping charges seems a little farfetched but is only a minor quibble in this dramatic ripped-from-the-headlines story. RECOMMENDED.

Keywords: Children of Gay Parents, Divorced Parents, Family Relations, Lesbian Mothers, Custody Cases, Homophobia, Bisexuality.

SNYDER, LAUREL. *Penny Dreadful.* Illus. by Abigail Halpin. New York, NY: Random House, 2010. 304p. ISBN: 9780375861994. OCLC #: 436387136. Ages 8–12. FORMAT: Hardcover. AWARDS: None. REVIEWS: BKLST, BCCB, KS, LMC, PW, SLJ.

Ten-year-old Penelope Grey lives a dull, uneventful life with her busy mother and father in a mansion in the city and spends her days lost in the pages of books. Everything changes when her father quits his job. Soon the family runs out of money and her parents sink into a deep depression. One day a telegram arrives telling Penelope's mother that she has inherited a family home in rural Thrush Junction, Tennessee. Seeing this as the answer to their financial problems, the family moves to Tennessee to start anew. Everyone falls in love with the small town, quirky townsfolk, and the rambling house. Penelope changes her name to Penny in an effort to be more adventurous, and makes several friends — including one with two mothers. Just when things start to look up, Penny and her family learn that their new house comes with its own pile of debt. Although her mother gets a job, the family is still in financial trouble. Penny decides that she'll save the day by gathering her friends and hunting for treasure. They fail to find the gold but Penny does discover rich bonds of friendship that can save the family. Written in a style similar to *The Penderwicks* (Birdsall 2005), this heartwarming story — full of adventure, hidden treasure, and several colorful neighbors — introduces readers to a loving community that just happens to include a lesbian couple. Soft black-and-white illustrations complement various scenes in the narrative and lend a classic touch to the book. Perfect for both school and public libraries. RECOMMENDED.

Keywords: Children of Gay Parents, Community Relations, Family Relations, Lesbian Mothers, Individuality.

WALLIAMS, DAVID. *The Boy in the Dress.* Illus. by Quentin Blake. New York, NY: Razorbill/Penguin, 2009. 231p. ISBN: 9781595142993. OCLC #: 318408074. Ages 9–12. FORMAT: Hardcover. AWARDS: Cooperative Children's Book Center Choices 2010, Rainbow List 2010; Stonewall Book Awards 2011, Children's and Young Adult Honor Book. REVIEWS: BKLST, BCCB, KS, PW, SLJ, VOYA. (Originally published in the United Kingdom.)

Twelve-year-old Dennis is different from other boys. He does not mind a good cry and welcomes hugs from his mates. He also has a penchant for fashion magazines and really wants to play dress-up — in girls' clothing. The star soccer player for his school, Dennis is well liked by his classmates but receives little attention from his depressed, recently divorced working-class father. When he is caught with a copy of *Vogue* under his mattress, Dennis is reprimanded by his father. When he is dared to wear an orange dress and heels to school by an older girl he fancies, the boy is expelled and barred from playing in the soccer championship. His problems are eventually resolved and Dennis learns that it is okay to be different, even if he is a boy who likes fashion and wearing dresses. Walliams's jovial text puts a light-hearted spin on a sensitive topic and Blake's humorous sketches extend the audience of the book to include reluctant readers. The book is not without flaws (the ending is too clean), but it does cover important aspects of gender nonconformity often absent from children's literature for intermediate readers. RECOMMENDED.

Keywords: Cross-Dressing, Gender Identity, Gender Nonconformity, British Literature, Great Britain, Family Relations, Single Parents, Individuality, School Relations.

WILSON, BARBARA. *A Clear Spring.* New York, NY: Feminist Press CUNY, 2002. 173p. ISBN: 9781558612778. OCLC #: 47054693. Ages 8–12. FORMAT: Hardcover. AWARDS: None. REVIEWS: BKLST.

Eleven-year-old Willa is traveling to visit her Aunt Carmen, Aunt Ceci and her partner Jane, cousins, and uncle for the summer in Seattle. At first she is a little nervous about her trip as she has not seen the relatives in a long time and is afraid that her cousins might not like her. Her fears are unfounded and she develops a rich relationship with her relatives, especially Jane, who piques Willa's interest in eco-sleuthing. Someone is polluting the salmon stream in a nearby park and wreaking havoc on the grounds. With the help of her two cousins, Willa solves the mystery and catches the bad guy. The writing seems forced at times and the eco-friendly message is heavy-handed. But the book does depict empowering, self-sufficient females and a very healthy, positive lesbian relationship between Aunt Ceci and Jane. The question, however, is which message is the strongest. ADDITIONAL SELECTION.

Keywords: Lesbian Aunts, Gay Relatives, Family Relations, Mixed Race Families, Latinos, African Americans, Individuality, Single Parents, Ecology.

WILSON, JACQUELINE. *My Brother Bernadette.* Illus. by David Roberts. London (UK): Egmont, 2001. 45p. ISBN: 9780749742232. OCLC #: 63188344. Ages 6–9. FORMAT: Hardcover. AWARDS: None. REVIEWS: None.

Poor Bernard is ridiculed by his dad and called a "softie" for not being tough like other boys. He's called Bernadette by neighborhood bully Big Dan and other kids because he has longish hair and likes to sew. To make matters worse, he and his sister have to spend the entire summer at summer camp with these guys! Life is miserable until Bernard gets a reputation for being a good fashion designer and is asked to create the costumes for the camp's play, which bears resemblance to

Grease. He gets his revenge when he creates a jacket for Big Dan and embroiders the name Daisy Dan along with several pink daisies on the costume. Wilson's engaging text and Roberts's droll illustrations are sure to attract beginning readers who are gender-variant, bullied, or have a penchant for fashion. RECOMMENDED.

Keywords: Bullying, Gender Identity, Gender Nonconformity, Family Relations, Individuality, School Relations, Costume Design, Fashion Design, British Literature, Great Britain.

WYETH, SHARON DENNIS. *Tomboy Trouble.* Illus. by Lynne Woodcock Cravath. New York, NY: Random House, 1998. 48p. ISBN: 9780679981275. OCLC #: 35450461. Ages 7–9. FORMAT: Hardcover. AWARDS: Best Children's Books of the Year, 1999, Bank Street College of Education, United States. REVIEWS: SLJ.

Eight-year-old Georgia likes to play baseball, but her long hair gets in the way. She goes to the hairdresser and has her hair cut very short. When she wears her baseball cap, Georgia looks very much like a boy, and when she starts a new school at the end of the summer, several students think she is a boy and bully her when she stands in the girls' line for recess, lunch, and so forth. Georgia explains that she loves her hair short and that she wears boys' clothes because that is what she likes. One day she meets a new classmate, Robin, who has long blonde hair and shares many of Georgia's interests. When they are playing together at recess, Georgia learns that Robin is actually a boy who loves long hair. While the story verges on being didactic, it is a good introduction to the topic of gender identity and is particularly useful in early chapter-book format. RECOMMENDED.

Keywords: Bullying, Gender Identity, Gender Nonconformity, Family Relations, Individuality, School Relations, Tomboys, Transgender.

YOUNGMILLER, CRISTIAN. *Everybody Has Those Thoughts: So It Doesn't Mean You're Gay.* Illus. by Andrew Toutant. Lexington, KY: CreateSpace, 2010. 48p. ISBN: 9780982713280. OCLC #: n.a. Ages 9–12. FORMAT: Paperback. AWARDS: None. REVIEWS: None.

Jack is a thirteen-year-old banana who has a problem. When he was playing a game of Truth-or-Dare with his friends, an apple and a grape, he told them that his strangest dream was kissing his best friend Billy. Then when Billy was dared to kiss Jack, the banana boy got a hard-on. His friends called him gay and now he's sad and confused. His dad, a doctor, takes him for a game of mini-golf and explains to Jack the Kinsey Scale as well as how the brain makes you dream unusual things. The writing is very didactic and the target audience for the book is difficult to determine. The childlike cartoon illustrations and large font with double-spaced lines give the book the feel of an early chapter book. However, the vocabulary is advanced and the treatment of the topic is one for older children. The book attempts to explain that being gay is okay but that straight people (or bananas) can have gay thoughts too. With so many better books on this topic, libraries will want to give this one a pass. NOT RECOMMENDED.

Keywords: Sex Education, Homosexuality, Kinsey Scale, Self-Published Literature.

CHAPTER 8

Informational Books, Biographies, and LGBTQ Children's Media

This chapter includes more than forty resources for children ages birth to eleven that depict same-sex parents, queer relatives, nontraditional families, gender-variant children, and influential LGBTQ historical figures. They are organized in the following categories:

> Nonfiction Books and Biographies
> Other Media
> > Films
> > Coloring Books
> > Music Recordings
> > Magazines
> > E-Books

For additional information on these entries, see p. 85.

Nonfiction Books and Biographies

ANTOLÍN VILLOTA, LUISA. *Virginia Woolf: La escritora de lo invisible.* Illus. by Antonia Santolaya. Madrid, Spain: Hotelpapel Ediciones, 2008. Unpaged. ISBN: 9788493617813. OCLC #: 433959761. Ages 6–10. FORMAT: Hardcover. AWARDS: None. REVIEWS: None. The text is in Spanish but there is an English translation by Elena Riudavets at the back of the book.

Beginning with her childhood and following her life as an accomplished writer, this accessible picture-book biography introduces young children to the life and literary world of Virginia Woolf. Readers learn about Woolf's struggle to find her own identity in a male-dominated world and about her passion for collecting words. Her relationship with Vita Sackville-West is not mentioned, but the book does give a nod to Woolf's *Orlando*, which is said to be a semi-autobiographical work based on her love affair with Vita and which at the very least portrays a transgender character. The English translation has numerous grammatical errors; however, the Spanish text draws readers into the magical world of words and books that illuminated Woolf's life. Likewise, the accompanying collage illustrations are child-friendly and imbued with surrealism. Perfect for both school and public library collections, particularly those in need of Spanish-language materials representing famous LGBTQ individuals. RECOMMENDED.

Keywords: Gay Role Models, Individuality, Biographies, Lesbian Authors, Virginia Woolf, Spanish Literature.

BRIMNER, LARRY DANE. *The NAMES Project.* New York, NY: Children's Press/Grolier, 1999. 32p. ISBN: 9780516209999. OCLC #: 40251688. Ages 8–12. FORMAT: Hardcover. AWARDS: None. REVIEWS: None.

Initiated in 1987, the NAMES Project AIDS Memorial Quilt was created as a way to help relatives and friends of AIDS victims grieve and remember their loved ones. It was also used as a political protest against the U.S. government's lack of attention to the AIDS epidemic. Beginning in 1988, the quilt traveled across the nation to raise awareness of the impact of the disease on American lives. At almost every stop, more panels of deceased persons with AIDS were added. Eventually the quilt became too big to display and was shown in its entirety for the last time in 1996. Soon afterward, NAMES Project coordinators began shipping out portions of the quilt to schools, museums, and libraries interested in creating exhibits. These traveling exhibits are still available today. The AIDS epidemic may not be as rampant today as it was in the 1980s and 1990s, but the disease still ravages many lives and this accessible book with detailed black-and-white and full-color photographs, provides elementary children with factual information about America's war on AIDS and the attempts to remember the many victims of the disease. Younger children will be especially interested in the panel created by elementary school children in Santa Cruz, California, in remembrance of children's author Arnold Lobel. This would be the ideal book to pair with the picture book *A Name on the Quilt: A Story of Remembrance* (Atkins), which describes how a girl and her family prepare a panel for the AIDS Memorial Quilt to honor the memory of her uncle. HIGHLY RECOMMENDED.

Keywords: Memorial Projects, Death, AIDS, NAMES Project AIDS Memorial Quilt.

CAREY, BILL. *Fairy Tales for the 21st Century: A Same-Sex Retelling of Two Classic Stories, Suitable for Children of All Ages.* Raleigh, NC: Lulu.com, 2008. 29p. ISBN: 9780557036608. OCLC #: n.a. Ages 7–11. FORMAT: Paperback. AWARDS: None. REVIEWS: None.

Taking two well-known fairy tales, Carey makes minor adjustments so that children in rainbow families or children who themselves are lesbian or gay can finally have traditional tales that reflect their lives. The first story, "Sleeping Beauty," is much the same as the commonly known version except that Sleeping Beauty must be kissed by a princess in order to break the spell. Also, there are eleven wise women and at least two of them are lesbians as they allow Sleeping Beauty to rest in their bed for her hundred-year nap. In the second story, "Cinderallen," readers are introduced to a gay version of Cinderella in which Prince Charming decides to marry a man instead of a woman. Allen is a poor commoner forced to cook and clean for his stepmother and three stepbrothers. As in the most commonly known version of the story, Allen is not allowed to attend the ball held by the prince but is rescued by magic; this time in the form of the ghost of his mother rather than a fairy godmother. Naturally, both stories have happy endings and the same-sex relationships are a non-issue. The book's pages are mainly long passages of double-spaced text accompanied by either poorly placed clipart or copyrighted photos from the Web. While there is a need for fairy tales for rainbow families this offering is lukewarm at best. NOT RECOMMENDED.

Keywords: Fairy Tales, Princes, Gay Men, Princesses, Lesbians, Stepfamilies.

CHRISTENSEN, BONNIE. *Fabulous! A Portrait of Andy Warhol.* New York, NY: Henry Holt, 2011. Unpaged. ISBN: 9780805087536. OCLC #: 645889815. Ages 7–11. FORMAT: Hardcover. AWARDS: None. REVIEWS: BKLST, HB, KS, PW, SLJ.

Filled with reproductions of Warhol's paintings, this picture-book biography describes various guiding events in Andy's life from a young age. His childhood struggles with bullying and illness are highlighted, as well as his later determination to make a name for himself. His Factory is mentioned briefly, ignoring the drug use and sexual activities that took place there. Includes an author's note, bibliography of resources for children, teens, and adults as well as a Warhol Time Line of important events. One of the few biographies on Warhol for younger children, this accessible title would pair well with *Uncle Andy's* (Warhola) or *Uncle Andy's Cats* (Warhola). RECOMMENDED.

Keywords: Artists, Biographies, Gay Role Models, Individuality, Andy Warhol.

COMBS, BOBBIE. *ABC: A Family Alphabet Book.* Illus. by Desiree Keane and Brian Rappa. Ridley Park, PA: Two Lives Publishing, 2000. Unpaged. ISBN:

9780967446813. OCLC #: 46451903. Ages 2–6. FORMAT: Paperback. AWARDS: None. REVIEWS: None.

Readers follow children and diverse families from A to Z as they engage in various activities such as playing ball, gardening, going to the beach, and visiting the zoo. A variety of rainbow families are represented including single-parent, two moms, two dads, and biracial same-sex families. Combs's simple text is appropriate for beginning readers and the cartoon illustrations provide a cheerful extension. Like *123: A Family Counting Book*, this picture book is perfect for assisting older preschool and early elementary school children as they seek reflections of their families in their books. Appropriate for school and public library collections. RECOMMENDED.

   Keywords: Adoption, Gay Fathers, Family Composition, Lesbian Mothers, Children of Gay Parents, Family Relations, Asian Americans, African Americans, Latinos, Mixed Race Families, Extended Families, Differently Able Individuals.

COMBS, BOBBIE. *123: A Family Counting Book.* Illus. by Danamarie Hosler. Ridley Park, PA: Two Lives Publishing, 2000. Unpaged. ISBN: 9780967446806. OCLC #: 51595866. Ages 3–6. FORMAT: Paperback. AWARDS: None. REVIEWS: BL.

From 1 to 20 children count a variety of objects in this picture book: dogs, bubbles, books, toys, fireflies, and so forth. However, the counting is not the real focus of this vibrantly illustrated exploration of families. Rather, through detailed illustrations representing various ethnicities, races, and cultures, children are introduced to the variety of forms a family can take. Two moms, two dads, extended families, and biracial families are just a few of the structures depicted. While the images are too detailed for younger children, this book will help older preschool and early elementary school children see affirming reflections of their families. Ideal for both school and public libraries. RECOMMENDED.

   Keywords: Gay Fathers, Family Composition, Lesbian Mothers, Children of Gay Parents, Family Relations, Asian Americans, African Americans, Latinos, Mixed Race Families, Extended Families.

DRESCHER, JOAN. *Your Family, My Family.* New York, NY: Walker and Co., 1980. 32p. ISBN: 9780802763839. OCLC #: 5892508. Ages 3–8. FORMAT: Hardcover. AWARDS: None. REVIEWS: BKLST, BCCB, SLJ.

One of the first U.S. informational picture books to include same-sex families in its coverage of diverse families, Drescher's offering describes single-parent families, foster families, extended families, families with grandparent caregivers, stepfamilies, and rainbow families. Families are presented in two-page spreads using simple text and a detailed black-white-and-orange line illustration. One spread describes a family with two mothers; another shows a family that includes a man and an androgynous partner who could easily be another man. The book is not as dated as one would expect and gives young children a glimpse into the lives of selected diverse families. RECOMMENDED.

Keywords: Adoption, Family Composition, Lesbian Mothers, Children of Gay Parents, Gay Fathers, Family Relations, African Americans, Extended Families, Single Parents, Divorced Parents, Stepfamilies, Grandparent Caregivers, Foster Parents.

EDMONDS, BARBARA LYNN. *When Grown-Ups Fall in Love.* Illus. by Matthew Daniele. Eugene, OR: Hundredth Munchy Publications, 2000. Rev. ed. Unpaged. ISBN: 9780965670012. OCLC #: 48381054. Ages 4–8. FORMAT: Paperback. AWARDS: None. REVIEWS: None.

In an effort to explain to children the different types of families and to normalize those that have two moms or two dads, Edmonds's picture book describes various family compositions. Unfortunately, the narrative includes vocabulary and concepts above the comprehension and reading ability of the target audience. For instance, many beginning readers and young children would struggle with the following line, "A family is where peace begins and dreams are fantasized, a peace that spreads from home to home, 'til dreams are realized." Daniele's muted cartoon illustrations add little to the story and probably would not attract the attention of young children. The book includes a space for children to write a story about their own family and a reproduced black-and-white version of the story that children can color. Although well meaning, this book is not very useful or practical for libraries. NOT RECOMMENDED.

Keywords: Gay Fathers, Family Composition, Lesbian Mothers, Children of Gay Parents, Family Relations, Self-Published Literature.

GORDON, SOL. *All Families Are Different.* Illus. by Vivien Cohen. Amherst, NY: Prometheus Press, 2000. Unpaged. ISBN: 9781573927659. OCLC #: 43667370. Ages 6–10. FORMAT: Paperback. AWARDS: None. REVIEWS: None.

All families are different — there is no such thing as a "normal" family! This is the premise of this lengthy look at family composition. Readers are introduced to families from different socioeconomic levels, religions, races, cultures, and lifestyles. At least one of the presentations includes a family with lesbian mothers. Cohen's black-and-white pen-and-ink illustrations provide representations of all types of diversity but do little to extend the text. Overall the informative but bland presentation may do little to inspire children to celebrate their families. A better choice for libraries would be *The Great Big Book of Families* (Hoffman). ADDITIONAL SELECTION.

Keywords: Family Composition, Lesbian Mothers, Children of Gay Parents, Family Relations, Latinos, African Americans, Mixed Race Families, Extended Families, Differently Able Individuals, Single Parents, Divorced Parents, Stepfamilies, Grandparent Caregivers, Foster Parents.

GREENBERG, KEITH ELLIOT. *Zack's Story: Growing Up with Same-Sex Parents.* Illus. by Carol Halebian. Minneapolis, MN: Lerner, 1996. 32p. ISBN: 9780822525813. OCLC #: 34410987. Ages 8–12. FORMAT: Hardcover. AWARDS: None. REVIEWS: BKLST, BL, HB, SLJ.

In this photo-essay, eleven-year-old Zack explains what it is like to have two mothers and describes the various things he does with them and his extended family and friends. He recalls how his mom met his second mother after his parents divorced and details how he felt during this period. Readers learn about the fun things he does with his moms including playing ball, going to Gay Pride, and attending Lambda family functions. He also mentions how it bothers him to hear his friends and classmates use the word "faggot" to demean someone. The book ends with Zack learning that his moms will soon be having a baby. The accompanying color photos add interest to the story but also date the text as photo illustrations tend to do. At times the narrative becomes too lengthy and slightly didactic. Nonetheless, there are so few books that describe the experiences of children in rainbow families that libraries may want to consider this title. ADDITIONAL SELECTION.

Keywords: Family Composition, Family Relations, School Relations, Lesbian Mothers, Children of Gay Parents, Gay Pride, Divorced Parents, Stepparents.

GRIFFITH, VICTORIA. *The Fabulous Flying Machines of Alberto Santos-Dumont.* Illus. by Eva Montanari. New York, NY: Abrams, 2011. Unpaged. ISBN: 9781419700118. OCLC #: 694172102. Ages 8–10. FORMAT: Hardcover. AWARDS: None. REVIEWS: BKLST, BCCB, KS, PW, SLJ.

Despite being the muse of John Cartier's first wristwatch for men, "Father of Flight," Alberto Santos-Dumont is not well-known outside France and South America. Propelled by his idealistic dreams that his flying inventions would bring about world peace, Alberto worked tirelessly to develop the world's first self-propelled flying machine, which according to Brazilian scholars was a feat he accomplished. Unfortunately, his aeronautical accomplishments and inventions have been overshadowed by those of the Wright brothers. Nonetheless, the Brazilian dandy charmed Parisian society with his personal flying machines, particularly the dirigible that he used to run errands and travel about Paris. Griffith's engaging, accessible text and extensive author's note and list of further reading materials provide readers with the facts and allow them to judge Alberto's accomplishments for themselves. Montanari's period, mixed-media illustrations have a life of their own, drawing in reluctant readers. Whether or not Santos-Dumont was gay or bisexual is debatable; Brazilian historians often choose to ignore his sexuality entirely. Griffith does not disclose this information either, although the additional readings include information about Santos-Dumont's homosexuality. For more information about the inventor's sexuality, consult http://www.glbtq.com/social-sciences/santos_dumont_a.html. RECOMMENDED.

Keywords: Biographies, Gay Role Models, Individuality, Alberto Santos-Dumont, Airplanes.

HARRIS, ROBIE H. *It's Not the Stork! A Book About Girls, Boys, Babies, Bodies, Families, and Friends.* Illus. by Michael Emberley. Cambridge, MA: Candlewick Press, 2006. 59p. ISBN: 9780763600471. OCLC #: 61758705. Ages 4–9. FORMAT: Hardcover. AWARDS: American Library Association Notable Children's Book 2007; Best Children's Books of the Year, 2007, Bank Street College of Education,

United States; Cooperative Children's Book Center Choices 2007. REVIEWS: BKLST, BCCB, HB, KS, LMC, SLJ.

Young children are curious. They want to know where babies come from, how boys are different from girls, and what makes a family. Using age-appropriate text and questions for young children, Harris addresses topics such as male and female body parts, reproduction, family composition, "okay and not-okay touches," and relationships. The text is straightforward and written at a level for young children, although scientific words are used. Emberley's cartoon illustrations leave nothing to the imagination but are appropriate for an informational book about the human body and reproduction. Some parents will not want to share this book with their children, but many will find various sections helpful to explain topics that invariably arise with young children. Rainbow families will appreciate the mention, albeit brief, of families with two moms or two dads. RECOMMENDED.

Keywords: Adoption, Gay Fathers, Family Composition, Lesbian Mothers, Children of Gay Parents, Family Relations, School Relations, Asian Americans, African Americans, Latinos, Indians, Single Parents, Mixed Race Families, Extended Families, Grandparent Caregivers, Uncles, Aunts, Children with Disabilities, Differently Able Individuals, Individuality, Gender Roles, Sex Roles, Sex Education, Pregnancy, Human Reproduction.

HARRIS, ROBIE H. *It's Perfectly Normal: Changing Bodies, Growing Up, Sex, and Sexual Health.* Illus. by Michael Emberley. Cambridge, MA: Candlewick Press, 2009. 3rd updated ed. 96p. ISBN: 9780763644833. OCLC #: 314838062. Ages 10–14. FORMAT: Hardcover. AWARDS: American Library Association Notable Children's Book 1995; Bulletin of the Center for Children's Books Bulletin Blue Ribbons 1994; Cooperative Children's Book Center Choices 1994. REVIEWS: BKLST, BCCB, HB, KS, PW, SLJ.

One of the most challenged, defaced, and stolen informational children's books in the United States, this classic title presents children ages ten and up with straightforward answers to common questions about sexuality, human reproduction, relationships, families, AIDS, and more. While some parents may object to the content of the book's text and droll illustrations, these features never provide developmentally inappropriate information for tweens, and this revised 15th Anniversary Edition ensures that the content is accurate. Readers learn, among other things, that it is okay to have same-sex attractions, have same-sex parents, or have intercourse with someone of the same sex. Of course, they learn all of this information with regard to heterosexual relationships as well. Although it is sure to be challenged or go missing from their collections, this is an important title for both school and public libraries serving all types of families. RECOMMENDED.

Keywords: Adoption, Gay Fathers, Family Composition, Extended Families, Lesbian Mothers, Children of Gay Parents, Family Relations, School Relations, Asian Americans, African Americans, Latinos, Indians, Native Americans, Indigenous People, Single Parents, Mixed Race Families, Grandparent Caregivers, Uncles, Aunts, Children with Disabilities, Differently Able Individuals, Individuality, Gender Roles, Sex Roles, Sex Education, Pregnancy, AIDS, Human Reproduction.

HARRIS, ROBIE H. *It's So Amazing: A Book About Eggs, Sperm, Birth, Babies, and Families.* Illus. by Michael Emberley. Cambridge, MA: Candlewick Press, 1999. 81p. ISBN: 9780763600518. OCLC #: 40433137. Ages 7–11. FORMAT: Hardcover. AWARDS: American Library Association Notable Children's Book 2000; Best Children's Books of the Year, 2000, Bank Street College of Education, United States; Cooperative Children's Book Center Choices 2000. REVIEWS: BKLST, BCCB, HB, KS, PW, SLJ.

Intended for children too old for *It's Not the Stork* (Harris) and too young for *It's Perfectly Normal* (Harris), this nonfiction book presents information about sexuality, animal and human reproduction, human anatomy, family composition, and "okay and not okay touches" for children ages seven to eleven. The information is more detailed than *It's Not the Stork* and is age-appropriate for the intended audience. Harris covers questions asked by children in this age range and describes relationships and attractions (some children in the older end of the range will just be beginning to have attractions to each other). Family compositions are described in great detail with illustrations of a diverse array of families. Masturbation, AIDS, and contraception are briefly mentioned. Emberley's humorous illustrations are good for reluctant readers and keep the text from taking itself too seriously. Rainbow families will appreciate the straightforward discussion of same-sex attractions and the normalcy that is presented. RECOMMENDED.

Keywords: Adoption, International Adoption, Gay Fathers, Family Composition, Extended Families, Lesbian Mothers, Children of Gay Parents, Family Relations, School Relations, Asian Americans, African Americans, Latinos, Indians, Native Americans, Indigenous People, Single Parents, Mixed Race Families, Extended Families, Grandparent Caregivers, Uncles, Aunts, Children with Disabilities, Differently Able Individuals, Individuality, Gender Roles, Sex Roles, Sex Education, Pregnancy, AIDS, Human Reproduction.

HAUSHERR, ROSEMARIE. *Celebrating Families.* New York, NY: Scholastic, 1997. Unpaged. ISBN: 9780590489379. OCLC #: 34283670. Ages 4–8. FORMAT: Hardcover. AWARDS: Cooperative Children's Book Center Choices 1997; Jane Addams Children's Book Award, Honor Book, 1998. REVIEWS: BKLST, BL, SLJ.

Using a series of vignettes, Hausherr introduces readers to fourteen different families in the United States by way of their children. Each two-page spread shows a child holding a photograph or picture of his/her family. Small tidbits about each family are provided as well as one color and one black-and-white photograph. The families are racially, economically, and religiously diverse and include parents who are lesbian, differently abled, incarcerated, divorced, single, and foster. The book is sure to spark discussions — why is one child's dad in jail and why is another one's mother in a wheelchair, for example? The pictures are somewhat dated, but this is still a sound addition for public and school libraries. *Note:* The Library of Congress and WorldCat cataloging information for this title includes the subject headings "problem families" and "dysfunctional families." Libraries will not want to use these classifications as they imply that there is something wrong with the families profiled in the book. RECOMMENDED.

Keywords: International Adoption, Family Composition, Lesbian Mothers, Children of Gay Parents, Family Relations, Family Tree, Latinos, African Americans, Mixed Race Families, Extended Families, Differently Able Individuals, Single Parents, Christian Families, Divorced Parents, Stepfamilies, Grandparent Caregivers, Foster Parents, Homeless Families, Incarcerated Parents.

HERON, ANN, AND MEREDITH MARAN. *How Would You Feel If Your Dad Was Gay?* Illus. by Kris Kovick. Boston, MA: Alyson Wonderland, 1991. 32p. ISBN: 9781555831882. OCLC #: 24122131. Ages 7–11. FORMAT: Hardcover. AWARDS: Lambda Literary Award Finalist, LGBT Children's/YA Category, 1992. REVIEWS: HB, LBR, PW, SLJ.

Eight-year-old Jasmine and her eleven-year-old brother Michael have three dads, which is quite different from most kids in their elementary school. Before Father's Day, Jasmine tells her class that she has three dads — her two gay dads and her stepfather. Some of her classmates call out derogatory terms and her teacher does nothing to stop them. Later that day, her brother Michael is teased on the playground and called "faggot" and "gay" because word has spread that he has two gay dads and the kids assume he must be gay too. When Noah, a child with a lesbian mother, tries to stick up for Michael, he's called gay as well. Jasmine and Michael's dad visits the school and tells the principal that he needs to hold sensitivity training sessions for the teachers and students. The dad reasons that allowing children to make hurtful remarks about gay people is just as bad as allowing them to make slanderous comments about him because he is black. The principal agrees and later holds an assembly on diverse families. The text is straightforward but didactic at times and the uneven, almost garish line illustrations detract significantly from the quality of the book. Librarians and educators could read passages from the book, which would certainly spark discussion about what it means to have a parent who is gay or to live in a "nontraditional" family. ADDITIONAL SELECTION.

Keywords: African Americans, Family Composition, Family Relations, School Relations, Teasing, Lesbian Mothers, Children of Gay Parents, Gay Fathers, Divorced Parents, Stepparents, Father's Day, Anti-Gay Sentiment.

HOFFMAN, MARY. *The Great Big Book of Families.* Illus. by Ros Asquith. New York, NY: Dial, 2011. Unpaged. ISBN: 9780803735163. OCLC #: 489014435. Ages 4–9. FORMAT: Hardcover. AWARDS: None. REVIEWS: BKLST, BCCB, KS, PW, SLJ. (Originally published in the United Kingdom.)

Families come in all shapes, sizes, religions, ethnicities, compositions, and colors in this informational picture book that examines various aspects of family life, from housing, feelings, hobbies, clothes, and pets, to jobs and holiday celebrations. Readers learn that some children are adopted, others are foster children, and some are only children. Interracial as well as same-sex families are depicted in addition to a variety of nontraditional families. Asquith's bright, cheery cartoon illustrations are packed with details that invite children to explore the pages for reflections of their own families. One illustration shows a child dressed as a Native American complete with buckskin and feathers, and librarians or caregivers will want to address this stereotype when sharing the book. The book is recommended for both school and public libraries; the one reservation is the image of the Native American. RECOMMENDED.

Keywords: Adoption, Gay Fathers, Family Composition, Lesbian Mothers, Children of Gay Parents, Family Relations, School Relations, Asian Americans, African Americans, Latinos, Native Americans, Indians, Single Parents, Mixed Race Families, Extended Families, Homeless Families, Grandparent Caregivers, Foster Parents, Uncles, Aunts, Children with Disabilities, Differently Able Individuals, Cross-Dressing, Gender Nonconformity.

HUGHES, SUSAN. *No Girls Allowed: Tales of Daring Women Dressed as Men for Love, Freedom and Adventure.* Illus. by Willow Dawson. Toronto, ON: Kids Can Press, 2008. 80p. ISBN: 9781554531776. OCLC #: 180689406. Ages 8–12. FORMAT: Hardcover. AWARDS: Best Books for Kids and Teens 2009, Canadian Children's Book Centre; Norma Fleck Award for Canadian Children's Non-Fiction 2009. REVIEWS: BKLST, KS, LMC, SLJ, VOYA. Positive review included in the Canadian publication *CM: Canadian Review of Materials,* published by the Manitoba Library Association.

Everything is not as it seems in this graphic-novel-style collective biography that profiles seven females (young women and girls) who dressed as men for freedom, power, financial gain, and family honor. Spanning from 1470 BCE to 1862 and covering various continents and cultures, the short entries detail the lives of these individuals and provide just enough information to whet the appetite of reluctant readers. An afterword and list of further reading supply additional contextual elements for readers wanting more on these gender-bending young people. The black-and-white graphic illustrations complement the straightforward narratives, extending the book's appeal. Gender-variant children will certainly find a role model among this diverse crowd. RECOMMENDED.

Keywords: Cross-Dressing, Gay Role Models, Gender Identity, Gender Non-conformity, Sex Roles, Individuality, Transgender, Biographies, Canada, Canadian Literature, African Americans, Egyptians, Chinese, Vikings, Jews, Women Soldiers.

HYMAN, TRINA SCHART. *Self-Portrait: Trina Schart Hyman.* Reading, MA: Addison-Wesley, 1981. Unpaged. ISBN: 9780201093087. OCLC #: 7246658. Ages 8–12. FORMAT: Hardcover. AWARDS: None. REVIEWS: HB, SLJ.

Sprinkled with illustrations from her various picture books, Hyman's autobiography or self-portrait follows her childhood, entrance into art school, marriage and divorce, "friendship" with Barbara Rogasky, and budding career as a children's book illustrator. Although never explicitly described in the book as a lesbian couple, Barbara and Trina were known by many to be a couple, and Hyman captures their relationship in some of her other children's book illustrations. Rainbow families "reading between the lines" will notice that Hyman places herself and Rogasky in the illustrations of Rogasky's *Winter Poems* and in John Updike's *A Child's Calen-*

dar. With so few biographies of LGBTQ role models, Hyman's accessible offering is perfect for both school and public libraries. HIGHLY RECOMMENDED.

Keywords: Lesbian Mothers, Children of Gay Parents, Gay Role Models, Biographies, Lesbian Artists, Lesbian Illustrators, Lesbian Authors, Trina Schart Hyman.

JENNESS, AYLETTE. *Families: A Celebration of Diversity, Commitment, and Love.* Boston, MA: Houghton Mifflin, 1990. 48p. ISBN: 9780395470381. OCLC #: 19554496. Ages 8–12. FORMAT: Hardcover. AWARDS: Cooperative Children's Book Center Choices 1990. REVIEWS: BKLST, BCCB, HB, KS, SLJ, PW.

Based on a traveling exhibition created by the Children's Museum in Boston, this collection of interviews and black-and-white photos profiles seventeen unique families across the nation. Readers meet children whose parents are divorced; children with two moms or two dads; those living in extended families, communes, and religious communities; and children who have been adopted or live with foster families. Each family profile includes a short narrative, mostly from the child's point of view, and then one or two photographs depicting the family. When the book was first published, it was challenged because of its positive depiction of gay families; over the years its depiction of sex roles and its photographs have dated the book. A more current title using a similar approach is *Families* (Kuklin). ADDITIONAL SELECTION.

Keywords: Gay Fathers, Family Composition, Lesbian Mothers, Children of Gay Parents, Mixed Race Families, Single Parents, Divorced Parents, African Americans, Asian Americans, Latinos, Single Parents, Extended Families, Differently Able Individuals, Cuban Americans, Mexican Americans, Adoption, Bilingual Families, Foster Parents, Cambodian Americans, Widows, Inuit.

JONES, CARRIE. *Sarah Emma Edmonds Was a Great Pretender: The True Story of a Civil War Spy.* Illus. by Mark Oldroyd. Minneapolis, MN: Carolrhoda, 2011. Unpaged. ISBN: 9780761353997. OCLC #: 646630438. Ages 8–11. FORMAT: Hardcover. AWARDS: None. REVIEWS: BKLST, BCCB, HB, KS, SLJ, PW.

As a way to escape her abusive father, who had always wished she was a boy, Canadian-born Sarah Edmonds crossed the U.S. border to become a Bible salesman. Quickly realizing that she could sell more wares as a man, she dressed in men's clothing and pretended, not for the first time, to be a man instead of a woman. Not long afterward, she decided to heed the president of the United States' plea for men to serve in the Civil War. Rejected at first, she eventually was able to enlist and after a short time became a trusted spy serving the Union Army. Unfortunately, she contracted malaria and decided to seek medical attention outside the army hospital lest they discover her true gender. After recovering, she could not rejoin her fellow soldiers because everyone thought she had deserted. Instead she became a nurse in a civilian hospital. Jones's narrative gives readers a glimpse into Edmonds's life and then directs them to a small number of recommended books. Oldroyd's painted illustrations are hazy at times and vary in quality, particularly in the depictions of Edmonds, who looks different in all the spreads. Compared with *Nurse, Soldier, Spy: The Story of Sarah Edmonds, A Civil War Hero* (Moss) this book's storytelling is slightly better, but the illustrations and additional informational sources are lacking in appeal and depth. Collectively, the two resources provide a clearer picture of Edmonds that would be appealing to gender-variant or queer children. ADDITIONAL SELECTION.

Keywords: Cross-Dressing, Gay Role Models, Gender Identity, Gender Nonconformity, Sex Roles, Individuality, Sarah Edmonds, Biographies, Civil War, Women Soldiers.

KAY, VERLA. *Rough, Tough Charley.* Illus. by Adam Gustavson. Berkeley, CA: Tricycle Press, 2007. Unpaged. ISBN: 9781582461847. OCLC #: 71126702. Ages 6–9. FORMAT: Hardcover. AWARDS: Amelia Bloomer List 2008; Notable Social Studies Trade Books for Young People 2008, a cooperative project of the National Council for the Social Studies (NCSS) and the Children's Book Council. REVIEWS: BKLST, KS, PW, SLJ.

Noted for his riding abilities and timeliness as a stagecoach driver, Charley Parkhurst was one tough feller to be reckoned with! He fought off bandits, saved a stagecoach from a collapsed bridge, ran a stage stop in his later life, and accomplished a host of other feats common to men during the mid- to late 1800s. Although everyone thought the unmarried Charley was a man, he was actually a woman who lived as a man most of her life and demonstrated to the world that a woman could do just about anything that a man could do. It wasn't until Charley's death that the secret was discovered. Kay's rhyming text, paired with Gustavson's detailed oil illustrations, captures some of the highlights in Charley's life. Although historical references would have been appreciated, a timeline of known facts is included and the title would pair well with *Riding Freedom* (Ryan) for even more information on Parkhurst. This book is perfect for gender-variant and transgender children or children with transgender or gender-variant family members. HIGHLY RECOMMENDED.

Keywords: Cross-Dressing, Gay Role Models, Gender Identity, Gender Nonconformity, Sex Roles, Transgender, Individuality, Charley Parkhurst, Biographies.

KRAKOW, KARI. *The Harvey Milk Story.* Illus. by David Gardner. Ridley Park, PA: Two Lives Publishing, 2001. Unpaged. ISBN: 9780967446837. OCLC #: 50283613. Ages 7–10. FORMAT: Hardcover. AWARDS: Cooperative Children's Book Center Choices 2003. REVIEWS: KS.

The first children's book to profile gay rights activist Harvey Milk, this straightforward biography follows the life of Milk from his childhood until his assassination in 1978. Readers learn about the politician's passion for equal rights for all people, including gays and lesbians. Although the text never ventures into didacticism, this biography, like many children's biographies, focuses on Milk's strong points rather than profiling him as a multidimensional man. Gardner's soft watercolor illustrations are the perfect accompaniment to the text, providing extra informational detail. Included are an epilogue, author's notes, and a bibliography for further reading. Considering the lack of children's biographies on gay role models, this book is needed in both public and school libraries. HIGHLY RECOMMENDED.

Keywords: Gay Rights Activists, Biographies, Gay Role Models, Gay Men, Harvey Milk, Gay Politicians, Gay Liberation Movement, Jewish Americans.

KRULL, KATHLEEN. *Giants of Science: Leonardo da Vinci.* Illus. by Boris Kulikov. New York, NY: Viking, 2005. 128p. ISBN: 9780670059201. OCLC #: 58526318. Ages 8–12. FORMAT: Hardcover. AWARDS: American Library Association Notable Children's Book 2007; National Science Teachers Association Outstanding Science Trade Books for Students 2006. REVIEWS: BKLST, BL, HB, KS, LMC, PW, SLJ.

Written in a chatty, easily accessible, and highly interesting style that will engage even reluctant readers, this chapter biography profiles one of the world's greatest artists and scientists. Krull describes his illegitimate birth and lack of formalized education, follows many of his major scientific accomplishments and activities, and mentions his death and what became of his papers afterward. While many books about da Vinci focus on his artistic abilities, Krull has chosen to profile his amazing scientific feats. She also discusses accusations of homosexuality when da Vinci was a young man, as well as his subsequent trial and release. Krull notes that da Vinci was probably gay as he had close relationships with men, but none with women. This point is laudable as many children's books choose to ignore his sexuality. **HIGHLY RECOMMENDED.**

Keywords: Biographies, Gay Role Models, Gay Men, Leonardo da Vinci, Gay Scientists, Gay Artists.

KUKLIN, SUSAN. *Families.* New York, NY: Hyperion, 2006. 40p. ISBN: 9780786808229. OCLC #: 62863972. Ages 7–11. FORMAT: Hardcover. AWARDS: American Library Association Notable Children's Book 2007; Best Children's Books of the Year, 2007, Bank Street College of Education, United States; Cooperative Children's Book Center Choices 2006. REVIEWS: BKLST, BL, BCCB, HB, KS, LMC, SLJ.

One of the best informational children's books available on family composition, Kuklin's work highlights fifteen families of varying races, religions, sexualities, sizes, and so forth. For each family, a child was interviewed and a portion of the transcript is profiled along with multiple full-color photographs of the family. The transcripts are in the words of the children, so the writing is very accessible to elementary-age children. The strength of the collection lies in the sheer breadth of families covered. Children will enjoy studying families like their own and reading about those similar to those of their classmates. A two-mom family and a two-dad family are highlighted in the mix. **HIGHLY RECOMMENDED.**

Keywords: International Adoption, Family Composition, Lesbian Mothers, Children of Gay Parents, Gay Fathers, Korean Americans, Japanese Americans, Chinese Americans, Asian Americans, Egyptian Americans, Trinidadian Americans, Stepfamilies, Divorced Parents, Mixed Race Families, Extended Families, Single Parents, African Americans, Indians, Christian Families, Jews, Muslims, Down's Syndrome, Differently Able Individuals, Immigrants.

MADDERN, ERIC. *The Fire Children: A West African Creation Tale.* Illus. by Frané Lessac. New York, NY: Dial, 1993. Unpaged. ISBN: 9780803714779. OCLC #: 26808913. Ages 5–8. FORMAT: Hardcover. AWARDS: None. REVIEWS: BCCB, HB, PW, SLJ.

Nyame the sky-god becomes lonely and decides to create the Earth, the moon and stars, and all the living creatures on the Earth. One day as Nyame is looking at his beautiful work the two spirits that have been living inside him, one male and one female, decide to jump out of Nyame's mouth and onto the Earth. Soon the two spirits create children out of clay and bake them on a fire at varying lengths to create a multicolored race of people. Although the book is written about the Akan people of West Africa, with the help of an adult young readers may be able to read between the lines and identify Nyame as a two-spirit person — as he would be known among First Nation and Native American cultures. Children would then see two-spirited people as powerful creators of life. Given the scarcity of children's literature about two-spirit people, this book would work for both school and public library collections. ADDITIONAL SELECTION.

    Keywords: Gender Identity, Two-Spirit People, Folklore — West Africa, Creation Stories, Race.

MILLER, HILLARY ALICE. *My Family Is Special: Family.* Raleigh, NC: Lulu. com, 2009. Unpaged. ISBN: n.a. OCLC #: n.a. Ages 3–5. FORMAT: Paperback. AWARDS: None. REVIEWS: None.

Although the intent of this book is to demonstrate the diversity in family compositions and to introduce children to biracial and same-sex families, the lack of illustrations and the placement and formatting of the text severely limit the audience and usefulness of this picture book. Huge white spaces are present above the various descriptions of families, which might give children an opportunity to draw their own interpretation of the families described. However, for a library this would not be practical. NOT RECOMMENDED.

    Keywords: Gay Fathers, Family Composition, Lesbian Mothers, Children of Gay Parents, Family Relations, African Americans, Latinos, Single Parents, Mixed Race Families.

MILLER, JENIFER INGERMAN. *A Family Has in It the People You Love.* Lexington, KY: CreateSpace, 2008. Unpaged. ISBN: 9781440421075. OCLC #: 430330152. Ages 3–8. FORMAT: Paperback. AWARDS: None. REVIEWS: None.

Simple text, numerous black-and-white photographs, and cartoon illustrations combine to introduce young readers to the concept of family and the many different forms that it can take: single parent, extended family, lesbian mothers, gay fathers, nuclear, and so forth. The quality of the book is average for a self-published title and the photographs include both archival and current. The use of cartoon animals is jarring when juxtaposed with these photographs. With so many other high-quality books about family composition available, libraries will want to give this one a pass. NOT RECOMMENDED.

Keywords: Gay Fathers, Family Composition, Lesbian Mothers, Children of Gay Parents, Family Relations, African Americans, Single Parents, Mixed Race Families, Extended Families, Grandparent Caregivers, Aunts.

MORRIS, ANN. *Families.* New York, NY: HarperCollins, 2000. 32p. ISBN: 9780688171995. OCLC #: 41834902. Ages 3–7. FORMAT: Hardcover. AWARDS: None. REVIEWS: BKLST, BL, KS, SLJ.

As in her many other informational titles, Morris uses full-color photographs and simple text. In this offering, she presents families from around the world participating in a variety of activities from the mundane to holidays and celebrations. At the end of the book, she provides supplementary information, describing the types of family represented and where they are situated in the world. A world map is included. Unfortunately, as noted by K.T. Horning in her presentations on LGBTQ children's literature, the single photo of a same-sex family with lesbian mothers is missing from the list of cited photographs. As a result, children in rainbow families (as well as children in other family types) miss the opportunity to see a lesbian household identified. This one oversight, whether purposeful or not, detracts from the strength of this book for rainbow families. ADDITIONAL SELECTION.

Keywords: Adoption, Family Composition, Lesbian Mothers, Children of Gay Parents, Asian Americans, Canadians, Foster Parents, Stepfamilies, Mixed Race Families, Extended Families, Single Parents, Ethiopians, Inuit, Vietnamese, African Americans, Latinos, Puerto Ricans, South Koreans, Native Americans, Brazilians, Saudi Arabians, Russians, Indians, Japanese, Jews.

MOSS, MARISSA. *Nurse, Soldier, Spy: The Story of Sarah Edmonds, A Civil War Hero.* Illus. by John Hendrix. New York, NY: Abrams, 2011. 48p. ISBN: 9780810997356. OCLC #: 639521181. Ages 8–12. FORMAT: Hardcover. AWARDS: None. REVIEWS: BKLST, BCCB, HB, PW, SLJ.

In an attempt to escape an arranged marriage, Canadian-born Sarah Edmonds cut her hair, dressed in men's clothes, and crossed the U.S. border to join the Union Army. Known to her fellow soldiers as Frank Thompson, Sarah became a nurse and trusted spy during the Civil War. Later in life, she left the army and married a man, resuming her life as a woman. In Moss's offering, readers glimpse one specific episode in Frank's life as a spy and are directed toward additional resources and a lengthy author's note for more information about Sarah Edmonds. Hendrix's pen-and-ink and acrylic illustrations and hand-drawn type, representative of period "wanted" broadsides, add depth and a historical feel. The storytelling is brief and at times lacks the depth needed to hold the attention of older readers. Hendrix's depiction of Frank disguised as a southern slave stops short of racial stereotyping. Considering that Frank disguised herself as many different types of people for her spy missions, one wonders why she chose to capture this particular instance, which is borderline offensive. The fact that Sarah eventually reclaims her female identity and marries a man makes the book less effective for gender-variant children than *Rough, Tough Charley* (Kay). ADDITIONAL SELECTION.

Keywords: Cross-Dressing, Gay Role Models, Gender Identity, Gender Non-conformity, Sex Roles, Individuality, Sarah Edmonds, Biographies, Civil War, Women Soldiers.

PARR, TODD. *The Family Book.* New York, NY: Little, Brown, 2003. Unpaged. ISBN: 9780316155632. OCLC #: 51060139. Ages 2–7. FORMAT: Hardcover. AWARDS: None. REVIEWS: SLJ.

The world is filled with many different types of families: gay families, stepfamilies, adopted families, single-parent families, nuclear families, and biracial families. Using engaging age-appropriate text, this informational book helps young children understand that their family is special regardless of its composition and the traits of its members. Parr's signature bold illustrations are juxtaposed against equally bright backgrounds that will attract the eye of preschool and early-childhood students. This is a perfect choice for all types of families in school and public libraries. HIGHLY RECOMMENDED.

Keywords: Adoption, Family Composition, Gay Fathers, Lesbian Mothers, Children of Gay Parents, Single Parents, Mixed Race Families, Stepfamilies, Grandparent Caregivers.

PARR, TODD. *It's Okay to Be Different.* New York, NY: Little, Brown, 2001. Unpaged. ISBN: 9780316155625. OCLC #: 44812233. Ages 2–7. FORMAT: Hardcover. AWARDS: None. REVIEWS: BL, HB, KS, PW, SLJ.

Children often worry about being different: having a different type of family, liking different things than their peers, looking different than those around them, and so forth. As in his other books, Parr uses simple, accessible language and relatable situations to help very young children feel good about themselves and their environment. On one of the pages, there is a fleeting line that it's okay to have different moms or different dads. With a depiction of two moms and two dads on the page, this could be interpreted that it is okay to have lesbian moms and gay dads. Parr's signature bold illustrations pop against equally bright backgrounds and complete this delightful book that is perfect for rainbow families as well as other types of families in school and public libraries. HIGHLY RECOMMENDED.

Keywords: Adoption, Family Composition, Gay Fathers, Lesbian Mothers, Children of Gay Parents, Individuality, Differently Able Individuals.

PARR, TODD. *We Belong Together: A Book About Adoption and Families.* New York, NY: Little, Brown, 2007. Unpaged. ISBN: 9780316016681. OCLC #: 179683900. Ages 2–7. FORMAT: Hardcover. AWARDS: None. REVIEWS: BKLST, BCCB, KS, SLJ.

Simple, cheerful illustrations and straightforward text describe the reasons why several families adopted their children. Single parents, gay dads, lesbian moms, and biracial nuclear couples are all presented in happy families excited and eager to adopt a child. Parr's books are appropriate for preschool children and present diverse families in a manner that is easily understood by young children. HIGHLY RECOMMENDED.

Keywords: Adoption, Family Composition, Gay Fathers, Lesbian Mothers, Children of Gay Parents, Family Relations, Single Parents, Mixed Race Families.

ROTNER, SHELLEY, AND SHEILA M. KELLY. *I'm Adopted.* Illus. by Shelley Rotner. New York, NY: Holiday House, 2011. Unpaged. ISBN: 9780823422944. OCLC #: 649419507. Ages 3–7. FORMAT: Hardcover. AWARDS: None. REVIEWS: HB, KS, PW, SLJ.

Colorful, detailed photographs and simple text introduce young children to the concept of adoption (both domestic and international) and provide visual examples of diverse family compositions including single parent, two mothers, two fathers, mother and father, and extended family. Children and caregivers from a variety of ethnic and racial groups are attractively depicted in the photograph collages on each two-page spread. Ideal for public and school libraries, this concept book is sure to attract both children and adults in rainbow families. A particular strength of the book is that it "shows" in pictures rather than "tells" in the text. RECOMMENDED.

Keywords: Gay Fathers, Family Composition, Lesbian Mothers, Children of Gay Parents, Mixed Race Families, Single Parents, African Americans, Asian Americans, Latinos, Extended Families, Adoption, International Adoption.

RYAN, PAM MUÑOZ. *One Hundred Is a Family.* Illus. by Benrei Huang. New York, NY: Hyperion , 1994. Unpaged. ISBN: 9781562826727. OCLC #: 28722389. Ages 4–8. FORMAT: Hardcover. AWARDS: None. REVIEWS: BL, PW, SLJ.

Encouraging readers to count from 1 to 10 and then in multiples of 10 up to 100, this concept book presents readers with a variety of family compositions to explore, from mixed-race to same-sex to extended and beyond. Ryan's text highlights various activities that families do together and Huang's endearing watercolor illustrations encourage children to search through the illustrations to find all the different types of families and people presented. RECOMMENDED.

Keywords: Family Composition, Lesbian Mothers, Children of Gay Parents, Family Relations, Asian Americans, Chinese Americans, African Americans, Mixed Race Families, Extended Families, Differently Able Individuals, Single Parents.

SCHAFFER, PATRICIA. *Chag Sameach! (Happy Holiday).* Berkeley, CA: Tabor Sarah Books, 1986. Rev. ed. Unpaged. ISBN: 9780935079166. OCLC #: 12552003. Ages 5–8. FORMAT: Paperback. AWARDS: None. REVIEWS: None.

Using a series of black-and-white photographs and straightforward text, this informational picture book introduces young readers to various Jewish holidays. The text describes how families celebrate the highlighted holiday, and the photographs depict diverse families including nuclear, mixed-raced, and same-sex. Unfortunately, the format of the book is not attractive and will be a hard sell for young children. Although this is one of the few children's books to present a lesbian Jewish family, the overall quality of the book does not merit its addition to collections. NOT RECOMMENDED.

Keywords: Children of Gay Parents, Lesbian Mothers, Jewish Holidays, Asian Americans, Latinos, Mixed Race Families, Jews.

SKUTCH, ROBERT. *Who's in a Family?* Illus. by Laura Nienhaus. Berkeley, CA: Tricycle Press, 1995. Unpaged. ISBN: 9781883672133. OCLC #: 30979383. Ages 3–7. FORMAT: Hardcover. AWARDS: None. REVIEWS: PW, SLJ.

What makes a family? Readers discover that families can consist of single dads, divorced parents, two moms, two dads, nuclear, or extended. They also learn that sometimes you look like members in your family and other times you don't. On the very last two-page spread, they finally learn that what makes a family is people who love you. The stilted, poorly written text, although ambitious, falls flat, and the comparison between human and animal families is jarring. Similarly, the static illustrations are uneven in quality and hold little appeal for young children. The two rainbow families mentioned are not given the respect of being a child's two dads or two moms; rather, in each case it is the parent and a "partner," discrediting the parental role of the other mom or dad. NOT RECOMMENDED.

Keywords: Gay Fathers, Family Composition, Lesbian Mothers, Children of Gay Parents, African Americans, Asian Americans, Latinos, Single Parents, Extended Families, Animal Families.

SNOW, JUDITH E. *How It Feels to Have a Gay or Lesbian Parent.* Binghamton, NY: Harrington Park Press, 2004. 110p. ISBN: 9781435280113. OCLC #: 227033497. Ages 8–14. FORMAT: Hardcover/Library Binding. AWARDS: None. REVIEWS: BKLST, BL, SLJ.

In this collection of more than thirty personal narratives, children from as young as seven to young adults in their late twenties and early thirties describe their feelings, coping mechanisms, school and family life, and relationships after they discovered that at least one of their parents was LGBTQ. Religious gay bashing, homophobia, and intense emotional pain are described, as are questions about the young people's own sexuality. Readers learn that children in rainbow families come from all backgrounds and vary in how they relate to their parents. Many of the stories deal with the pain of divorce (the author worked as a psychologist with the courts). As in any collection of stories and personal narratives, the quality varies but any child of any age in a rainbow family should be able to find at least one story that resonates. Considering the wide age range of the children and youth profiled, some of the information may be inappropriate for younger children. RECOMMENDED.

Keywords: African Americans, Latinos, Family Composition, Family Relations, School Relations, Lesbian Mothers, Children of Gay Parents, Gay Fathers, Bisexuality, Divorced Parents, Stepfamilies, Homophobia, COLAGE.

SOLOMON, SHARON. *Cathy Williams, Buffalo Soldier.* Illus. by Doreen Lorenzetti. Gretna, LA: Pelican, 2010. Unpaged. ISBN: 9781589808010. OCLC #: 567099903. Ages 8–11. FORMAT: Hardcover. AWARDS: None. REVIEWS: HB, KS, LMC.

One of the first documented women to enlist in the United States Army, Cathy Williams dressed as a man and fought alongside other African Americans as a Buffalo Soldier after the Civil War. This picture-book biography describes Cathy's transformation from young slave girl to washerwoman in the Civil War to soldier and eventually owner of a laundry business. Although the book holds great potential for providing gender-variant children with an African American role model, the affected text and predominantly expressionless illustrations limit the book's accessibility. The lack of historical notes limits its usefulness, although a timeline is provided. NOT RECOMMENDED.

Keywords: Civil War, Cross-Dressing, Gay Role Models, Gender Identity, Gender Nonconformity, Sex Roles, Individuality, Cathy Williams, Biographies, African Americans, Buffalo Soldiers, Female Slaves, Women Soldiers.

STAFFORD, ANIKA. *Aisha's Moonlit Walk: Stories and Celebrations for the Pagan Year.* Boston, MA: Skinner House Books/Unitarian Universalist Association, 2005. 81p. ISBN: 9781558964853. OCLC #: 57193376. Ages 6–11. FORMAT: Paperback. AWARDS: None. REVIEWS: None.

Aisha and her friend Heather (a girl with two mothers) take readers on a tour of various pagan holidays in this collection of stories, craft ideas, discussion questions, and guide for parents/educators. Eight holidays are introduced with a short story involving Aisha and Heather followed by questions and craft suggestions. The holidays are Samhain, Winter Solstice, Brigid's Day, Spring Equinox, Beltaine, Summer Solstice, Lammas, and Fall Equinox. The stories vary in quality but do help children make a personal connection to the highlighted holiday. Unfortunately, the layout of the black-and-white book is very off-putting, with few visuals and many lengthy pages of double-spaced text. Brief suggestions for additional reading are provided, with a focus on Unitarian Universalists. Considering there are few, if any, other books that include rainbow families in a discussion of pagan holidays, libraries may want to consider this title for their collections. ADDITIONAL SELECTION.

Keywords: Children of Gay Parents, Lesbian Mothers, Neopaganism, Holidays, Friendship, Unitarian Universalists.

TAX, MEREDITH. *Families.* Illus. by Marilyn Hafner. Boston, MA: Little, Brown, 1981. 32p. ISBN: 9780316832403. OCLC #: 6666792. Ages 4–8. FORMAT: Hardcover. AWARDS: None. REVIEWS: BKLST, BCCB, KS, PW, SLJ.

Six-year-old Angie takes young readers on an exploration of various types of human and animal families seen in New York City. Mostly she uses her various classmates to introduce stepmothers, adopted children, extended families, and single parents. She politely introduces a lesbian couple as her friend Susie's mother and "godmother." When her friends discover Susie does not have a dad, the boys in her class fight over who can be her father — because she *has* to have a father. Children will relate to Tax's accessible text and Hafner's complementary pen-and-ink illustrations. Unfortunately, some of the illustrations are dated and Hafner did not use the correct Spanish form of "Happy Birthday" in her illustrations of a Puerto Rican child's anniversary. NOT RECOMMENDED.

Keywords: Adoption, Family Composition, Lesbian Mothers, Children of Gay Parents, Family Relations, African Americans, Extended Families, Latinos, Puerto Ricans, Single Parents, Divorced Parents, Stepparents, Grandparent Caregivers.

TURNER, ROBYN. *Rosa Bonheur.* Boston, MA: Little, Brown, 1991. 32p. ISBN: 9780316856485. OCLC #: 22207941. Ages 8–12. FORMAT: Hardcover. AWARDS: Children's Book Center Choices 1991. REVIEWS: BKLST, HB, KS, SLJ.

Part of the Portraits of Women Artists for Children series, this detailed picture-book biography profiles French artist Rosa Bonheur, including her relationship with her "lifetime friend" (read, partner) Nathalie Mica. The informative text describes her childhood, adult life, and eventual death, with significant emphasis on her artistic style and subjects. Bonheur's lifetime friend is mentioned as the artist's traveling companion and a photograph of their château is presented as the place where "they lived the rest of their lives." The book never expressively states the two women were a couple. Rainbow families willing to read between the lines are introduced to a lesbian role model that will empower young women today. RECOMMENDED.

Keywords: Biographies, Gay Role Models, Lesbian Artists, Rosa Bonheur, French Artists, Lesbian Couples.

WALTER-GOODSPEED, DEE DEE. *At My House What Makes a Family Is Love.* Illus. by Jim Morrison. Bloomington, IN: AuthorHouse, 2006. 23p. ISBN: 9781425924263. OCLC #: 156935172. Ages 4–8. FORMAT: Paperback. AWARDS: None. REVIEWS: None.

What makes a family is love! Whether you have foster parents, two moms, or grandparents as caregivers, the important thing is that you are loved. This simple picture book profiles families of varying compositions in diverse living arrangements: condos, houses, mobile homes, or no homes (homeless). While the text is appealing and sure to spark discussion, the illustrations are uneven in quality, often using garish depictions of the families. If libraries use this book, it is recommended that children create their own illustrations. A better choice for libraries on a similar topic is *The Great Big Book of Families* (Hoffman). ADDITIONAL SELECTION.

Keywords: Gay Fathers, Family Composition, Lesbian Mothers, Children of Gay Parents, Single Parents, Mixed Race Families, Extended Families, Homeless Families, Grandparent Caregivers, Foster Parents, Divorced Parents.

WARHOLA, JAMES. *Uncle Andy's: A Faabbbulous Visit with Andy Warhol.* New York, NY: Putnam, 2003. Unpaged. ISBN: 9780399238697. OCLC #: 50204285. Ages 5–9. FORMAT: Hardcover. AWARDS: Best Children's Books of the Year, 2004, Bank Street College of Education, United States; Cooperative Children's Book Center Choices 2004; Children's and Young Adult's Book Award, 2004, Primary Nonfiction, International Reading Association. REVIEWS: BKLST, BCCB, KS, PW SLJ.

In this illustrated memoir, Jamie and his country bumpkin family take a special trip to New York in August 1962 to visit his grandmother and famous Uncle Andy (Warhol). Uncle Andy's house is full of interesting things — twenty-five cats all named Sam, half-finished art, junk remnants for art projects, and pop art sculptures. The story explains the influence that Uncle Andy had on Jamie's future career as an artist and readers will be inspired by Warhola's detailed spreads and may want to create their own art from "found" objects. Uncle Andy's sexuality is never discussed, but the book does present a gay role model for children in rainbow families. RECOMMENDED.

Keywords: Artists, Family Relations, Gay Role Models, Gay Uncles, Individuality, Andy Warhol.

WINTER, JONAH. *Gertrude Is Gertrude Is Gertrude Is Gertrude.* Illus. by Calef Brown. New York, NY: Atheneum, 2009. Unpaged. ISBN: 9781416940883. OCLC #: 79860283. Ages 4–8. FORMAT: Hardcover. AWARDS: Bulletin of the Center for Children's Books Blue Ribbons 2009; Cooperative Children's Book Center Choices 2010; Rainbow List 2010. REVIEWS: BKLST, BCCB, KS, LMC, PW, SLJ.

This nonsensical picture-book biography invites young readers to a party at the house of Gertrude Stein and Alice B. Toklas. Not just any party but the party of parties that everyone who is everyone attends. Guests include Basket the poodle and artists and writers such as Pablo Picasso, Henri Matisse, and Ernest Hemingway. Winter's prose varies in length and subject, paying tribute to Stein's own writing style. Brown's abstract illustrations mirror the artwork of famous artists who attended Stein and Toklas's many parties. The integration of art and text creates a whimsical work that takes itself none too seriously and would work well as a read-aloud for younger children or as a springboard into modernist writing and art for older children. The author's note mentions Gertrude and Alice's longstanding relationship, although it does not say that they were partners. RECOMMENDED.

Keywords: Biographies, Gay Role Models, Lesbian Authors, Gertrude Stein, Alice B. Toklas, Lesbian Couples.

Other Media

Films

The films in this section include live-action and animated selections that can be used with children up to eleven years of age. Some films are aimed at educators or other adults, but include portions that are highly relevant to elementary children. *Rick and Steve: The Happiest Gay Couple in All the World,* created and directed by Q. Allan Brocka, and *Queer Duck*, written and created by Mike Reiss and directed by Xeth Feinberg, are not listed. The first uses Lego-like characters and the second one is animated, but in each case the content is intended for adults, much like the animated programs *The Simpsons* and *Family Guy.*

BERLINER, ALAIN, AND CHRIS VANDER STAPPEN. *Ma vie en rose (My Life in Pink).* Culver City, CA: Sony Pictures, 1997. 88 minutes. Color. French with English, Spanish, and French subtitles. ISBN: 9780767836623. OCLC #: 46673735. RATING: R. Ages 10–12. FORMAT: DVD. AWARDS: Best Foreign Language Film, Golden Globe; Outstanding Film, GLAAD Media Awards;

FIPRESCI Prize, Sarajevo Film Festival; Best Feature Film, Seattle Lesbian & Gay Film Festival. REVIEWS: None.

One of the few movies to depict a transgender child, this slice-of-life French film profiles seven-year-old Ludovic and his family as they navigate the choppy waters of a suburban community that is both homophobic and intolerant of Ludovic's gender-variant behavior. Ludovic is a typical self-absorbed seven-year-old who cannot understand why everyone makes a big deal of his cross-dressing and playing with dolls, particularly since he knows he is really a girl. When he announces to his friends and family that he plans to marry the boy next door and then proceeds to have a pretend ceremony complete with his own gown, a downward spiral of ostracization begins for Ludovic and his family. Particularly poignant is the scene in which one boy is no longer allowed to sit next to Ludovic at school because his parents have told him that he will go to hell if he interacts with Ludovic. The movie has a rating of "R" in the United States, but most other countries give it the equivalent rating of PG-13 for language (there is one instance of a four-letter word when the mother becomes distraught). This would be a perfect movie for parents and preteens to watch together and to spawn discussion of societal views about homosexuality, transgender, and gender nonconformity. The character of Ludovic is wonderfully portrayed and viewers almost forget he is a boy pretending to be a girl. HIGHLY RECOMMENDED.

Keywords: Family Relations, School Relations, Gender Nonconformity, Transgender, Gender Identity, Cross-Dressing, French Films, France.

BORTMAN, CAMOMILE, LESBIAN AND GAY PARENTS ASSOCIATION (SAN FRANCISCO, CA), GAY AND LESBIAN PARENTS COALITION INTERNATIONAL. *Both of My Moms' Names Are Judy: Children of Lesbians and Gays Speak Out.* San Francisco, CA: Lesbian and Gay Parents Association, 1994. 10 minutes. Color. English. OCLC #: 155140087. RATING: Not Rated. Ages 8 and up. FORMAT: VHS/DVD. AWARDS: None. REVIEWS: None.

This short documentary features interviews with early-grade-school children who have two moms or two dads. These children, from a variety of racial and ethnic groups, discuss how it feels to be bullied because of their parents' sexuality, how their schools often ignore their family dynamic in the curriculum, and how they want things to change. A brief segment discusses the lack of books about their families in their classrooms. The simplicity and brevity of this film allows it to serve a twofold purpose: as an educational tool to prompt discussions of rainbow families among elementary school children and as a training tool for educators serving the needs of rainbow families. RECOMMENDED.

Keywords: Children of Gay Parents, Family Composition, Family Relations, Gay Fathers, Homosexuality and Education, Lesbian Mothers, School Relations, Documentaries, Elementary Schools, Curriculum, Professional Development.

COHEN, HELEN, AND DEBRA CHASNOFF. *It's Elementary: Talking About Gay Issues in School.* Harriman, NY: New Day Films, 2008. 78 minutes. Color. English. ISBN: 9781574482065. OCLC #: 213376856. RATING: Not Rated.

Ages 10–12. FORMAT: 2 DVDs. AWARDS: Best Documentary, San Francisco International Lesbian and Gay Film Festival; Best Documentary, Santa Barbara Lesbian and Gay Film Festival; Juror's Choice Award, Charlotte Film Festival; Best Educational Film, Northern Lights International Film Festival; Documentary of the Year, GLAAD Media Awards; Best Documentary, Chicago Lesbian and Gay Film Festival. REVIEWS: None.

The first DVD is the original 1996 version of this film, which describes how educators in six elementary and middle schools address topics relating to LGBTQ individuals and families with children in first grade and up. One segment of the documentary showcases teachers using the picture book *Asha's Mums* to broach the topic of same-sex parents. It also includes *It's Still Elementary,* which looks at the impact of *It's Elementary* on some of the teachers and students ten years after they were featured in the original film. The second DVD includes a shorter, 1997 version of *It's Elementary* intended for use in professional development settings. The film was created for adults but certain segments can be shown to upper elementary students to begin a discussion on LGBTQ families. RECOMMENDED.

Keywords: Children of Gay Parents, Family Composition, Family Relations, Gay Fathers, Homosexuality and Education, Lesbian Mothers, School Relations, Documentaries, Elementary Schools, Curriculum, Professional Development.

COHEN, HELEN, AND DEBRA CHASNOFF. *That's a Family: A Film for Kids About Family Diversity.* San Francisco, CA: Respect for All Project/Women's Educational Media, 2000. 36 minutes. Color. English. ISBN: 9781574481297. OCLC #: 145501893. RATING: Not Rated. Ages 7–11. FORMAT: DVD. AWARDS: National Council on Family Relations Media Award. REVIEWS: None.

A combination of live-action interviews and animated segues, this appealing collection profiles elementary-age children from various types of families: mixed-race, same-sex, intergenerational, single-parent, adoptive, and so forth. Parents include two moms, two dads, one mom and one dad, grandparents, and one parent. For each family, the children describe how the family was formed and what they think about it; they also define terms that may be unfamiliar to other children, such as "gay." The various family types are divided into easy-to-locate chapters on the DVD for librarians and educators wanting to focus on a specific family for a program or lesson. A discussion and teaching guide covers each family type presented, provides extension activities, and suggests children's books and professional resources on the topic. This would be an ideal film to pair with *Families* (Kuklin). HIGHLY RECOMMENDED.

Keywords: Children of Gay Parents, Family Composition, Family Relations, Gay Fathers, Homosexuality and Education, Lesbian Mothers, School Relations, Documentaries, Elementary Schools, Curriculum, Professional Development, Mixed Race Families, Adoption, International Adoption, Stepfamilies, Divorced Parents, Single Parents, Grandparent Caregivers, African Americans, Latinos, Asian Americans, Guatemalan Americans, Chinese Americans, Muslims, Jews, German Americans, Filipino Americans, Bilingual Families.

MAXWELL, ANDREA, AND TAMMY STONER. *Dottie's Magic Pockets.* Los Angeles, CA: Pink Pea, 2007. 50 minutes. Color. English. ISBN: n.a. OCLC #: 248739533. RATING: Not Rated. Ages 2–5. FORMAT: DVD. AWARDS: None. REVIEWS: SLJ.

When Dottie's son goes to school and her partner goes to work, the lesbian mom reaches inside her magic pockets and pulls out special glitter that brings her house to life with puppets, songs, dancing, and more. This DVD includes two episodes: "Doing the Flower" and "Beat Beet." In the first episode, children learn the importance of individuality and being proud of your own unique self. The episode also includes a lesbian couple with a new baby and two daddy caterpillars and their children. In the second episode, young children are introduced to several homophones and taught the difference between them. This episode also includes a gay character who is sad because his boyfriend is out of town. Rainbow families are effortlessly integrated into each of these episodes and the same-sex parent issue never arises. The catchy songs and repetitive nature of the programs are appropriate for young children and the mixture of live action, animation, and puppetry are sure to hold their attention as well. Additional information on the show is available from http://www.dottiesmagicpockets.com/. RECOMMENDED.

Keywords: Family Relations, Individuality, Gender Roles, Sex Roles, Gay Men, Lesbians, Children of Gay Parents, Gay Fathers, Lesbian Mothers, African Americans.

SCAGLIOTTI, JOHN, AND DAN HUNT. *Oliver Button Is a Star.* Monson, MA: Hunt & Scagliotti Productions, 2001. 56 minutes. Color. English. ISBN: n.a. OCLC #: 58995121. RATING: Not Rated. Ages 6 and up. FORMAT: DVD/VHS. AWARDS: None. REVIEWS: BKLST.

Using Tomie dePaola's *Oliver Button Is a Sissy* as a springboard for discussing gender variance in children, this multimedia production includes animated scenes from the book; a live production of the book by the Twin Cities Gay Men's Chorus; commentary from dePaola, Ann Bancroft, Bill T. Jones, and Kevyn Aucoin about growing up as gender-variant children; and scenes from a first grade classroom where the teacher uses Oliver Button to discuss gender nonconformity with her young students. There is something here for everyone (children, teachers, librarians, and parents) but particularly important are dePaola and the other actors' descriptions of being bullied, beaten, or teased for being different. Each of them details how society refused to let them be themselves. HIGHLY RECOMMENDED.

Keywords: Family Relations, Individuality, School Relations, Teasing, Bullying, Gender Identity, Gender Nonconformity, Gender Diversity, Gender Roles, Sex Roles, Cross-Dressing, Gay Authors, Tomie dePaola, Tomboys, Dance, Documentaries, Elementary Schools, Curriculum, Professional Development, Lesbians, Gay Men.

SPADOLA, MEEMA. *Our House: Kids of Gay and Lesbian Parents.* New York, NY: First Run Features, 2008. 56 minutes. Color. English. ISBN: n.a. OCLC #: 212933289. RATING: Not Rated. Ages 11 and up. FORMAT: DVD. AWARDS: Best Documentary, New York Lesbian and Gay Film Festival. REVIEWS: Library Journal, Entertainment Weekly.

Profiling rainbow families across the United States, this documentary highlights what it is like to be the child of gay and lesbian parents in rural, urban, and suburban areas as well as in various religious, ethnic, and racial communities. Interviews include children and parents and cover topics such as homophobia, religious acceptance, bullying in schools, gay marriage, and so forth. The presentation is well rounded, depicting both the joys and sorrows of being in a rainbow family. The real-life coverage will spark discussions about gay rights, anti-gay sentiments, and much more. RECOMMENDED.

Keywords: Family Relations, School Relations, Teasing, Bullying, Homophobia, Documentaries, Children of Gay Parents, Lesbian Mothers, Gay Fathers, African Americans, Spanish Americans, Mormons, International Adoption, Divorced Parents, Stepfamilies.

TOWNE-COLLEY, MARGAUX, AND JOHN EDWARDS. *Buddy G, My Two Moms and Me: The Lost Rings.* Omaha, NE: Us2 LLC, 2007. 11 minutes. Color. English. ISBN: n.a. OCLC #: 432048832. RATING: Not Rated. Ages 2–5. FORMAT: DVD. AWARDS: None. REVIEWS: None.

Based on Margaux Towne-Colley's son and his relationship with his lesbian mothers, this computer-animated program follows five-year-old Buddy G and his next-door neighbor Owen as they have outdoor adventures fueled by huge doses of imagination. While they are playing, Owen decides that he wants to "borrow" rings that belong to Buddy G's mothers. Unfortunately, he loses them and the two boys must work together to find the rings, with the help of Buddy G's computer called Socrates, before they get into big trouble. The animation and catchy songs are appealing to young children, who will be hungry for more after watching this short episode. The two-mom aspect is naturally integrated into the storyline. Additional information on the show is available from http://www.buddyg.tv/. RECOMMENDED.

Keywords: Family Relations, Children of Gay Parents, Lesbian Mothers, Friendship, Truthfulness.

VASQUEZ, JAMES, AND JOBIN SEBASTIAN. *Ready? Ok!* New Almaden, CA: Wolfe Video, 2009. 93 minutes. Color. English. ISBN: 9781934676271. OCLC #: 318462156. RATING: Not Rated. Ages 11 and up. FORMAT: DVD. AWARDS: Best Feature, Seattle LGBT Film Fest; Best Narrative Feature Film, Out San Diego. REVIEWS: None.

Fourth-grader Josh is quite enthusiastic about cheerleading, much to the chagrin of his mother and the faculty at his Catholic school, who believe that cheering is for girls. While he does receive taunts from the boys at school, Josh is quite happy to spend his time with his female classmates planning dance routines, braiding hair, and being his artistic self. Ever the young entrepreneur, the boy decides to apply to cheerleading camp and raise money for his cause. His single mother is preoccupied with work and has little time for her son, her twin brother who sometimes lives with the family, and her firecracker mother. However, when she loses her job, Josh's mother decides to take stock of her family relationships and, with the help of a gay neighbor, decides to be supportive of her son's penchant for dolls, dresses, and cheerleading. This heartwarming family comedy is one that will reinforce individuality and raise questions about what really makes a family. The film does contain one fleeting reference to pot and porn but that should not deter parents from sharing this movie with their children. RECOMMENDED.

Keywords: Family Relations, Divorce, Single Parents, Individuality, School Relations, Gender Identity, Gender Nonconformity, Gay Neighbors, Cross-Dressing.

WGBH BOSTON AND COOKIE JAR ENTERTAINMENT, INC. IN ASSOCIATION WITH MARC BROWN STUDIOS. *Buster's Outdoor Journeys. (Postcards from Buster).* Hollywood, CA: Pink Pea, 2007. 50 minutes. Color. English. ISBN: n.a. OCLC #: 248739533. RATING: Not Rated (U.S.); G (Canada). Ages 3–8. FORMAT: DVD. AWARDS: None. REVIEWS: None.

Similar to the other programs in the *Postcards from Buster* series, this collection follows Buster and his dad as they travel across the United States introducing young children to various aspects of daily life. Four episodes are included here: "Meet Me at the Fair" highlights a county fair in Indiana, "The Giant Pumpkin" explores a pumpkin farm in Oregon, "Bayou, By Me" profiles a Louisiana Bayou, and "Sugartime!" introduces children to the process of making maple syrup in Vermont. This program was pulled from many PBS stations around the nation because it included the "Sugartime!" episode, which has children with two mothers. To make it more obvious that funders of *Postcards from Buster* didn't approve of the "Sugartime!" episode, each of the other three episodes includes a statement that funding was provided by a Ready to Learn Cooperative Agreement from the U.S. Department of Education through the Public Broadcasting Service. This statement is missing from the "Sugartime!" episode and the DVD case notes that "Sugartime!" did not receive this funding. There are special features for each of the other three episodes on the DVD but not for "Sugartime!" All this controversy aside, the program is average in quality and children in rainbow families would have to listen closely to the "Sugartime!" episode to even discern that the mothers are lesbian. Nonetheless, with the lack of children's television programming that represents rainbow families, this DVD is still recommended. RECOMMENDED.

Keywords: Family Relations, Sex Roles, Children of Gay Parents, Lesbian Mothers, Maple Syrup, Pumpkins, County Fairs, Bayous, Rabbits.

Coloring Books

BLACK, LIBBY, AND JENNIFER LOVVORN. *My Family, Your Family, Our Family.* Self-Published, 2004. Unpaged. ISBN: n.a. OCLC #: 237609318. Ages 4–8. FORMAT: Paperback. AWARDS: None. REVIEWS: None.

Eight LGBTQ families are presented in this informational coloring book about family composition. Readers are introduced to single parents, lesbian mothers, gay fathers, biracial families, stepfamilies, extended families, and of course the children. The text is very basic and children can infer — based on the illustrations and some of the names — that a broad diversity of ethnicities and races are represented. According to the back of the book, some of the characters are bisexual and transgender as well. While the intentions of this book are laudable, the end product is not very engaging. The illustrations look as if they were created by taking photographs and outlining/tracing over various facial features. The result is very little detail and considerable white space. NOT RECOMMENDED.

Keywords: African Americans, Asian Americans, Indian Americans, Adoption, Family Composition, Family Relations, Lesbian Mothers, Mixed Race Families, Children of Gay Parents, Self-Published Literature, Bisexual Parents, Transgender Parents.

BROWN, FORMAN. *The Generous Jefferson Bartleby Jones.* Illus. by Leslie Trawin. Boston, MA: Alyson Wonderland, 1991. Unpaged. ISBN: 9781555831981. OCLC #: 25166748. Ages 4–8. FORMAT: Paperback. AWARDS: None. REVIEWS: SLJ.

Jefferson Bartleby Jones (Jeff to his friends) has two dads, Pete and Joe, who he loves to visit. During the week he lives with his mother but at weekends his dads are all his, taking him to the zoo, the farm, and many other wonderful places. Jeff's friends only have one dad each, and their dads are often too busy working to spend time with them. Jeff generously lends his dads out to take his friends to the zoo and farm. One Sunday, Jeff accidentally schedules both of his dads to spend time with his friends and there is no one at home for him. Jeff is angry at first but soon his dads and friends come back to get him and buy ice cream for everyone. The rhyming text is forced at times and the sentence structure may be hard for young children to read. Trawin's line illustrations are lackluster at best and do little to extend this coloring storybook. NOT RECOMMENDED.

Keywords: Family Relations, Gay Fathers, Children of Gay Parents, Divorced Parents.

BUNNELL, JACINTA. *Sometimes the Spoon Runs Away with Another Spoon Coloring Book.* Illus. by Nathaniel Kusinitz. Oakland, CA: PM Press, 2010. Unpaged. ISBN: 9781604863291. OCLC #: 555670679. Ages 4–8. FORMAT: Paperback. AWARDS: None. REVIEWS: None.

"Diddle Diddle Dumpling, my son John, Went to bed with a pretty dress on, One shoe off and one shoe on, Diddle Diddle Dumpling, my son John." This rhyme is just one of many rhymes, proclamations, and tongue-in-cheek observations in this contemporary look at gender. Readers see gender-variant children adopting their own pronouns to describe themselves, Prince Charming looking for the owner of a glass slipper so he can buy his own pair, and the Little Mermaid searching for another boot that will empower her to start over with her own voice and a pair of legs. These are certainly not your mother's nursery rhymes and it's about time! The ready-to-color images depict a variety of children and storybook characters ready to tackle to society's view of gender. Based on anecdotes from real children, this coloring book could be used during library programming to spark discussions about gender or to affirm the lives of gender-variant children. A list of questions about gender is also provided. RECOMMENDED.

Keywords: Gender Nonconformity, Gender Identity, Individuality, Transgender, Cross-Dressing, Gender Diversity, Sex Roles, Gays, Lesbians, Queer Rhymes, Differently Able Individuals.

BUNNELL, JACINTA, AND IRIT REINHEIMER. *Girls Will Be Boys Will Be Girls Will Be . . . : A Coloring Book.* Berkeley, CA: Soft Skull Press, 2010. Unpaged. ISBN: 9781932360622. OCLC #: 62881461. Ages 4–8. FORMAT: Paperback. AWARDS: None. REVIEWS: None.

From GAGA (Girls Against Gender Assignment) to nurturing men to genderless toys to revolutionary women, this nonconformist coloring book presents readers with a variety of gender-variant children who refuse to be boxed in by society's gender expectations. The collection derives from twenty contributors who sketched their own cartoon illustrations to accompany an affirming statement for gender-nonconforming and transgender children. The illustrations vary in quality but overall the text and illustrations combine to create an important and empowering book. RECOMMENDED.

Keywords: Gender Nonconformity, Gender Identity, Transgender, Individuality, Cross-Dressing, Gender Diversity, Sex Roles, Differently Able Individuals.

BUNNELL, JACINTA, AND JULIE NOVAK. *Girls Are Not Chicks Coloring Book.* Oakland, CA: PM Press, 2009. Unpaged. ISBN: 9781604860764. OCLC #: 316058266. Ages 4–8. FORMAT: Paperback. AWARDS: Amelia Bloomer List 2011. REVIEWS: None.

The first in a series of "genderific" coloring books for contemporary children, this offering provides positive gender-role models for girls, demonstrating that girls can do anything. Readers meet a modern Rapunzel, Miss Muffet, and ballerina who are determined to show the world that they won't sit around and wait for some boy to come and save them. A combination of empowering text and ready-to-color illustrations highlighting "gurl power," this is a good resource to spark discussion and use for library programming with all families. RECOMMENDED.

Keywords: Gender Nonconformity, Gender Identity, Individuality, Cross-Dressing, Gender Diversity, Sex Roles.

CLARKE, CHERIL. *My Family! A Multi-Cultural Holiday Coloring Book for Children of LGBT Families.* Illus. by Aiswarya Mukherjee and Suraj Singh. Sicklerville, NJ: My Family!/Dodi Press, 2010. Unpaged. ISBN: 9780976727347. OCLC #: n.a. Ages 4–11. FORMAT: Paperback. AWARDS: None. REVIEWS: None.

Multiracial families with two moms and two dads, as well as extended families, are represented in this coloring book that highlights holidays such as Christmas, Hanukkah, and Kwanzaa. Unfortunately, whereas some of the other coloring books listed here have a distinct narrative, this one showcases random images of varying quality. Many of the illustrations are too small and detailed for young children, and older children may not find the book engaging. While the concept is commendable, the overall execution is poor. NOT RECOMMENDED.

Keywords: Family Relations, Gay Fathers, Lesbian Mothers, Children of Gay Parents, Self-Published Literature, African Americans, Mixed Race Families, Kwanzaa, Christmas, Hanukkah.

GONZALEZ, MAYA CHRISTINA. *Gender Now Coloring Book: A Learning Adventure for Children and Adults.* San Francisco, CA: Reflection Press, 2010. 49p. ISBN: 9780984379910. OCLC #: n.a. Ages 4–12. FORMAT: Paperback. AWARDS: None. REVIEWS: None.

Chock-full of vocabulary, facts, details, and activities relating to transgender children, famous transgender people in history, and transgender animals, this informational resource and coloring book provides a window for preschool and elementary school children to explore the concept of gender and to choose a gender that matches their own. Readers and their caregivers are introduced to the six kids of the gender team, who take them on a journey to explore the ins and outs of gender identity. Pages range from simple matching activities for younger children to detailed historical accounts for older readers. Topics such as intersex, two-spirit, and gender diversity in other cultures are also explored. Gonzalez's kid-friendly illustrations extend the age range of the book but do contain nudity that may offend conservative parents. Regardless, the topic of the book is very important and rarely covered in children's literature. Librarians will appreciate the extensive lists of resources on transgender at the back of the book. RECOMMENDED.

Keywords: Gender Nonconformity, Gender Identity, Individuality, Transgender, Self-Published Literature, Intersex, Cross-Dressing, Gender in History, Gender Diversity, Two-Spirit People.

JOHNSON-CALVO, SARITA. *A Beach Party with Alexis.* Boston, MA: Alyson Wonderland, 1991. Unpaged. ISBN: 9781555832308. OCLC #: 29370157. Ages 4–8. FORMAT: Paperback. AWARDS: None. REVIEWS: None.

School is out and Alexis wants to have a beach party with all her friends! The young African American girl creates invitations and soon the big day arrives. Alexis and her two moms go shopping and then to the beach to set up for the party. As guests gather, readers are introduced to various types of families. Although this is a party, the text doesn't quite capture the festive atmosphere but rather reads as a play-by-play of the action. The illustrations of racially diverse children are average in quality but add an aspect to this coloring storybook that is not often available in books about rainbow families. Libraries may want to consider adding the book to a parenting section for this reason alone. ADDITIONAL SELECTION.

Keywords: African Americans, Family Composition, Family Relations, Lesbian Mothers, Grandparent Caregivers, Mixed Race Families, Children of Gay Parents.

WILLHOITE, MICHAEL. *Families: A Coloring Book.* Boston, MA: Alyson Wonderland, 1991. 48p. ISBN: 9781555831929. OCLC #: n.a. Ages 2–7. FORMAT: Paperback. AWARDS: None. REVIEWS: None.

One of the first coloring books for children to depict gay families, Willhoite's title introduces readers to a variety of family types both human and animal. The text is sparse and the illustrations are average at best. While the book might be appropriate for rainbow families to share together, it offers little for library collections or programs, and those seeking reflections of gender-nonconforming or transgender children will be disappointed by the traditional gender images of girls with dolls and boys playing ball. ADDITIONAL SELECTION.

Keywords: Family Composition, Children of Gay Parents, Gay Fathers, Lesbian Mothers, Latinos, African Americans, Asian Americans, Single Parents, Divorced Parents, Stepfamilies, Adoption, Extended Families, Gay Uncles, Aunts.

Music Recordings

NASH, SUZI. *Rainbow Sprinkles: Songs for Our Children Celebrating Our Diverse Lives.* Pennsauken, NJ: Disc Makers, 2005. 30 minutes. English. ISBN: n.a. OCLC #: 77562451. Ages 2–5. FORMAT: Compact Disc/MP3 Download. AWARDS: None. REVIEWS: None.

"Families come in different ways, some are straight and some are gay!" With this opening line sung in a country western style, young children immediately know this song collection is different than most. Celebrating the joys of growing up in rainbow families, the songs represent diverse genres and vary greatly in quality. Some of the songs are preachy and forced (such as "Just the Way I Am") while others flow freely. Regardless, this diverse collection is sure to have something for everyone and will have children clapping and snapping along to at least a few of the songs. "Uncle Mike" celebrates an uncle who is transgender; other songs are vague enough about sexualities to be inclusive of parents and children who identify as bisexual. RECOMMENDED.

Keywords: Family Relations, Individuality, Gender Nonconformity, Children of Gay Parents, Gay Fathers, Lesbian Mothers, Gay Relatives, Lesbian Aunts, Transgender, Transgender Uncles, Bisexuality.

STONER, TAMMY. *The Super Secret Seashell Cave.* Los Angeles, CA: Dottie's Magic Pockets, 2009. 1 hour 18 minutes. English. ISBN: n.a. OCLC #: 505653638. Ages 2–5. FORMAT: Compact Disc/MP3 Download. AWARDS: None. REVIEWS: None.

Twenty-four tracks follow Dottie and her friends on an adventure to the sea. The quality of the songs varies but for the most part they are catchy and age-appropriate for preschool children. This is more of a sing-along story than an actual CD of individual songs and would allow children to take the lesbian mom and her friends along for a road trip to their own sea adventure! Additional information on the show and CD is available from http://www.dottiesmagicpockets.com/. RECOMMENDED.

Keywords: Family Relations, Individuality, Gender Roles, Sex Roles, Gay Men, Lesbians, Children of Gay Parents, Gay Fathers, Lesbian Mothers.

THOMAS, MARLO. *Free to Be You and Me.* New York, NY: Arista, 1972/2006. 46 minutes. English. ISBN: n.a. OCLC #: 70902215. Ages 4–8. FORMAT: Compact Disc/Download. AWARDS: None. REVIEWS: None.

Produced as a music recording and book and later as a television program for children in 1974, this subversive collection of songs challenges gender roles and gender stereotypes while promoting children's individuality. The songs highlight girls who want to do traditional male activities and boys who want to participate in traditional female activities. What boys and girls can wear and what types of toys they play with are also addressed. A cover of *William's Doll* is among the recording's offerings. The cast includes numerous well-known actresses and actors. Both the television program and the music recording have been remastered and rereleased for a new generation of children. There are many positive messages that gender-variant children will find affirming. HIGHLY RECOMMENDED.

Keywords: Family Relations, Individuality, Gender Roles, Sex Roles, Gender Nonconformity, Gender Diversity, Cross-Dressing.

Magazines

MATANAH, LAURA. *Rainbow Rumpus: The Magazine for Youth with LGBT Parents.* Minneapolis, MN: Rainbow Rumpus. Ages 6–12. FORMAT: Online. AWARDS: None. REVIEWS: None. URL: http://www.rainbowrumpus.org.

Established in 2005, this volunteer-based online magazine is one of the few magazines available for children in rainbow families. According to the magazine's Web site, Rainbow Rumpus produces "over 25 new stories each year, along with articles, essays, music and video created by both young people and professional artists." Rumpus's advisory board includes well-known LGBTQ authors Marion Dane Bauer, Nancy Garden, Gregory Maguire, and Jacqueline Woodson. Information for LGBT parents as well as articles and e-books for children in rainbow families is provided. This is an excellent resource for both school and public libraries. HIGHLY RECOMMENDED.

Keywords: Family Relations, Individuality, Gender Roles, Children of Gay Parents, Gay Fathers, Lesbian Mothers.

E-Books

Various Web sites present different formats of e-books that represent rainbow families. Some of these electronic books offer PDFs that can either be read online or printed and read like a traditional book. Other e-books are only available online and must be read using electronic devices like Kindles, Nooks, and iPads. These e-books may include sound or the ability to "turn pages."

ONG por la No Discriminación — Created by an anti-discrimination organization in Spain, this Web site includes downloadable e-books (free PDFs) of gay-themed picture books in English and Spanish. The books were originally published in Spanish and have been translated into English. The quality of the translations and books varies from title to title. The four books available, all written by M. Luisa Guerrero, are *Seelie, el hada Buena, El viejo coche/The Old Car, La Princesa Ana/Princess Anne,* and *Marta y la sirena/Marta and the Mermaid.* URL: http://www.ong-nd.org/editorial_nd_conjunto_ingles.html.

Rainbow Rumpus' Printable Picture Books and Early Readers — Representing a variety of ethnicities and races, these picture books and beginning reader books represent both lesbian and gay households. The titles include *Baby Maria* (written by Mike Huber and Illus. by Jackie Urbanovic), *Same, Same* (written by Amy E. Brandt and Illus. by Jackie Urbanovic), *The Boy Who Captured the Moon* (written by Patt Ligman and Illus. by Jackie Urbanovic), and *Ta-cumba Goes By Himself* (written by Mike Huber and Illus. by Christine Thornton). The four books vary in quality and include activities and discussion questions. URL: http://rainbowrumpus.org/htm/printable.htm.

SEARS, JESSICA MAY. *Amazing Mommies.* Good As You Books, 2009. Ages 4–8. FORMAT: Online. COMPATIBILITY: Kindle, iPad. AWARDS: None. REVIEWS: None. FEATURES: Page Turn, Color Illustrations.

Using mixed media and line illustrations, this e-book follows a young girl named Flora who has two mommies. She describes the many things they do together and then decides to visit her friends' houses to see what types of families they have. The narrative is didactic at best and the line illustrations appear to be filled-in coloring book pages. NOT RECOMMENDED.

Keywords: Children of Gay Parents, Lesbian Mothers, Family Composition.

VAN GILS, CONNIE. *Bill Sanders.* Illus. by Roel Seidell. Narrated in English by Mary-Ann Jacobs. Software developed by Michel Boezerooij. 2011. Ages 4–8. FORMAT: Online. COMPATIBILITY: iPhone, iPod, iPad. AWARDS: None. REVIEWS: None. FEATURES: Narrated Story, Page Turn, Color Illustrations. For more information, visit: http://www.billsandersapp.com/en/home.html.

Bill is different from the other boy frogs who love girls; he prefers to watch the boy frogs in water ballet and is in love with a boy frog named Ted. When his cousin and the other frogs discover Bill's penchant for boys, they laugh and throw stones at him. Bill runs away to Paris and becomes a famous performer in a gentleman's club. As Bill's fame grows, the other frogs decide he's not so bad and ask him to come back to their ditch (pond). Bill arrives in a new car, with golden jewels and a haughty attitude. Recalling how mean the other frogs were to him when he was younger, Bill decides to leave and not come back. As he is about to go, Ted hops up and flatters his way into Bill's heart and lily pad where they kiss, laugh, and live happily ever after. Bright watercolor illustrations are pleasing to the eye, the narration is clear, and the navigation is simple. Unfortunately, the rhyming is forced and the narrative is overly didactic and touches on adult themes such as male performers in gentlemen's clubs. While there are few interactive, narrated LGBTQ e-books for children, libraries and parents will want to look elsewhere. NOT RECOMMENDED.

Keywords: Individuality, Frogs, Homosexuality, Performers, Dancers, Gay Frogs.

PART 4

✳

Resources

CHAPTER 9

Resources for Educators, Librarians, and Rainbow Families

Many useful resources are available to assist educators, librarians, and rainbow families (adults and children) in learning more about LGBTQ children's literature, library services to rainbow families, LGBTQ parenting, and inclusive classrooms for children in rainbow families. This chapter presents a variety of recommended articles, books, films, and Web sites intended for librarians, teachers, educators, children in rainbow families, and/or parents/caregivers in rainbow families. Best practices, book lists, parenting strategies, and more are included. Web sites are annotated to provide additional information about the purpose or scope of the resource.

Print Resources: Articles and Books

LGBTQ Parenting

Alpert, H. *We Are Everywhere: Writings By and About Lesbian Parents.* Freedom: Crossing Press, 1988.

American Psychological Association. *Lesbian and Gay Parenting,* 2005. Accessed August 14, 2011, at:
http://www.nclrights.org/site/DocServerAPADocumentonLesbianandGay
Parenting2006.pdf?docID=5381.

Arnup, K. *Lesbian Parenting: Living with Pride and Prejudice.* Charlottetown, Canada: Genergy Books, 1995.

Barret, Robert L., and B. Robinson. *Gay Fathers: Encouraging the Hearts of Gay Dads and Their Families.* Lexington, MA: Lexington Books, 1990.

Benkov, Laura. *Reinventing the Family: The Emerging Story of Lesbian and Gay Parents.* New York, NY: Crown Publishing, 1994.

Berk, Brett. *The Gay Uncle's Guide to Parenting: Candid Counsel from the Depths of the Daycare Trenches.* New York, NY: Three Rivers/Crown Publishing, 2008.

Bernstein, Robert A. *Families of Value: Personal Profiles of Pioneering Lesbian and Gay Parents.* New York, NY: Marlowe and Co., 2005.

Boenke, Martha, ed. *Trans Forming Families: Real Stories About Transgendered Loved Ones.* 3rd ed. Washington, DC: PFLAG Transgender Network, 2008.

Brickley, Margie. *Opening Doors: Lesbian and Gay Parents and Schools.* San Diego, CA: Family Pride Coalition, 1999.

Brill, Stephanie, and Rachel Pepper. *The Transgender Child: A Handbook for Families and Professionals.* San Francisco, CA: Cleis Press, 2008.

Brodzinsky, David, and Adam Pertman, eds. *Adoption by Lesbians and Gay Men: A New Dimension in Family Diversity.* New York, NY: Oxford University Press, 2011.

Burke, P. *Family Values: Two Moms and Their Son.* New York, NY: Random House, 1993.

Chasnoff, Debra. "Gay Parents Do Exist: Letting the Rabbit Out of the Hat." *Social Education* 69, no. 4 (2005): M2.

Chesler, Phyllis. *Mothers on Trial: The Battle for Children and Custody.* Chicago, IL: Lawrence Hill Books, 2011.

Children's National Medical Center. *If You are Concerned About Your Child's Gender Behaviors: A Guide for Parents.* Washington, DC: Children's National Medical Center, 2003. Accessed on May 15, 2011, at: **http://www.childrensnational.org/files/PDF/DepartmentsandPrograms/ Neuroscience/Psychiatry/GenderVariantOutreachProgram/GVParent Brochure.pdf.**

Clifford, Denis, Frederick Hertz, and Emily Doskow. *A Legal Guide for Lesbian and Gay Couples.* Berkeley, CA: NOLO, 2007.

Clunis, D. Merilee, and G. Dorsey Green. *The Lesbian Parenting Book: A Guide to Creating Families and Raising Children.* New York, NY: Seal Press, 1995.

Cole, Ellen, Esther Rothblum, and Janet Wright. *Lesbian Step Families: An Ethnography of Love.* Binghamton, NY: Harrington Park Press, 1998.

Cooper, Leslie, and Paul Cates. *Too High a Price: The Case Against Restricting Gay Parenting.* New York, NY: American Civil Liberties Union Foundation, 2006. Accessed on May 15, 2011, at: **http://www.aclu.org/lgbt/gen/30472res20070711.html#4.**

Corley, Rip. *Final Closet: The Gay Parents' Guide for Coming Out to Their Children.* Miami, FL: Editech Press, 1990.

Dansky, Steven. *Nobody's Children: Orphans of the HIV Epidemic.* Binghamton, NY: Harrington Park Press, 1997.

Davis, Laura, and J. Keyser. *Becoming the Parent You Want to Be: A Sourcebook of Strategies for the First Five Years.* New York, NY: Broadway Books, 1997.

Drucker, Jane. *Families of Value.* New York, NY: Plenum Press, 1998.

Drucker, Jane. *Lesbian and Gay Families Speak Out: Understanding the Joys and Challenges of Diverse Family Life.* Cambridge, MA: Da Capo, 2001.

Dunne, Gillian A. *Living "Difference": Lesbian Perspectives on Work and Family Life.* London, UK: Haworth Press, 1998.

Ehrensaft, Diane. *Gender Born, Gender Made: Raising Healthy Gender-Nonconforming Children.* New York, NY: The Experiment, 2011.

Evelyn, Just. *Mom, I Need to Be a Girl.* Imperial Beach, CA: Walter Trook Publishing, 1998. Available full-text for free at:
http://ai.eecs.umich.edu/people/conway/TS/Evelyn/Evelyn.html.

Fakhrid-Deen, Tina, and COLAGE. *Let's Get This Straight: The Ultimate Handbook for Youth with LGBTQ Parents.* Berkeley, CA: Seal Press, 2010.

Garner, Abigail. *Families Like Mine: Children of Gay Parents Tell It Like It Is.* New York, NY: HarperCollins, 2004.

Gillespie, Peggy, and Gigi Kaeser. *Love Makes a Family: Portraits of Lesbian, Gay, Bisexual and Transgender Parents and Their Families.* Amherst, MA: University of Massachusetts Press, 1999.

Ginott, Haim G. *Between Parent and Child: The Best-Selling Classic that Revolutionized Parent-Child Communication.* New York, NY: Three Rivers./Crown, 2003.

Glazer, Deborah F., and Jack Drescher. *Gay and Lesbian Parenting.* New York, NY: Haworth, 2001.

Goldberg, Abbie E. *Lesbian and Gay Parents and Their Children: Research on the Family Life Cycle.* Washington, DC: American Psychological Association, 2010.

Golombok, Susan. *Parenting: What Really Counts?* Philadelphia, PA: Routledge, 2000.

Goss, Robert, and Amy Strongheart. *Our Families, Our Values.* New York, NY: Hayworth Press, 1997.

Gottlieb, Andrew. *Sons Talk About Their Gay Fathers.* Binghamton, NY: Harrington Park Press, 2003.

Green, Jesse. *The Velveteen Father.* New York, NY: Villard, 1999.

Hart, Melissa. *Gringa: A Contradictory Girlhood.* Berkeley, CA: Seal Press, 2009.

Herrera, Diana. *Women in Love: Portraits of Lesbian Women and Their Families.* Boston, MA: Bulfinch Press, 1998.

Hertz, Frederick. *Legal Affairs: Essential Advice for Same-Sex Couples.* New York, NY: Henry Holt, 1998.

Howey, Noelle, and Ellen J. Samuels. *Out of the Ordinary: Essays on Growing Up with Gay, Lesbian, and Transgender Parents.* New York, NY: St. Martin's Press, 2000.

Infanti, Anthony. *Everyday Law for Gays and Lesbians and Those Who Care About Them.* Boulder, CO: Paradigm, 2008.

Johnson, Suzanne M., and Elizabeth O'Connor. *For Lesbian Parents: Your Guide to Helping Your Family Grow Up Happy, Healthy, and Proud.* New York, NY: Guilford, 2001.

Johnson, Suzanne M., and Elizabeth O'Connor. *The Gay Baby Boom: The Psychology of Gay Parenthood.* New York, NY: New York University, 2002.

Lev, Arlene Istar. *The Complete Lesbian and Gay Parenting Guide.* New York, NY: Berkley Books, 2004.

Lewin, Ellen. *Lesbian Mothers: Accounts of Gender in American Culture.* Ithaca, NY: Cornell University Press, 1993.

Lindsay, Sally. *Welcome to Our Family: A Baby Journal for LGBT Families.* Illus. by Laura Shepard. Ridley Park, PA : Two Lives Publishing, 2004.

McGarry, Kevin. *Fatherhood for Gay Men: An Emotional and Practical Guide to Becoming a Gay Man.* New York, NY: Harrington Park Press, 2003.

MacPike, Loralee. *There's Something I've Been Meaning to Tell You.* Tallahassee, FL: Naiad Press, 1989.

Mallon, Gerald P. *Lesbian and Gay Foster and Adoptive Parents: Recruiting, Assessing, and Supporting an Untapped Resource for Children and Youth.* Washington, DC: Child Welfare League of America, 2006.

Martin, April. *The Lesbian and Gay Parenting Handbook: Creating and Raising Our Families.* New York, NY: HarperCollins, 1993.

Menichiello, Michael. *A Gay Couple's Journey Through Surrogacy: Intended Fathers.* Binghamton, NY: Haworth Press, 2006.

Miller, Claudia. "Two Moms, Two Dads, When Young Children Ask Us Questions About Gay and Lesbian Families, We Can Give Age-Appropriate and Support Explanations." *Children's Advocate* Jan.–Feb. (2001). Accessed on May 15, 2011. Available at:
http://www.4children.org/issues/2001/january_february/two_moms_ two_dads/.

Moraga, Cherrie. *Waiting in the Wings: Portrait of a Queer Motherhood.* Ithaca, NY: Firebrand, 1997.

Morgen, Kenneth. *Getting Simon: Two Gay Doctors' Journey to Fatherhood.* New York, NY: Bramble Books, 1995.

Movement Advancement Project, Family Equality Council, and Center for American Progress. *All Children Matter: How Legal and Social Inequalities Hurt LGBT Families (Full Report).* October 2011. Accessed February 10, 2012, at:
http://action.familyequality.org/site/DocServer/AllChildrenMatterFull Final10212011.pdf?docID=2401.

National Gay and Lesbian Task Force. *Family Policy: Issues Affecting Gay, Lesbian, Bisexual and Transgender Families.* New York, NY: National Gay and Lesbian Task Force Policy Institute, 2004. Accessed August 14, 2011, at:
http://www.thetaskforce.org/downloads/reports/reports/FamilyPolicy. pdf.

Pepper, Rachel. *The Ultimate Guide to Pregnancy for Lesbians.* 2nd ed. San Francisco, CA: Cleis Press, 2005.

PFLAG. *Our Trans Children*. Washington, DC: PFLAG, 2007. Accessed on August 16, 2011, at: **http://www.pflag.org/fileadmin/user_upload/Publications/ OTC_5thedition.pdf.**

Pierce-Buxton, Amity. *The Other Side of the Closet: The Coming-Out Crisis for Straight Spouses and Families*. Revised and expanded ed. New York, NY: John Wiley, 1994.

Pies, Cheri. *Considering Parenthood: A Handbook for Lesbians*. Minneapolis, MN: Spinster's Book Co., 1988.

Pollack, Sandra, and Jeanne Vaughn. *Politics of the Heart: A Lesbian Parenting Anthology*. Ithaca, NY: Firebrand Books, 1987.

Priwer, Shana, and Cynthia Phillips. *Gay Parenting: Complete Guide for Same-Sex Families*. Far Hills, NJ: New Horizon, 2006.

Rafkin, Louise. *Different Mothers: Sons and Daughters of Lesbians Talk About Their Lives*. San Francisco, CA: Cleis Press, 1990.

Reddy, Maureen, Martha Roth, and Amy Sheldon. *Mother Journeys: Feminists Write About Mothering*. Minneapolis, MN: Spinsters Ink, 1994.

Ricketts, Wendell. *Lesbians and Gay Men as Foster Parents*. Portland, ME: National Child Welfare Resource Center, 1991.

Rizzo, Cindy, and Jo Schneiderman. *All the Ways Home: Parenting in the Lesbian and Gay Community—A Collection of Short Fiction*. Norwich, VT: New Victoria Publishers, 1995.

Savage, Dan. *The Kid: What Happened After My Boyfriend and I Decided to Go Get Pregnant*. New York, NY: Penguin, 1999.

Schulenburg, Joy. *Gay Parenting: A Complete Guide for Gay Men and Lesbians with Children*. Garden City, NJ: Doubleday, 1985.

Schwartz, Lita Linzer, and Florence W. Kaslow. *Welcome Home! An International and Nontraditional Adoption Reader*. New York, NY: Haworth, 2003.

Sember, Brette McWhorter. *Gay and Lesbian Parenting Choices: From Adopting or Using a Surrogate to Choosing the Perfect Father*. Franklin Lakes, NJ: Career Press, 2006.

Sherbourne Health Centre. *LGB Parenting for Family Friends*. Toronto, ON: 2009. Accessed on May 15, 2011, at: **http://www.lgbtqparentingconnection.ca/resources.cfm?mode=3& resourceID=12a2a00a-3048-8bc6-e8d5-794efa3fcbb6.**

Sherbourne Health Centre. *Transsexual Transgender (ts/tg) Parenting: Basic Information for Our Friends and Families*. Toronto, ON: 2009. Accessed on May 15, 2011, at: **http://www.glhv.org.au/files/sherbourne_trans_parenting.pdf**

Snow, Judith E. *How It Feels to Have a Gay or Lesbian Parent: A Book by Kids for Kids of All Ages*. Binghamton, NY: Harrington Park Press, 2004.

Strah, David, and Susanna Margolis. *Gay Dads: A Celebration of Fatherhood*. Photographs by Kris Timken. New York, NY: Penguin, 2003.

Swallow, Jean, and Geoff Manasse. *Making Love Visible*. Freedom, CA: The Crossing Press, 1995.

Tasker, Fiona L., and Susan Golombok. *Growing Up in a Lesbian Family.* New York, NY: Guilford Press, 1997.

Wells, Jess. *Lesbians Raising Sons.* New York, NY: Alyson Publications, 1997.

Weston, Kath. *Families We Choose: Lesbians, Gays, Kinship.* New York, NY: Columbia University Press, 1991.

Wright, Janet M. *Lesbian Step Families: An Ethnography of Love.* Binghamton, NY: Harrington Park Press, 1998.

Library Programs and Services to Adults in Rainbow Families

Albright, Meagan. "The Public Library's Responsibilities to LGBT Communities: Recognizing, Representing, and Serving." *Public Libraries* 45, no. 5 (2006): 52–56.

American Library Association Office for Intellectual Freedom. *Access to Library Resources and Services Regardless of Sex, Gender Identity, Gender Expression, or Sexual Orientation: An Interpretation of the Library Bill of Rights.* Chicago, IL: American Library Association, 2002. Accessed on May 15, 2011, at:
http://www.ala.org/ala/issuesadvocacy/intfreedom/librarybill/ interpretations/accesslibrary.cfm.

Gough, Cal, and Ellen Greenblatt. "Gay and Lesbian Library Materials: A Book Selector's Toolkit." In *Public Library Collection Development in the Information Age,* ed. by Annabel Stephens, pp. 151–170. Binghamton, NY: Haworth Press, 1998.

Gough, Cal, and Ellen Greenblatt. *Gay and Lesbian Library Service.* Jefferson, NC: McFarland, 1990.

Gough, Cal, and Ellen Greenblatt. "Gay and Lesbian Library Users: Overcoming Barriers to Service." In *Diversity and Multiculturalism in Libraries,* ed. by Katherine Hoover Hill, pp. 197–213. Greenwich, CT: JAI Press, 1994.

Hill, Nanci Milone. "Out and About: Serving the GLBT Population @ Your Library." *Public Libraries* 46, no. 4 (2007): 18–24.

Maxwell, Lynne. "Building Rainbow Families." *Library Journal* 133, no. 6 (2008): 54–57.

Quinn, J., and M. Rogers. "New Push for Gay and Lesbian Programming." *Library Journal* 117, no. 10 (1992): 19.

Ritchie, Catherine, David Fettke, and Dale McNeill. "GLBT: Programming at the Dallas Public Library." *Public Libraries* 47, no. 2 (2008): 50–54.

Rothbauer, Paulette. "Locating the Library as Place Among Lesbian, Gay, Bisexual, and Queer Patrons." In *The Library as Place: History, Community, and Culture,* ed. by John Buschman and Gloria Leckie, pp. 101–116. Westport, CT: Libraries Unlimited, 2007.

Seborg, Liesl. "Sharing the Stories of the Gay, Lesbian, Bisexual and Transgendered Community: Providing Library Service to the GLBT Patron." *PNLA Quarterly* 70, no. 1 (2005): 15–17.

Silverrod, Nancy. "San Francisco's GLBT Service Challenges." *Public Libraries* 46, no. 4 (2007): 22–24.

Simpson, Stacy H. "Why Have a Comprehensive and Representative Collection? GLBT Material Selection and Service in the Public Library." *Progressive Librarian* 27, (Summer 2006): 44–51.

Library Collections and Services for Children in Rainbow Families

Alexander, Linda B., and Sarah D. Miselis. "Barriers to GLBTQ Collection Development and Strategies for Overcoming Them." *Young Adult Library Services* 5, no. 3 (2007): 43–49.

Austin, Patricia. "Opening the Door to Tolerance." *Book Links* 19, no. 2 (2010): 42–45.

Chambers, Bradford, ed. "Homophobia and Education: How to Deal with Name-Calling." *Interracial Books for Children Bulletin* 14, no. 3/4 (1983): 3–38.

Chapman, Elizabeth, and Briony Birdi. "Fiction for All." *Public Library Journal* 23, no. 1 (2008): 8–11.

Curry, Ann. "If I Ask, Will They Answer?" *Reference and User Services Quarterly* 45, no. 1 (2005): 65–75.

Farrelly, Michael Garrett. "Serving Gay Youth @ Your Library." *Public Libraries* 45, no. 4 (2006): 40–41.

Ford, Michael Thomas. "Gay Books for Young Readers: When Caution Calls the Shots." *Publishers Weekly* 241, no. 8 (1994): 24.

Garden, Nancy. "Gay Fiction for Kids: Is Anyone Out There Publishing It?" *Lambda Book Report* 6, no. 4 (1997): 25.

Garden, Nancy. "Lesbian and Gay Kids' Books Under Fire." *Lambda Book Report* 4, no. 7 (1994): 11.

Herbeck, Joyce. "Creating a Safe Learning Environment: Books for Young People About Homosexuality." *Book Links* 14, no. 3 (2005): 30.

Howard, Vivian. "Out of the Closet . . . but Not on the Shelves? An Analysis of Canadian Public Libraries' Holdings of Gay-Themed Picture Books." *Progressive Librarian* 25 (Summer 2005): 62–75.

Naidoo, Jamie Campbell. *Focus on My Family: An Analysis of Gay-Themed Picturebooks and Public Library Services for LGBTQ Children and Children with Same-Sex Parents.* Paper presented at the annual conference of the American Library Association, Chicago, IL, July 2009. PowerPoint available at: **http://presentations.ala.org/images/b/b3/DRG_Naidoo.ppt**.

Schrader, Alvin M. "'I Thought I'd Find Myself at the Library': LGBTQ Services and Collections in Public and School Libraries." *PNLA Quarterly* 72, no. 1 (2007): 4–9.

Spence, Alex A. "Controversial Books in the Public Library: A Comparative Survey of Holdings of Gay-Related Children's Picture Books." *Library Quarterly* 70, no. 3 (2000): 335–379.

Historical and Critical Analyses of LGBTQ Children's Literature

Albright, Lettie K., and April W. Bedford. "From Resistance to Acceptance: Introducing Books with Gay and Lesbian Characters." *Journal of Children's Literature* 32, no. 1 (2006): 0–15.

Bronski, Michael. "Positive Images and the Stupid Family: Queer Books for Kids?" *Radical America* 25, no. 1 (1993): 61–70.

Bruhm, Steve, and Natasha Hurley. *Curiouser: On the Queerness of Children.* Minneapolis, MN: University of Minnesota Press, 2004.

Butler, Charles. "Experimental Girls: Feminist and Transgender Discourses in Bill's New Frock and Marvin Redpost: Is He a Girl?" *Children's Literature Association Quarterly* 34, no. 1 (2009): 3–20.

Casement, Rose. "Breaking the Silence: The Stories of Gay and Lesbian People in Children's Literature." *New Advocate* 15, no. 3 (2002): 205–213.

Chick, Kay. "Fostering an Appreciation for All Kinds of Families: Picture Books with Gay and Lesbian Themes." *Bookbird* 46, no. 1 (2008): 15–22.

Clyde, Laurel, and Marjorie Lobban. "A Door Half Open: Young People's Access to Fiction Related to Homosexuality." *School Libraries Worldwide* 7, no. 2 (2001): 17–30.

Clyde, Laurel, and Marjorie Lobban. *Out of the Closet and Into the Classroom: Homosexuality in Books for Young People.* Deakin, ACT, Australia: ALIA, 1992. The third edition of this book was never published but is available in full-text for free from the Macquarie University Library: **http://voyager.mq.edu.au/vwebv/holdingsInfo?searchId=167&recCount=50&recPointer=0&bibId=1279365.**

Crisp, Thomas. "Setting the Record 'Straight': An Interview with Jane Severance." Children's Literature Association 35, no. 1 (2010): 87–96.

Day, Frances Ann. *Lesbian and Gay Voices: An Annotated Bibliography and Guide to Literature for Children and Young Adults.* Westport, CT: Greenwood Press, 2000.

Esposito, Jennifer. "We're Here, We're Queer, But We're Just Like Heterosexuals: A Cultural Studies Analysis of Lesbian Themed Children's Books." *Educational Foundations* 23, no. 3/4 (2009): 61–78.

Flanagan, Victoria. *Into the Closet: Cross-Dressing and the Gendered Body in Children's Literature and Film.* New York: Routledge, 2007.

Garden, Nancy. "Writing About Gay and Lesbian Characters in a Changing World." *Book Links* 14, no. 3 (2005): 28–29.

Herzog, Ricky. "Sissies, Dolls, and Dancing: Children's Literature and Gender Deviance in the Seventies." *The Lion and the Unicorn* 33, no. 1 (January 2009): 60–76.

Hoosen, Vanessa. "True Love or Just Friends? Flemish Picture Books in English Translation." *Children's Literature in Education* 41, no. 2 (2010): 105–117.

Huskey, Melynda. "Queering the Picture Book." *The Lion and the Unicorn* 26, no. 1 (2002): 66–77.

Jackson, Sue, and Susan Gee. "'Look Jane', 'No You Look John': Constructions of Gender in Early School Reader Illustrations Across 50 Years." *Gender and Education* 17, no. 2 (2005): 115–128.

Kidd, Kenneth, and Michelle Ann Abate, eds. *Over the Rainbow: Queer Children's and Young Adult Literature*. Ann Arbor, MI: University of Michigan Press, 2011.

Lester, Neal. "(Un)Happily Ever After: Fairy Tale Morals, Moralities, and Heterosexism in Children's Texts." *Journal of Gay and Lesbian Issues in Education* 4, no. 2 (2007): 55–74.

Mallan, Kerry. *Gender Dilemmas in Children's Fiction*. New York: Palgrave Macmillan, 2009.

Mendell, Patricia, and Patricia Sarles. "'Where Did I Really Come From?' Assisted Reproductive Technology in Self-Published Children's Picture Books." *Children and Libraries* 8, no. 2 (2010): 18–29.

Naidoo, Jamie Campbell. "Representation in Queer Children's Books: Who's In and Who's Out." In *Diversity in Youth Literature: Opening Doors Through Reading,* ed. by Jamie Campbell Naidoo and Sarah Park. Chicago, IL: American Library Association, 2012.

Newman, Lesléa. "The More Things Change . . . : Heather Has Two Mommies Turns 20." *Publishers Weekly* 256, no. 42 (2009): 58.

Norton, Judy. "Transchildren and the Discipline of Children's Literature." *The Lion and the Unicorn* 23, no. 3 (1999): 415–436.

op de Beeck, Nathalie. "Diversity Breeds Controversy." *Publishers Weekly* 252, no. 17 (2005): 32–33.

Salem, Linda C. "Literature with GLBTQ Characters, Themes, and Content." In *Children's Literature Studies: Cases and Discussions* by Linda Salem, pp. 103–120. Westport, CT: Libraries Unlimited, 2006.

Tunks, Karyn Wellhousen, and Jessica McGhee. "Embracing William, Oliver Button, and Tough Boris: Learning Acceptance from Characters in Children's Literature." *Childhood Education* 82, no. 4 (2006): 213–218.

Wolf, Virginia L. "The Gay Family in Literature for Young People." *Children's Literature in Education* 20, no. 1 (1989): 51–58.

Yampell, Cat. "Alyson Wonderland Publishing." *Bookbird* 37, no. 3 (1999): 31–33.

Children of Rainbow Families in the Classroom

Baker, Jean M. *How Homophobia Hurts Children: Nurturing Diversity at Home, at School, and in the Community*. Binghamton, NY: Harrington Park Press, 2002.

Biegel, Stuart. *The Right to Be Out: Sexual Orientation and Gender Identity in America's Public Schools*. Minneapolis, MN: University of Minnesota Press, 2010.

Blackburn, Mollie V., and Caroline T. Clark. "Becoming Readers of Literature with LGBT Themes: In and Out of Classrooms." *Handbook of Research on Children's and Young Adult Literature*, pp. 148–164. New York, NY: Routledge, 2011.

Blaise, Mindy. *Playing It Straight: Uncovering Gender Discourse in the Early Childhood Classroom.* New York, NY: Routledge, 2005.

Burrill, Melany. *All God's Children: Teaching Children About Sexual Orientation and Gender Diversity.* Fort Wayne, IN: LifeQuest, 2009.

Cahill, Betsy, and Rachel Theilheimer. "'Can Tommy and Sam Get Married?' Questions about Gender, Sexuality, and Young Children." *Young Children* 54, no. 1 (1999): 27–31.

Campos, David. "Buster Bunny as a Teaching Tool: A Lesson from the Controversy over an Animated Rabbit." *Journal of Gay and Lesbian Issues in Education* 4, no. 2 (2007): 93–97.

Casper, Virginia. "Very Young Children in Lesbian- and Gay-Headed Families: Moving Beyond Acceptance." *Zero to Three* 23, no. 3 (2003): 18–26.

Casper, Virginia, and Steven B. Schultz. *Gay Parents, Straight Schools: Building Communication and Trust.* New York, NY: Teachers College Press, 1999.

Casper, Virginia, Harriet Cuffaro, Steven Schultz, Jonathan Silin, and Elaine Wickens. "Toward a Most Thorough Understanding of the World: Sexual Orientation and Early Childhood Education." In *Gender in Early Childhood,* ed. by Nicola Yelland, pp. 72–97. New York, NY: Routledge, 1996.

Clay, James. "Creating Safe, Just Places to Learn for Children of Lesbian and Gay Parents: The NAEYC Code of Ethics in Action." *Young Children.* 59, no. 6 (2004): 34–38.

Clay, James. "Working with Lesbian and Gay Parents and Their Children." *Young Children* 45, no. 3 (1990): 31–35.

Cooley, Robin. "Beyond Pink and Blue." Rethinking Schools Online 18, no. 2 (2003). Accessed May 15, 2011, at:
http://www.rethinkingschools.org/archive/18_02/pink182.shtml.

Corbett, Susan. "A Complicated Bias." *Young Children* 48, no. 3 (1993): 29–31.

Dykstra, Laurel A. "Trans-Friendly Preschool." *Journal of Gay and Lesbian Issues in Education* 3, no. 1 (2005): 7–13.

Emfinger, Kay. "Rethinking Welcoming Literacy Environments for LGBT Families." *Childhood Education* 84, no. 1 (2007): 24–28.

Flores, Gabriel. *Teachers' Attitudes in Implementing Gay-Themed Literature as Part of a Balanced Multicultural Education Curriculum.* Ann Arbor, MI: ProQuest, 2009. Accessed on May 15, 2011, at:
http://gradworks.umi.com/3370947.pdf.

Fox, Robin. "One of the Hidden Diversities in Schools: Families with Parents Who Are Lesbian or Gay." *Childhood Education* 83, no. 5 (2007): 277–281.

Gelnaw, Aimee. "Belonging: Including Children of Gay and Lesbian Parents — and All Children — in Your Program." *Childcare Information Exchange* 163 (2005): 42–44.

Goldman, Linda. *Coming Out, Coming In: Nurturing the Well-Being and Inclusion of Gay Youth in Mainstream Society.* New York, NY: Routledge, 2008.

Greever, Ellen, Patricia Austin, and Karyn Welhousen. "*William's Doll* Revisited." *Language Arts* 77, no. 4 (March 2000): 324–330.

Herbeck, Joyce. "Creating a Safe Learning Environment: Books for Young People About Homosexuality." *Book Links* 14, no. 3 (2005): 30–34.

Hermann-Wilmath, Jill M. "Full Inclusion: Understanding the Role of Gay and Lesbian Texts and Films in Teacher Education Classrooms," *Language Arts* 84, no. 4 (2007): 347–356.

Janmohamed, Zeenat, and Ryan Campbell. *Building Bridges: Queer Families in Early Childhood Education.* Toronto, ON: Atkinson Centre for Society and Child Development, 2009.

Kissen, Rita. *Getting Ready for Benjamin: Preparing Teachers for Sexual Diversity in the Classroom.* Boulder, CO: Rowman and Littlefield, 2003.

Klinger-Lesser, Lee, Tracy Burt, and Aimee Gelnaw. *Making Room in the Circle: Lesbian, Gay, Bisexual, and Transgender Families in Early Childhood Settings.* San Rafael, CA: Parent Services Project, 2005.

Kosciw, Joseph, and Elizabeth M. Diaz. *Involved, Invisible, Ignored: The Experiences of Lesbian, Gay, Bisexual, and Transgender Parents and Their Children in Our Nation's K–12 Schools.* New York, NY: Gay, Lesbian, and Straight Education Network, 2008.

Kwasnica, Judy. *Count Me In: Gender Equity in the Primary Classroom.* Toronto, ON: Green Dragon Press, 1995.

Lakey, Jennifer. "Teachers and Parents Define Diversity in an Oregon Preschool Cooperative — Democracy at Work." *Young Children* 52, no. 4 (1997): 20–26.

Lamme, Linda L., and Laurel A. Lamme. "Welcoming Children from Gay Families into Our Schools." *Educational Leadership* 59, no. 4 (2001): 65.

Lamme, Linda L., and Laurel A. Lamme. *Welcoming Children from Sexual-Minority Families into Our Schools.* Bloomington, IN: Phi Delta Kappa Educational Foundation, 2003.

Lesbian and Gay Parents Association. *Overcoming Homophobia in the Elementary Classroom: A Workshop for Educators and Administrators.* San Francisco, CA: Lesbian and Gay Parents Association, 1996.

Letts, William, IV, and James Sears. *Queering Elementary Education: Advancing the Dialogue About Sexualities and Schooling.* Boulder, CO: Rowman & Littlefield, 1999.

Lewis, Eleanore Grater. "What Mother? What Father?" *Young Children* 51, no. 3 (1996): 27.

Lipkin, Arthur. *Beyond Diversity Day: A Q&A on Gay and Lesbian Issues in Schools.* Boulder, CO: Rowman & Littlefield, 2003.

Lipkin, Arthur. *Understanding Homosexuality, Changing Schools.* Boulder, CO: Westview Press, 1999.

Robinson, Kerry. "Making the Invisible Visible: Gay and Lesbian Issues in Early Childhood Education." *Contemporary Issues in Early Childhood* 3, no. 3 (2002): 415–434.

Robinson, Kerry, and Criss Jones Diaz. *Diversity and Difference in Early Childhood Education.* Berkshire, England: Open University Press, 2006.

Rowell, Elizabeth. "Missing! Picture Books Reflecting Gay and Lesbian Families: Make the Curriculum Inclusive for All Children." *Young Children* 62, no. 3 (2007): 24–30.

Schall, Janine, and Gloria Kauffmann. "Exploring Literature with Gay and Lesbian Characters in the Elementary School." *Journal of Children's Literature* 29, no. 1 (2003): 36–45.

Stewig, John Warren. "Self-Censorship of Picture Books About Gay and Lesbian Families." *The New Advocate* 7, no. 3 (1994): 184–192.

Swartz, Patti Capel. "Bridging Multicultural Education: Bringing Sexual Orientation into the Children's and Young Adult Literature Classrooms." *Radical Teacher* 66, (2003): 11–16.

Swartz, Patti Capel. "It's Elementary in Appalachia: Helping Prospective Teachers and Their Students Understand Sexuality and Gender." *Journal of Gay and Lesbian Issues in Education* 1, no. 1 (2003): 51–71.

Walling, Donovan. *Open Lives, Safe Schools: Addressing Gay and Lesbian Issues in Education.* Bloomington, IN: Phi Delta Kappa Educational Foundation, 1996.

Williams, Karen, and Margaret Cooney. "Young Children and Social Justice." *Young Children* 61, no. 2 (2006): 75–82.

Woog, Dan. *School's Out: The Impact of Gay and Lesbian Issues on America's Schools.* Boston, MA: Alyson Publications, 1995.

Miscellaneous Information and Statistics About Rainbow Families

Albin, Tami, and Jennifer Church-Duran. "Queering the Web: Gay, Lesbian, Bisexual, Transgendered, and Queer (GLBTQ) Resources." *C&RL News* 69, no. 8 (2008): 466–469.

Gates, Gary J. "New Census Bureau Data Show Annual Increases in Same-Sex Couples Outpacing Population Growth." The Williams Institute, UCLA, 2010. Accessed May 15, 2011, at:
http://www.law.ucla.edu/williamsinstitute/pdf/ACS2009presser.pdf.

Gates, Gary J. "Same-Sex Couples and the Gay, Lesbian, Bisexual Population: New Estimates from the American Community Survey." Williams Institute, UCLA, October 2006. Accessed May 15, 2011, at:
http://escholarship.org/uc/item/8h08t0zf.

Gates, Gary J., and Jason Ost. *Gay and Lesbian Atlas.* Washington, DC: The Urban Institute, 2004.

Human Rights Campaign. *Transgender Basics.* Washington, DC: Human Rights Campaign, 1998.

Human Rights Campaign. *Transgender 101: An Introduction to Issues Surrounding Gender Identity and Expression.* Washington, DC: Human Rights Campaign, 1998.

James, Susan Donaldson. "2 Million Kids Raised by Gay Couples Are at Risk, Says Study." ABC News, November 2, 2011. Accessed February 10, 2012, at:

http://abcnews.go.com/Health/children-sex-parents-harmed-anti-gay-laws-study/story?id=14862339.

Journal of LGBT Youth Editor. "The (Re)Searching of Queer Youth." *Journal of LGBT Youth* 5, no. 3 (2008): 1–3.

Perrin, Ellen C. *Sexual Orientation in Child and Adolescent Health Care.* New York, NY: Springer Science and Business Media, 2002.

Ponton, Lynn, M.D. "What Does Gay Mean? How to Talk with Kids About Sexual Orientation and Prejudice." National Mental Health Association, 2011. Accessed on May 15, 2011, at:

http://www.nmha.org/whatdoesgaymean.

Powell, Brian, Catherine Bolzendahl, Claudia Geist, and Lala Carr Steelman. *Counted Out: Same-Sex Relations and Americans' Definitions of Family.* New York, NY: Russell Sage Foundation, 2010.

Rottnek, Mathew. *Sissies and Tomboys: Gender Nonconformity and Homosexual Childhood.* New York, NY: New York University Press, 1999.

Wilkinson, Stephanie. "Drop the Barbie! If You Bend Gender Enough, Does It Break?" Brain, Child: The Magazine for Thinking Mothers (2001). Accessed on May 15, 2011, at:

http://www.brainchildmag.com/essays/fall2001_wilkinson.htm.

Periodicals for Rainbow Families

Gay Parent Magazine — This relatively inexpensive magazine, available in both print and online formats, is directed toward LGBTQ parents across the nation. Contents include book reviews, personal parenting stories, information about rainbow family vacations and events, and gay-friendly school information.
http://www.gayparentmag.com/

Pink Parenting — Launched in summer 2011, this UK magazine for LGBTQ parents and rainbow families provides parenting tips, new articles, surrogacy and adoption information, and more for today's modern queer family. Available by online and print subscription.
http://www.pink-parenting.com/

Rainbow Rumpus — Billed as the only online literary magazine for children with gay and lesbian parents, this interactive and informative Web site includes book reviews, short stories, e-books, children's art, activities, and more. Rainbow Rumpus has a sister site, Rainbow Riot, that is an online literary magazine just for teens.
http://www.rainbowrumpus.org/
http://rainbowriot.org/teens

Educational Films

Both My Moms' Names Are Judy. San Francisco Lesbian and Gay Parents Association, 1994. DVD, 10 min.

Camp Lavender Hill (documentary). Michael Magnaye and Tom Shepard, 1997. VHS, 28 min.

Daddy and Papa. Johnny Symons, 2002. DVD/VHS, 57 min.
http://www.daddyandpapa.com/

The Family Journey: Raising Gender Nonconforming Children and *I'm Just Anneke.* Jonathan Skurnik, 2010. DVD, 26 min. total (2 films approx 13 min. each).
http://www.youthandgendermediaproject.org/Home.html

In My Shoes: Stories of Youth with LGBT Parents. Jen Gilomen and COLAGE Youth Leadership and Action Program, 2005. Online. 31 min.
http://www.colage.org/inmyshoes/

It's Elementary: Talking About Gay Issues in School. Debra Chasnoff and Helen Cohen, 1996. DVD/VHS, 78 min. or 38-min. training version. Re-release in 2007 includes *It's STILL Elementary.*
http://www.groundspark.org

No Dumb Questions: A Documentary Film. Melissa Regan, 2003. DVD, 24 min.
http://www.nodumbquestions.com/

Our House: A Very Real Documentary About the Kids of Gay and Lesbian Parents. Meema Spadola, 2000. VHS/DVD, 60 min.
http://www.itvs.org/ourhouse

That's a Family! Debra Chasnoff and Helen Cohen, 2000. DVD/VHS, 35 min.
http://www.groundspark.org

Online Resources

Organizations and Foundations

COLAGE: People with a Lesbian, Gay, Bisexual or Transgender Parent — Formerly known as Children of Lesbians and Gays Everywhere, this parent organization with numerous chapters across the United States is part social media community/ support group and part information clearinghouse for resources relating to children with LGBTQ parents. Various booklists, brochures, and online resources are provided in addition to several types of social media boards.
http://www.colage.org/

Family Equality Council — Formerly the Family Pride Coalition and Rainbow Families, this organization developed from the merger of the two organizations to create a one-stop, information-packed Web site for both children and adults in rainbow families. The site includes a wealth of resources from guides for LGBTQ parents who want to make sure their children have inclusive schools to levelized lists of children's books to LGBT research reports to "My Family Loves Me: Drawings from America's Children," a 64-page collection of family profiles from children in rainbow families.
http://www.familyequality.org/

The Gay and Lesbian Alliance Against Defamation (GLAAD) — A non-profit organization dedicated to ending media stereotypes of the LGBTQ community, which includes children and adults in rainbow families.

http://www.glaad.org/

The Gay, Lesbian and Straight Education Network (GLSEN) — A national organization seeking to create safe learning environments for all children in the United States, including children in rainbow families. The organization produces various reports, such as a survey of the climate of U.S. schools that highlights bullying, homophobia, and other harmful social factors for children. Also included on the Web site are educator resources, booklists, and links to other like-minded organizations.

http://www.glsen.org/

Lambda Legal — One of the nation's largest organizations dedicated to protecting and fighting for the legal rights of LGBTQ individuals in the United States. Covers various legal issues such as adoption, marriage, and employment and health benefits.

http://www.lambdalegal.org/

National Gay and Lesbian Task Force — One of the nation's oldest LGBT advocacy groups and part of a think-tank on current issues influencing the LGBT community, the task force provides reports, suggestions, and profiles on topics relevant to rainbow families such as parenting and adoption, youth concerns, marriage and family recognition, etc.

http://thetaskforce.org/

PFLAG: Parents, Families and Friends of Lesbian and Gays — This national nonprofit organization with numerous chapters across the United States is a support group for the LGBTQ community and those who love and care for members of this community. The organization's Web site features fact sheets, reports, curricular resources, book lists, pamphlets and brochures, and much more relating to the creation of welcoming and inclusive spaces for all members of the LGBTQ community.

http://community.pflag.org/

TransKids Purple Rainbow Foundation — A nonprofit organization dedicated to promoting and funding research relating to serving transgender children and youth. The site includes various recommended books, research reports, and organizations, all relating to transgender topics.

http://www.transkidspurplerainbow.com/index.htm

Blogs

Accepting Dad — One of the few blogs written by a dad of a gender-variant child, this helpful blog serves as both a support group and resource for other parents with gender-variant children. Entries include book reviews, links to newspaper articles and reports on gender-variant children, and accounts of parenting a gender-variant child. A list of recommended books and links to other blogs and professional organizations for parents of gender-variant children are also provided.

http://www.acceptingdad.com/

Born This Way — A wonderful space for both children and adults in rainbow families, this blog allows users (mostly adults) to post picture of themselves as gender-variant children along with a story describing their childhood or the picture. This upbeat blog radiates a message that everything will turn out all right, helpful for children and youth in rainbow families, particularly those who are queer or gender-variant.

http://www.BornThisWayBlog.com

Diversidad Afectivo-Sexual — Developed by Víctor Díez Mazo, this Spanish-language blog includes links to numerous Spanish-language LGBTQ and gender-variant children's books, educational resources, and other information for those interested in teaching children about rainbow families. The second link is for another blog by Mazo that highlights a few gender-variant and LGBTQ children's e-books along with a few related activities.

http://diversidadafectivosexual.blogspot.com/

http://recursosdiversidadafectivosexual.blogspot.com/search/label/libros

Donor Offspring: Books for Children — Created by Patricia Sarles, this informative blog provides bibliographies of children's books about artificial insemination, surrogacy, and in vitro fertilization. Sarles lists books for single parents as well as lesbian and gay parents. Many of these books are not categorized in library catalogs and online book stores in ways that indicate that they cover these topics, making this blog even more important. Children's books listed on the site can be shared with donor offspring.

http://booksfordonoroffspring.blogspot.com/

Gay-Themed Picture Books for Children — Created by Patricia Sarles, this extensive Web site lists numerous children's picture books with LGBTQ content. Each book includes a cover of the photo and then a blurb about the book from either the Library of Congress, Books in Print, or publisher catalogs. Although Sarles does not provide a review of the books, the list is helpful for rainbow families, educators, and librarians seeking the titles of LGBTQ picture books. Links to various LGBTQ organizations, booklists, and other resources are all provided. This is a great place for rainbow families and librarians to begin! Highly recommended.

http://booksforkidsingayfamilies.blogspot.com/

I'm Here. I'm Queer. What the Hell Do I Read? — Developed by author and speaker Lee Wind, this is the blog for resources relating to queer literature for LGBTQ youth. Although the focus of the site is primarily young adult literature, Wind does include recommendations of children's books with LGBTQ family members/themes as well as a list of queer-related "Picturebooks I Wish Had Been Read to Me When I Was a Little Kid!" Information about bullying in schools and queer youth in the news is also provided.

http://www.leewind.org/

Mombian: Sustenance for Lesbian Moms — Developed by lesbian mother Dana Rudolph, this one-stop blog provides information on lesbian parenting; book reviews of LGBTQ parenting and children's resources; links to information relating to LGBTQ politics in matters of parenting, adoption, etc.; and "diversions" in the form of fun information of interest to lesbian mothers. Although the site is geared toward lesbian caregivers, the information is relevant to other caregivers in rainbow families.

http://www.mombian.com/

Q-ntos Homoparentales — A Spanish-language blog that provides an annotated listing of various LGBTQ fairytales and children's books for rainbow families.
http://q-ntos.blogspot.com/

Rainbow Books: GLBTQ Books for Children and Teens — The blog of the Rainbow Project, which is a joint project of the Gay, Lesbian, Bisexual, and Transgender Round Table and the Social Responsibilities Round Table of the American Library Association. Past lists of Rainbow Books are available as well as current titles that have been suggested or nominated for the Rainbow List.
http://glbtrt.ala.org/rainbowbooks/

Raising My Rainbow: Adventures in Raising a Slightly Effeminate, Possibly Gay, Totally Fabulous Son — Often witty and rarely dull, this blog describes a mother's ups and downs raising C. J., a gender-variant boy. While the blog's creator doesn't include resources like the "Today You Are You" blog, it is a perfect complement and would serve as inspiration and support for other parents of gender-variant children.
http://raisingmyrainbow.com/

Today You Are You: Love, Yoga, Parenting, and Gender Diversity — Created by Jennifer Carr, the author of the transgender children's book *Be Who You Are!*, this blog records her joys and frustrations parenting a gender-variant child in a society that does not always approve of gender nonconformity. She also includes resources specifically for and about transgender children and their families.
http://todayyouareyou.com/

Book Lists and Librarian/Educator Resources

The Children's Peace Education and Anti-Bias Library — Provides a searchable database of anti-bias picture books to use with young children to promote understanding of topics such as racial identity, gender roles, culture and language, and family composition.
http://www.childpeacebooks.org/cpb/

The Diversity Center of Santa Cruz — This extensive Web site offers a listing of various types of community as well as informational resources for the LGBTQ community. Of particular interest to rainbow families and the librarians and educators serving them is the lengthy list of recommended children's and young adult books and professional reading, primarily on the topic of gender identity and transgender individuals.
http://diversitycenter.org/programs/transgender-program/transgender-resources/children/

GLBT Resources for Children: A Bibliography — Complied by public librarian Nancy Silverrod for the Gay, Lesbian, Bisexual, Transgender Round Table (GLBTRT) of the American Library Association, this annotated list includes picture books, novels, informational books, magazines, movies, and parenting resources for rainbow families.
http://www.ala.org/ala/mgrps/rts/glbtrt/popularresources/children.cfm

Pinkbooks — Contains an extensive listing of bibliographies relating to LGBTQ characters in children's literature and LGBTQ topics in young adult literature.

Both fiction and nonfiction titles are presented, along with a list of resources for LGBTQ youth.

http://www.pinkbooks.com/

Rainbow Reading: Gay and Lesbian Characters and Themes in Children's Books — Contains an annotated bibliography of LGBTQ picture books, intermediate novels, and young adult novels. Also includes the webmaster's reflective insights on some of the books.

http://www.windowsill.net/gaybooks.html

Rainbow Sauce — This Web site offers links to various annotated lists of queer media, including queer reads in the following categories relevant to rainbow families: children's books for gay parents, children's books for lesbian parents, children's books for gay and lesbian parents, lesbian parenting, and gay parenting.

http://www.rainbowsauce.com/queerreads.html

Tackle Homophobia — Supported by the United Kingdom's Paul Hamlyn Foundation, this comprehensive Web site provides educators and librarians with resources, educational activities, annotated booklists, and extensive lists of UK organizations that combat homophobia in children and youth ages four to eighteen. Many of the resources are relevant to educators around the world.

http://www.tacklehomophobia.com/

Welcoming Schools — Sponsored by the Human Rights Campaign Foundation, this up-to-date site is chock full of lesson plans, teaching points, librarian tips, extensive bibliographies (of books for all ages covering a broad spectrum of LGBTQ topics), and other resources for creating welcoming environments for rainbow families. Particularly useful is a free 93-page guide to creating inclusive educational environments for children in rainbow families. Highly recommended.

http://www.welcomingschools.org/resources/

LGBTQ Book Distributors (U.S. and Non-U.S.)

A Fortiori — This Spanish publisher based in Bilbao produces a series of picture books entitled Cuentos en favor de TODAS las familias. These children's books include numerous alternative types of families including rainbow families.

http://afortiori-bilbao.com/editorial/documents/catalogo_familias.html

Berkana — The online portion of this gay and lesbian bookstore in Madrid, Spain, includes many children's books with LGBTQ content. Many of the Spanish-language books mentioned throughout this book and in the "Additional Non-U.S. Picture Books with LGBTQ Characters" section below can be purchased from Berkana. The link below is to the section of the Web site devoted to children's books.

http://www.libreriaberkana.com/libros/materias/cuento-infantil/1/

La Cabane de Suzon — This French online bookstore has numerous children's titles available, including many of the LGBTQ French-language picture books listed in the "Additional Non-U.S. Picture Books with LGBTQ Characters" section below.

http://www.lacabanedesuzon.fr/

Learn to Include — This is the Australian publisher and distributor of the easy-to-read Learn to Include series about a lesbian couple, their daughter, and friends who include another gay family. The Web site includes a free 44-page teachers' manual that accompanies these picture books and describes how to use them in the classroom. Many of the activities are tied to Australian teaching standards.

http://www.hotkey.net.au/~learn_to_include/

My Family! — This is a lesbian-owned publisher of children's picture books and coloring books featuring LGBTQ characters that are African American, Jewish, Latino, and from other diverse groups. One of the co-owners is an author of many of the books, and in 2011 the company began distributing LGBTQ picture books by other publishers and authors.

http://www.myfamilyproducts.net/en/

ONG por la no discriminación — This Spanish-language Web site includes LGBTQ Spanish-language picture books, information about LGBTQ children's plays, and various other resources against discrimination. Some of the books available on the Web site can be downloaded for free and others are available for purchase for library and classroom collections.

http://www.ong-nd.org/index2.html

Two Lives Publishing — Formerly a publisher and distributor of an extensive list of children's and parenting resources for rainbow families, this company now distributes the Learn to Include Series and offers the Two Lives Publishing titles for sale. Using an Internet archive tool such as the Wayback Machine (http://www. archive.org/web/web.php), librarians can input the publisher URL below and access an archived PDF of Two Lives Publishing's catalog that includes an extensive listing of LGBTQ children's books and parenting resources that would be useful for collection development.

http://www.twolives.com/books.html

General Web Sites About Promoting Acceptance and Understanding of Rainbow Families

"Això era i no era dues mares . . ." — This is the name of a Spanish Rainbow Family children's program that was offered by the Central Public Library in Gandia, Spain, and sponsored by the Educant per a la ciutadania, educant contra la discriminacion. A program description and colorful poster are available at http://www.lgtb. es/item.php?id=123. Spanish language handouts and activities to accompany the LGBTQ children's books used in the program can be downloaded at:

http://www.lgtb.es/descarrega.php?id=405&arxiu=Pinten_families_diversitat. pdf

Around the Rainbow — This Canadian organization provides support for children and adults in the LGBTQ and two-spirit communities. This highly recommended Web site features extensive curriculum guides, training information for educators, book lists for various age groups and types (children, young adult, parents, educators), as well as a listing of online resources. Many resources are available in both English and French.

http://www.aroundtherainbow.org/

Camp Aranu'tiq — Located in southern New England and named after the Chugach (Yup'ik, an indigenous people of Alaska) word for two-spirit, this summer camp for transgender and gender-variant children ages eight to fifteen provides a safe-zone environment where children in the gender borderlands are comfortable to explore their identity. The nonprofit, volunteer-based organization also has a blog that highlights various camp activities and advisory board members, who include Chaz Bono.

http://www.camparanutiq.org/home.html

Families Like Mine — The companion Web site to Abigail Garner's book of the same name, this includes stories from children of LGBTQ parents, LGBTQ parenting resources, links to LGBTQ organizations for children of LGBTQ parents, and much more.

http://familieslikemine.com/

Gay Dads Australia: A Resource for Gay Dads and Those Thinking of Becoming Dads — This helpful Australian resource provides information about surrogacy, adoptions, and current news relating to gay parenting. Personal stories from gay dads are included as well as a list of recommended children's picture books and parenting books and movies.

http://gaydadsaustralia.com.au/

Gender Spectrum — Founded by the authors of the definitive book on transgender children, *The Transgender Child: A Handbook for Families and Professionals*, this site includes information about how to create gender-inclusive environments that are welcoming to children and teens who are gender-nonconforming. Resources include tips and connections for parents, youth, and educators, as well as legal information and news about gender laws in the United States.

http://www.genderspectrum.org/

KQED Bay Area Mosaic LGBT Studies — Part of the public media Web site for Northern California, this section provides lesson plans for grades K to 6 that assist educators as they seek to incorporate lessons and curriculum units relating to rainbow families and family diversity.

http://www.kqed.org/w/mosaic/gaylesbian/index.html

LGBTQ Parenting Connection — This Canadian network of organizations provides a wealth of information relating to LGBTQ parenting including a downloadable brochure series entitled Queer Parenting Info, free downloadable posters, bibliographies of recommended books, links to research articles and other LGBTQ organizations for rainbow families, a calendar of events for Canadian rainbow families (such as a Dykes Planning Tykes parenting course and a Queer Family Halloween Hullabaloo), and much more.

http://lgbtqparentingconnection.ca/home.cfm

Love Makes a Family — Both a book and a traveling exhibit, this historical piece from Peggy Gillespie, the cofounder and director of Family Diversity Projects, provides first-person interviews and accounts of children and adults in rainbow families. Organizations can schedule the exhibit, which includes striking black-and-white photos of LGBTQ families.

http://www.familydiv.org/lovemakesafamily.php

Out for Our Children — This UK-based community organization is composed of lesbian parents concerned about making nurseries and preschools welcoming for LGBTQ families. The Web site contains numerous book lists, extensive downloadable lesson plans and classroom activities, information about UK laws relating to rainbow families, and free downloadable posters that include rainbow families.
http://www.outforourchildren.co.uk/

Proud Parenting — Both a social network site and information resource center, this resource provides LGBTQ parents with news stories; helpful advice relating to education, parenting, surrogacy, and adoption; and personal stories from parents in rainbow families.
http://www.proudparenting.com/

The Rainbow Babies — Part community support group and part information central, this site provides information about LGBTQ parenting, adoption, pregnancy, surrogacy, and more. Also included are personal stories from parents in rainbow families and reviews of LGBTQ children's books and parenting books.
http://www.therainbowbabies.com/

Rainbow Families Council — This Australian volunteer community organization provides information to LGBTQ adults interested in adopting and starting families. Particularly useful parts of the Web site are the attractive "Who's in Your Family?" full-color posters and information sheets. These can be downloaded for free and used in libraries, early childcare facilities, schools, and other organizations.
http://rainbowfamilies.org.au/

Safe Schools Coalition — An international organization based in Seattle, Washington, the Safe Schools Coalition provides resources, advice, bibliographies, lesson plans, hotline numbers, and considerable information for teachers, educators, information professionals, parents, caregivers, and LGBTQ youth who want to make schools around the world safe and welcoming for all LGBTQ individuals.
http://www.safeschoolscoalition.org/safe.html

Soulforce — This organization is dedicated to nonviolent resistance to religious and political oppression of LGBTQ individuals. The organization's Web site includes news stories, reports, and various resources that highlight religious bigotry toward the LGBTQ community and offer nonviolent suggestions for fighting this bigotry. Many of Soulforce's activities involve emphasizing the actions and damaging influences of the group called Focus on the Family, which strives to eradicate the LGBTQ community by the use of misguided religious force and propaganda related to U.S. "family values" (read: heterosexual nuclear families).
http://www.soulforce.org/

Ten Oaks Project — A non-profit, volunteer-driven Canadian organization, Ten Oaks Project provides safe-zone, gay-friendly activities and programs for children and youth in rainbow families. Activities include camps and events for children who self-identify as LGBTQ or have LGBTQ parents.
http://www.tenoaksproject.org/default.aspx

Time for Families — This site includes information about same-sex adoptions, newsbytes related to LGBTQ parenting, videos relating to LGBTQ parents and children, as well as personal stories and family photos from rainbow families.

http://timeforfamilies.com/family-matter/family-stories/

TransActive Education and Advocacy — One of the first organizations in the United States to address the topic of transgender children, their families, and educational concerns, this Portland, OR-based advocacy group provides many wonderful resources about transgender individuals, gender nonconformity and gender identity in children. Lesson plans, community resources, training information, and tips for creating inclusive environments for these children and their families are included along with news and current events.

http://www.transactiveonline.org/index.php

TransParentcy — An informational and support Web site providing transgender parents and their children with various resources including helpful links and custody information. The stated purpose of the site is to dispel erroneous myths about the harmful influence of transgender parents on their children.

http://www.transparentcy.org/

Single-Parent Picture Book Bibliography

This bibliography includes selected children's picture books featuring single parents that could also be used with rainbow families. It does not list all the picture books with single parents but selects books that have special child appeal.

Although these books do not include a parent who is LGBTQ, the sexual orientation of the single parent is not divulged and no other parent is mentioned, making these books suitable for single lesbian mothers, gay fathers, and bisexual or transgender mothers or fathers. In a few of the books, a single aunt or single uncle caregiver is described.

Ackerman, Karen. *By the Dawn's Early Light.* New York, NY: Atheneum, 1994.

Andreae, Giles. *I Love My Mommy.* Illus. by Emma Dodd. New York, NY: Hyperion, 2010.

Bauer, Marion Dane. *My Mother Is Mine.* Illus. by Peter Elwell. New York, NY: Simon & Schuster, 2001.

Bauer, Marion Dane. *The Very Best Daddy of All.* Illus. by Leslie Wu. New York, NY: Simon & Schuster, 2004.

Bennett, Kelly. *Dad and Pop: An Ode to Fathers and Stepfathers.* Illus. by Paul Meisel. Somerville, MA: Candlewick Press, 2010.

Brown, Peter. *Children Make Terrible Pets.* New York, NY: Little, Brown, 2010.

Bruchac, Joseph. *My Father Is Taller than a Tree.* Illus. by Wendy Anderson Halperin. New York, NY: Dial, 2010.

Caines, Jeannette. *Just Us Women.* Illus. by Pat Cummings. New York, NY: HarperCollins, 1982.

Carlson, Nancy. *It's Going to Be Perfect.* New York, NY: Viking, 1998.

Curtis, Jamie Lee, and Laura Cornell. *My Mommy Hung the Moon: A Love Story.* New York, NY: HarperCollins, 2010.

Downey, Roma. *Love Is a Family*. Illus. by Justine Gasquet. New York, NY: Harper-Entertainment, 2001.

Eichler, Margrit. *Martin's Father*. Illus. by Bev Magennis. Chapel Hill, NC: Lollipop Power, 1971.

Fallens, Bronny, and Muntsa Vicente. *My Super Single Mum*. Elwood, Vic. (Australia): Bronny and Muntsa, 2011.

Gutman, Anne. *Daddy Cuddles*. Illus. by George Hallensleben. San Francisco, CA: Chronicle Books, 2005.

Gutman, Anne. *Daddy Kisses*. Illus. by George Hallensleben. San Francisco, CA: Chronicle Books, 2003.

Gutman, Anne. *Mommy Hugs*. Illus. by George Hallensleben. San Francisco, CA: Chronicle Books, 2003.

Gutman, Anne. *Mommy Loves*. Illus. by George Hallensleben. San Francisco, CA: Chronicle Books, 2005.

Kasza, Keiko. *A Mother for Choco*. New York, NY: Putnam, 1992.

Katz, Karen. *Daddy Hugs*. New York, NY: Simon & Schuster, 2007.

Katz, Karen. *Mommy Hugs*. New York, NY: Simon & Schuster, 2006.

Kemp, Jane, and Clare Walters. *Dad Mine*. Illus. by Dawn Apperly. New York, NY: Little, Brown, 2003.

Kemp, Jane, and Clare Walters. *Mom Mine*. Illus. by Dawn Apperly. New York, NY: Little, Brown, 2003.

Ketteman, Helen. *Mama's Way*. New York, NY: Dial, 2001.

Kroll, Virginia L. *Beginnings: How Families Come to Be*. Illus. by Stacey Schuett. Morton Grove, IL: Whitman, 1994.

Lacámara, Laura. *Floating on Mama's Song/Flotando en la canción de mama*. Illus. by Yuyi Morales. New York, NY: HarperCollins, 2010.

Lindsay, Jeanne W. *Do I Have a Daddy? A Story About a Single-Parent Child*. Buena Park, CA: Morning Glory Press, 2000.

Milord, Susan. *If I Could: A Mother's Promise*. Illus. by Christopher Denise. Cambridge, MA: Candlewick Press, 2008.

Morales, Yuyi. *Little Night/Nochecita*. New Milford, CT: Roaring Brook Press, 2007.

Newman, Lesléa. *Daddy's Song*. Illus. by Karen Ritz. New York, NY: Henry Holt, 2007.

Newman, Lesléa. *Just Like Mama*. Illus. by Julia Gorton. New York, NY: Abrams, 2010.

Numeroff, Lisa. *What Daddies Do Best*. Illus. by Lynn Munsinger. New York, NY: Simon & Schuster, 1998.

Numeroff, Lisa. *What Mommies Do Best*. Illus. by Lynn Munsinger. New York, NY: Simon & Schuster, 1998.

Parr, Todd. *The Daddy Book*. New York, NY: Little, Brown, 2002.

Parr, Todd. *The Mommy Book*. New York, NY: Little, Brown, 2002.

Perkins, Lynne Rae. *Home Lovely*. New York, NY: Greenwillow, 1995.

Pfister, Marcus. *Happy Birthday, Bertie!* New York, NY: North-South, 2010.

Polacco, Patricia. *Something About Hensley's*. New York, NY: Philomel, 2006.

Ryder, Joanne. *My Father's Hands*. Illus. by Mark Graham. New York, NY: Harper-Collins, 1994.

Ryder, Joanne. *My Mother's Voice*. Illus. by Peter Catalanotto. New York, NY: HarperCollins, 2006.

Sartell, Debra. *Time for Bed, Baby Ted*. Illus. by Kay Chorao. New York, NY: Holiday House, 2010.

Schotter, Roni. *Mama, I'll Give You the World*. Illus. by S. Saelig Gallagher. New York, NY: Schwartz and Wade, 2006.

Schwartz, Amy. *Willie and Uncle Bill*. New York, NY: Holiday House, 2012.

Smalls, Irene. *Father's Day Blues: What Do You Do About Father's Day When All You Have Are Mothers?* Illus. by Kevin McGovern. Stamford, CT: Longmeadow Press, 1995.

Smalls, Irene. *Jonathan and His Mommy*. Illus. by Michael Hays. New York, NY: Little, Brown, 1992.

Soetoro-Ng, Maya. *Ladder to the Moon*. Illus. by Yuyi Morales. Somerville, MA: Candlewick Press, 2011.

Stein, David Ezra. *Interrupting Chicken*. Somerville, MA: Candlewick Press, 2010.

Tarpley, Todd. *How About a Kiss for Me?* Illus. by Liza Woodruff. New York, NY: Dutton, 2010.

Thomas, Eliza. *The Red Blanket*. Illus. by Joe Cepeda. New York: Scholastic Press, 2004.

Williams, Vera B. *A Chair for Always*. New York, NY: HarperCollins, 2009.

Williams, Vera B. *A Chair for My Mother*. New York, NY: HarperCollins, 1982.

Williams, Vera B. *Something Special for Me*. New York, NY: Greenwillow, 1983.

Woodson, Jacqueline. *Our Gracie Aunt*. Illus. by Jon J Muth. New York, NY: Jump at the Sun, 2002. (The aunt in the story is single and becomes the children's caregiver.)

Yolen, Jane. *My Father Knows the Names of Things*. Illus. by Stéphanie Jorisch. New York, NY: Simon & Schuster, 2010.

Ziefert, Harriet. *31 Uses for a Mom*. Illus. by Amanda Haley. New York, NY: Putnam, 2003.

Ziefert, Harriet. *33 Uses for a Dad*. Illus. by Amanda Haley. New York, NY: Putnam, 2004.

Zolotow, Charlotte. *A Father Like That*. Illus. by Leuyen Pham. New York, NY: HarperCollins, 2007.

Additional Non-U.S. Picture Books with LGBTQ Characters

This bibliography lists additional children's picture books published outside the United States with LGBTQ content. These books were not listed elsewhere because they were not available for interlibrary loan. However, information on distributors for most of these books is provided in the "Online Resources" section of this chapter. These books are not translated into English.

Apellániz, Arancha. *La princesa valiente*. Illus. by Mabel Piérola. Barcelona (Spain): Ediciones Bellaterra, 2009. Spanish.

Bertouille, Ariane, and Marie-Claude Favreau. *Ulysse et Alice*. Montréal (Canada): Éditions du Remue-ménage, 2006. French.

Brière-Haquet, Alice. *La princesse qui n'aimait pas les princes*. Illus. by Lionel Larchevêque. Arles (France): Actes Sud Junior, 2010. French.

Chabbert, Ingrid. *La fête des deux mamans*. Illus. by Chadia Loueslati. Palaja (France): Les petits pas de Ioannis, 2010. French. Available at http://www.lespetitspasdeioannis.com/.

Christos. *Dînette dans le tractopelle*. Illus. by Mélanie Grandgirard. Saint-Mandé (France): Talents Hauts, 2009. French.

Cruz, Esther Elexgaray. *El Día de la rana roja*. Illus. by Raúl Domínguez Pazo. Bilbao (Spain): Editorial A Fortiori, 2005. Spanish.

David, Morgane. *J'ai deux papas qui s'aiment*. Paris (France): Hatier, 2007. French.

Douru, Muriel. *Cristelle et Crioline*. Paris (France): KTM Éditions, 2011. French.

Douru, Muriel. *Dis . . . mamans*. Paris (France): Éditions gaies et lesbiennes, 2003. French.

Douru, Muriel. *Un mariage vraiment gai*. Paris (France): Éditions gaies et lesbiennes, 2004. French.

Facchini, Vittoria. *Moi, j'aime pas les garçons*. Paris (France): Circonflexe, 2001. French.

Guerrero, M. Luisa. *Marta y la sirena/Marta and the Mermaid*. Alicante, Spain: ONG por la No Discriminación, 2009. Bilingual English/Spanish text.

Guerrero, M. Luisa. *Seelie, el hada Buena*. Alicante, Spain: ONG por la No Discriminación, 2008. Spanish.

Guerrero, M. Luisa. *El viejo coche/The Old Car*. Alicante, Spain: ONG por la No Discriminación, 2008. Bilingual English/Spanish text.

Hense, Nathalie, and Ilya Green. *Marre du Rose*. Paris (France): Albin Michel Jeunesse, 2009. French.

Herrera, Carmen. *Piratas y quesitos*. Illus. by Luis Filella. Bilbao (Spain): Editorial A Fortiori, 2005. Spanish.

Honoré, Christophe. *Je ne suis pas une fille à papa*. Illus. by Antoine Guilloppé. Paris (France): T. Magnier, 1998. French.

Lacombe, Benjamin. *Longs cheveux*. Saint-Mandé (France): Talents Hauts, 2006. French.

Lenain, Thierry. *Mademoiselle Zazie: Mademoiselle Zazie a-t-elle un zizi?* Illus. by Delphine Durand. Paris (France): Nathan, 1998. French.

Lesaffre, Laetitia. *Barbivore*. Saint-Mandé (France): Talents Hauts, 2008. French.

Lorenzo, Manuel R. *Ana y los patos*. Illus. by Bernardo Erlich. Bilbao (Spain): Editorial A Fortiori, 2005. Spanish.

Mélo. *Imagier Renversant*. Illus. by Sébastien Telleschi. Saint-Mandé (France): Talents Hauts, 2006. French.

Montero, Beatriz. *Tengo tres mamás.* Illus. by Luis Tobalina. Madrid (Spain): Ediciones La Librería, 2007. Spanish.

Olten, Manuela. *Niños valientes.* Barcelona (Spain): Ediciones Serres, 2006. Spanish.

Olten, Manuela. *Les p'tits mecs.* Translated by Echte Kerle. Paris (France): Seuil Jeunesse, 2006. French, translated from Spanish.

Reixach, Laura. *Cebollino y pimentón.* Barcelona (Spain): Ediciones Bellaterra, 2010. Spanish with an English translation at the end of the book.

Roger, Marie-Sabine, and Anne Sol. *A quoi tu joues?* Paris (France): Éditions Sarbacane; Amnesty International, 2009. French.

Scotto, Thomas. *Jérôme par coeur.* Illus. by Olivier Tallec. Arles (France): Actes Sud Junior, 2009. French.

Spagnol, Estelle. *La catcheuse et le danseur.* Saint-Mandé (France): Talents Hauts, 2010. French.

Texier, Ophélie. *Jean a deux mamans.* Paris (France): L'École des loisirs, 2004. French.

Tisseron, Serge, and Aurélie Guillerey. *Le mystère des graines à bébé.* Paris (France): A. Michel Jeunesse, 2008. French.

Selected Creators of LGBTQ Children's Books

A selected list of authors and illustrators of children's literature presenting children and adults in rainbow families. Some key creators are omitted because information about them is not readily available.

* Sarah Brannen — http://sarahbrannen.yellapalooza.com/
* Henry Cole — http://www.henrycole.net/
* Linda deHaan — http://www.lindadehaan.com/biography.html
* Tomie dePaola — http://www.tomie.com/
* Nancy Garden — http://www.nancygarden.com/
* Maya Christina Gonzalez — http://www.mayagonzalez.com/about.html and http://www.reflectionpress.com/gendernow/coloring.html
* Rigoberto González — http://www.rigobertogonzalez.com
* Heather Jopling — http://www.nicknamepress.com/index.htm
* Lucia Moreno Velo — http://morenovelo.blogspot.com/ and http://www.topka.es/topkabooks/
* Lesléa Newman — http://www.lesleakids.com/index.html and http://www.lesleanewman.com/
* Vanita Oelschlager — http://vanitabooks.com/
* Todd Parr — http://www.toddparr.com/
* Johnny Valentine (pseudonym for Sasha Alyson) — http://www.glbtq.com/sfeatures/interviewsalyson.html and http://www.sashaalyson.com/
* Michael Willhoite — http://www.michaelwillhoite.com/

Author Index

This index provides access by author to the titles listed in Parts 1, 2, and 3 of this book. Also see the Subject Index for authors highlighted in Parts 1 and 2.

Title Index

This index focuses on materials for LGBTQ children. It covers titles included in Parts 1, 2, and 3 of this book as well as titles in the "Single-Parent Picture Book Bibliography" and "Additional Non-U.S. Picture Books with LGBTQ Characters" sections of Part 4. An asterisk indicates that the title is highly recommended.

Keyword Index

This is a listing of keywords used in the bibliographic entries in Part 3 of this book. See the accompanying Subject Index for wider access to subjects discussed throughout the book.

Subject Index

Also use the Keyword Index, which provides a listing of keywords used in the bibliographic entries in Part 3 of this book.

About the Author

Dr. JAMIE CAMPBELL NAIDOO is an endowed assistant professor at the University of Alabama School of Library and Information Studies and director/founder of the National Latino Children's Literature Conference. He teaches and researches in the areas of early childhood literacy, culturally diverse children's literature, and library services to Latino families. He is active in REFORMA and has chaired both the Pura Belpré and Américas Award committees. He is also the editor of *Celebrating Cuentos: Promoting Latino Children's Literature and Literacy in Classrooms and Libraries* (Libraries Unlimited, 2011).